COLLECTIONS

OF THE

MASSACHUSETTS HISTORICAL SOCIETY

SEVENTH SERIES — VOL. IX

Committee of Publication

CHARLES FRANCIS ADAMS
EDWIN FRANCIS GAY
GEORGE PEABODY WETMORE
WORTHINGTON CHAUNCEY FORD

COMMERCE
OF
RHODE ISLAND

1726 — 1800

VOL. I
1726 — 1774

BOSTON
PUBLISHED BY THE SOCIETY
MDCCCCXIV

PREFATORY NOTE

THE letters and papers printed in these volumes formed a part of the commercial correspondence of four generations of a Newport mercantile house. The last of the principals was Christopher Grant Champlin, who died in 1840 or 1841, leaving his home on Spring Street, Newport, to Christopher Grant Perry. The house, on his death, passed to Hon. Duncan C. Pell, and, known as the Pell House, remained standing until it was demolished a few years ago, to make way for the building of the Young Men's Christian Association.

On tearing down the old house the contractor, Manuel, found in the attic some five boxes of manuscripts, the records of mercantile activity from the early part of the eighteenth century. Manuel claimed ownership of the papers, and his claim appears to have been allowed. Attempts were later made to buy the entire collection by Dr. Horatio R. Storer and Mr. George Champlin Mason, but without success; and the papers, apparently with little selection or judgment, entered upon a process of dispersal. A part of the collection went to the Newport Historical Society; another selection found its way to the Rhode Island Historical Society; but the larger part appeared in the auction room and was secured by our colleague, Hon. George Peabody Wetmore. What is in existence constitutes but a small part of the original accumulation, and the loss is regrettable, because so few great collections of commercial correspondence for the colonial period remain. The Stephen Collins Papers, and the Ellis and Allen Papers in the Library of Congress are the more notable, but they are of later date and no part of them has as yet been printed. Through the generous interest of Mr. Wetmore these two volumes of the Rhode Island Papers are published, the first important contribution in print to the history of the commerce of a British

American colony. The more interesting letters in the private collections of Mr. Mason and Dr. Storer and in the collections of the Newport and Rhode Island Historical Societies are, through the courtesy of the owners, included in these volumes.

Neither the connection nor the limits of each division of the papers are clearly marked. The earlier letters were of the Redwood family, originally of Antigua, but later of Newport. The house of Ayrault of Newport entered about the middle of the eighteenth century, as also that of Lopez. To the second half of the century, the firms of Lopez and Champlin contribute the larger part.

The historical value of the collection lies in the detailed statement at first hand of commercial routes, usages and development. The markets of the West Indies, Europe and the British colonies of North America, prices, currencies, conditions of credit, insurance and hiring and sailing of vessels; nature of the cargo and manner of disposing of it; the initiative and responsibility of captains charged with the disposal of one cargo and the obtaining of another, whether for cash or by barter; port charges and customs, smuggling and bribery of officials, — these are some of the many matters dealt with, and not in general terms, but by specific examples. The range of dealings is wide; the sugars and rum of the West Indies; logwood from Honduras; salt from Spain and the West Indies; whale oil and spermaceti, in the crude form or in candles; lumber, staves and casks; live stock, flour and rice, the catalogue would be a long one, and the groups will indicate the importance and direction of the trade. The names of ships and of their captains supply material for the history of commercial and industrial enterprise.

Two branches deserve mention, the purchase and manufacture of spermaceti, which were controlled by agreements among the large manufacturers in New England as closely as by any trust agreement of later times; and the African slave trade, of the greatest importance to Newport, in the decline of which that place lost its commercial position. The cargo of a slave ship from Newport, the manner of dealing with the slave stations on the African coast, and the prices of slaves, quoted in rum in Africa, and in pounds sterling in the West Indies, are here to be found. The action of the first Continental Congress in checking this trade affronted the Rhode Island merchants; but this action and the War of Independence put an end to the traffic, and other lines of trade relation were exploited.

The changes in the nature and direction of colonial commerce are indicated. Sugars, whale oil, lumber and ships constituted the leading articles until the trade acts of Great Britain fostered an illegal trade with the foreign West Indies and Holland. As sugars declined in importance flour and flaxseed took their place, the flour going to Spanish ports, the flaxseed to Ireland. The war from 1775 to 1783 compelled the merchants to change their commerce; for English markets, the principal outlet in the past, were now closed to American ships, and no small risk attended a direct trade with Europe. The Dutch and Spaniards offered some market, and the French went through the form of attempting to draw to themselves the trade lost to Great Britain. Concessions were made on whale oil and tobacco; but the opposition of French interests to real concessions, such as would enable the American shipper to compete successfully, was too great to be overcome, and the French markets remained protected and closed markets. Russian ports on the Baltic offered fairer prospects, besides offering materials, like canvas and cordage, wanted in America. India and China tempted the enterprising.

A few of the more interesting and unusual pieces are reproduced, as well as some of the more representative signatures.

CHARLES FRANCIS ADAMS
EDWIN FRANCIS GAY
GEORGE PEABODY WETMORE
WORTHINGTON CHAUNCEY FORD

BOSTON, September 15, 1914

OFFICERS

OF THE

MASSACHUSETTS HISTORICAL SOCIETY

APRIL 9, 1914

President
CHARLES FRANCIS ADAMS . . . . LINCOLN

Vice-Presidents
JAMES FORD RHODES . . . . BOSTON
JOHN DAVIS LONG . . . . HINGHAM

Recording Secretary
EDWARD STANWOOD . . . . BROOKLINE

Corresponding Secretary
WILLIAM ROSCOE THAYER . . . . CAMBRIDGE

Treasurer
ARTHUR LORD . . . . PLYMOUTH

Librarian
SAMUEL ABBOTT GREEN . . . . GROTON

Cabinet-Keeper
GRENVILLE HOWLAND NORCROSS . . . . BOSTON

Editor
WORTHINGTON CHAUNCEY FORD . . . . CAMBRIDGE

Members at Large of the Council
WILLIAM VAIL KELLEN . . . . COHASSET
FREDERICK JACKSON TURNER . . . . CAMBRIDGE
GAMALIEL BRADFORD . . . . WELLESLEY HILLS
CHARLES PELHAM GREENOUGH . . . . BOSTON
JOHN COLLINS WARREN . . . . BOSTON

RESIDENT MEMBERS

1860.
Hon. Samuel Abbott Green, LL.D.

1867.
Charles Card Smith, A.M.

1873.
Hon. Winslow Warren, LL.B.
Charles William Eliot, LL.D.

1875.
Charles Francis Adams, LL.D.

1876.
Hon. Henry Cabot Lodge, LL.D.

1877.
John Torrey Morse, Jr., Litt.D.

1881.
Rev. Henry Fitch Jenks, A.M.

1882.
Arthur Lord, A.B.
Frederic Ward Putnam, S.D.

1884.
Edward Channing, Ph.D.

1887.
Edwin Pliny Seaver, A.M.

1889.
Albert Bushnell Hart, LL.D.

1890.
Abbott Lawrence Lowell, LL.D.

1891.
Hon. Oliver Wendell Holmes, LL.D.
Henry Pickering Walcott, LL.D.

1893.
Hon. Charles Russell Codman, LL.B.
Barrett Wendell, Litt.D.
James Ford Rhodes, LL.D.

1894.
Rt. Rev. William Lawrence, D.D.
William Roscoe Thayer, Litt.D.

1895.
Hon. Thomas Jefferson Coolidge, LL.D.
Hon. William Wallace Crapo, LL.D.

1896.
Granville Stanley Hall, LL.D.

1897.
Rev. Leverett Wilson Spring, D.D.
Col. William Roscoe Livermore.
Hon. Richard Olney, LL.D.
Lucien Carr, A.M.

1898.
Rev. George Angier Gordon, D.D.
John Chipman Gray, LL.D.
Rev. James DeNormandie, D.D.
Andrew McFarland Davis, A.M.

1899.
Archibald Cary Coolidge, Ph.D.
Charles Pickering Bowditch, A.M.

1900.
Melville Madison Bigelow, LL.D.

RESIDENT MEMBERS

1901.
Thomas Leonard Livermore, A.M.
Nathaniel Paine, A.M.
John Osborne Sumner, A.B.
Arthur Theodore Lyman, A.M.

1902.
Henry Lee Higginson, LL.D.
Brooks Adams, A.B.
Grenville Howland Norcross, LL.B.
Edward Hooker Gilbert, A.B.

1903.
Franklin Benjamin Sanborn, A.B.
Charles Knowles Bolton, A.B.
Samuel Savage Shaw, LL.B.
Ephraim Emerton, Ph.D.
Waldo Lincoln, A.B.
Frederic Jesup Stimson, LL.B.
Edward Stanwood, Litt.D.
Moorfield Storey, A.M.

1904.
Roger Bigelow Merriman, Ph.D.
Charles Homer Haskins, Litt.D.

1905.
Hon. John Davis Long, LL.D.
Theodore Clarke Smith, Ph.D.
Henry Greenleaf Pearson, A.B.
Bliss Perry, LL.D.

1906.
Edwin Doak Mead, A.M.
Edward Henry Clement, Litt.D.
William Endicott, A.M.
Lindsay Swift, A.B.
Hon. George Sheldon.
Mark Antony DeWolfe Howe, A.M.
Arnold Augustus Rand, Esq.

1907.
Jonathan Smith, A.B.
Albert Matthews, A.B.
William Vail Kellen, LL.D.

1908.
Frederic Winthrop, A.B.
Hon. Robert Samuel Rantoul, LL.B.
George Lyman Kittredge, LL.D.
Charles Pelham Greenough, LL.B.
Henry Ernest Woods, A.M.

1909.
Worthington Chauncey Ford, A.M.
William Coolidge Lane, A.B.

1910.
Hon. Samuel Walker McCall, LL.D.
John Collins Warren, M.D., LL.D.
Harold Murdock, Esq.
Henry Morton Lovering, A.M.
Edward Waldo Emerson, M.D.
Hon. Curtis Guild, LL.D.
Frederick Jackson Turner, Litt.D.
Gardner Weld Allen, M.D.

1911.
Henry Herbert Edes, A.M.
George Hubbard Blakeslee, Ph.D.
George Hodges, LL.D.
Richard Henry Dana, LL.B.
George Foot Moore, LL.D.
Gamaliel Bradford, Litt.D.
Justin Harvey Smith, LL.D.

1912.
John Spencer Bassett, Ph.D.
Malcolm Storer, M.D.
Edwin Francis Gay, Ph.D.

1913.
Charles Grenfill Washburn, A.B.

1914.
Frederick Lewis Gay, A.B.
Thomas Franklin Waters, A.M.
Zachary Taylor Hollingsworth, Esq.
Chester Noyes Greenough, Ph.D.
Joseph Grafton Minot, Esq.

HONORARY MEMBERS

1896.
Rt. Hon. Viscount Bryce, D.C.L.

1899.
Rt. Hon. Sir George Otto Trevelyan, Bart., D.C.L.

1901.
Pasquale Villari, D.C.L.

1904.
Adolf Harnack, D.D.
Rt. Hon. Viscount Morley, D.C.L.

1905.
Ernest Lavisse.

1907.
Rear-Admiral Alfred Thayer Mahan, D.C.L.

1908.
Henry Adams, LL.D.

1910.
Eduard Meyer, Litt.D.

1911.
Hon. Andrew Dickson White, D.C.L.

CORRESPONDING MEMBERS

1875.
Hubert Howe Bancroft, A.M.

1878.
Joseph Florimond Loubat, LL.D.
Charles Henry Hart, LL.B.

1879.
Franklin Bowditch Dexter, Litt.D.

1883.
Rev. Charles Richmond Weld, LL.D.

1896.
Hon. James Burrill Angell, LL.D.

1897.
Hon. Woodrow Wilson, LL.D.
Hon. Joseph Hodges Choate, D.C.L.

1898.
John Franklin Jameson, LL.D.

1899.
Rev. William Cunningham, LL.D.

1900.
Hon. Simeon Eben Baldwin, LL.D.
John Bassett Moore, LL.D.

1901.
Frederic Harrison, Litt.D.
Frederic Bancroft, LL.D.
Charles Harding Firth, LL.D.
William James Ashley, M.A.

1902.
John Bach McMaster, LL.D.
Albert Venn Dicey, LL.D.
John Christopher Schwab, Ph.D.

1903.
Rev. Arthur Blake Ellis, LL.B.
Auguste Moireau.
Hon. Horace Davis, LL.D.

1904.
Sir Sidney Lee, LL.D.

1905.
William Archibald Dunning, LL.D.
James Schouler, LL.D.
George Parker Winship, A.M.
Gabriel Hanotaux.
Hubert Hall.

1906.
Andrew Cunningham McLaughlin, LL.B.
Hon. Beekman Winthrop, LL.B.

1907.
Hon. James Phinney Baxter, Litt.D.
Wilberforce Eames, A.M.
George Walter Prothero, LL.D.
Hon. Jean Jules Jusserand, LL.D.
James Kendall Hosmer, LL.D.

1908.
John Bagnell Bury, LL.D.
Rafael Altamira y Crevea.
Hon. James Wilberforce Longley, D.C.L.

Henry Morse Stephens, Litt.D.
Charles Borgeaud, LL.D.

1909.
Lyon Gardiner Tyler, LL.D.
Clarence Bloomfield Moore, A.B.

1910.
Edward Doubleday Harris, Esq.
Charles William Chadwick Oman, M.A.

1911.
Samuel Verplanck Hoffman, Esq.
William Milligan Sloane, LL.D.

1912.
Rear-Admiral French Ensor Chadwick.
William MacDonald, LL.D.

1913.
John Holland Rose, Litt.D.

1914.
Hon. George Peabody Wetmore.

Commerce of Rhode Island

[1726–1800]

JONAS LANGFORD TO ABRAHAM REDWOOD [1]

Antig[ua] 4th Decemb: 1726.

Deare Cousin Abrah. Redwood,[2]

I RECEIVED yours about a week after Capt. Browne[3] sail'd from our Island, otherwise should have sent an answer by the same opportunity. I note the Contents of your Letter and according to your desire have spoke to the Governour[4] about the money you wrote to him for and he assured me that he had ordered you the same and was willing for your Coming over provided you had your Fathers Consent. I am glad to hear of your good health which mercy we at present enjoy. pray make our loves acceptable to your

---

[1] The original is in the Newport Historical Society.

[2] Abraham Redwood, the elder, born in Bristol, England, 1665, traded between London and Jamaica. In 1687 he settled in Antigua, where he married Mehetable, daughter of Jonas Langford, and thus became possessed of a large sugar plantation on the island, the Cassada Garden, with many slaves. In 1715 he removed to Salem, Massachusetts, and later to Newport, Rhode Island. He died there January 17, 1729, aged 64 years. This letter is addressed to his son, Abraham.

[3] John Browne.

[4] Edward Byam, commissioned as Lieutenant-Governor of Antigua January 28, 1715, and again October 17, 1727. Antigua was one of the Leeward Islands, and John Hart held the governorship of these Islands, 1721–1727.

Brother and Sister and all our relations and believe I am with great Cincerity your Loving Kinsman,

[Endorsed,] By Capt. Bell.[1]

JONAS LANGFORD TO ABRAHAM REDWOOD JR.

Deare Cousin Abraham Redwood,

SINCE my last by Capt. Bell wherein I inform'd thee that I had spoke to the Governour to remit to thee the money thou wrote to him for, which he promised me he would by the next oppertunity have not had any from thee, but have heard by Capt. Browne that thou hast had a severe fitt of Sickness, but now pretty well recovered of the same, and if so with the advice of thy Father and the rest of thy friends, I would have thee come over and look into thy affairs that thou mayst have some notion how and after what manner we gett our Bread in these parts. I write thus free to thee as being one of the nearest relations I have, and would not have thee be lost as the rest of thy Brothers were in Road Island. pray make my respects acceptable to all my relations and accept the same thy self from thy Loving Kinsman.

JONAS LANGFORD

ANTIGUA, 10th, March, 1726/7.

[Endorsed] By Captain Browne.

---

[1] Captain William Bell commanded the sloop *Elizabeth and Mary*, of Rhode Island, and was taken by the French off the coast of Martinico in 1727. *New England Weekly Journal*, July 10, 1727.

William Hillhouse to Abraham Redwood, Jr.

Antegua, July 21th, 1727.

Sir,

By Edwa'd Byams Esq. order I heave sent you enclosed a bill of Loading for one bag of Cotton wich came to hand after the Gouenor had got the bills of Loding for the six hhd. of Rome and had enclosed them in his Letter, therefor he desired me to send you it with an acc't. thereof which is as onder nath wich is all at present from, sur, your Most Humbell Servant To Command,

WILL. HILLHOUSE

Invoise of one bag of Cotton shiped by Edwad Byam Esqr one the Schooner *Mercy* Capt. Richard Gill, Master, one acc't. of Mr Abram Redwood Jun. being markd as Margin [A.R.] etc.

295 Neat Cotton at 10d. per	£ 14.15.-
To the Bagg	£ 0. 8.
To 4½ per Cent	£ 4.8
To warfage	£ .9
	£ 15. 8.5
To the Enumarat. Duty	12.7
	£ 16.01.0

WILL HILLHOUSE.[1]

Sarah Parson to Abraham Redwood[2]

Antigua, the 23d November, 1728.

Respected Kinsman Abraham Redwood,

HAVEING the good fortune by my sons marring to bee still nearer related then before makes me take the Liberty to give the a few Lines; and understanding thy Interest hear is like to be in thy one posesion in a short time, I have

---

[1] In 1727 Manchester was said to contain at least fifty thousand persons, and its prosperity rested upon the manufacture of cotton in all its varieties. This industry, evidences of which are found at Manchester as early as 1635, owed its preëminence to immigrants from Antwerp about 1685, and drew its material "from beyond the sea." The cotton wove thin came from the Levant, and fustians were the principal product. As early as 1727 the eastern cotton had been largely supplanted by cotton from the English colonies in America.

[2] The original is in the Newport Historical Society.

this Request to the to lett my husband have the management of it, whoe I belive the may trust and find him verry just and honest to thee in that affair, and the may give the Governer a hint that my self being thy Relation the was willing my husband should have the offer off it. If the writes to Cousin Langford he will I know forward it he being our perticular friend; but I beg thy favor that none of them may know that I write to the, because it may make some people that are now uppon it our Enimis as wee are strange but may only signifye that the hears my husband meets with noe seafareing buisness which put the uppon imploying him in thy affairs, soe that will be verry sufficient for a Reason soe Dr. Cousin I beg thy Consideration and a speedy anser before any one tryes to intercept us with kind Loue to thy self and spouse I am thy Verry Obliged Kinswoman,

Sarah Vaxfon

pray my Loue to all my new Relation as well as old ones as the hast fredom.

Rowland Frye to Abraham Redwood, Jr.

Sir   London, 18 April, 1729.

I HAVE by order of Mr. Edward Byam Esq. the Governour of Antigua, sent to Boston Certain Lead and Iron Work for your Account amounting to £91:0:9 as per Invoice and Bill of Lading enclosed. there will be no Vessell from hence for some time, bound directly to Rhode Island, or should I have sent the Goods to this place, but was directed if there was not, to send them by the first Ship to New England, and have also ensured £100 on the said Goods which at 2 per Ct. policy and Commission is £2:14:6.

I have also ensured per order of Governour Byam £80 on Capt. Davis to this place at the same Premio. The charge is £2:4:6. The Ship[1] arrived yesterday with 8 Casks[2] of Sugar for your account, which I shall dispose of to your best advantage and will then transmitt you the Account of Sales per Capt. Hammerden[3] I am, Sir,

Your most humble Ser
Row'd Frye

Sir

ON the other side is Copy of what I wrote you by Capt. Hammerden. this encloses Copy of the Invoice and 2d Bill of Lading.

I have sold your 8 Casks Sugar per Davis at 25/ and hope to send you the Acct. Sales very shortly. I am Sir, Your most humble Servant   ROW'D FRYE

London 8, May, 1729.
[Endorsed,] Per Capt. Henderson via Boston.

JONAS LANGFORD TO ABRAHAM REDWOOD

Deare Cousin,

BY Capt. Pearce I was favoured with thine, and perceive that thou intendst to give thy partes that feell to thee by they Fathers death to thy mother.[4] I am not at all against thy being kind to her and her Children but I

---

[1] The *Parham Gallry.*

[2] A cask, hogshead or chest of sugar contained twelve hundred pounds — more or less. These eight casks gave a net sale of £60. 14. 6.

[3] "On Tuesday morning the 22d Currant, a New Ship Burthen about 180 Tons, Francis Hammerden Commander, lying at the Long-Wharffe [Boston], took fire as is supposed by a Candle, and was burnt, the Value whereof is reckoned about Two Thousand Pounds." *New England Weekly Journal*, August 28, 1727.

[4] His father had married for a second wife Patience (Howland) Phillips, daughter of Joseph Howland, of Duxbury, Mass. As Jonas Langford Redwood, the eldest son, had been killed in 1724, by a fall from a horse, Abraham inherited the Antigua property.

would have thee be well inform'd what Estate thou art master of and then thou mayst be as liberall as thou pleaseth. I return thee my hearty thanks for thy kind present of Cheeses, and am with due regard to thy self, Wife, and family, they assured friend and Loving Cousin,

JONAS LANGFORD

Antigua, 27th of Sept., 1729.

P. S. I understand that thou hast an undoubted right to 2 thirds of they Fathers Negroes, and thy Mother the other third during her life; so that if thou canst buy her third, it would be better than any Body else should have them. Vale.

WILLIAM HILLHOUSE TO ABRAHAM REDWOOD

Antegua, Aprill 4th, 1729.

SUR, according to Edward Byam, Esqr. order I heare in put you a bill of Loding for a Negro Mane named John which came from Road Island he has promised a great amendment and I wish he may come saf to your Hands which is all from your Most Humbell Servant to comand.

WILL HILLHOUSE

HENRY BONNIN TO ABRAHAM REDWOOD

Antigua, the 21st August, 1729.

Sir,

I REC'D yours directed in the absence of Capt. Rob't Carr to me, and as per bill of Ladeing I have rec'd the Ninty bbs. of Flow'r, Twenty Seven Boxes of Sope and Seven boxes [of] Candels, and shall disposte of them to your best advantage as soone as possible and make you returns by same Sloop, not haveing an oppertunity to dispose of her as order'd. Nor is their any Salt at Anguilla or St. Martins or likely to bee. Shingles, and Stave unsold. You loste Fifteen Sheep the rest have solde at Thirteen Shill's each. Flower is at Eighteen but sells slowly. Our Cuntry produce of all sorts is scarce and dear, Rum from Twenty One pence to Two Shill's, Sugar 22/6 per Cwt at your owne Estate, Cotton 10½ pence per pound, Mollasses none to be had, unless should happen any from Guardeloupe. We have had noe Advice whear Capt. Rob't Carr is arrived but hope him well. My Deligence shall not be wanting for the Dispatch of your Sloop, unless a Chapman should offer. in the Interim I remain with Respects Your Oblidged

Humble Servant
Henry Bonnin

P. S. Capt. Dan'l Pearce arrived the 14th Instant.

[Endorsed,] To Mr. Abraham Redwood, Merchant at New Porte Rhodeisland. Per Capt. Tillinghast, Q. D. C.

ROWLAND FRYE TO ABRAHAM REDWOOD

Sir,

I WROTE you lately by Capt. Shewell since which I have honoured your Bill £180:13:4 to Mr. George Byam. as the Crop is now over I propose to send your Account Current by the next Ship.

Sugar still bears a low price and there does not seem to be any prospect of its rising, for the French have supplyed the foreign Markets, and we have a large Quantity on hand.[1]

---

[1] The value of imports into Great Britain from Antigua in 1730 was £268. 801, and of exports to that island, £32. 582. The exports to New England in the same year were £208. 196, and the imports, £54. 701. The two divisions nearly balanced the movement. The custom house year ran from Christmas to Christmas. Anderson, *Origin of Commerce*, IV. 36.

About 1725 the French began to supply, in considerable quantities, the European markets with sugars from their colonies of Martinico, Hispaniola, etc. This commerce had hitherto been almost monopolized by the English, a small quantity coming from Portuguese Brazil. The Dutch colony of Surinam also came into the market. The imports into London, for one month, May, 1730, of sugar from the American colonies was 1421 hogsheads; but in the year 1731 the re-exports from London of colonial sugar amounted to 58. 446 cwt. The British colonies on

We beleive that there will be a Governour soon appointed;[1] there are 2 or 3 Persons talked of, but I cannot learn who will have it. I am, Sir, Your most humble Servant,

ROW'D FRYE

London, 9 December, 1730.
[Endorsed,] Per C. Lightfoot.

RICHARD NUGENT TO ABRAHAM REDWOOD

Antigua, 7th January, 1730/1.

Dear Sir,

I MUST once more return you my hearty thanks for all favours perticularly for your kind recommendation in my favour, to my Brother,[2] he has ever since treated me more like a Father then a Brother. I am well assured it's on your Account only, for before he almost heated me, and I must own it was in some Measure my owne fault; but for the future, hope shall take care to meritt the Carractor you gave him of me. I am sure he loves you intirly, for in all companey he talkes of you after the handsomest manner, and tells them how much he's obliged to you for renting him Land, when at the same time you refused others. I understand Young Mr. Langford designes to quitt your Estate in a little time. I am not sertain whether he designes it or not; but its publickly talkt of here. if he should, I know my Brother would verry read'ly take the same charge,

---

the American continent, however, supplied their needs in sugar, rum and molasses, by importing from the Dutch and French sugar colonies, and also brought in European goods and manufactures, in contravention of the navigation laws. English merchants dated this illegal trade from 1715, and in 1731 their complaints led to the preparing of a bill prohibiting the importation of sugar, rum or molasses, of the plantations of foreign nations (except Portuguese), into Britain or Ireland, or any of the King's Dominions in America, under forfeiture of lading, ship and furniture. The terms of the bill and the arguments raised are summarized in Anderson, *Origin of Commerce*, III. 177.

[1] Lord Londonderry, appointed governor of the Leeward Islands in 1728, died September 12, 1729. William Matthew, the Lieutenant Governor, acted until October 30, 1733, when he was appointed governor, and held the office until his death, August 14, 1752.

[2] Walter Nugent.

on him, and would be glad to have it in his power, to doe you any Service. if you don't take care you'l loose your Money in Giles Watkins's Hands. I believe if you would write to my Brother he would putt you in a way how to gett it, for I heard him say it was a pitty you should be so treated, and he protested had he power he would make him pay it imeaditly. I give you this Hint for your Goverment. I hope in a little time, to have the Honour of takeing you by the Hand. Pray my kind Service to your good Spouse,[1] Mrs. Betty, Content, and the Little Ones, not forgetting Captain John Browne, and all freinds, and please to accept the same from him that is with great Esteem, Worthy Friend

P. S. I begg you'l not mention anything of the above, to any body. I am Yours, R N.

ROWLAND FRYE TO ABRAHAM REDWOOD

Sir,

I WROTE you lately to Antigua and sent your account current, but I since understand that you are at Rhode Island, and now enclose you there a Copy of it, which I hope you will find to be right, the Ballance is £715:17:8d in your Favour.

I have honoured your Bill to Thomas Richardson for £140: — tho' I have had no advice of it. I beleive it would be proper for the future to send advice, when you

---
[1] Martha Coggeshall.

draw, least any one should forge your hand or alter the Tenour of your Bill.

Sugar bears but an indifferent Price with us nor are they likely to be high this year, there is so much of the last Crop on hand. Midling sell at 21/ to 23/ very good to 26/ per Ct. I am, Sir, Your most humble Servant,

Row'd Frye

London, 17 February, 1730/31.
[Endorsed,] Per C[apt.] Holmes.

Walter Nugent to Abraham Redwood

Antigua, 11th March, 1730/1.

Worthy Sir,

The above is coppy of my last. This goes via Boston to advise of your Granmothers[1] Death in Barbadoes, fourteen days agoe, and that your kinsman Jonas Langford has taken possesion of his Popeshead Estate, and designes [to] quitt yours, in five or six days. I offred my Service to take care of your Estate in his roome, but he tells me, the Governour has promist young Major Tomlinson,[2] untill he has your final Determination, whome you'l chuse. I have nothing to say against the Gentleman, but you are best Judge which of us, you scincearly believe has your Interest most at heart. you always told me, and I don't in the least doubt your Honour, that you would serve me in any thing in your Power. its now in your Power to serve me and your self alsoe. Just now he came to me and told me he came from the Governor where he was making Interest to Manage your Estate, and desired the favour of me to give him a line to you in his favour. I told him he must excuse me; for I was in hopes you would come and settle your Estate your self, which I heartly wish, it may suit with your Conveniency so to doe; but if you did not, I did not in the least doubt, but you would give me

---
[1] Mrs. French? See the next letter.
[2] John Thomlinson, Jr.

the preference at which he was a little Surprized, and made answer that then he must depend upon the Governors recommendation only, for he had no Interest with you himself, and indeed I don't think he can reasonably expect it, considering the Treatment you mett with when at Antigua.

I now make you a tender of my Service, and you may depend none will serve you more just. I will write you more at large per Captain Carr, which sailes in 10 days; Several makes Interest for him to the Governor. as for my part I have not, nor shall not depend, or speak to any but your self, and as you always have been my freind, I am in hopes you will still continue. you may depend I shall study to merritt your favours, consider I shall not keep any of your Negroes out of your feild. I have House Negroes enough of my own, and that advantage only will be considerable in your way, as you want a great many more then you have to settle your Estate. you was pleased to order the Governor at two different times to lett me have Land, for which I return you my hearty thankes, although I am not certain whether I shall have any or not as yett. therefore I am sure if you don't give him positive orders to give me the Management of your Estate I am sure he will give it to Tomlinson. my Brother Richard presents you and your good family with his Service. he setts out next week for New York, where he goes in order to settle an Account for me there. I have money in the hands of Colonel Nathaniel Gilbert of that place — between one and 200 £ this money. I shall order it to be remitted to you, if he has not already shipt it to me. my Brother meets Captain Carr at your Island to come back with him. I will say more of this affaire in my next. your Sloop, Captain Pope, is not yett arrived. when he does you may depend I shall doe him all the Service in my power. you'l have several letters in favour of Tomlinson. I pray make no answer to them, untill Captain Carr arrives. I have by this tired your patience with my Nonsense, but I hope you'l excuse it. my Spouse joynes with me, in our best

COMMERCE OF

cts to your good Lady, and please to accept
self, for I am

)pie via Boston sent before.

JONAS LANGFORD TO ABRAHAM REDWOO

[Antigua, March

Couzin,

)URS [I] receiv'd by Capt. Pope[1] with one a lit
th of which you charge me with a neglect in
Now to justifye myself in that particular an
e blame to the Captains of your vessels; fo
;eing their Duty; in whom I have confided tv
your absence vizt. one by Capt. Thodey[2] (
)ther (via Boston) both which I thought
'd ere now; They both giving melancholy
 the Condition of our Island; not haveing
to do us any service for these twelve mor
1 'has reduc'd your Crop to less than half w

---

ncis Pope.
aptain William Thody was in command of a sloop *Endeavour*
at St. Lucia in 1727. *New England Weekly Journal*, July 10

pected, and am affraid will ruin the next years Crop entirely; if not a Season very speedily. I mention'd the Death of my Father to you in my last which you have not receiv'd, but find by your Letter you have heard of the same. I have since taken possession of the Popes head Plantation which fell to me by Death of Mrs. French, which has oblidg'd me to quitt your Estate, the management of which you were so kind to trust me with and have given all my accounts to the Governour in order to be sent by this Opportunity which I hope will meet with Approbation. The Governour has thought proper to let Mr. Thomlinson, Junior, have the management of your Estate whom I am certain is one of the best planters we have in these parts; and a Gentleman thàt will do you as much Justice as if you were upon the spot your self; Therefore hope for your own advantage you will continue him there, notwithstanding some misunderstanding happen'd between you whilst in this Island; in relation to the Cains upon your Land, which he was oblidg'd to pay for; and if the Governour thought him not a proper person he never would have fixed him there contrary to the Interest of him who he has always studied. So with Love to Wife and Family and same to self, I remain your Loving Kinsman,

JONAS LANGFORD

P. S. I shall send by this opportunity tenn gallons of Arrack;[1] and three dozen bottles of Citron Watter[2] also what things you sent for by Mr. Lovell who is just arriv'd. my Watch is broke; and can't perswade my Mother to sell her Negroe boy Jonny; but shall desire the Governour to send Charles.

---

[1] A word of Eastern origin applied to any spirituous liquor of native manufacture, but in the West Indies meant a liquor distilled from sugar, fermented with the cocoa-nut juice. Johnson defined it, "a spirit procured by distillation from a vegetable juice called toddy, which flows by incision out of the cocoa-nut tree." It does not appear to have been an article of import into Great Britain from the West Indies; but rackee (*raqi*) from Turkey, practically the same sort of spirit, is mentioned in the customs tables.

[2] Properly a liquor distilled from the rind of citrons.

Issabella Langford to Abraham Redwood[1]

Antigua, April 7, 1731.

Dear Cosen,

Yours I received and am glad to hear of your safe arrival with your family. I wish you joy of your second son health and happiness attend you and yours. I return you thanks for your present of apples. Capt. Car sent me a few apples in a handkerchief but weare good for nothing; however your good will was never the less. we have not seen him since he came. my Mother returns thanks for all favours receiv'd, particular[ly] for her half part of a Horse.[2] I understand the other half for my Sister Betty. I need not writ you thee misfortun that has befallen our family since you left us. I understand you have heard of the Death of my Dear Father, which is a very great trouble to us, in particular to my Dear Mother who would have wrot to you, but her troubles being very great have defer'd itt to the next oppertunity. she gives her kind love to you and yours. my brothers and sisters gives their loves to all your family. pray make my love and service exceptable to your good Spoues, and my littel Cosens, and except the same from your sinceare and loveing Cosin. I have sent you by this oppertuni[ty] a Cagg of tamrons.[3] my Mother gives her kind love to Cosin Whipple[4] and will writ by the next oppertunity. my Sow lies in with nine piggs and am in hopes I have not made so bad a bargain as you thought I had. Yours,

Isabella Langford

---

[1] The original is in the Newport Historical Society.
[2] The export of horses to the West Indies centred in Connecticut, and continued an important commerce until the War of Independence. In the act of 1731 the sending of horses or lumber from the American continent to foreign sugar colonies was prohibited, to the end of placing these colonies at a disadvantage in producing sugar.
[3] Tamarind, the fruit of the *Tamarindus Indica*.
[4] Joseph Whipple married Sarah, sister of Abraham Redwood.

Walter Nugent to Abraham Redwood

Antigua, April the 11th, 1731.

Worthy Sir,

The above is a Coppy of mine to you by way [of] Boston and New Yorke to which I reffer you. This goes by Capt. [Carr] to advise you I have yours per Capt. Pope with a Gould Watch to be [sold] I'll doe my Endeavours to gett it don. you have not limitted me t[o a] price, so that I can't well tell what to demand for it. I will alsoe [¹] all the Service in my power, but am afriad he will make no gr[eat] it, all soarts of goods being now a drugg, for People have not any [ ] the weather being so very Dry; if I had seen him before he had [ ] advise him to goe farder to seeke a Markett; but he tells me he [had no] discresionally orders for that purpose, which with Submission to you, Sir, is wrong,   for I take him to be a serious sober discreet Gentleman, and such men should have orders in case they should arrive here to markett as he now has, to proceed farder. I have looked out for [a] Pipe of wine for you, but could not meet with any that was good en[ough for] you. I shall send you one by Captain Pope, with the hollands. my brother goes [per Capt.] Kerr. I design'd to send him to New york — but the affair I was sending him about, I had an account of it's being don.   Incloased I send you a Letter to Collonel Nathaniel Gilbert, which please to seale and forward by the Post.   I send you two Negroes;[2] if you like them keep them and give my Account credit for what you think they are worth.   the Negroe man is a Peice of a Saylor and a fine Papa Slave — cost thirty pounds Sterling out of the Ship.   the Negroe woman is a fine Slave.   I had another which is a better wather, but suspected somthing I entended against her, on which shee's given us the Slip

---

[1] Mutilated.
[2] In this year Paul Dudley printed at Boston his *Essay on the Merchandize of Slaves and Souls of Men*. Massachusetts imposed a duty of £4 a head on negroes, but the King in 1732 issued an order that no new duty should be laid on them. *Belcher Papers*, I. 256.

this morning, but hope to have her againe before Pope sailes. note, this woman I now send I bought her from one John Wilson and paid him forty-five pounds Cash. I now understand his title is not good, and am advised to ship her off. if you like her I will warrant her to you. Pay Captain Kerr six or eight pound for his Sivellity to my brother; he would not take any thing from me here. I am sorry you'r disapointed in the Limmons, Orringes and Lymes I sent you. if the Fellow ever comes here, I will make him dearly pay for them. I am sorry I can't send you any now except a feiw by my brother, which am afear'd they will not keep. I have sent you two Caggs of Tamerins, one ditto of Sweetmeats, mixt with Ginger, Twelve bottles of Sittron Watter, of which I begg your Acceptance. I have also sent one Cagg of Tamerins to your brother-in-law Mr. Coggshell.[1] I begg you'l deliver it to him to whom I present my humble Service. Altho: unknown, I am verry much obliged to him for his Sivellity to my brother when there.

Mrs. Nugent joynes me with our best respects to your good Lady and Little ones. Accept the same your good selfe for I am sincearly Your Most Obliged Humble Servant,

WALTER NUGENT

Pt. St. note by Collonel Gilbert's Letter you are to keep the bills untill such time you have his Advise of my bills being accepted. Please to lett my brother have any thing he wants on my Account.

FRANCIS POPE TO ABRAHAM REDWOOD[2]

Dear freind　　　　　　　　　　Antigua May 12th 1731.

I HAVEING this good oppertunity by Capt. Bennett to let you know that I have disposed of all my Cargo, only good part of the Chese I cant sell, for the markett is very dull　I have sold as my Neighbowrs has done, but have not as yett got in my Debts as yet; and as for my horses

[1] David Coggeshall.
[2] The original is in the Newport Historical Society.

will turn out at about eaight pound foreteen shillings per head but however it cant be help now, for there was three Newlondon men arived after I landed. they landed there horses and sold for tow pistoles a head and three which is very true but however I shall make what Dispach I can If it pleases God to sale next Sunday for I pray excuse my lying so long hear, twas not for my Desire. If I could a heard of any Salt down to Leward I would bin allmost by this at home but however I hope you will not take a mis in what I have done for the best I could to your advantage. I have got in about tweenty Cask of hog Suger and Rum. so more next, onely that Capt. Newgent came to town to day, where wee got by our self and drink you and your Wife good health. No more at present but shall conclude this Instant with Love to you both and Children. I hope your self and good Family do enjoye health as I hope from the allmighty to find in. tell then I am, Sir, your most humble Servant and affectionate freind

FRANCIS POPE[1]

Kind Love to Brother Abraham and his Wife and famely. Pray excuse bad wrighting.

Deare freind I pray you wont see my Wife want any thing that you can due for her.

ROWLAND FRYE TO ABRAHAM REDWOOD

Sir, London, 15 May, 1731.

My last was 20 March by Capt. Carey advising you that I had honour'd your Bill £50. —. — to Jos: Jacob. I have since your favor 9th Febry with a Power of Attorney to receive some Legacy for you, and I have been with the Widow of Mr. John Field, who is willing to pay any Legacy that shall appear due to you, and I beleive she is also in such circumstances as to be able to do it, but at present seems to be a stranger to the Affair. Mr. Richard Part-

---

[1] Francis Pope is a signer of the petition to Earl of Bellomont, September 26, 1699, on a church in Rhode Island, together with Pierre Ayrault. Probably father to the ship captain. Mason, *Annals of Trinity Church*, Newport, 11.

ridge,[1] to whom I deliver'd the enclosed letter, informs me that he has already received the Legacy for his Friend, and believes that you have made a Mistake in your letter of Attorney, for he apprehands that there are two Legacys due to you, whereas you only impower me to receive one for £38: 10: — which fell to you by the Death of your Brother Jonas Langford Redwood   the other is the Legacy of £154: — : — left [by] your Brother Wm. Redwood,[2] of which you take no Notice in your letter of Attorney, nor is there any proof of his Death. Mr. Walter Newberry also informs me that he has received both those Legacys, and advises me to write you and get an explanation of this from you before I receive the Legacy of £38: 10: so that I beg you will let me know how the Case stands, and I will then finish your Business withal the Dispatch imaginable.

I have honour your Bill for £60. to Jos: Jacob, one for £100. and another for £50. payable to John Freebody. pray be so good as to advise me when you draw any Bills, least there might be otherwise some mistake or some forged Bills be brought to me for Acceptance, for at present I only believe they are of your Drawing by the hand writing.

Since the above I have rec'd yours 21 November, via Antigua, with orders for sundry Goods, all which I am getting ready and will send by the first good opportunity to Boston or Rhode Island; but I beleive it will be sometime hence before they can all be finished fit for you. however I will loose no time. I hope you have received your Account Current dated 21 January last, and shall observe to send it once a year. if you would have it oftener be pleased to let me know. I have received none of your Sugar yet, but beleive we shall have some Ships in very soon, tho' the price is so low that I am afraid they will not answer your expectation. I am Sir,   Row'd Frye

P. S. I have taken my Brother Samuel (whom I beleive you knew in Antigua) to be in Partnership with me, and hope you will continue to favour us with your Correspond-

---

[1] Merchant of London, and later agent of Rhode Island.
[2] He had died October 31, 1712, aged sixteen.

ence as when I was without a Partner. Copy per Capt. Clarke.

ELIZA LANGFORD TO ABRAHAM REDWOOD

Antigua, May the 16, 1731.

Dear Cousen,

YOURS I received by Capt. Pope, and am well pleased to hear of your safe arrival and that you with your Family enioy a perfect state of health I pray God keep you so, that yours may not be left as I and mine are, for we are like Sheep without a Shepherd. he had his failings as well as others but I may say I have lost the best of Husbands and my Children the best of Fathers. my troubles are unknown. I pray God soporte me under all my afflections. I hope he has receiv'd true satisfaction for his Good deeds don upon Earth there being but few that has left a better carrecter behind them he departed this life the thirty of november after three days illness of the Collick. Dear Cousin I hope that we shall still keep a true freindship for each other and when ever we meet again you shall find as hearty a wellcome to me as ever.

I thank you for all favours received Particular your last which is a Horse betwixt Betty and my self he has no mark so we weare oblidge to take any that Pope would give us. he is a small black horse. Pray make my Love and Service exceptable to your good spouse and Family, except the same from her who is your

Loveing Cousen

Eliza Langford

the Children gives their kind Loves to you and yours. I have sent you by Capt. Pope 1 Kegg of tamarind markt A R   1 Kegg of Sweatmeats markt A R.

Edward Byam to Abraham Redwood

Antigua, the 22nd of May, 1731.

Sir,

My last was by Capt. Carr of the 7th of April in which I gave you an account; the Arbitrators upon second thoughts and the extreame dry weather had awarded Mr. Gamble to pay you £102. and to deliver up the land the 25th of May. I alsoe advised I had paid your bil on me to said Carr for £200, and that I had sent you by him 90 bar. Sugar and ten hheads of rum amounting to £310. 1. 2¼. there was alsoe some goods sent you that Mr. Lovell brought out for you according to your order, amounting to about £90; I gave Capt. Carr £20 od mony to lay out for you at St. Kits in case there being none to be purchasd here, but at an extravagant price £20 or £22 per Cent. I am now to inform you that your Crop is almost over   all that is now made or likely to be made will not be sufficient to pay your debts here and buy provisions and cloaths for your Slaves. Abundance of your canes by means of the dry weather are soe short they will not be fit to be cut this year. if we finde them of any length in July to be sure they shall be ground. Mr. Burke nor my selfe has rec'd one shilling from Gamble Watkins or Tomlinson, occasiond by the great drought. a day of fast was appointed the 19th of May to beseech the Almighty to turne his wrath from us. God was graciously pleased to send us a fine Season the 17th and some the 19th, which put some watter in our ponds[1] and greatly refreshd the canes, which gives hopes of a Crop the next year. Your Manager sticks close to your plantation, soe that if we have tollerable weather you may expect to make a good quantity of Sugar the ensuing year. With boath our kind respects etc.

Edward Byam

---

[1] The Indian name for Antigua was Jamaica. "It is a singular circumstance that this word, which in the language of the larger islands signified a country *abounding in springs*, should in the dialect of the Charaibes, have been applied to an island that has not a single spring or rivulet of fresh water in it." Edwards, *History of the British Colonies in the West Indies*, I. 473. Antigua was subject to excessive droughts, and the settlers early resorted to cisterns for holding the rain water.

Debts you owe Capt. Leily £148; Mr. Langford on ball'a about £229; bill of exchange to George Byam, £90 Sterl. or £139; Lovell about 90 — besides plantation char[ges].

Port Charges, Antigua [1]

1731. Port Charges of the Sloop *Abraham & Jonah*		Dr.
To Cash pd. for Plantation Bonds		£0. 6.0.
To Do. pd. the Navill Officer		0.14.0.
To Do. pd. the Collector		1. 3.0.
To Do. pd. for 1 Barrill Turpintine		1. 0.0.
To Do. pd. in the Powder Office		3. 9.0.
To Do. pd. the Searchers		0.14.0.
To Do. pd. in the Custom House		2. 2.0.
To Do. pd. the Comptrowler		0.14.0.
To Do. pd. for the List of Men		0.10.6.
To Do. pd. the Navell Officer		1. 9.6.
To Do. pd. the Clerke		0.14.0.
To Greenwitch Hospitall		1. 0.9.
To Do. for Exchange		0. 1.6.
To Do. pd. the Fort to pass		0. 3.0.
To Do. pd. the Liquor office		0. 3.6.
To Do. pd. the Waiter for Indosing Cocketts		0. 7. .
		£14.11.9.

Antigua, May 24th, 1731.
 Errors Excep'd per me,
  Francis Pope

Edward Byam to Abraham Redwood

Antigua, June the 18th, 1731.

Sir,

I REC'D a letter of yours of the 29th of March. this is said to be sent by the way of Boston, but came here from Rhoad Island (and delivered me by Capt. Newgent,) in which you are pleased to mention that you had rec'd a letter from me last January by which letter you understood that Mrs. French was dead (who dyd in Feb:) and you desire that I would put Capt. Newgent into the Managment of your plantation. Capt. Carr I am informd was arrivd

---
[1] The original is in the Newport Historical Society.

with you about ten days before this Vessell saild, in w[hich sen]t you a letter of the 7th of Aprill, and allsoe the Coppy of another letter dated the 12th of March, [in w]hich I acquainted you that I had plac'd a Manager on your Plantation with the likeing and approbation of your Kinsman Mr. Langford.

I cannot help being much surprisd first that you should write a letter said to goe by way of Boston that came directly from Rhoad Island, and at the same time is pleasd to take noe notice that you had rec'd my letters of the 12th of March or 7th of Aprill. I have noething to say against Capt. Newgent but that he may manage very well, and as the estate is your owne you may put on who you pleasd upon it. But I think there was noe Necessity for this cunning; for since you had a mind he should be put on your plantation, if you had plainly writ to me that Collo. Tomlinson should be displac'd, and the other put in his stead it woud have bin more sinceare and I woud have done it.

When Capt. Newgent came to me and shewd me your letter I desird he would excuse me from giving him the charge of your plantation until I did hear farther from you on that head. If he had desird the managment before I had agreed with the other he might have had it. But how far soe much artifice may consist with dealing as wee would be dealt by I leave you to judge. Now I beg leave youl be so good as to consider wheather or not you have not usd me very unkindly. I pray you to observe that in making up your Account I could have charg'd you (and it would have bin allowd me) five per Cent for paying about the sum of £7000 which would have amounted to here £350, as you may perceive by the debit part of your account. I gave you £50 Sterling in the bil of a £1000, for which I chargd but 50 per Cent and the exchange was 55. This you may remember I told you. I had reason to believe this might have obtained the small favour of the continuance of an Agent I had plac'd, until his il managment or unfaithfulnes should have deserv'd his being displacd.

But as I finde I can be of noe service to you I desire youl please to appoint another Attorny, and soe I wish you a great deal of prosperity from, Sir, Your humble Servant

EDW. BYAM

You are sensible I overpaid £487. for which I have your bond. this I shall discount with Mrs. Burke.

ROWLAND FRYE TO ABRAHAM REDWOOD

London, 30 July, 1731.

Sir

MY last was 26 Ulto. by Captain Forster since which I am not favour'd with any from you. I have by this Opportunity sent the Goods you orderd which I hope will go safe and prove to your Satisfaction. the Amount is £215: 12:8 as by Invoice and bill of Lading enclosed.

I could meet with no Master that was willing to carry the Horses. They insisted on £10 Sterling for each besides your finding all the Hay, Corn, etc. as I did not send the Horses I thought it was to no Purpose to send the Coachman; because if you are willing to give that Freight he must go over to take care of them. his Wages will be £15. Sterling per Annum, a Livery, his Passage and all Charges to be paid by you, for which Consideration he is to be bound to you for 3 Years[1] You will be pleased to let me have your Directions in this Affair, for til then I cannot venture to send them upon such high terms.

I shall be glad to hear that the Iron Gates and Stone Work are as you directed, the Workmen inform me your

---

[1] It was not unusual to obtain such servants from England. In 1733 Governor Belcher asked for a good footman: "I must pray you to be very carefull in making choice of this servant, that he be sober, honest, well understanding his business, that can shave and dress a wig well, and do every thing about a gentleman, that would go to the same church with me — not one bred to the Church of England. ... My footman that will be out of his time in three months has twenty pounds a year, this money, wages, besides a livery, dyett, etc., which are worth at least £60 a year more." *Belcher Papers*, I. 271. He complained later that his servants were all free, and set up for themselves. *Ib.*, 380.

Directions were not so perfect as could be desired, however that everything was performed in the best manner, and the Stone Work fitted to the Gates, that there cannot well be a mistake in putting them up.

Flower potts are not now in Fashion; so that I have now sent you two pine apples of a new sort of stuff which wears as well as stone, and comes very cheap; for in stone they would cost above £12. if you do not like them, they will probably serve for some other place about your house, and I will then send you any sort you please to order. There are 1 M of Bricks more than you order'd, but as you did not mention what sort they were to be, I first shipped Grey Stocks.[1] I was afterwards informed that the Coins should be of Red Bricks, and have therefore sent 1 M of them. I hope it will be no loss to you as the Charge of them is not very great. These things are what I am no great judge of, and if any thing should be amiss I hope you will be so good as to excuse it, for I do assure you that I have used my utmost Endeavours to get everything in a handsome manner, and as cheap as possible, they being all bought with ready Money.

Governour Byam writes me that he shall not be able to ship me any of your Sugar by reason of the dry weather. the Market is still so bad that I believe it has been for your Advantage to pay them away there. it is to be hoped the Market will mend soon as the Crops fall short in several Islands.

I have now taken my Brother Samuel into partnership and shall beg leave for the future to subscribe our Names jointly. I am, Sir,

Row'd Frye

P. S. I have not yet had an answer to mine about your letter of Attorney.

Copy per Captain Homans.

---

[1] The English brick in 1724 was 9 inches in length, $4\frac{1}{2}$ inches in breadth, and $2\frac{1}{4}$ inches in thickness. *London Gazette.*

Rowland Frye to Abraham Redwood

Sir, London, 13 August, 1731.

I WROTE you lately by Captain Homans who carried all the Goods you order'd, which I hope you have received in good order. this serves to enclose copy of the Invoice and 2d Bill of Lading for them.

As you desired your Acct. Current I have now been able to finish it and have sent it you accordingly. the Ballance is two shillings and 3*d.* in your Favour. you will observe that I have received no money by virtue of your Letter of Attorney, because I wait for your farther Instructions about it.

We have had several ships from Antigua but no news about the crops, only they have had some fine Rains. Sugars are still low, and there is no prospect of the Markets mending till the latter end of the year. I am, Sir, Your most humble Servant

ROW'D FRYE [1]

Henry Clinton to Abraham Redwood

Sir, Antigua, 5th October, 1731.

THIS goes per the *Charming Nancy,* Jas. Slocombe, Master, with four Hhds. Rum, Seven Hhds. Molasses, and Twelve Kegs Sweetmeats. I desire you'l ship the produce in Lumber and Stock, or any thing you'l judge to my advantage. The Bearer brings you Major Nugents Atty; in case my Cargo be not sufficient he will be accountable for the Remainder. I should on all Occasions be glad to serve you and am with Respect, Your Mo: Hunble Servant,

HENRY CLINTON

I beg youl send 2 Thousand white oak heading; 4 Thousand white oak staves; One Hhead Buck wheat. What-

---

[1] Beginning with September, 1731, on the enforcement of the British acts of trade in New England, see the *Belcher Papers,* printed in 6 *Mass. Hist. Collections,* VI. VII. The papers run to 1643.

ever Charge the Master may be at in respect to Carpenters work Please to advance. There are 13 Ca: Sweetmeats.[1]

ROWLAND AND SAMUEL FRYE TO ABRAHAM REDWOOD

Sir, London, 3 March, 1731 [1732.]

ON the other side is a copy of what we wrote you by Capt. Bonner. we have since received the Goods for your Legacy and have enclosed you an Invoice and Bill of Lading for them. The Goods amounted only to £151. and the Remainder, being three pounds, was paid us in money. We have also sent your Account Current, as you desired to have it frequently, the Ballance is £459: 17: 3 in our favour. we hope it is to your satisfaction, but if there be any mistakes please to let us know and they shall be rectify'd. We cannot yet meet with any Captain that will carry your Horses.[2] there are several Ships would carry them to Antigua if you could afterwards conveniently transport them to Rhode Island. Our Sugar Market is still very dull, and it is to be feared will not be better this Crop. We are Sir etc.
ROW'D AND SAM'LL FRYE

P. S. There is a Bounty on the eight peices of Norwich Crapes of six pence per pound as they are made of worsted and silk.[3] the charge of the Debenture is about 20/, so

---

[1] Governor Belcher describes the New Hampshire export trade in 1631 in words which will apply to New England in general: "The chief trade of the Province continues (as for many years past) in the exportation of masts, yards, bowsprits, boards, staves, and rafters for England, but principally to Spain and Portugal, and some to the Charribee Islands, with lumber and refuse fish, and the better sort of fish to Spain, Portugal, Italy, etc. Some sloops and small vessells go in the winter (with English and West India goods) to Virginia, Maryland and Carolina and return with corn and flesh." *Belcher Papers*, I. 71.

[2] "We have been endeavoring to get some captain to carry your coach-horses, but cannot persuade any one of them to do it. They say there is a great risque in it, and they will loose their Freight unless they bring them alive; if you please to make some agreement with any captain there, we can get the Horses in a weeks time, and otherwise we are afraid we shall never be able to send them." *Rowland and Samuel Frye to Abraham Redwood*, April 26, 1732.

[3] Silk stuffs mixed with grogram-yarn, incle, cotton, or worsted, having at least two-thirds parts of the ends, or threads of the warp, silk or enough silk to be obvious

that there will be a small matter coming to you, for which you shall have Credit as soon as we receive it.

Copy per Homans.[1]

JOHN TOMLINSON, JR. TO ABRAHAM REDWOOD

Sir, [Antigua, April, 1732.]

THIS by Capt. Pope incloses you a Bill of Lading for Forty Hhdds. and three Barrels of Rum, with sixty one Barrels of Sugar, which goods I hope will come safe to hand; The Barrels of Rum markt 41. and 42. are what I made for your own peculiar use, and wish they may please you; I think they want nothing but Age. 43 is a Cask of Highwines for fear some of the Rum shou'd have lost part of its strenght before it gets to you.

The Governour has given Capt. Nugent a Lease for your Land. I beleive he writes you by this opportunity.

After a miserable spel of dry-weather God has blest us with such plentiful Showers, that our next years Crop that was just upon dying, begins now to look fresh: The Rains will be of vast service, even to this years Crop, both as to quality and quantity.

I shall wait your further orders about your Works, not having had a line from you since my two former, one by way of New York, the other directly to your Island; and whatever your orders are they shall be punctually followed. I have sent you a dosen pounds of Bohea Tea,[2] and a Barrel of Herrings, for Mrs. Redwood, according to a memorandum of Collo. Gunthorpe's.[3]

My Wife desires Mrs. Redwoods acceptance of three Cags of sweet meats, with two dosen Pint-Bottles of Citronwater, Oranges, and Lemons, none to be had, the dry

---

and apparent to the customs officer, the silk to be double the value of the bounty, received six pence a pound bounty on export. It was first allowed in 1722.

[1] A captain also appearing in *Belcher Papers*, I. 213.

[2] Bohea is derived from the name of two ridges of hills in the province of Fuhkien, China, whence tea was first imported into England. Early in the eighteenth century it was the name of the finest kinds of black tea.

[3] John Gunthorp. See next letter.

weather having been so very severe that they dropt from the trees before they were half grown; I am, Sir, Your most assured Friend and Humble Servant

        JOHN TOMLINSON, JUN'R.

 I have bought you a pipe of Wine according to your order. I have shiped to Messrs. Frye's Eighty Hhdds. of Sugar and shall follow your orders in shipping on.

JOHN GUNTHORP TO ABRAHAM REDWOOD

Deare Abraham,   Antigua, April the 23th, 1732.

 I SHOULD have wrote to you by several oppertunities since my arrival here, if my indisposition had not prevented me, which continued very severely upon me ever since I left you till about fourteene days agoe, from which time I have beene upon the recoverie and am now in hopes I shall live to see you again; We have had an exceeding dry spell of weather from November till the begining of this month, but thank God now its as favourable as we can desire:

 I have sent you by your Sloope my Spanish Stone Colt which I hope will be acceptable to you, as I think him as compleate a beautie as any of his Species, when he is in goode order, and has beene the moste admird litle Creature here, we have had among us. My Son tells me he discoverd a litle lamness in his right foote or shoulder when he carried him downe to towne, which hapend as we immagin from his breaking loose from the boy that led him and scampering about for some time before they could catch him again; but if itt continues and should prove in the shoulder, make the Farrier putt in a French Rowill[1] below the Setting on the Shoulder, and turn him to grass, and he'l soone be well; The Old Horse is in fine order and pritty well, and much admired by my Wife, who takes her self abundance of care of him; I think you [I] have sent you what you gave me a Memorandum for, and I assure you my goode Friend, Pope should have carried Mrs. Redwood and

---

[1] A seton inserted in the flesh of an animal.

yourself a plentifull share of the several sort of fruits of this Island if any were to be had, and noe oppertunitie shall escape me when I can have itt in my power to oblidge you therwith or any thing else. Jack Tomlinson tells me he now writes you the mortifieng account of the Governours signing Newgent a Lease for your Lands contrary to your request to him, which I think is not verie kind, however you may make that voide by a Course of Law when you please, as your Attorney Tomlinson did not consent thereto. If time or my health would admit, I would write more fully upon the occasion and demonstrat to you how great a sufferer you are and will be thereby during the Lease; but perhaps I may be thought officious and too busie therein, and it were more advisable not to concern myself therewith; I should not doe Captain Pope justice if I did not acquaint you of his Diligence in your bussiness, and singular care and regard to your interest, and take my word for itt, that whenever you part with him, you will scarse meet with his equal for fidelity to serve you; but of that I dare say you have no thoughts. I am in hopes you will dispatch him back again immediately, and let me have fraight on board the Sloope for what I have to bring from Rhoade Island, according to your promise. Pray excuse me to Major Martin for not writing to him by this oppertunity, and my Landlord also, but I will not slip the next if I am able; my Wife joyns with me in our best respects to Mrs. Redwoode and your self, and beleive me to be, Dear Abraham,

*Yr. Sincere Friend
and affect Humser:
Jno. Purthorp*

ROWLAND AND SAMUEL FRYE TO ABRAHAM REDWOOD

Sir,

THE above was wrote you by Ct. Carey who carried 3000 of Red Stock Bricks for your Account, which we hope you received in good order. this encloses the 2d Bill of Lading.

We have lately received 10 hhds. of your Sugar by Capt. Stewart, 20 hhds. by Draper, and 18 hhds. by Sutcliffe. they are come to a most miserable market, nor is there any prospect of its being better. pretty good Sugars sell now for 16/ per C. as yours are but indifferent we shall not be able to get so much for them, tho' our best endeavours shall not be wanting. We shall render you the Accounts Sales of all your Sugars as soon as they can be made out.

We have not received any letter from you of late so have nothing further to add but to assure you that we are, Sir, Your most humble Servants

ROW'D AND SAM'LL FRYE

London, 5 July, 1732.

[Endorsed,] Per Capt. Winslow.

JOHN GUNTHORP TO ABRAHAM REDWOOD

Antigua, July the 24th, 1732.

Deare Abraham,

THOUGH you have not wrote to me by Pope or any other oppertunitie since my last to you, yet you may perceive by this I am unwilling to drop a Correspondence with a Friend I have contracted an intimacy with, and entertain so good a regard for, as let me assure you I doe for your self, and notwithstanding your refusal to fraight my frame and Roofe in your sloope this last trip she has made, according to your repeated and faithfull promises to me, which alone engadged me to bespeake itt, yet am I far from cherishing any ill will, or harbouring the least resentment against you for itt, as I have mett with noe disapointment thereby; However let me once more advise you as a sincere and real Friend to be always punctual to your word and strictly observant of your Promises, which will never faile of gaining you the goode Esteeme of every bodie, and mai[n]tain to your self a distinguishing Character, meritorious without spott, or blemish; and for this I am [persuaded] you have goode Nature [enough] to hold me excusable;

I beg leave to recommend the Bearer Mr. John Pigott, Son to old Major Pigott of our Island, to your Friendship and favour, and if you can be any way servisable to him by assisting him to gett an Employment in the Command of some goode Vessel; I shall take itt as a very greate favour, for He is truely a young Gentleman of Meritt, being, very modest, sober, industrious, a brisk Sayler, and goode Artist, which I aver to be the Character given to me of him by two Captains of Men of War, he had the honour to serve under as Midship Man for four years last past. Capt. Malbone[1] I am in hopes will provide for him, and use your interest with him to that end. My Wife joyns with me in our best respects to Mrs. Redwoode, and accept the same from, My goode Friend, Your Affectt. Humble Servantt

JNO. GUNTHORP

FRANCIS POPE TO ABRAHAM REDWOOD

Antigua, July 25th day, 1732.

Sir,

THESE come to accquant you that I am safe arrived at Antigua in thurty one days after I left you, where wee have landed all your fraims in good order, and all the rest of my Lumber and as for our Staves being in so great demand when I was here last voyage that now they wont give more then four pounds for the best that brought here; and as for your Hups the major[2] wants them all for the

---
[1] Godfrey Malbone. See p. 49, infra.
[2] Thomlinson.

Plantation, and the most part of the Staves, so that I shall have nothing to sell but the Shingles and sum of the Board, if I can sell them so have nothing strange to wright you, only that wee are all well in good helth, thank God, and shall make all the despach I can. I shall get about forty hhgds. in by night from Arter Willkerson upon freight for Rhode Island. I have had no Goods from the Plantation not as yet; so if the major dount detain me here, I hope to sale in three or four days after Capt. Casey; so I shall conclude your affectionate friend till Death,

FRANCIS POPE

My kind Love to you and your Wife and Children.

[Endorsed,] These per Capt. Casey.

ROWLAND AND SAMUEL FRYE TO ABRAHAM REDWOOD[1]

London, 6 September, 1732.

Sir,

OUR last was by Capt. Croker with Invoice and 2d Bill of Lading for the Horses, etc. sent you in the *Britannia*. enclosed is copy of the Invoice for them.[2]

We are now to acknowledge your Favours 9th and 17 June, advising us of your Bills for £100 pay'a to Jonathan Thurston for £110 to Mr. John Brown, both which are honoured.

We are obliged to you for your Recommendation of Mr. Brown and shall take care that he have no reason to complain of our usage.

Enclosed is Account Sales for 10 hhds. Sugar per Stewart. Nett Produce £46. 2. 6, as also copys of Sales for your

---

[1] The original is in the Newport Historical Society.

[2] "We have at last got an opportunity to send your Horses and Capt. Draper has promised to take a great deal of Care of them, and to encourage him thereto we have given him £1. 11. 6 for his Prim[age] and Trouble. The Horses are thought to be very good and cost 50 Guineas. As the charge will be as much on ordinary ones as those that are very good, we thought you would not grudge the Expence." *Rowland and Samuel Frye to Abraham Redwood*, July 31, 1732.

Sugars by Davis, Oliver, Ion and Draper.[1] we cannot yet make out the Accounts for the 18 hhds. per Sutcliff, nor the 12 hhds. per King, but you may expect them in our next.

Our Market has mended a little, but is still very bad. if there be not something done to encourage an Exportation, the Colonys will suffer very much. We are, Sir, Your most humble Servants,

Row'd & Sam'll Frye

Rowland and Samuel Frye to Abraham Redwood

London, 8 February, 1732/3.

Sir,

Our last was 10 October. since which we have your's of the same Date, and are glad to hear the Horses cam to you in good order. Enclosed is Invoice and Bill of Lading for all the Goods you order'd, amounting to £154. 16. 4. we hope you will receive them in good order. we were forced to guess at the sizes of the Shoes, Gloves, etc. for want of your sending the measures. there is a Drawback on Linnen,[2] Muslin and Haberdashery, for which you shall have credit as soon as we receive the money.

You have also Account Sales for 12 hhds. Sugar per King, 18 hhds. per Sutcliff, and 10 hhds. per Coulter, with Copy of Sales for 10 hhds. per Stewart. these compleat the sales of all the Sugars sent us this year for your account. We have now likewise sent your Account Current, Ballance due to us being £612. 4. 11. after you have received this Account, we believe you will not be surprised that we have not paid the Bills, you drew on us lately, to the value of £450. We should be very proud to serve you, and would

---

[1] The details were given in a letter of July 31: 10 hhd. per Davis, £52. 2. 10; 8 hhd. per Ion, £39. 18. 1; 10 hhd. per Oliver, £42. 19. 2; and 20 hhd. per Draper, £88. 0. 6. The market was still very low, and the Sutcliffe shipment, "very ordinary," might sell for 13/.

[2] In Massachusetts bounties were offered to raisers of hemp and flax. *Belcher Papers*, I. 69. Rhode Island, in 1728, paid a bounty of 2d a pound to Samuel Clarke of Jamestown, on 1227 pounds of hemp raised, water rotted and dressed by him. *Newport Historical Magazine*, IV. 84.

have readily honoured your Bills, but it does not suit us to let so much money lay abroad, and sugars clear at present so little that it must be some time before they could discharge so large a Debt. therefore hope you will excuse us. if a small sum will at any time be of service to you, you may freely command it.

When we settled with the Executors of Mr. John Field and received the Legacy due to you by the death of your Brother William, you never mentioned any thing to us of any other Legacy, altho' we wrote you on this head, nor have you sent over any proofs of his Death. we will enquire of these persons about it and write you their answers in our next.

There is no such thing as a good Coachman to be got, they are very scarce and have great wages here, so that it will be much more for your advantage to get one from Boston. We are, Sir, Your most humble Servants

Row'd and Samuell Frye

Jacob Long [1] to Abraham Redwood

Saint Johns, Antigua, March the 14. 1732 [1733.]

Sir,

In my to last Letters I acquainted you of my proceding, which I dont doupt but you have received them; one by the way of Phillidelphia, the other by the way of New York. Antigua his now a scorching for want of Rain. there has binn no Rain not this three Mounth. Rum his att this time fiveteen pence for Cash and Sixteen pence for Goods Sugers from fifteen Shillings to twelf and sixpence per Hundread. White oak Staves and heedding his in great demand. other Lumber his not much wonted. Candles are in demand, and I belive will be all this year. the Ships not being arived that ware exspected fraight his not yet brock from fore Shillings, but exspect to brack every day. Capt. Pope his now a taking in and I hope will be redy to

---

[1] He had commanded the sloop *Diligence*, of Rhode Island, taken by the French on the coast of Martinico in 1727. *New England Weekly Journal*, July 10, 1727.

saile by the first of Aprill. Your Mill has binn going night and day this five weeks and has made a great Deel of Suger. I shall take all dilligent Care to ship my Affects of your Sloup and Cargo has soon as possoble one board your Sloup.

Mr. Jonas Langford his married to Ashing Wanners Daughter.

Sir, your Humble Servant to command,
JACOB LONG

[Endorsed,] Per Capt. Braton.

FRANCIS POPE TO ABRAHAM REDWOOD[1]

Sir,   Antigua, March 19th day, 1732 [1733.]

THESE Lines is to acquant you of my safe Ariveall in Antigua tweenty-eight days. So after a long and tedious Passage I have dun according to your Orders left on the Plantations six oxen, and two died upon the passage, and my horses; for major tomlinson taken them for the Mill, for your plantations suffred for want of them; and the most part of my Cargoe and the rest I shall dispose of as soon as I possibly can, and to the best advantage. as for the Cropps in this Island they are but poore, by reason of the great want of Rain, which is so much that water is not to be got for Drinking. as for my Candles I came to a good markett at 12 pence, and the rest of my Cargoe but indifferant. I shall take ten hogsed to day in, and the rest of my Cargoe as soon as possible, which I hope will be in three weeks after this, if Capt. Long does not detain me upon the account of shipen his goods for I must weaight tell the fifteen of April. so my freaind, as for going for mill timber for the mill, major tomlinson he thought would not ben for your advantage, and he could not du it for I have gone according to his Orders as you have direcked me in my orders, so have no more to wright at present, but shall conclude Your very most humble Sarvant,

FRANCIS POPE

---
[1] The original is in the Newport Historical Society.

my Love to you both and your Children and all them that ask after poor Frank.

wee all well at present, I thank God for it; only wee lost David, died the thursday after wee come out.

[Endorsed,] these pr Capt. Clark.

JOHN TOMLINSON, JR. TO ABRAHAM REDWOOD

Sir,   Antigua, March 21: 1732/3.

I AM now to acknowledge the favour of several of yours, and shall follow your Orders, as near as can be.

The occasion of your Sloop being detain'd here so long, has been intirely owing, to the great Rains we had after Xmas, which continued untill the middle of Feb: so that no mills were at work, till about that time; However as the Rains were general over all the Islands; I hope your Effects will come to so good a Market as to make amends, for the long time she has been out.

Inclosed is a Bill of Lading for Sugar, Rum,[1] One peece of

---

[1] Rum was sent in large quantities to Great Britain, but could not find a market in France, as brandy, the local product, received protection. The rum and molasses of the French islands could profitably be sold only on the American continent, and the British factors complained that the Americans sold lumber, provisions and horses to the English islands, and spent the proceeds in buying sugar and molasses of the French islands, "whereby the French are enabled to increase their settlements, and also their negro trade," and the prices of slaves and produce were thus enhanced. In former years the British islands obtained their provisions and supplies from the mother country; but now the chief benefit of the northern colonies to the kingdom was their ability to satisfy the islands, and their trade should be confined to the British islands. That four-fifths of the profits of the sugar islands centred in Great Britain, and one-fifth in the northern colonies, and that one-fifth, estimated to be about £300,000 per annum, was largely expended in the French islands. In reply it was asserted that the British sugar islands could not supply the molasses and rum needed for the Indian trade and the fisheries; that the principal imports from the French islands were molasses, which was made into rum, silver and cocoa. The silver was sent to England in payment for supplies, and was the only ready money obtainable by the colonies; that to prohibit imports of molasses from islands other than the British would destroy an important shipping industry, create a monopoly and greatly reduce the fisheries, the trade in peltry and the commercial connections with the mother country. Anderson, *Origin of Commerce*, III. 181. The controversy continued until 1733, when Parliament, for the encouragement of the British sugar islands, passed an act imposing duties

Sheeting Holland, One Cag of preserv'd Ginger, four of Sweet-meats, Two dosin quart Bottles of Citron water, One Dosin pints ditto, all which I hope will come safe to Hand and be to your satisfaction.

As we have no likelyhood of Sugars mending in their price in England, I think you're very much in the right for ordering the greatest part of your Sugars to be shipt to your self.

We have no news here, worth mentioning to you, not so much as any certainty of a New General, which gives us no uneasiness, since we are so happy as to have Gov: Byam over us. The Sugars numbred 29 to 36 are all strain'd; but I think 29 and 35 are the brightest.

I am now straining, and design to strain all, if I can but supply myself with straining Cloths, which are now very scarce.

I hope this will find you and Family in good Health; which is the hearty wish of, Sir, Your most Obliged Friend and Humble Servant,

JOHN TOMLINSON, JUNIOR

My Wife joyns with me in our best respects, to your self and Lady. I have sent you two Barrels of Oranges, but I am very much afraid (they are so ripe) that they wont keep till the vessel arrives; but the Captain has promist to take all the care that can be.

FRANCIS POPE TO ABRAHAM REDWOOD

Sir,   Antigua, June 28th day, 1733.

THESE few Lines comes by Capt. Thomas, that I have got in seventy five hhg of Rum and Suger, beside twenty teirces of Suger; and hope, if it pleases the allmighty God

---

on products of foreign sugar colonies, other than Portugal, imported into any of the British plantations in America, viz.: nine pence per gallon on rum, six pence per gallon on molasses, and five shillings on every hundred weight of sugars and paneles, — "to be paid down in ready money by the importers, before the landing of the merchandise." 6 Geo. II. c. xiii.

with my Liberty, I hope to sale in about four or five days after Capt. Thomas, and hope by night to have in about ninety hhgs. in. I wood a rote you by Capt. Scott,[1] but Bennett and he both saled in one day for Rhoad Island, and I gave my letter to Bennett. and pray Sir you wood be so good as to deliver my letter to my Wife. So, Sir, Major tomlinson, being in town yesterday, I was saying to him that I could not despose of my Candles, he told me I had better to sell them for sevenpence then to leve them. So, Sir, I wood not dew nothing to your Disadvantage upon no account, what ever trust you put in me yesterday bringing down Rum from the plantation your Cattle being verey poor that two of them died in the path a come to the town, wich will be sumthing of hendrenc of my not saleing so soon as I thought to saled four days after Bennett so, Sir, I have nothing farther to wright you at present, being all well at present I thank God. With my Love and Service to you and all friends,

Francis Pope

I shall bring about ten hhgs. upon the deck for Capt. Gardner.[2]

[Endorsed,] These per Capt. Thomas.

Rowland and Samuel Frye to Abraham Redwood

Sir,

We are now to acknowledge your Favour 21 May enclosing a Certificate of the Death of your Brother William Redwood. We thereupon applyed to Mrs. Field, who is Executrix to the Estate, but could get no satisfactory answer from her. she complains of her being left very much involved and that she has paid several Legacys which the Law could not have obliged her to do. had you sent

---

[1] Perhaps Joshua Scott, an "honorary" member of the Fellowship Club, August 7, 1753. This club admitted only such persons as were or had been commanders of vessels, and met monthly in one of the public houses in Newport. A list of the members from 1753 to 1850 is in *Newport Historical Magazine*, IV. 167.

[2] William Gardiner?

us at first a regular account of this Legacy we might have recover'd it as well as the former one; but now we cannot tell how we shall succeed, but we shall apply to Mr. Walter Newberry, who may possibly do us some service.

We were in expectation you would not have taken it amiss that we did not pay all your Drafts on us, as they amounted to so considerable a Sum; but would have thought yourself obliged to us for advancing you £612. 4. 11 at a time, when all the merchants refused to advance any thing for their West India correspondents; sugars being then so low and the Islands in so declineing a condition. we have been enquiring after the rest of your Bills but cannot hear any thing of them, therefore suppose they are sent back. Mr. Tomlinson has shipped us 20 hhds. of your Sugar by Blair, and 12 hhds. by Capt. Sherburne. Enclosed is account of Sales for the first parcel. Nett Produce £157. 0. 4; the others are not yet landed.

Our market is a little better than it was last year, and if there be much Exportation Sugars will still rise.

We have nothing further to add but that we shall be proud of the Continuance of your Favours, and we shall always take care to execute faithfully what you entrust us with. We are, Sir, Your most humble Servants,

Row'd and Sam'll Frye

London, 20 July, 1733.

Rowland and Samuel Frye to Abraham Redwood

London, 29 August, 1733.

Sir,

Our last was by Capt. Homans, since which we have not heard from you. we have again applyed to Mrs. Field about your Legacy of £38: 10: 0, but perceive the Certificate you sent us is for Mr. Wm. Redwood, whereas the Legacy is due to your Brother Jonas Langford Redwood. we have already rec'd £154. 0: 0 for the Legacy due to your Brother William, and should have rec'd this at the same time had you sent us a proper authority.

Mrs. Field says if the Legacy is due she will pay it but must first consult Mr. Walter Newbury, as she is a Stranger to the Affair; and therefore we should have a Letter of Attorney from you to impower us to receive the money and also a Certificate of Jonas Langford Redwood's Birth and Burial, and that the Legacy is now due to you. however we believe you need not put your self to this expence till you hear from us whether Mrs. Field will pay the Legacy or not.

Enclosed is Copy of Sales for 20 hhds. of Sugar by Blair. the 12 by Sherburne are sold but at 17/6 per C. they proving very indifferent, and hope to send the sales in our next. we have lately rec'd 20 hhds. by Whipple, and Thirty by Draper, both which we shall take care to dispose of at the height of our Market. If there be any of your Bills in town unpaid we shall take care to discharge them all, for, as we promised, we are still ready to supply you with two or three hundred pounds when it may be of Service, tho' our affairs will not permit us to advance a large Sum.

There has been a Storm in the Leeward Islands which has done them a good deal of Damage, and we believe it will make Sugars rise here.[1] We are, Sir, etc.,

Row'd and Samuel Frye

Copy per Capt. Cary.

ROWLAND AND SAMUEL FRYE TO ABRAHAM REDWOOD

Sir,

On the other side is a Copy of our last by Capt. Cary, since which we have not heard from you, but have received 10 hhds. more of your Sugar by Tomlinson; as they are not landed we cannot write you how they prove. however shall take care to get the most for them that our Market will afford. the 30 hhds. by Draper and 20 by Whipple are sold at 18/6d per C. The accounts shall be rendred of the whole in our next, if possible; at present they cannot be made out, because we have not yet settled with the Buyers.

---

[1] An account of the hurricane, which struck the islands June 30, 1733, is in the *New England Weekly Journal*, August 13, 1733.

when the whole crop is completed we shall observe to send your Account Current.

We have honoured your Draft for £115 to Simon Peese, which is the only Bill we can hear of in Town, or they should also have been paid.

We have not yet had any particular answer from Mrs. Field about your Brother's Legacy, but shall let you know as soon as we have.

Our Market has been mended lately, pretty good Sugars now sell at 22 and 23 sh. per C. We are, Sir, Your most humble Servants,

Row'd and Sam'll Frye

London, 6 October, 1733.

Francis Pope to Abraham Redwood

Antigua, December 8th day, 1733.

Sir,

THESE come to acquaint you by Capt. Scott that I am safe arrived att Antigua, twenty nine days after I left you, where upon my passage I have had verey bad weather. I lost you 25 hoggs and three Sheep, and like to come to a poor markett for everything that I have brought here, thoug you gave me large orders if I like the markett to stay but howver you cant blame me for staying by Reson that Major Tomlinson has stopt me to land all my Lumber for the use of your Plantasion, and the Crops is like to be verey backward by reson of a blast that been amunks them the major told me that you have had a peice of Cain blasted that wood a made you fifty hhd of good Suger but my desine is to sell all for redy Cash and come away as soon as possable. here is look for a ship from the Cape devards [Verde] with Salt, which I hope to by a Loade and come direckly home. I cant tell you of anything to put in the Sloop, if it should please the allmighty God that the Sloop getts well home, but Shingles and hoops will be the best article that you can send as for horses will not dou. Sheep att 20 shilling, Beeff att fifty, Chese at 9 pence, Candles seven, Soap at Sixpence. I cant wright you nothing larger at present then to lett you no that I have sold but verey little. I being well att present, I shall conclude with Love and Service to you both and Children. I pray excuse short wrighting.

FRANCIS POPE

[Endorsed,] these per Capt. Scott.

ROWLAND AND SAMUEL FRYE TO ABRAHAM REDWOOD.

Sir, London, 12 February, 1733/4.

OUR last was 6th October per Captain Hammerden since which we have received your Favour 27 August, but it could not be answer'd sooner as there was no ship bound to that Part.

Enclosed are Account Sales for your Sugars by Draper, Whipple, Shirburne, Tomlinson, and Davis, which compleats the Accounts of all that we have received from your plantation this last crop. We were obliged to abate 6 s. per hundred on 20 hhds. after they were sold, because on delivery they did not answer their samples by that value. As all your affairs with us are now finished we have sent your Account Current. there is a Ballance of £44: 9: 5 still due to us. You will observe that we have paid your Bill for £115, to Simon Pease, and wish it had suited us to pay your two other Drafts, of £402. 10 to Hen: Collins and £60 to Dan: Ayrault.[1] We should have readily done it, only the apprehensions of a speedy war with France deterred us, knowing how much the Islands lay exposed to an Invasion from the French.[2] but should there be a settled peace you may depend on our serving you on any other occasion.[3]

---

[1] Daniel Ayrault, son of Pierre, born c. 1676–77 and died June 25, 1764. He married Marie Robineau, who died in 1729.

[2] In 1736 Antigua had a militia of 1500 men, with two forts and seven batteries, and the total force in the Leeward Islands amounted to 3.772 white men.

[3] The war of the Polish Succession broke out in August, 1733, and involved so France as to make any hostile movements against England's American possessions unlikely. Belcher feared that Great Britain might become involved, and asked that a small naval force be maintained at Boston. The presence of the French at Cape Breton threatened the safety of the commerce of New England. *Belcher Papers*, I. 418

Antego Sugars sell now from 17 to 24 s per Ct. according to their Goodness. We are, Sir, Your most humble Servants

       Row'd and Samuel Frye

Francis Wilks to Abraham Redwood [1]

London, 26 November, 1734.

Sir,

Since the foregoing Copy of my last no Ships have arrived from your parts. this only serves to advise you that I have rec'd a bill of Lading for 26 hhds. of Sugar shipt for your Account by Mr. Thomlinson of Antigua, on board the Ship *Godfrey*, Cap. John Draper, to my consignment, which ship is safe arrived at Falmouth in the West of England, tho' I understand she sprung a leak at Sea for which she put in at Newfoundland. hope your Sugars by her rec'd no damage, and I should be very glad to know if hereafter I must make Insurance on any goods that shall receive advice of being shipt to me on your account, or not. Sugars remain still at a stand. the Sugar refiners have left of working for above two months past, but now have begun again, and are even now resolved not to give the last high prices.[2] as soon as these Sugars on board of Draper are landed shall dispose of the whole to your best advantage and discharge your draft on me; being with great respect Sir, Your most obedient Servant,

            Fra. Wilks

---

[1] In the *Belcher Papers* are a number of letters from Belcher to Francis Wilks.

[2] "All our sugar islands together are thought annually to produce 85,000 hogsheads of sugar, each hogshead containing twelve hundred weight, or in all, 1,200,000 hundred weight. Of which Great Britain was thought to consume annually 70,000 hogsheads . . . [or] nine pounds and a half of sugar to each person. . . . It is computed that 300 sail of shipping go annually from Great Britain to the sugar islands, beside those which go thither from our American colonies, and that about 4,500 seamen are employed in navigating them; and that there is annually exported thither to the value of £240,000 in British manufactures." Anderson, *Origin of Commerce*, III. 203.

SAMUEL EVELEIGH TO GODFREY MALBONE

[South Carolina,] September the 12th, 1735.

Sir,

If the Book of Samples of Beads has come to your hands from Mr. Thos. Leech of Pensilvania, desire you'l return it me by the first Oppertunity, and also write me if you want those Gooseberry beads I formerly advised you of which lye at Barbadoes, or any other (haveing a large quantity of divers Sorts by me).

The Season for our Rice this last Summer has been extraordinary good, and tho the Bugg formerly mention'd, has done much damage to several Plantacons, yet its universally concluded, wee shall make above Twenty Thousand Bbls. more this year than the last.[1]

There has been imported into this place since the 25th of March last Twenty-four Hundred Negroes, which have sold very well, tho' the greatest part upon Credit, and several others are still expected.

I sent you a small Parcell of Goods per Capt. Chas. Wickam the fourteenth of September, 1734. desire you'l ballance that Account primo Oppertunity in Cheese, best Butter, and Tallow, and you'l oblidge, Sir, Your Humble Servant,

Sam Eveleigh

---

[1] In 1733 it was stated that the rice "exported from South Carolina to Spain and Portugal was become so cheap in those two countries as to have put almost an entire stop to the importation of that commodity from Venice and other parts of Italy; so far as to give ground to hope that Carolina might soon engross all the trade of Europe for that fine grain. Anderson, *Origin of Commerce*, III. 200. In 1730 rice was made a non-enumerated commodity, and so capable of direct export from Carolina to the Mediterranean, without being first landed in Great Britain. 3 Geo. II. c. xxix. Nine years later the exports from South Carolina reached 71,484 barrels, and in 1740, 91,110 barrels.

P. S. I desire you'l send me Two of the best Dolphin Cheeses.

[Endorsed,] Mr. Godfrey Mallbone, Merchant, Rhode Island.[1]

Francis Wilks to Abraham Redwood

London, 12 July, 1736.

Sir, I have received your favors of the 28th of april from Antigua and observe its Contents   herewith you have your account current ballance in my favor £16. 18. 2, which on examining I hope you will find agreable   am sorry to acquaint you that one Hans Steger to whom I sold 20 hhds. of your Sugar is broke; he was a person when sold him your Sugars in perfect Credit and not refused by any body. the state of the affair and what he paid on Account you'll see by your account current.   a great many other Sugar Merchants are concernd in this unhappy affair, and am apt to think for account of Gent[leme]n in Antigua. Mr. Hill is £700, Mr. Gerrish upwards of £500, with several others.   there is a Statute of Bankrupt taken out whereby all his effects are seized, and hope the creditors will have a handsome dividend, of which shall acquaint you farther hereafter. I am concern'd for this unhappy accident, and do assure you that as before mentiond the person was not deny'd credit by any body.   the information you had of Sugars being at 30/ was intirely wrong   the price is nothing near it   the finest St. Kitts Sugars have not been sold for more than 25/; Antigua's are now sold from 20 to 23/ as in quality.   I have paid your draft of £60 in favor of Jno. Freebody, also £300 in part of the £900 to Henry Collins the person who has this draft will keep it till you send farther effects, which as soon as they come to hand shall be applyd to discharge the remainder of said draft.   am obliged to you for your farther Consignments by Captains Watts and Davis, and your promises of assisting Captain Bulkley in

---

[1] In a later letter he is called Captain.

his lading on my account. you may depend on my study for retaliations of these favors, but misfortunes will happen to the most carefull. I am with due respect, Sir,

Mr. Z. Bourryan being absent.

Herewith you have sundry accounts sales for 62 hhds. of Sugar for which is credit given in your account current.

12 hhds. of Sugar per the *Chesnutt*	Hammett		£97.12. 8
10 . . . . . . per the *Sarah*	Lowthorp	. . .	68.11. 2
20 . . . . . per the *Parham Club*	Davis	. . . .	121. 4.11
10 . . . . . per the *Joseph*	Gorman	. . . .	86.10. 1
10 . . . . . per the *Success*	Snelling	. . . .	78.13.—

JOHN CAHOONE, JR. TO AYRAULT?[1]

Sir, Anamabo,[2] Octob^r the 27th, 1736.

AFTER My Respects to you: these may Inform how it is with me at present. I bles god I Injoy my health very well as yett: but am like to have a long and trublesom Voyge of it, for there never was so much Rum on the Coast at one time before, Nor the Like of the french shipen — never seen before for no. for the hole Coast is full of them. for my part I can give no guess when I shall get away, for I purchest but 27 Slaves since I have bin hear, for slaves is Very Scarce. we have had Nineteen sail of us at one time in the Rhoad: so that these ships that are said to Cary prime Slaves off is now forced to take any that Comes.

---

[1] Original in the possession of Mr. George C. Mason, in *Reminiscences*, II. 104.

[2] Anamaboe, or Anamabu, was an English fort on the coast of Guinea. It now lies in the Gold Coast, about eleven miles east of Cape Coast Castle. This neighborhood was much divided among the European powers, and the French, Dutch, Portuguese and English had forts within a few miles of one another, stations for obtaining slaves from the interior. As late as 1764 it was stated with truth that the Europeans knew nothing of the river courses or of the interior country.

heair is 7 sail of us Rume men that we are Ready to Devur one another; for our Case is Despart: So, I begg that you will exist my family in what they shall want for I no not when I shall git home: to them myself. I have had the misfortune to Bury my Chefe Mate on ye 21st of September, and one man more; and lost the Negro man, primus, and Adam Over board on my pasedge one three weeks after another: that makes me now Very weak handed: for out of what is left theair is two that is good for nothing — Cap Hamond hath bin heair six months and has but 60 Slaves on bord — my harty sevice to yr Spouse and family — I am y's to Com, JOHN CAHOONE, JR.

This day we are Informed Capt Handy heth cast away his Sconer to windward.

SNOW "GRAY HOUND"[1]

To all People to Whom these Presents shall come: John Tillinghast and Nathaniel Potter, both of Newport in the County of Newport in the Colony of Rhode Island, etc., Merchants, send Greeting: Whereas Nathan Bull of said Newport, Mariner, by One Charter Party bearing Date the Second Day of August, A.D. 1740, did Demise, Grant, and Lett unto Peter Bourse,[2] George Goulding,[3] and Joseph Whipple, all of s'd Newport, Merchants (a Com'tee appointed by Act of Assembly,)[4] the Snow *Gray Hound*, burthen about one hundred and eight Tuns, in order to transport therein some of the Soldiers raised to go against the Spaniards into some part of the West Indies; which said Snow was to be fitted, tackled, and apparelled as in and by said Charter Party is expressed, and then to be appraised by two indifferent Men to be chosen by both Parties. Now Know Ye That we, the said John Tillinghast and Nathaniel Potter,

---

[1] The original is in the Newport Historical Society.

[2] Peter Bours, died September 20, 1761, aged fifty-six years. He is frequently mentioned in Mason, *Annals of Trinity Church*, Newport.

[3] George Goulding married Mary (Ayrault) Cranston, a daughter of Daniel Ayrault.

[4] *Rhode Island Col. Rec.*, IV. 574.

being chosen by both Parties, have view'd said Snow, examin'd the Accounts of Charges and Disbursments, etc., when fitted as aboves'd ready for sailing, and maturely considered the same. We are of Opinion, and it is our sincere Judgement That said Snow, when she went to Sea, with all her Appurtenances and fitted as aforesaid, was justly and honestly worth the sum of Two Thousand Eight Hundred Pounds in good and passable Bills of Publick Credit of the Colony of Rhode Island. In Witness whereof We have hereunto set our Hands and Seals, the Eighth Day of October, in the fourteenth Year of his Majesties Reign Anno Dom: 1740.

JOHN TILLINGHAST
NATH'LL POTTER

These are to certify, the Hon'ble the Principal Officers and Commissioners of his Majesty's Navy, That the *Greyhound*, Robert Oliver, Master, burthened One hundred and eight Tons, belonging to North America, was employed as a Transport in the Service of this Expedition to the seventeenth day of May last, at which time he was discharged from the said Service; and in passing his victualling Account to that time with the Commissary for Stores, it appears he is Debtor One Pound fifteen shillings and seven pence half penny Sterling, which he hath paid to the said Commissary, and that the said Master hath conformed to the Terms of his Agreement made with Colo. Gooch dated on board of the *Vere* Transport this Twelfth of June, 1741.

WILLIAM FURNEL TO ABRAHAM REDWOOD

Sir, Antigua, October 13th, 1742.

I AM not a little supprised (although at same time ought not to be) to find that per letter from Mr. Stephen Bayard, a man of good character, and would not write a wrong thing, although you have done to your Brother Dan'el Lawrance, that your Attorneys had paid the money, due said Lawrance unto his Attorneys, how could you have the face or assurance to write any such false thing when was not paid. I cant gett the money due from your own Estate due to me and Comp[any], and dont see how can pay others. this may be practable in you to keep your own C'n and imagine to hunt others: in that case you are mistaken. no I cant get the Money due from your own Estate, about one hundred and sixty pounds due long enough, but will sue next year, and then law will give it me. and further that the Debt was dis'd. its not many I owe to (but if any) but thats oweing to such long winded Gentlemen as you, as keeps one out of their money year after year. I fancy I shall not give you that oppertunity, and find men of a more generous temper then to study to write what is not just. Mr. Thomas Shephard of this Island made me a payment 15th May last and not before, which your Attorneys knows perfectly well was not before, of one hundred and ninety three pounds one shilling and four pence, which I have transferred neat proceeds unto Mr. Stephen Bayard to pay a Sterling bill for what in my hands, but I expect'd to have paid it to Maj'r Martin but would not meddle, but chuse I should remitt it, as have done per this Conveyance, as I think you could have the least Reason to be guilty of such ungenerous action to your Abused Humble Servant,

WM. FURNEL

ROBERT MORRIS TO GODFREY MALBONE[1] AND SAMUEL VERNON

Gentlemen, New Providence,[2] March 18th, 1744/5.

MY last was from St. Anns,[3] January the 25th; the 26 about 10 in the Morning sailed, the 14th of February about 12 saw a Sail of Cape Antons, which we took in about six

---

[1] Godfrey Malbone is said to have been a native of Virginia, who came to Newport about 1700. After some years at sea he inherited sufficient property to become independent, and engaged in commerce and privateering. He died February 22, 1768. Mason, *Annals of Trinity Church, Newport,* 54 *n.*

[2] The most important of the Bahama Islands, having Nassau, the seat of government of the islands.

[3] Probably Jamaica.

hours. She belongd to Nanz, came from Logan,[1] and designed to touch at the Havana. her Cargo is by the Manifest about 250 Hhds. of Sugar, some Indigo, some Hides and Tobaco. the Captain says she is richer then we expect. She was taken in Concort with the Brigantine. She must be condem'd here, but dont propose discharging the Cargo, as the officers will compute the Duties, by the weight of a few Casks; and as I have appl'd to Major Stewart am in hopes the Duties will be very moderate, of which he'l advise. as I am now bound on a Cruse, in Concort with a Snow and Sloop, as you'l see by the inclosed, to intercept if possible a Fleet of 16 Sail bound from Cape François.[2] The Company was for dividing here, but put them off. this is short and goes by way of Boston, but shall write more fully by way of Carolina Disr (?) Youl excuse heaste. I am, Gentlemen,

Your Humb.^e Servt
Robert Morris

[Endorsed,] Capt. Godfrey Malbone and Mr. Sam'l Vernon, Merchants in Newport, Rhode Island.

John Thomlinson[3] to Abraham Redwood

Sir, London, the 18 March, 1744 [1745.]

SINCE my last to you I have sold your Sugars that were then comed to hand this year vizt. 38 Casks. they were

---

[1] Léogane, Hayti.
[2] Now Cape Haytien, a seaport town on the north coast of Hayti. Before Louisburg the English ships were said to have taken in July of this year three French ships from the East Indies, prizes valued at £800,000. *Law Papers*, II. 5.
[3] John Thomlinson was a merchant in London, who served as agent of New Hampshire for some years. See *Belcher Papers* and *New Hampshire Provincial Papers*.

very low and wanted Colour. the first 18 hhds. I sold at 31/6 per Cent, and the other 20 hhds per Dickinson was so much worse that I never could get above 29/ for them; so was obliged to keep them untill very lately. the many Sugar Ships that have been lost and taken rose the price of sugars, so that I got 32/ per Cent for them; that is, I have sold them at that price and shall soon send you those Sales. Collo. Thomlinson advised me that he had shipd me ten hhds of your Sugar by Capt. Cuizack and desired me to insure them as usual; but the ship by which he advised me thereof was taken and carried into France, and when the Letters came to hand from France, Capt. Cuizack was given over for lost, so that I could not get a peney Insurance made on him. I had since advice from Mr. Thomlinson of 20 hhds of your sugar ship'd on board the *Bolan*, Capt. Payne, and 10 hhds on board the *Black Ann*, both which I made insurance upon, and the *Bolan*, Capt. Payne, is taken and carry'd into France. And the *Black Ann* has been taken, and is retaken and carryd into Bristoll by a privateer however you will be pretty safe in both those Adventures, only Collo. Thomlinson has not yet sent me duplicates of Bills of Ladings for those Sugars to prove that they were aboard. Therefore must write to him to do it, as I must have them to prove that these Sugars were on board before I shall recover the Insurance; and I shall also write to him, (and I would have you to do the same) always to take care to write for insurance in time and by two or three Conveyances, and to send Bill of Lading and Invoice of all the Sugar he ships by at least three Conveyances so long as this war continues.

I have not for several Months past had the Favour of a Line from you, and here is now brought to me by Richard How your Bill of Exchange dated the 14th of November, 1744, in Favour of Mr. Joseph Jacobs for £250 Sterling, and I hear there is another of your Bills on me in Town, but has not been brought to me yet. as I have no advice of either of those Bills I have told Mr. How, as I shall also tell whoever brings the other, that as soon as I have advice of them

I shall accept and pay them, and I must begg of you both for your own safety and mine that whenever you draw on me that you will at the same time give me advice of what Bills you draw; for I know nobody that will or can with safety pay any Bill without advice, and very ill consequences have, and may attend the payment of Bills without proper advice.

The account of the Jamaica Hurycane is but just comed here,[1] and thereupon Sugar is greatly advanced, and I hope it will keep up as the freights and insurance must now continue very high during this French war. I think I have not farther to add, save that I am with very great respect, Sir, Your most humble Servantt

JOHN THOMLINSON

Inclosed is the sales of all your Sugars that are come to hand as on the other side, Neat proceeds of 384 hds. being £548. 16. 1.

[Endorsed,] with Magazines. Per Capt. Adams. Q. D. C.

ROBERT KING TO STEPHEN AYRAULT[2]

Perth Amboy, May 11th, 1745.

Dear Cuzen Stephen,

WE are heartily concern'd to finde that we are not likely to be favoured with Cuzen Susannah's Company untill that she changes her minde of apprehention of danger. hope you'l send a line on your hereing from the f[orce] on the Expedition.[3] it is but a narrow low way of thincking that those of Pencilv'a and of this province who should consider so publick an undertaking of so great consequence but not likely to doe any thing in either province, under the pretence of the thing not being recommended by his Maj[es]tie, etc.

---

[1] It had occurred October 20, 1744. An account of it is given in the *Boston Weekly News-Letter*, January 17, 1745.
[2] Third son of Daniel Ayrault, born 1709 and died in 1794. His wife Ann was daughter of Peter Bours.
[3] Against Louisburg.

Thay have been tould that the advantages to these Colloneys would be great if that they had once the Brittish Standerd fixed up there, but it seems equal to some people who governs as thay can purchuss their peac whoever is over them. we shall be glad to here of Cuzen Goulding's recovary and of the young Ladie you mention to have been indisposed lately. Be pleased to pay our Complyments to Brother and all the family round, and to Cuzen Ellias when you write that the Blessing of the Almighty God may attend their great undertakeing is the hea[r]ty wishis of, D'r Stephen, your affectionate Kinsman and humble Servant

ROBT. KING

[Endorsed,] To Mr. Stephen Ayrault, Merchant, at Guest Newport.

JOHN THOMLINSON TO ABRAHAM REDWOOD

Copy per Adams. London, the 1st May, 1746.

Sir,

I HAVE here to acknowledge your favour of the 29th January adviseing of your Draft in favour of Mr. Joseph Jacobs for £200 Sterling, which is accepted, and when due will be duely paid. I have also Mr. Thomlinson's Favour of the 1st March last from Antigua inclosing me Bill of Lading for 16 hhds of Sugar per Capt. Colshare who is safe arriv'd at Dartmouth without haveing any Insurance on 'em, and I hope he will arrive here safe; And the Sugars will if good fetch a good Price. the Average on the *Black Anne* is not yet settled by the Owners, so that we cannot yet send you the Sales of the 30 hhds of Sugar in her. As soon as that is done you shall have 'em. I am with great Esteem, Sir, Your humble Servant,

JOHN THOMLINSON

JOHN THOMLINSON TO ABRAHAM REDWOOD

Sir, London, the 30th May, 1746.

BUT nine days since I received your several Letters all upon one half sheet of paper of the 15th of October the 14th of February and 10th of March last with the Duplicate of

Wait Tripp's Appeal, etc. But never had the Original or the other Letters of the 6th of September, or 5th of December, or the first Copy of Mr. Benjamin Hazard's Case which accompanyd the same, as you will see by my Letters since wrote to you and Mr. Hazard; and you will also see that I had received a duplicate of Mr. Hazard's Case, and have put it into the best Lawyers' Hands, as I have likewise done Mrs. Wait Tripp's Case, and I shall use my utmost Endeavours to get both of them brought on to a hearing as soon as possible; but those appeals are sometimes very teadious. Notwithstanding Mr. Banester has wrote Mr. Harrison that I had rec'd John Jones Letter and was to carry on his Case I assure you Mr. Jones never wrote me one word about it, but has sent it to Mr. Baker, and Mr. Baker by his Lawyer has delivered it at the Councel office in order to proceed in the prosecution thereof, and which I had notice of from the Council office to appear for Mr. Hazard; so then I was obliged to give Mr. Hazard's papers to my Lawyer, and the Cause is on the List and will, I suppose, be heard in its turn: but when that will be it is impossible for me to say, but no endeavours of mine shall be wanting to get both that and the other over as soon as possible. It would be worth your while to prevail with Mr. Harrison, whom I take to be a very honest and good man, to give you a sight of that letter of Mr. Banister's. it is dated the 21st of September, and a duplicate thereof was intercepted in some ship taken or retaken and shewn about here; and a Friend of mine told me what it contain'd relating to me and several others; but I would not believe a word of it as Mr. Banister had been all along, and was to all Appearances for Months after the writeing of that Letter, upon the best and friendlyest Terms with me, and proposeing to help me into very advantagous Scheemes of Trade with several of the most considerable Gentlemen in Carrolina both North and South. But to convince me the said Letter in his own hand writing was brought me and I had the Liberty only to read it over, and I find it has been shewn to others and some has had the Liberty to take Copys of it. But the chief concern it gave me was to think that Mr. Banister was capable of writeing such a Letter more then for any prejudice it might do me. Mr. Banister I find knows that I and some others have seen it but have not taken any notice to him of it or do I think it worth while any further then to vindicate my self when any part thereof is mention'd to me.

The defrence you mention to be between the sales of the Sugars in Capt. MacDaniell and my Account Currant, arose from an error in the freight, and you will see that by my Letter to you of the 26 of October, 1743, so that your Account Currant is right as it stands. You will see by the above Copy that your Bill of £200 in favour of Mr. Joseph Jacobs mett with due Honour. Capt. Colshare in whom your Sugars therein mention'd [are,] has got no farther then Portsmouth. I wish they were safe up. I think they would sell well, as the last I sold was some belonging to judge Gourdon of Antigua and not very fine. the price was 45/ per Cent. I have some more of his which I have been bid the same price for, but am in hopes of getting more, as so many of our Sugar Ships have been lately taken. I have just settled the Average on the Ship *Black An* with the owners, and here send you the Sales; in which you will see that you are only charged with 1 and $\frac{3}{4}$ per Cent. the Money paid for $\frac{1}{3}$d of Value of said Sugars at Bristoll to the Recaptors was charged to your Account Currant at the time it was paid, and as 10 hhds. of the 30 were insured, we shall now settle for the Money paid for Account of the said Ten with the Insurers, and give your Account Credit for the same and shall very soon send you your Account Currant. I am with great Esteem, Sir, Your most humble Servant

JOHN THOMLINSON

N. B. The freight instead of £21. 10. 7 should have been £24. 0. 7 (per McDaniel).

WHITE LOVELL TO ABRAHAM REDWOOD[1]

Dear Cousin: Antigua, Sep'r 26, 1747.

THE Island having had dry Weather for some time past, which probably you might hear of, suppose the Postage from Boston will not be thought much of when you are acquainted that about this day sevenight[2] we had a small Hurricane which did no considerable Damage in this Isld, and have continued Rains since, so that the ponds are filled and thereby a fine Prospect for the Crop which before was in great Danger. Our Family are pretty well only tired with nursing Issabell. She hath now been given over by the Doctors fourteen weeks and only supported by good Attendance, and is considerably better her first Disorder was a Lax, tho I think she never was perfectly will since the Measles. As to the Commodores affairs, leave them to Coll Thomlinson who was one of the Committee, but by his flying from his Accusers 'tis plain he would not bring his Deeds unto the Light, and he hated the Light because his Deeds were Evil. My best Love and Respects attend my Cousin, with Cousin Hitty, and the rest. I am your affectionate and obliged Kinsman

White. Lovell

After I had sealed this Letter we recd terrible accounts from St. Chris:, St. Eustatia, etc.

MATHIAS JONES TO SAMUEL AND WILLIAM VERNON[3]

Gentlemen,   Nevis, April 4th, 1748.

I AM favour'd with yours per Capt. Richards of the 11th February last, and am sorry to hear of your very ill and unjust Treatment by Capt. Carr and Frye. these Cap-

---
[1] The original is in the Newport Historical Society.
[2] September 13. See *Boston Weekly Post Boy,* October 26, 1747.
[3] See Mason, *Annals of Trinity Church, Newport,* 153 n.

tains brought in here a French privateer sloop of Eight Carriage and Tenn Swivell guns and other warr like stores, and put them into my hands when they went on another Cruize, with full power from under their hands to dispose of them at publick vendue to the highest bidder, which was done, as per inclosd account more fully will appear; and as to the privateer sloop they themselves sold to one Capt. Cradock and self for £350 Current money, and wee to run the risque of her being claimd, which said sume of £350 was paid them as per their receipt on the Register, which they took out in their names after Condemnation now by me, and which I shewd Capt. Richards, Copy of which receipt I have now inclosd, for your further satisfaction. they made a Flagg of Truce of this their prize before they sold her to us, for which the publick of this Island paid, paying all Charges carrying their said prisoners to Guardolopa, £100 Currancey. as to the bill remitted by Capt. Frye was paid by Capt. Cradock in part discharge of the sloop sold to us, which was the only bill they reced here. all the papers and accounts I deliver'd Capt. Carr and have both their receipts for all the Transactions, Copys of which I now inclose you. every step towards receiveing the head money was taken before our Governour, and am afraid it will be impracticable to procure the like, without one of the Captains or other chief officers of one of the said two privateers being on the spot. however rest fully satisfy'd I shall do every thing to serve you in this affair. I am with best respects,

Pent Your mo. Obed. Serv
S. Mathias Jones

[Endorsed,] Per Capt. Bragton. [Brayton?]

JOHN REYNELL TO ABRAHAM REDWOOD[1]

Philadelphia, 2nd Sept'r, 1748.

Esteemed Friend Abraham Redwood,

SHOULD have writ thee per Capt. Pearce, and acknowledged the Receipt of thy favour of 20th of 5 mo:, inclosing a Bill of Exchange for £40. Sterling, but that James Logan, junior, who had been for some time in a declining Condition had concluded to go in the Vessell to Rhode Island for his health, but she sail'd sooner than was expected, and left him and the Letters that were to have gone by him: It was well for the Ladd, I believe, that it happen so, for he has had a bad Fever almost ever since, tho' we hope is now a little better, and in a likely way in time to get well again; but its very probable if he had gone in Pearce, he would have dyed on the Passage. Was glad to hear thou and Family were in good health. I and the rest of mine through mercy are partakers of the same favour; Jonas has been indisposed with a great Cold, had a Bleeding at his Nose, and something of a Fever, but is got quite well, tho' it has made him look paler and thinn. Sometime before thine came to hand, we had advice of a Cessation of Arms with France, on which Bills immediately fell to 70 per Cent. which was the highest price given when thine came, and accordingly have credited thy Account at that Exchange, since are fallen to 65 per Cent. My Wife joyns with me in kind Respects to thee and Spouse, and am Thy Assur'd Fr'd

John Reynell

P. S. We have just come over from London a Latin School Master of our Society, which Fr'ds here sent for in order to have their Children instructed in that and the Greek Language.

J. R.

---

[1] The original is in the Newport Historical Society.

JOHN THOMLINSON TO ABRAHAM REDWOOD

Sir, London, the 16 of May, 1750.

This serves only to enclose you Bill of Loading and Invoice for the Goods you were pleased to order, except the two peices of Callicos which I could not gett printed in Time. as soon as done shall send them. The Bill now in parliament for regulating and restraining the Paper Currancy in America, has for some time past, and do's still take up a good deal of my time,[1] that I can not at present enlarge, only shall refer you to the Bearer Captain Richards for a particular account of what difficultys we have mett with in that affair, and in what Sittuation that Bill at present is, and am with true Esteem, Sir, Your Most humble Servant

John Thomlinson

[Endorsed,] Per Captain Richards, Q. D. C.[2]

DAVID LINDSAY TO AYRAULT?[3]

Gentlemen, Anamaboe, 20 Febu., 1752.[4]

This third of mine to you, and now I am to let you Know my proceed'gs Since my Last Daited 3th Jan.[y]; and I have Gott on bord 61 Slaves and upards of thirty ounces of Goold,

---

[1] See Davis, *Currency and Banking in the Province of the Massachusetts Bay*, I. 258.

[2] Imports from New England into Great Britain in year 1750 were valued at £48. 455; exports to that region, £343. 659.

[3] Original in the possession of Mr. George C. Mason, in *Reminiscences*, II. 106.

[4] In order to extend and improve the trade with Africa Parliament enacted in 1750 a law, 23 George II. c. 31, the preamble of which read: "That the trade to and from Africa being very advantageous to Great Britain, and necessary for the supplying her plantations and colonies with a sufficient number of negroes, at reasonable rates, ought, for that reason to be free and open to all his Majesty's subjects: it was therefore enacted, that it shall be lawful for all the King's subjects

and have Gott 13 or 14 hhd' of Rum yet Left on bord, and God noes when I shall Gett Cleare of it ye trade is so very Dull it is actuly a noof to make a man Creasey my Cheef mate after making foor or five Trips in the boat was taken Sick and Remains very bad yett then I sent Mr. Taylor, and he got not well and three more of my men has sick. James Dixson is not well now, and wors, then I have wore out my Small Cable, alto ockam, and have ben oblige to buy one heare; for I thought the conciquance of yr Intrust on bord this vessel was Two great to Rusk with bot a cable to trust to. therefor I begg you not Blam me in so doeing. I should be Glad I coold Com Rite home with My slaves, for my vesiel will not Last to proceed farr we can See Day Lite al Roond her bow under Deck. however I hope She will carry me Safe home once more. I need not inlarge. heare Lyes Captains hamlet, James, Jepson, Carpenter, Butler, Lindsay; Gardner is Due; Ferguson has Gone to Leward all these is Rum ships. Butler is in a brig with 150 hhds from Barbados belong to Cape Coast Castle. Ivve sent a small boye to my Wife. I conclude with my best Endevors for intrust, Gentlemen, your faithful Servant at Command.

DAVID LINDSAY

N. B. on the whole I never had so much trouble in all my voiges I shall Write to barbadoes in a few days.

SAILING AGREEMENT[1]

IT is agreed between Philip Wilkinson[2] and Comp. on the one part and Richard Penmure on the other, That the said Philip Wilkinson and Comp. oblige themselves to fitt and

---

to trade to and from any place in Africa, between the port of Sallee, in South Barbary, and the Cape of Good Hope, without any restraint whatsoever, except as herein after expressed." The claims and possessions of the Royal African Company passed to this new company, "The Company of Merchants trading to Africa," but the trade became open to all, and so remained.

[1] The original is in the Rhode Island Historical Society.

[2] A merchant associated with Daniel Ayrault, Jr. Mason, *Annals of Trinity Church*, Newport, 73 n.

load the Sloop *Charming Polly* with such Cargoe as they shall think proper and send her to St. Vincents where the said Penmure obliges himselfe to dispose of the Cargoe if he can. If not to proceed to Dominico and their sell what he can, and proceed from thence to St. Eustatia and dispose of any part of the Cargoe he may have left, as also what goods he may be obliged to take in pay for his Cargoe at St. Vincents or Dominico, and when the whole is invested into money to proceed with all possible dispatch to the Island of Highspanola (without any goods whatsoever) and their invest the neat proceeds of hir Cargoe in good Molasses, best Muscovado sugars and Indigoe. In considerat. of which (and his obtaining a french pass) he is to have Twelve per Cent Commission on the Original Cargoe but no Commission on the sails of such goods as he may be oblidged to take in pay for his Cargoe at St. Vincents or Dominico, which are to be sold at St. Eustatia, said Penmure also to have the Monthly Wages of Twenty five pounds per month (Old Tenor) and to have his board paid here by said P. Wilkinson & Co. from the date hereof untill he sails. At the return of the Vessell to Rhode Island all acco'ts are to be setled and the Ballance paid every Voiage. Said Penmure to have Tenn hogsheads Privelidge in said Sloop and an allowance of four peices of eight a week for his Expences whilst at Highspanola, Tenn peices of Eight for Cabin Expences for his Passage home and Thirty pounds all'd him here for his Sea Stores etc. also to be allowed Tenn Pistoles or Three hundred Liveres for all the Port Charges at Highspanola. and should he have the misfortune to loose any of his people so as to make it absolutely needfull to ship hands there, the said Wilkinson & Compe are to make good any reasonable agreement he may make with them. Dated at Newport on Rhoad Island, December first, 1752.

RICHD PENMURE

JOHN MANWARING TO ABRAHAM REDWOOD

Sir, Antigua, June 11th, 1753.

As I had the pleasure of your acquaintance here and presumeing on the civillity's you was please to shew me likewise, I take the freedom to acquaint you that yesterday departed this life your old worthy friend John Tomlinson,[1] Esquire, and was this morning interred and as his death must oblige you to appoint some other person here, not only as your Attorney, but also to take care of your estate; and as I am no stranger to Plantation concerns, (haveing liv'd upon severall estates here) I take the liberty to make you a tender of my services, which if proves acceptable to you may depend that no person will take more care of your interest in every shape then what I shall do, and as reasonable in my terms.

I submit the matter to your consideration and shall be proud to hear of your own and Familys health. I am, Sir,

Your obedt humble Servant

John Manwaring

SAILING ORDERS

Captain Newport, May 1st, 1755.

OUR snow *Venus* of which you are Master being loaded and ready to sail, we order, that you improve the first favourable Wind and Weather, and proceed to the Port, where

---

[1] The son had formed a partnership in London, Thomlinson, Trecothick and Company, which became in 1762, Trecothick, Apthorp and Thomlinson. Barlow Trecothick was later prominent among the English merchants with American connections during the stamp and other tax agitations.

you are to deliver your Cargo at, agreeable to your Bills of Loading, make all possible despatch in order to compleat your Voyage, agreeable to the Instructions herewith given you, which desire you'll observe as particular as possible, its our Opinion its best to go North about, best to avoid an Enemy and your Men from an Impress,[1] dont speak with any Vessil in your Passages without their is absolute necessity of it, neither lay out any Money on your Vessil, if can be avoided, as you well know our Voyage depends upon Frugality. You have ten small cask of Rum on board, which dispose of in the best manner you can for the proceeds bring home any thing you think will answer best, be cautious dureing the Voyage to avoid any danger — especially shou'd there be a Warr you must suspect every Vessil you see to be your Enemy, even when you return upon this Coast. I need say no more, as you well understand every difficulty that may happen by being incautious. It is agreed that you shall have in lieu of Primage,[2] etc. Twelve Pounds Stg., to be paid in Urope, and also Two shilling and Six pence sterling per Day while in port. We wish you a good Voyage and safe return and are yours, etc.[3]

The foregoing is Copy of my Orders which I promise to observe.

Wm Pinnegar [signature]

---

[1] In Queen Anne's war an act of Parliament was passed forbidding impressment of seamen in the English colonies in America; but in 1716 and again in 1740 the crown law officers decided that the act expired at the end of the war. *Law Papers*, I. 112, 116.

[2] Primage was a customary allowance made by the shipper to the master and crew of a vessel for loading and care of the cargo. It has become a percentage addition to the freight, paid to the owners or freighters of the vessel.

[3] Pinnegar had made a voyage to Hamburg, for Vernon and Stevens, owners of the snow *Venus*, commencing September 10, 1754, and continuing until October, 1755.

Wilkinson and Ayrault to David Lindsay [1]

Newport, Aug. 15th, 1755.

Sr, you being master of our Schooner *Siraleone* and ready to sail, Our orders are that you Imbrace the first opportunity of wind and weather, and Proceed for the Coast of Affrica; where Bless God you arrive, there Dispose of your Cargoe on the best terms you can for Gold, slaves, etc. when you have finished your trade (which we desire may be with all convenient Dispatch) Proceed for the Island of Barbadoes, and if your Slaves will fetch Twenty Seven pounds, round, great and small, you may sell them. Though shoud it be a Warr we expect they will fetch a much better Price which we leave to you. as also to Proceed Directly from the Coast of affrica to St Christophere, If you think best. but if they will not sell at Barbadoes, If you goe there or to St Christophere, you will proceed without loss of time for the Island of Jamaica, or else where as you will have Letters of Direction Lodged for you at Barbadoes or St. Christophere. you are to have five out of six for your Coast Commissions and five per Cent sales in the West Indies and five per Cent for the Goods you purchase for return. Your chief mate and second mate are to have Two slaves each Privilege and five for yourself. we wish you a good Voiage and are your friends and most humble Ser^{ts}.

PHILIP WILKINSON
DANIL AYRAULT, JR.

Above is a Copy of order rec'd wch I promise to follow.

DAVID LINDSAY

Bill of Lading [2]

S. S.

Ship'd by the Grace of God, in good Order and well Conditione'd by Philip Wilkinson & Co, owners of the Schooner *Sieraleone*, in and upon the good Ship call'd the Schooner

---

[1] Original in the possession of Mr. George C. Mason, in *Reminiscences*, II. 146.

[2] A printed form filled in, in the possession of Mr. George C. Mason, in *Reminiscences*, III. 195.

Sieraleone wheref is Master, under God, for this present Voyage, David Lindsay, and now riding at Anchor in the Harbour of Newport and by God's Grace bound for the Coast of affrica, to say, Thirty eight hogsheads, seven large barrils and Twenty six halfe barrils of Rum. Tenn firkins Butter, one cask tobacco, Twenty one barrils and half Beef and Pork, one barril sugar, one barril flour and 15. 1-18 Bread. being marke'd and numbered as in the Margin, and are to be delivered in the like good Order, and well Condition'd, at the aforesaid Port of the Coast of Affrica (the Danger of the Seas only excepted) unto the said David Lindsay or to his Assignes, he or they paying Freight for the said Goods nothing, with Primage and Avarage accustomed. In witness whereof, the Master or Purser of the said Schooner hath affirm'd 3 Bills of Lading, all of this Tenor and Date; the one of which 3 Bills being accomplished the other two to stand void. And so God send the good ship to her desired Port in Safety. Amen. Dated in Newport, Aug. 16, 1755.

DAVID LINDSAY

HENRY LLOYD[1] TO AARON LOPEZ[2]

Sir, Boston, April 3d, 1756.

TALLOW is the only thing in demand that commands the Cash quick, is now 3/ and on the Rise; can have 3/8 per lb. for 40 or 50 Boxes Candles, 10 or 11 to the pound, if made of good Tallow, and without any mixture of Hoggs Fatt. Molasses 11/6 Cash; Sugar £12 to £16, and sell pretty readily. Cocoa about £30, Coffee 6/6, Pimento 9/; Ginger wanted for the Army, the last sold at £12. Cotton

---

[1] In 1774 Henry Lloyd was one of the addressers of Governor Hutchinson, and was then described as "merchant and contractor for the troops," and of Long Wharf, Boston. He went to Halifax in 1776, and was proscribed and banished in 1778. He removed to London and died there in 1795-96, aged eighty-six.

[2] Aaron Lopez came to Rhode Island in 1750 and died in 1782, aged fifty-one years. His father-in-law, Jacob Rodrigues Rivera, is said to have introduced the manufacture of spermaceti into America. *Newport Historical Magazine*, II. 98. His wife Abigail, died May 14, 1762. *Rhode Island Historical Magazine*, VI. 85, 90, 93.

wooll slow at 10/6. Bohea Tea about 32/ to 32/6 the difficulty of Importation is very great, the officers on an Information having been this day in pursuit of some I have by me, but having a Cockett[1] for it sav'd it, notwithstanding if you are determined to send any must caution against venturing too much in one bottom, as it is an unsettled point here whether in a Court of Admiralty, a Cockett will screen it, if can't be prov'd to be Legally Imported from Great Brittain, in short the Gentlemen here in fair Trade are determined to prevent the Importation of Hollands goods at all adventures, and tis probable may employ people to be on the look out.[2] I expect Mr. Folger in Town from Nantucket[3] in a few days, when shall engage what Head matter[4] I can for you. I am Your most H'ble Servt.

HENRY LLOYD

HENRY LLOYD TO AARON LOPEZ

Sir, Boston, May 3d, 1756.

HAVE rec'd yours of 30th ulto.; that you refer to per Mr. Pate never came to hand. observe what you say about purchasing Sperma Ceti of Mr. Quincey. when he comes to Town will make it my Business to see him, and make the offer you prescribe, but am very sure he will not take up with it, as I have had occasion but lately to t[reat] with him on that head, when he refus'd 12/6, and if I remember said he would not sell under 13/6. beleive can get of Mr. Langdon at 13/, which is the lowest I have been offer'd at any

---

[1] A document issued by the customs officer as a certificate that their merchandise had been duly entered and had paid duty.

[2] The privilege to import tea, under license, from any foreign parts, was repealed by 7 Geo. I. c. 21. § 12.

[3] Nantucket in 1756 had eighty vessels in the whale fishery, and the returns were 12,000 barrels, selling for £27,600.

[4] Spermaceti, a wax found in the head cavities of the sperm-whale (*Physeter macrocephalus*), where it is dissolved in the sperm oil while the creature is living. At a temperature of about 6°C. the solid matter separates in a crystalline condition; and the old method was to dig the brain from the cavity and separate the oil from it by dripping. The residue is crude spermaceti, of which an ordinary sized whale would yield twelve barrels.

time. if will do at that please to let me know your mind and I will procure what I can.

Mr. Rotch of Nantucket [1] is now here and offers me Head Matter, any quantities I may want at the usual premio over and above the price of Oyl and 2½ per Ct. Commissions, to be deliver'd at New Port, and will take the Oyl from which the Head Matter is extracted in part of pay either at the price of Oyl when the Head matter is deliver'd, or as it shall be when he receives it, which ever you choose at the time of purchase. Molasses is now 11/6 many people think will not be under, others that it will. I imagine that of the best quality may hold up to that, at least will not be under 11/. I am Your most Humble Servant

HENRY LLOYD

P. S. I have seen Mr. Quincey he will not sell his Sperma Ceti under 13/6 per lb., and Mr. Langdon has none to spare. since writing the above your favours inclosing a line from Messrs. Harts is come to hand. can by no means advise to sending any Tea without a proper Clearance, and if with [   ] then a Chest or two at a time by experienc'd Coasters. when your [   ] comes to hand will use my best Endeavours in [torn] in procuring the Sperma Ceti and that I shall use all the Caution I'm master of in the affair, well knowing the Gentleman's policy you mention. I imagine there will be no advantage taken of the 2 Baggs of Cocoa more then is mention'd in the Cockett. I am Your most Humble Servant

HENRY LLOYD

HENRY LLOYD TO AARON LOPEZ

Sir,   Boston, May 10th, 1756.

I DULY received your favour of the 7th current and observe Mr. Quincy's Terms are such as you can't comply with.

---

[1] Joseph Rotch (1704–1784) and his son, William (1734–1828), removed from Nantucket to New Bedford in 1765. The son is probably intended in the letter, and an autobiographical account of his experiences in the War of Independence is printed in the *N. E. Hist. Gen. Reg.*, XXXI and XXXII. See also Ricketson, *History of New Bedford*, 109.

when Mr. Rotch comes again shall let him know your proposals with Regard to Head Matter, and engage the 100 bbs. of him if I can on your Terms; but Question whether he will take the Oyl at New Port and be at the charge and risque of transporting it to Nantucket or round here.[1] have not yet had an answer from Capt. Folger. I must caution you against being too nice and critical with the Nantucket men, for I can assure you nothing can be done with them in that case, the only way is to make the best Terms you can with them, whenever you have occasion to purchase; but tis in vain to attempt to tye them down to any measures they don't like. Molasses still rubbs off at 11/6, but does not readily go off in quantities at that, am told some was sold last week at 11/. Sugars are on the fall, vast quantities already come in, and more expected soon, is now at £10 to £16 as in quality Mr. Heyman Levy has accepted my order in favour of Judah Hays. your Cocoa not come to hand; it is daily on the fall, was sold in small quantities last week at £25. I am Your most Hble Servant,

HENRY LLOYD

Per Mr. Bannister.

HENRY LLOYD TO AARON LOPEZ

Sir, Boston, June 14th, 1756.

I HAVE only time to acknowledge the Receipt of your favours of 3d and 11th current. the first inclosing Bill Lading for 35 hhds. Molasses per Stone, which with 5 more per him are come to hand, and hous'd, no one at present offering to purchase. the price is reduc'd to 10/6 some has been bought at 10/ but hope shall do something better with yours, if I can give a short Credit in which I must govern myself, as I shall need Cash to purchase head matter, between 60 and 70 bbs. of which I hope to ship you by Arey, who talks of sailing this Evening, 34 Casks of which is already on Board. the price will be from £145 to £147. 15/

---

[1] Rotch insisted that Lopez should take the head matter at Nantucket, and delivering the oil at Boston at Lopez's own charge and risk.

per Tonn for the Oil, £5. 10/ only per bbl. bounty for some, and £5 with 2 per cent. Commission and Freight for others. Oil has been rising every Day this week past, but hope is got to the heighth. Mr. Rotch's Son arriv'd last Saturday and says his Father will be able to ship some head matter per Arey. I advis'd you in my last I had sold the 10 hhds. Molasses, 9 hhds. at 11/ per Gallon and 1 at 11/6. fear 15 Baggs of your Cocoa will not sell on any reasonable Terms, for anything further must refer you to mine per last post which suppose you'l receive this week. I am Your most H'ble Servant,

HENRY LLOYD

HENRY LLOYD TO AARON LOPEZ[1]

Sir, Boston, June 28th, 1756.

I DULY rec'd your favours of 15th Current per Morton, with Bill Lading for 10 hhds. Molasses, which have stor'd, and 18th per Mr. Polock. Molasses still continues down at 10/ to 10/6, but if the News of Port Mahon's being beseig'd (as you have it in our papers) be confirm'd and a declaration of Warr should ensue[2] thereon, it must soon rise. shall not part with any till farther orders, unless am oblig'd to do it to secure a parcell of Sperma Ceti. there is about 20 or 30 bbs. come in this morning I hope to get, but depends wholly on the person to whom the Oil is sold. if to my Freind Mr. Apthorp who first bespoke it I shall have it. were it practicable to procure money on Interest I would do it, but all those who let have of late so generally put it out on Government security I know not where to go for £100. you may depend on my best endeavours to procure the 100 bbs. Head matter besides what I have sent, and if possible reconcile Mr. Folger who is expected here this week. he commands but little if any, more then comes in his own Vessells. Mr. Rotch is expected also, and tho' he

---

[1] The original is in the Newport Historical Society.
[2] War against France was declared May 18, 1756.

supplys so many manufactories, and has shipt considerable to Europe this Season, I dont despair of his complying with his promise for 200 bbs., part of which expect you'l receive per Arey. will do the best I can with the Cocoa but is so bad fear must be oblig'd to sell at a very under rate. have offer'd it at £22. 10/ and shall not refuse £20. I am Your most Humble Servant,

HENRY LLOYD[1]

HENRY LLOYD TO AARON LOPEZ

Sir, Boston, July 7th, 1756.

I RECEIVED your Favours of 5th current per Mr. Joseph De Lucena, advising of Weaver's arrival with your 5 bbls Head matter. I have now by me 60 barrills more for you and hope to be freequently picking up small parcells, which shall forward as opportunity presents, that you may have the advantage of returning your Oil while the market holds up. the present price is £160 per Tonn and can have so for yours per Arey if in seasonably.

I have not yet been under a necessity of selling your Molasses to disadvantage; but if a large quantity of Head matter offers and cant do otherwise must dispose of as much as such emergency will call for. you may depend on my utmost endeavours in Collecting as much as you have given orders for.

Mr. Rotch's Son is here and tells me they shall be able to send you a parcell of Head matter per the first Vessell bound from Nantucket to Newport, and will complete the order as soon as they can. Folger is not here, believe it too late to procure much from [him.] I am Your most h'ble Servant,

H. LLOYD

---

[1] "Sugars and all W. India produce are daily arriving and of course become dull; but if the advice from Port Mahon proves true tis probable a war will soon follow which will in a short time alter the price of goods. . . . Trading seems under great discouragements here, notwithstanding our navigation in general has been more successful than for many years past. Whether a war will operate to our advantage or not must be left to the event; but if the trade does not revive, we have but one way to save ourselves, and that is to retrench our expensive living." *Stephen W. Greenleaf to Wilkinson and Ayrault*, Boston, June 29, 1756. *R. I. Hist. Soc.*

HENRY LLOYD TO AARON LOPEZ

Sir, Boston, July 12th, 1756.

I'M to inform you I have shipt on Board the Sloop *Greyhound*, William Harris, who saild last Saturday 60 Casks Head matter which I wish safe to hand.[1] I have bought and am about purchasing 30 Casks more to go by Sturgis[2] who sails the last of this week; that per Harris cost from £158 to £160 per Tonn for the Oil, the last only £150 to which price Oil is now reduc'd. am sorry yours per Arey was not at market before it fell. I am Your most H'ble Servant,

HENRY LLOYD

P. S. What Oil is now at markett is like to go at £145. if so, part of the 30 bbs mentiond above will be at the same price for the oil.

HENRY LLOYD TO AARON LOPEZ

Sir, Boston, July 19th, 1756.

CAPT. ROTCH arriv'd yesterday and tells me they have shipt you 60 or 70 Casks Headmatter from Nantucket, and that it was by mistake and through forgetfulness of his Father that the 50 bbs they shipt Messrs. Harts was not shipt you. the report of a declaration of warr comes so many different ways leaves little room to doubt the truth of it. I shall therefore desist from selling your Molasses (unless a Bargain of Headmatter should offer) till I'm further advis'd from you. have sold only 9 hhds. at 11/, and believe can now get so for the remainder. Yours per Arey inclosing Bill Lading for 80 Casks Oil came duly to to hand.[3] the Oil sold at £146 per Tonn and this day is fallen to £140. have shipt on Board Capt. Sturgis for your Account 31 Casks Headmatter, 18 of which at £150

---
[1] Value £217. 14. 11¾ lawful money.
[2] Thomas Sturgis.
[3] The 80 casks sold for £196.5.11 lawful money.

for the Oil and 13 at £146, am promis'd 6 bbs more which will be at £140, or less, as it is daily falling. your damag'd Cocoa is still on hand but will probably sell to advantage, as tis likely most other sorts of goods will when warr is declard. I am Your most H'ble Servant,

HENRY LLOYD

P. S. I shall ship the 6 hhds. Fish to Mr. Levy,[1] per Wimble,[2] you order'd some time agoe, and shall forward the Sales of your Oil per Sturgis.

JAMES DUNCAN TO METCALF BOWLER[3] AND COMPANY[4]

Gentlemen, Honduras Bay, March 3d, 1757.

THIS being the first opportunity since I left you Gladly Embrace it to acquaint you of my safe arrivall here, after fifty one days passage. I touch'd at Musquito[5] agreeable to Orders, and offer'd part of the Briggtn to William Pitt, Esqr., but he refusing made the best of my way here, and have Desposed of all my Cargo except the Flour and Mosheets. the Baymen has stated the Price of Flour at 32/6 per C, which made me keep that article 'till the last, but am afraid shall be oblig'd to comply to get clear of it. Have now on board Ninety Tons Loggwood, and expect Twenty more to morrow, so that barring accidents shall sail in Twenty days from this date, and for many Reasons too tedious to mention, shall be oblig'd to touch at Rhode Island on my way to Amsterdam. I beg the favour of you to write to Mr. Deneauville,[6] or whoever you order the

---

[1] Hayman Levy.

[2] William Wimble, of sloop *Stamford*.

[3] Metcalf Bowler married Ann, daughter of Major Fairchild, and after an adventurous career in commerce, privateering, and the American War of Independence, died in Providence, 1789, where he kept a house of entertainment, the "Queen's Head." Mason, *Annals of Trinity Church, Newport*, 107 n.

[4] The original is in the Rhode Island Historical Society.

[5] The English claimed a protectorate over the Mosquito Indians, and resorted to the coast for mahogany, log wood and other dye woods, but the claim was disputed by Spain. The Mosquito Coast is now a part of Nicaragua.

[6] Deneuville.

Vessell too, to make Insurance for my Acct. three thousand guilders; but if Insurance can't be had in Holland, then please to insure five hundred Dollars for my Acct. at Rhode Island (from here to Rhode Island, and no where else) I have receiv'd all my old debts except one craft load Wood, which expect to have on board to morrow, and was much better than purchasing the Wood now; for they are so well supply'd both at the shoar, and here, that the people are not sensible of a War yet. but the times will soon alter, and as there will be a plenty of Loggwood in the Old River for some months yet, and should there be the least appearance of a Spanish War (which God forbid) and 'tis agreeable to every one concern'd, I should be glad to take another voyage this way, before we go to Hollond, as I have a Letter on board from Mr. Pitt to Mr. Bowler, giving him his particular reasons for not taking a part of the Briggtn this Voyage, and some assurances that he will be concerned with him the next Voyage, and as the Trade of the Shoar increases much with the Spaniards, if we can once get a Vessell in there, am well Assured 'twill prove very Advantagious. however the whole is with you to Determine, and I shall use my utmost Endeavours for the Advantage of the Present Voyage, and remain with due Regards, Gentlemen, your very Humb Servt.

JAMES DUNCAN

P. S. Inclos'd you have a Copy of a Letter I rec'd at Black River from the Captain of the *Wager* Man of War, to the Inhabitants of the Bay. The *Wager* was bound to Port Mahon (a new Settlement about 35 Leagues to the Southward of this Place) to demand all the English Prisoners there, and satisfaction for 3 Vessells Lately taken by Don Palma. Am in some hopes of receiving the Wood for Mr. Allen's note, and if I do shall ship it to Holland.

Addressed to Messrs Metcalf, Bowler and Company, Owners of the Briggantine *George* in Rhode Island. Per favour Captain John Coddington.

Power of Attorney[1]

KNOW all men by these presents that We the Subscribers being the officers Mariners and Company now belonging to the Brige *George* a Private man of Warr, Whereof Benjamin Wanton[2] is Commander belonging to Newport in the County of Newport and Colony of Rhode Island, Do hereby Constitute and make Christopher Champlin Junr of Newport aforesaid merchant, jointly and severally our Sole Agent or Attorney, for us and in our names and stead and to our uses to ask demand sue for levy and require, recover and receive of and from all and every person and persons of in and to all and every the prizes, goods wares and merchand'zes moneys and effects, and things of every nature and kind whatsoever that shall or may be taken or siezed by the said Brige *George* during her intended cruize from her sailing from Newport untill her arrival there again, as well in consortship with other private vessells of Warr or otherwise Giveing and hereby Granting unto our said Attorney our full and whole power strength and authority in and about the premisses and to take and use all due course and process both in law and equity to recover the same, on receipt thereof or any part or parcell thereof in the Name of us and each of us as the case may require to make proper acquittances and lawfull discharges for the same, and We do hereby invest our said attorney with full power and authority to do and to perform all and every lawfull act, and acts, thing and things necessary to effect the ends aforesaid with full power to make and substitute one or more attorney or attorneys under him and again at pleasure to revoke or displace them. In Witness Whereof We have hereunto sett our hands and seals this eighteenth day of June in the Thirtieth Year of the Reign of our Sovereign Lord George the Second King of Great Britain &c. and in the year of our Lord one thousand [seven hundred] and fifty seven. N. B. Whatsoever Coin the Prize, or Prizes shall be sold for, the shares shall be paid out in the same.

---

[1] The original is in the Rhode Island Historical Society.
[2] Baptized September 10, 1733.

Mr. Champlin: Our people have not all sign'd this, by Reason there was a good many on Board each Prize, so that 'twas impossible to get it done through so much confusion, but make no manner of doubt but they will all come into it, as there seems now not to be the least objection.

ANTHONY ATWOOD
THOMAS M°GUAR
JAMES × GWIN'S MARK
THOMAS BORDEN
BENJ. REED
ROBERT HOWARD
BOUTWILL HOWARD
ROBERT ×^his_mark HOLDEN
MALEKIAH ×^his_mark GRINNELL
THOMAS COOPER
RICHMOND CRANSTON
JOHN HUBBARD
JOHN WEEDEN
JOHN THOMPSON
WM. HAMOND FOR JAMES JOHNSON AND SON
BENJAMIN LOUD
MILLER FROST

Witnesses.
JOHN BALL
ISRAEL AMBROSE

JOHN HAMMOND
ROBERT PATTERSON
REUBEN GREEN
JOHN BROWN
JOSEPH PHILLIPS
BENJ. WANTON
JOB EASTON
ROBERT DUNBAR
ISRAEL AMBROSE
DAN^L DUNCAN
JAMES LEACH
JAMES TOSH
SAMUL UNDERWOOD
HEZEKIAH EGGLESTON
WM. THURSTON
JOHN NICKLESS
JOHN BALL
WILLIAM EASTON
JOHN CHASE
ROGER BROWN
JOSIAS WALLACE
JOHN SHREFE
JOHN PRICE
WILLIAM GRAFTON
FRANCIS PURSE
LEVI SHEARMAN
NATHAN FANNING
DANIEL GRAY
JOHN VENABLES
JOHN PARRY
NICHOLAS ×^his_mark COGGESHALL

THOMAS ATTWOOD for my negro SCIPIO and Apprentice Boy JOHN HUBBARD
JAMES ROACH for WM. CATIAN &

Richard and Richard Oliver to Abraham Redwood

London, 11th January, 1759.

Sir,

HEREWITH you'll receive a Copy of what we wrote you by Captain Farr. Since then we have received Bills of Lading from Mr. Lavicount for Sugars ship'd per out 2d Leeward Island fleet viz.

 10 Hhd. per *Charming Polly*, Capt. Davis.
 10   per *Martha*, Capt. Bruce.
  5   per *3 Friends*, Capt. Allison.
 10   per *Dragon*, Capt. Warner.

All which arrived safe, but remain as yet unsold, owing to the dullness of our present market and the expectation of better prices. Tho yet the goodness of the future sales, depends greatly on the political measures, that may take place on the detention or release of the Dutch Captures we have made; but as our Ministry hath shewn a proper degree of spirit hitherto in the Conduct of our affairs, and have not yet granted the Dutch a general release of their ships (tho some have been given up), we hope the suspence of their determination on them may still give us the benefit of an exportation and thereby raise the value of our Sugars. The foreign demand always gives us great advantage in our Sales, and the exporters, ceasing to purchase as has been the case for some time past, has occasion'd the price being depreciated. You may depend on our mutual endeavours for your Interest, and that the best opportunity shall be attentively observed for the disposal of your Sugars. Your Approbation will always give us pleasure, as we should wish to merit it by making our Services agreeable to you.

We inclose you Sales of your 10 Hhds per Gladman, 10 per Lessly, 10 per Hooper, 10 per Coulter, 10 per Gilston, which we hope may be approv'd, the 10 per Hooper were almost dabs,[1] and those by Coulter and Gilston but little better. we can't help repeating that the general quality

---
[1] The refuse or sediment of sugar, a term still employed in the trade.

of your Sugars is extremely low and dark. the disposal of them we assure you hath had our Care.

Our R: O. Junior prays his Complements to your Son, whom he had the pleasure of knowing at Antigua; also desires to be remember'd to Mr. Whipple. We both join in our good wishes to every part of your family and remain with Regard,

Sir
Your most hum'l Servt
Richg Rich Oliver

THOMAS MARTIN TO ABRAHAM REDWOOD

Antigua, August 13th, 1759.

Sir,

I WROTE you some time past and since have sent several Copies, but never have been favord with an Answer. I take the liberty once more to request you would let me know if you incline to rent your Estate in this Island. If so I will give you Eighteen Hundred pounds Sterling money per Annum, on a Lease of fifteen, or as many Years longer as you like. Give you good Security here, and in LONDON, for the payment of the rent, and every other matter that is requisite on these occasions. Should this be agreeable, you'll be pleased to signify the same to your Attorneys, as I am always ready to make good my Proposals. This will be forwarded to you by Messrs. Devenport and Wintworth, Merchants in Piscataqua, whom I have requested to pray your Answer, as I've sent a Vessel to their Address, which will return immediately, and may bring it. I am, Sir, Your most Obedient Servant,

THOMAS MARTIN

FLAG OF TRUCE [1]

Colony of Rhode Island.

WHEREAS Thomas Remington of Newport in the County of Newport and Colony of Rhode Island aforesaid Master of the Schooner *Wind-Mill* is going with a Flag of Truce from this Colony unto the Island of Hispanola in the West Indies and carries with him Fifteen French Prisoners besides the Company of said Schooner, which including the said Thomas Remington amounts to Twenty five in number, And Whereas I the Subscriber am appointed by the General Assembly to examine every Flag of Truce that shall be fitted out of this port and also to see that no Goods be put on board contrary to law having therefore undertaken and performed the said service I do hereby certify that the Schooner aforesaid hath not on board any Goods contrary to law. These is indeed, Six Barrs Beef, four Barrils pork, one thousand weight of Bread, Six firkins Butter and Seventy Barrils of Flour, Which said Quantity of Provisions in my opinion is no more than a sufficiency for the subsistance of the said Thomas Remington his people and the said Prisoners in their voyage to the said Island of Hispaniola for him and his people whilst they tarry there and to support them in their voyage homewards with fifteen British subjects whom he is to bring from thence, if there be so many of them prisoners at the said Hispaniola. Given under my hand at Newport in the Colony aforesaid the Twenty second day of October, 1759.

WILLIAM READ [2]

OLIVER CHAMPLIN TO CHRISTOPHER CHAMPLIN [3]

Gen'm: Cape Fransway [Français], 19th Decemb., 1759.

I HAVING this opertunity Imbrace it to Inform you that 15 Days after we left you was taken by a small privater

---

[1] The original is in the Rhode Island Historical Society.
[2] *Rhode Island Col. Rec.*, VI. 173.
[3] The original is in the Rhode Island Historical Society.

belonging to this porte and have been plunderd and arived hear yesterday and libeld I being prisner at larg and mate; my people being Confind my triol will Come on in two or three days and by What Mr. Laveal says am in hopes shall Recover my vessel and moneys taken from me again.

Mr. Laveal says the greates Obstacle in the way is that their is no prisner no Letter to the Govenor but sase that he will do all in his power to have her Restord with the moneys taken from me and doubts not of success. had ther been a Letter to the Govenor it would [have] prevented her being throd into the Judges hands. . . .

OLIVER CHAMPLIN

W. GRANT TO CHRISTOPHER CHAMPLIN [1]

Monte Christo,[2] 28 Novem., 1759.

. . . THERE is now in the Roade about 45 sail and eight or ten Ready to sail, so we have a prospect of very good Times. Markets Rises and produce falls at a prodigious Rate, in particular Mollasses which is to be got now for 19 ps. 8/8. The Brigg *Hawk* from Antigua has Taken two Sloops and a Snow outward Bound and Carried them to port, which I belive will be attended with very Bad Consequence in case their are Condemned, as there is two or three more here and only Waite to hear of the fate of those already Carried to port, before they begin to make Reprisals. I am etc.

W. GRANT

WILLIAM LISTER TO CHRISTOPHER CHAMPLIN [3]

Dr. Sir,   New York, Feb'y 2d, 1760.

YESTERDAY I ariv'd here where I had the pleasure to hear of our Vessel being sail'd for port Louise.[4] Insurance

---

[1] The original is in the Rhode Island Historical Society.
[2] In San Domingo, near the mouth of the Grand-Yaque River.
[3] The original is in the Rhode Island Historical Society.
[4] Capital of the island of Mauritius, then known as the Île de France.

within this few days has rais'd much. I have got our Insura. done at 28 per Ct. all risques, which is 8 per Ct. more than has been given, owing to the bad success Flags has had lately several of which has been caried into dif't Ports, and if but one barrel of Provisions has been sold to the French they say that the Cargo will be condem'd.

if coming home and no Provisions can be prov'd to have been sold they are in hopes that they will be clear'd so that them few Bbs. of Flow'r endangers the Cargo both to and from port, and by what I can learn Insurance can't be obtain'd at and from Port Louis here now at less than 22 per Ct. or 24. they now make 8 per Ct. difer's between Vessell from the Mount that have cary'd Provision and them that have not. if you want any Insurance done here soon do not depen'd on Mr. Jamison as he will be in the Cuntry for a Mo. or six Weeks and I must return to my Dearest. this is the first time of my seeing my Uncle but not the First L'r to you but have not been Fav'rd with one from you. Please to derect to me at Burlington to the care of Mr. Franklin if by a Vessell to York.

I hope to be with you in Aprill if our Vessell is not taken. my Compliments to all Fr'ds. I remain Dr. Sr. yrs. etc.

WM. LISTER

RICHARD AND RICHARD OLIVER TO ABRAHAM REDWOOD

Sir, London, 18th March, 1760.

ABOVE is Copy of our Letter of 3d November: are still without any of your favours.

You have before this been advis'd the glorious success of our Squadron under Sir Edward Hawk in the defeat of that commanded by Monsieur Conflans destin'd with 18,000 land forces for Ireland.[1] We have now also the pleasure to write you that Thurot,[2] after landing and plundering in one of the Northern parts of Ireland, in his return was

---

[1] In November, 1759, off Belle Isle. See *Dictionary of National Biography*, XXV. 197.

[2] François Thurot (1727–1760).

met, engag'd, and overcome, by three of our Frygates having lost his Life during the Attack.

Tho we have constantly endeavord to push off your Sugars when the prices have been encouraging, from their low quality and the bad reputation of Antiguas this year we have not been able to dispose of more than your 10 Hhds. per Lusby at 42/6, Sales inclos'd; which tho' a good price for them is far inferior to such as we are able to render to our Friends in general. Our Market for our Natural Sugar has for some time been dull owing to the Foreign demand not being so sperited as expected, by supplys from Monte Christi and Guardaloup to foreign Marts immediately. The probability of the Malt Distillery being again open'd has also particularly contributed to hurt our Market for low Sugars, in reducing the price of Melosses; the distillers Petition has not however yet succeeded, and the City, on the other hand, we hope from their Petition will be able to continue that salutary and beneficial prohibition to which we attribute the Reformation among the People with their increased industry and uncommon sobriety.[1] having comply'd with Mr. Blyzard's Order for Goods on Account of your Estate we inclose you duplicate of Invoice forwarded to him by our Fleet but lately sail'd. We shall further ship by the next Fleet 40 Hhds. Beans directed by him. Having nothing further at present to add but our respects to your Family and wishes for your health and felicity, remain with sincerity and regard, Your Oblig'd Humble Servants,

RICHARD AND RICHARD OLIVER

The distillers have succeeded in their petition.

[Endorsed,] Per Capt. Whitson.

---

[1] "The high prices of spirituous liquors manufactured in Great Britain, wisely occasioned by some late statutes, having greatly lessened the consumption thereof amongst the commonalty, and thereby contributed very much to their health, sobriety and industry; for the prevention of the return of former mischiefs, an act of Parliament passed in the thirty-third year of King George II For preventing the excessive Use of Spirituous Liquors, by laying additional Duties thereon: and for encouraging the Exportation of British-made Spirits, etc. — Which law has further contributed to the said salutary end." Anderson, *Origin of Commerce*, III. 318.

W. Grant to Christopher Champlin[1]

Sir,   Monte Christo, 20th April, 1760.

I RECEIV'D yours of the 20 March, and likewise a Letter for Capt. Duncan, who is still at St. Domin'o. Yesterday I saw his Cooper, one Fish, who left him but 18 days from this date; from whom I have collected the following intelligence. That he Arrived at St. Domingo in 21 Days after he left Rhode Island, and after being there 10 Days landed his Fish which he sold at 8 ps. 8/8[2] per Q[uintal], also some dry goods which he landed chiefly Wollens were sold at a very good advance, but his Linnens are unsold, and that he expected to have permission to land his Flower every day, which in case he did was worth 12 ps. 8/8 per b'rll Capt. Duncan has been reduced almost to the grave by Sickness, but was entierly Recoverd before he left him, which in some measure detain'd him there. these are the most material affairs I learned from him and which I thought would give you the most satisfaction to know. As for times here they are so bad I dont care to say any thing about it. it is sufficient to tell you that Molasses is at 25 ps. 8/8 Brown Sugare 5 ps. 8/8 Communes 6 Whites 7:½ and Markets are as dull. but now I am writing about the times, I am almost Distracted and only wish to see you, which will be soon, to tell you I am, Sir, yours,

                                             W. GRANT

Spermicity Candles at St. Domingo 5 Rials.

David Jamison to Christopher Champlin[3]

Dear Sir,   New York, July 3d, 1760.

YOUR favour of the 24th of May I received some time ago, since which have had the pleasure of seeing Mr. Lister who informed me of the Contents of your Letter much to

---

[1] The original is in the Rhode Island Historical Society.

[2] The Spanish *peso duro* (hard dollar), bearing the figure 8, and of the value of eight reals.

[3] The original is in the Rhode Island Historical Society.

the same Purpose of yours to me, and am very sorry to find that our Voyage from which I had conceived great hopes, is likely to turn out so very ill, however when I consider that what we did, we imagined was for the best, all I can say is, that we are unfortunate, and that it's in vain to repine.

I am now about trying a Voyage to our own Islands (since Trading with the Enemy has turn'd out so very ill) and shall sail for St. Kitts[1] in about a week in a Sloop in which I am partly concerned myself, and therefore have sent you the enclosed Power of Attorney to enable you to dispose of my third part of the Schooner and Cargo in case she should arrive, as it will not answer for me to be concerned in a Vessell from Rhode Island and remain in this place, and make no manner of doubt but you will act as carefully for my Interest as tho' it were your own.

If the Schooner should arrive, and you dispose of my part of the Vessell and Cargo, desire you will remitt the N't Proceeds (in hard Cash) if possible together with the Accounts to James Duane,[2] Esq'r, Attorney at Law in this place, with whom I have left a Power to act for me in my absence.

Mr. Lister informs me in a Letter I received from him since his arrival at Rhode Island that the Stills we bought, are sold again for the same money, and that he shall receive the money in a little time. Therefore have desired him in a Letter which goes with this, to pay into your hands whatever he shall have left, after deducting what I owe him, which beleive will near discharge what I was deficient in the purchase of the Schooners Cargo, the Remainder am obliged to leave unpaid, till her Arrival or my Return from the West Indias which hope will be in a short time;

I am, wishing you all the Health of Body and Mind, Success in Trade, or whatever else your heart can desire Dear Sir, Your sincere Friend and hum: Serv:

DAVID JAMISON

---

[1] One of the Leeward Islands, now Saint Christopher.
[2] (1733–1797).

Richard and Richard Oliver to Abraham Redwood

London, 24th August, 1760.

Sir,

We beg leave to refer to our last of 23d June per the *Jupiter*, and copy per *New York Packet*. We are still without any of your favors, but hope no indisposition has prevented your writing. We now advise the arrival of our Leward Islands Fleet and the undermentiond Sugars on your Account.

  5 Hhds. per *London Packet*, Davis.
  5 Ditto per *Martin*, Hooper.
  5 Ditto per *Antigua Planter*, Gladman.
  5 Ditto per *Sally*, Lusby.

20 Hhds. and have Bill of Lading for 5 Hhd: more per the *Johnson*, Wm. Lessly, expected by the 2d Convoy to be look'd for the ensuing Month.

Our Market continues low and, as natural to expect on fresh supplys, fallen, but lower than we foresaw. We shall, therefore, still keep your 30 Hhds. formerly advis'd to be on hand in hopes of your Advantage their quality not having commanded a Price in proportion to other Sugars oblig'd our keeping them longer than desireable for taking the advantage of a bare Market; but this speculation from our Connexion with Guardaloup has not yet answer'd, and we had done better in selling, could we have foreseen that the prohibition on Corn Sperits would have been taken off.

We are affraid the quality of the above will not be better than usual, and for such, as indeed all Antiguas from their present general bad Reputation, we shall find it difficult to command a price in proportion to good Sugars to which the present demand is almost wholly confind, and some Dabs from Antigua sold lately at 25/6, some low Sugars at 29/, and good Midling at 35/. so great a falling off will be disagreable to all our Friends as well as it is to ourselves; but we must submit with the aggravation of an additional Duty. the finest St. Kitts Sugars now sells for

46/ which would this time 1[2] months have commanded 58/; lower Sugars have fallen in a still greater proportion. We hope for better times and shall you may be assur'd always act as we imagine most for your advantage.

Our German Affairs look badly. Cassell posess'd by the French, who have also enterd on some part of our Hanoverian Electorate. if the whole falls into their hands our affairs will wear a very different aspect from what they have done, and England on a Peace [will] feel the misfortune of a Continental connexion.

We pray our Compliments to your Family, and our Friend, your Son, and remain with real Esteem, Sir, Your Obliged and Obedient Humble Servants,

RICHARD AND RICHARD OLIVER

JAMES DUNCAN TO BOWLER AND CHAMPLIN [1]

Gent: Kingston, Jamaica, 14 Fbu 1760.

I TAKE this occasion by my brother John Duncan to inform you [of] my misfortune of being sent in here was taken aboute 10 Leagues to the westward of Cape St. Antony (the west end of Cuba) by the *Harwich* man of warr Will'm Marsh commander the 12th August at 4 o'clock in the morning. had the ill luck to fall just athwart his Bows. They did not discover us untill Daylight, when they gave us chase, then aboute 4 miles from us, the wind being light and flattering bro't him up with us at noone. he took possession of the vessell, took all my people on Board the man of warr, and man'd the Briggt. with his own people, and the next day put us under Convoy of the *port Royal* man of warr bound for Jamaica, where we arrived the 1st. Instant. I have applied to Mr. Moore and Several other principle Merchants to Lay in Claime for Vessell and

---

[1] The capture of merchant vessels offered little profit compared to the taking of a Spanish galleon or treasure ship. In Anderson (IV. 13) are given the returns from *La Hermione*, a Spanish register ship, condemned in the Admiralty Court November, 1762. The net proceeds were £519,705. The admiral received £64,963; the captain of one of two capturing vessels, £65.053; and each of three commissioned officers, £13.004.

Cargo but none of them cares to undertake, as I have no Letters of Credit. Mr. Livingston is in the Country, have apply'd to him in your Name and expect his answer tomorrow. if he Refuses shall petition the Judge for an appeal. if not granted shall enter a protest against his proceedings and take out a coppie of the Condemnation and proceed Home as soon as possible. I don't mean by Claiming to get the Vessell and Cargo clear, for they Condemn every thing that's sent in. all I can expect is the Benefitt of an appeal. Shall do my utmost to obtain it, as I am acting for other people as well as my selfe. was the whole Intrest my own I would put up with the first Loss. for the people here are such Villens and so united in these affairs they appraise the sugars at half the Value and take 'em to their own account. So that if we Recover we get nothing. The Agents have endeavored to prevent my Claiming by offering me my private adventure which is very considerable. . . . My being taken is a fatetal affair to me and a heavy strocke to you. But I have and shall continue to do my utmost for the General Intrest and remain, etc.

JAMES DUNCAN

JAMES DUNCAN TO BOWLER AND CHAMPLIN [1]

Gent'n,   New York, Dec'b'r 24th, 1760.

I ARRIVED here yesterday after all my misfortunes and am very sorry to hear there is no hopes of Redemtion, as I laid in a Claim for the Brigg and Cargo, the Charges of which amounts to near four hundred pounds Jamaica Currency I have drawn on you for One hundred and forty odd pounds that Currency the Ballance of Mr. Livingston acc't and make no doubt of your honoring the Bill altho I have been so unfortunate in my undertak'g am truly sensible of your loss as well as my own and know of no other way to get Satisfaction but to fitt out a small

---
[1] The original is in the Rhode Island Historical Society.

Vessell against the Jamaica men who have at least 40 Sail of Vessells runing up and down to Hispaniola. The Vessell is just puting off. I shall be with you in a few days. Till when Remain Gent'n Y'r Very humble Servt.

JAM'S DUNCAN

P. S. 15 Days ago we spoke with Capn. Cook and Capn. Fones[1] who told me Capn. Hubbs was to sail in 4 days. 18 days ago we brot. too an Antegua Privateer, bound to providence who had a Brigg'n in possesion which he retook from the French, Jere: Cranston Master. Cranston was on board the French privateer.

GEORGE CROSSWALL TO REDWOOD AND CHAMPLIN[2]

Gentlemen, Monte Christo, March the 8th, 1761.

IN a few hours after I left you I soon had a nother wind and asoon as it began to blow and rain it soon sett us to work amend'g our rags of sails, and never ceas'd mending from morning untill night untill our arrivall heare which was the 2nd of march; on the 17th and 18th we hade a violent gale of wind which lasted 40 hours att SSE to SSW. and in the extreamity of the gale our Mainsail splitt and tore the old from the new, and in the evening all hands att work amending of it (wett as it was). Before sun went down a very heavy sea broke on Board of us, which washt all the Lumber our Boatt, and Cambooss over board, and lay on hir beam ends for some time. it also drew the ring bolts that our Cambooss wase lasht to. had that same sea broke in on the Quarter Deck where every soull of us wase att work on the mainsaill we must have all gone as our boatt went. So Gentlemen you see the bad consequence in send'g a vesell to sea without sails sufficient for when others wase crouding for a merket I wase lying rouling in the trough of the sea, amending our shaterd rags. I shall gett some Canvass and putt my sails in good order before I

---
[1] Daniel Fones became a member of the Fellowship Club, October 2, 1753.
[2] The original is in the Rhode Island Historical Society.

leave this place. Youll pardon me for troubling you with the above subject.

When I arrived to my great joy, I found that our shade wase in demand and imediatly agreed for 200 Barrels of the same for 12 ps. 8/8 per Barrel. Butt when I came to deliver the same they opned a number of Barrels, and you must know they lookt but very indifferently; for they smelt musty being the pickel had run o't and had been long keept. But on the whole I have sold all of it, except 30 or 40 Barrels, which is the worst of the whole. I have offered them at 8 ps. 8/8 but no, they seem to have a sufficiensy of that Quality, and wase there a vessell to arrive now, I question whether or not she could sell. I have sold the Sperma Ceti at 5 Ryals, the tallow at 1 and $\frac{1}{4}$, and have but sold 8 Barrels Mackrell and them at 6 ps. 8/8 and $\frac{1}{2}$ Saltt fish unsold. the price current is but 3 to 3 and $\frac{1}{2}$ Suggars att present is very high, the best muscovado at 4 ps. 2 Ry^s. Molasses at 22 ps. and a great many wanting, but belive Suggars will fall in 3 or 4 weeks. am at a great Loss for want of a Boat and can get none as yett to purchase. I have nothing further to add. Butt shall write you by all convenient opportunitys, and am Gentlemen when I can serve Yours etc.,

GEORGE CROSSWALL[1]

Capt. Sweett sail'd a few days on Cruise before I arrived. I heare that Hobs is well below.

We have no account of Capt. Grant nor [Capt. Dan]iell Duncan as yett.

SPERMACETI CANDLE AGREEMENT[2]

It is proposed by Rich'd Cranch and Co to all the other Manufacturers of Spermaciti Candles within the limits of New England in North America that in order to promote their and our mutual advantage, We will all unite in the following articles of Agreement Viz:

---
[1] Of Newport.
[2] Original in the possession of George C. Mason.

First. That we will all unite ourselves for the full term of Seventeen Kalendar months from and after the date hereof, that is untill the fifth day of April, 1763, into one general Body, by the name of the United Company of Spermaciti Candlers, by which name we will respectively own and acknowledge each others as members.

2d. That we will respectively send Positive Orders to our respective Buyers of Head matter, not to give for head matter more than six pounds sterling per Ton, above the price of common merchantable Spermacity Body brown Oyl, when said orders shall not be forwarded to our respective Buyers till after the Fifth day of April next.

3d. That the current price of said common merchantable Spermaciti Body brown Oyl, shall at all times be determined by the curr. price given by the merchants of Boston for the London Market at the day the purchaser receives any Headmatter, but in case there be no current price settled at that day, by the merchants aforesaid, then the next following cur. price by them given for such Oyl, shall govern the price of said Head matter.

4th. That we will not at any time within Said Term by any means either directly or indirectly by Presents, Promises or otherwise give for Head matter more than six pounds Sterling per Tun above the price of such Common Oil as aforesaid, not receive any at a greater difference, which said price of said Oil shall be ascertained as aforesaid, nor will we either of us receive any head matter, which is acknowledged by the Seller to be pre engaged.

5th. That we will not at any time within the said Term by any means directly or indirectly either by present, Promises or otherwise give more than Two and half per Cent Comm' to any person or persons for Buying Head matter for us. Neither will we by any means or ways receive any head matter at any greater price or cost to us then Two and half per ct, Considered as Common or otherwise more than the six pounds sterling difference aforesaid.

6th. That we will not at any time within Said Term by any means either directly or indirectly by our selves or otherwise for us, sell within the Limits of New England our respective Spermaciti Candles for less value then one Shilling and Ten pence half penny Sterling per pound besides one shilling Sterling more for each box, each box to contain about a quarter of a hundred weight.

7th. That no one House in this United Company shall Receive and manufacture any Head matter either directly or indirectly for and upon the amount of any other person not concerned in the United Company, upon any terms whatsoever and neither of our houses shall add to their Company any new partners without the consent of the other Houses.

8th. That we will by one member at least from each House have Two General meetings during said Term at the best Tavern in Taunton, Viz. The first upon the first Tuesday in November, 1762, and the other on the first Tuesday in March, 1763, or if bad weather then the next fair day after each said Day in order to Consult about matters for our general interest, and the expenses of this Union, and the said General Meeting shall be paid in proportion to the number of manufacturers thus united and one member from each House at these General Meetings shall always bring these articles of Union so that if any alteration or addition should be agreed upon, the same may be annex'd thereunto, and such Members (meaning manufacturing) as at any time may neglect these General Meetings shall pay a fine of Eight Dollars, (a reasonable excuse excepted) and shall be bound to conform to what may be agreed upon by them who mett. Provided always that nothing shall be allowed or added to these Articles but by the universal consent of the members present.

9th. That whereas the manufacturers now united as aforesaid are more than sufficient for Manufacturing all the Head matter at any time brought or likely to be brought into New England. Therefore each of us shall from time to time use his utmost endeavour by all fair and honourable means to prevent the setting up any other Spermaciti works and that Obadiah Brown and Comp, together with any two or more of our Houses be empowered to call a special Meeting to be holden at Taunton to which notice we each respectively promise to adhere.

10th. That in case we find notwithstanding this present Union that the price of Head matter still keeps up above six pounds Sterling per tun above the price of such oyl as aforesaid, or in case Head matter should now come down to our Difference in price now agreed upon, and should again rise beyond our aforesaid difference of six pounds Sterling per Tun, above the price of Such oil aforesaid. Then in either case, we agree to fit out at least Twelve vessels upon our joint Concern to be employed in the Whale fishery, each manufacturer in this United Company to furnish and receive an equal proportion in and from said vessells, and we also agree to add to the number of these Vessells from time to time as many more as may then appear most proper.

11th. That if any one or more members of either House in this United Company shall at any time within said Term, either directly or indirectly do or Cause to be done any Act or thing Contrary to the plain Spirit and intention of either of these articles, and the same shall be come known (by the evidence of one Credible person under his hand) to either of the other members of either House in said United Company, he shall upon such evidence of malconduct immediately advise the other Houses of such breach of articles and the evidence thereof and thereupon the said United Company shall be immediately dissolved, and each House shall be at Liberty to act in the same manner as though these articles had never been.

12th. That each and every of these Articles shall be understood in the most simple plain and obvious meaning of the words, and no one member shall contrary to the Spirit and intention of these Articles endeavour to make any advantage of such in accuracy or want of expression as may have happened through haste or otherwise.

In Witness of our full Consent to each and every of the aforesaid Articles and declaring upon our Honour, Reputation and Character as Men, That we will throughout the said Term act agreeable to same We hereunto subscribe our names this Fifth day of November, 1761.

ROBERT JENKINS.	OBADIAH BROWN & COMP^Y
	RICHARD CRANCH & Co.
	NAPH HART & Co
	ISAAC STELLE & COMP
	THO ROBINSON & Co.
	AARON LOPEZ & Co.
	COLLINS & RIVERA
	EDWARD LANGDON & SON

The following are Names of the Gentlemen Concerned in the several Houses.

OBADIAH, NICHOLAS, JOSEPH JOHN & MOSES BROWN. THOMAS FLUCKER ESQ.	O. BROWN & CO.
NATHAN GORHAM, JOSEPH PALMER, R^D CRANCH & WILLIAM BELCHER	R^D CRANCH & CO.
HENRY COLLINS JACOB ROD RIVERA	COLLINS & RIVERA.
JOHN MAUDSLEY ISAAC STELLE & JOHN SLOCUM.	ISAAC STELLE & CO.
NAPHTALI, SAMUEL, ABRAM & ISAAC HART	NAPH: HART & CO.
THO^S & JOS ROBINSON WILLIAM RICHARDSON	THOS ROBINSON & CO.
AARON LOPEZ. SOLUS	A. LOPEZ.
EDWARD LANGDON & SON	EDW LANGDON & SON.

WILLIAM STEAD TO CHRISTOPHER CHAMPLIN

Sir, London, 28 February, 1762.

THE foregoing is Coppy of my last of the 30 September per *Polly*, Winn, via Newyork; since have been favour'd with yours of the 23 November per *Boscowen*, Jacobson, via Boston, and the 4 inclos'd Bills value £328.1. are all

accepted when paid shall credit your Account for the same. I am sorry you shou'd take it amis that Mr. Rome had my Power of Attorney which intimated to you, as I never yet doubted the honour and reputation of your House having had such a Character of it as to put it beyond all doubt; but when you consider the Goods sent you was charg'd at 12 Months Creditt, which is now upwards of 3 years standing, that you cannot blame me for asking for the Ballance; for had much rather be paid at the time agreed on than have any Interest to charge which is no sort of satisfaction to us at this time, when we can make much greater advantages of it out of trade. I am sorry that I cou'd give you no Satisfaction with regard to the Average in the *New Concert*, shou'd have been glad to have left it to Arbitration, but the Underwriters wou'd not agree to it, and believe your Remedy at Law would have been very uncertain as the Captain's Protest and Papers were defective. You may be sure I took all possible methods to obtain you satisfaction, but found it ineffectual. I make you a tender of my best services when ever you have further occasion for them, And am, Sir, Your most Humble Servant,
          WILLIAM STEAD

LAMAR HILL AND BISSET TO ABRAM REDWOOD

         Madeira, 5th June, 1762.

Esteemed Friend Abram Redwood,

WE were very sorry to learn that Captain Allen of New London, who carried your last years supply of wine, fell into the hands of the French, by which misfortune you were disappointed of it; but we hope you will have better success with the pipe we have now shiped by way of Salem, consigned as per Bill of loading inclosed to Richard Lechmere, Esquire, who we doubt not will forward it carefully to you, and that you will find its quality to your satisfaction, having been very carefully chosen. The Cost as at bottom is 40/ cheaper than the last year's, and we shall value for it on Trecothick, Apthorp & Thomlinson.

The heavy loss our House suffers by the Death of Richard Hill, our late affectionate and honored partner, will be perceived we hope by no alteration in the method of our Business, which shall be preserved on the same principle that established it, vizt. a steady view to the interest of our Constituents, by his Son and Son-in-Law, who are with much respect to you [and] your's, Your most obliged and obedient friends

LAMAR HILL & BISSET

No. A. R. 1. a pipe of wine £28.0.0
10 per Cent for the N: York gauge
of 120 Gallons £2.16.0
£30.16/ Stg.

Wheat 450 to 500 r[ei]s per Alquier
Corn 3[00] to 350 Do.
flour 3600 to 4$ per Quintal
Codd fish 4 to 4400 rs. per Do. not more than 10 or 1200 Quintals should come to fetch these prices.
New York wine [Rum] 95$ per pipe
West India Do. 62$ Do.

COLLINSON AND POTTENGER TO STEPHEN AYRAULT

London, August 3rd, 1762.

Worthy Friend Stephen Ayrault,

SINCE our last 30th April per Jacobson and Capt. Sutfield, via New York, have none of your further Favours. The Bills then mentiond to be accepted, vizt.

Joseph Clarke on Jos: Sherwood . . . . £200.——
Thos. Filtch on Richard Jackson, Esq. . . . . . . 90.—. 8

are now both paid and plac'd to your Credit, and for which remittance return our thanks.

Agreable to what we wrote at that time have now to hand you Invoice and Bill Lading for the Goods order'd, amounting to £263.9.3 ship'd on board the *Atlantic*, Nathan'l Adams, Mr., per Boston (no opportunity offering for your Port,) consign'd to Thos. Green, Esqr. as usual, to whom we forward one Bill Lading, desiring him to follow your directions in the forwarding them to Rhode Island. we wish them safe to hand and to your Satisfaction, which will give us pleasure to hear. Insurance from hence to Boston is done upon the best Terms, being 15 G[uinea]s, with returns as per Invoice, and the Risque is continued from Boston to Rhode Island at the old price 2 G's per Ct. which at this time is rather objected to, the Underwriters thinking it too little. We have now sent the Linnens you order'd on Mr. Lindsay's Account, (also that of your own,) which we hope may prove agreable. The Amount of Mr. Lindsay's Invoice exceeds the Bill remitted (by £*10.17.2.*) which was not intended. Therefore as we have wrote him, if you have no objection, will debit your Account with the same, for which shall wait your leave. Note what you say respecting the sundry Articles per Dymond. The Chair Nails short sent you shall have Credit for. we are sorry for the Complaint against the Kettles with respect to the heavy Bales, etc. that you should have the trouble of altering them. In any future parcel you may depend on our particular care to have them made lighter. The Frame Saws you mention were order'd [of] Smith and Loomes Comp'y, but at that time could not get any of that make; therefore ventured to send London Saws; which we were in hopes would have answerd very well; When the old Copper, etc., you mention comes to hand we will do the best w[e] can with it, and will settle your Account with the Executors [of] Mr. Rumsted, accordingly. hope ere this the Goods per Calef may be safe with you; The History of the House of Stuarts is not to be had. Agreable to your request have wrote the Invoice upon smaller and thiner paper which if it answers the purpose you will please to mention, and we will continue it.

Have now only to add our best wishes, and in hopes of hearing from you soon remain with all true Regard; Your Assured Friends,

COLLINSON AND POTTENGER

[Endorsed,] To Stephen Ayrault, Merchant at Rhode Island. To the Care of Thos. Green, Esqr., Merchant at Boston. Per Capt. Adams.

Sailing Orders for Africa[1]

Captain John Peck,   Newport, Octor. 29, 1762.

As you are at present master of the sloop *Prince George* with her Cargo on board and ready to sale you are to observe the following orders:

That you Imbrace the first fair wind and proceed to sea and make the best of your way to the windward part of the Coast of Affrica, and at your arrival there dispose of your Cargo for the most possible can be gotten, and Invest the neat proceeds into as many good merchantable young slaves as you can, and make all the Dispatch you possibly can.[2] As soon as your Business there is Compleated make the best of your way from thence to the Island of New Providence and there dispose of your Slaves for Cash, if the Markets are not too dull: but if they should [be], make the Best of your way home to this port, take pilates and make proper protest where ever you find it necessary. You are further to observe that all the Rum on board your Sloop shall come upon an average in case of any Misfortune, and also all the slaves in general shall come upon an Average in case any Casualty or Misfortune happens, and that no Slaves shall be brought upon freight for any person, neither Direct nor Indirect.

And also we allow you for your Commission four Slaves

---

[1] The original is in the Rhode Island Historical Society.

[2] "Newport, Sept. 5, 1763. By a gentleman who arrived here a few days ago from the coast of Africa, we are informed of the arrival of captains Ferguson and Wickham, belonging to Newport, who write very discouraging accounts of the trade upon the coast, and that upwards of 200 gallons of neat rum had been given per head for slaves, and scarcely to be got at any rate for that commodity. This must be felt by this poor and distressed government, the inhabitants whereof being at this time very large adventurers in that trade, having sent and about sending, upwards of 20 sail of vessels, computed to carry, in the whole, about nine thousand hogsheads of rum, a quantity much too large for the places on the coast where that commodity has generally been vended. We hear many vessels are also gone and going from the neighboring governments, likewise from Barbadoes, from which place a large cargo of rum had arrived before our informant left the coast, of which they gave 270 gallons for a prime slave." *Boston Gazette*, September 12, 1763.

upon the purchase of one hundred and four, and the priviledge of bringing home three slaves and your mate one.

Observe not neglect writing us by all opportunitys of every Transaction of your Voyage. Lastly be particular Carefull of your Vessell and Slaves, and be as frugal as possible in every expense relating to the voyage. So wish you a Good Voyage and are your Owners and humble Servants.

[No firm signature]

But further observe if you dispose of your Slaves in Providence lay out as much of your neat proceeds as will Load your Vessel in any Commodity of that Island that will be best for our advantage and the remainder of your Effects bring home in money.

ISAAC ELIZER
SAMUEL MOSES [1]

SPERMACETI CANDLE AGREEMENT [2]

WE the Subscribers, Manufacturers of Spermaciti Candles Being met together at Providence in N. E. this 13th Day of April, 1763, have agreed for ourselves and Partners Respectively (notwithstanding any alteration that may happen in our respective Houses within the term herein after mentioned) honorably to adhere and abide By the Following Articles — Viz.

First. That we will and hereby do unite ourselves into one Body for our General and Particular Interest for the full Term of one Year from and after the Date hereof, i.e. until the 13th Day of April, 1764.

Second. That we will not at any time within said Term By any Means either directly or indirectly By ourselves or others for us by Present, Promises or otherwise Pay or engage to Pay or Give for Headmatter more Than ten Pounds Sterling per tun above the Current Price of Common Merchantable Spermaceeti Body Brown oyl nor receive any Head-

---

[1] Preliminaries of peace between France and Great Britain were signed November 3, 1762. By the treaty Great Britain restored to France the islands of Guadaloupe, Mariegalante, Desirade and Martinico in the West Indies, and obtained Canada, the Grenadas, St. Vincent, Dominica and Tobago. Spain agreed to permit unmolested the cutting, loading and export of logwood from Honduras.

[2] Original in the possession of George C. Mason, in *Reminiscences*, I, 40.

matter at a Greater or Difference. Which said Price of said Common Oyl shall at all Times be ascertained by the Current Price Given by the Merchants of Boston for the London Market at the Day the purchaser receives any Headmatter. But in case There Be No Current Price Settled at that Day By the Merchants aforesaid then the next following Current Price by them Given for such Oyl shall Govern the Price of Said Headmatter.

Third. That from and after the Date hereof and until the s^d 13th day of April, 1764, we will Not by any means, Directly or indirectly receive or engage to receive Any Headmatter but only from the following Persons Who shall be our only Buyers or Factors for Headmatter during Said Term. Viz. Joseph and William Rotch, Sylvanus Macey and Co, Folger and Gardner, Robert and Jessie Barker, Obed Macey, Richard Mitchell and Jonathan Burnell, all of Nantucket, Henry Lloyd of Boston, George Jackson of Providence, and Benjamin Mason of Newport. And we will Not By any Means Directly or indirectly Give or allow our Said Factors More than two and a half per Cent Consideration as A Commission or otherwise for their Trouble.

Fourth. That all the Headmatter caught in North America And Brought into Any Port Thereof after the Date Hereof and until the Said 13th Day of April, 1764, Shall Be Considered as one Common Stocke or Dividend, Whether any of the Vessels are owned by any of us or not to be devided by our Said Factors to Each House of Manufacturers in the following Proportions. Viz.

Nicholas Brown and Co. 20 barrels out of Every 100 Barrels.
Thomas Robinson and Co. 13 ditto

Isaac Stelle and Co.	9 ditto
Aaron Lopez.	11 ditto
Moses Lopez.	2 ditto
Edward Langdon and Son.	4 ditto
Joseph Palmer and Co.	14 ditto
The Philadelphians.	7 ditto
Naphtali Hart and Co.	9 ditto
J. Rivera and Co.	11 ditto

And our Said Factors shall be directed under our Hands to divide the Headmatter caught this Year in the above Proportions in the Spring, Summer and Fall seasons, Excepting only that our Said Factors at Nantuckett Be directed to keep in their own Hands about four hundred Bbls of the Fall Headmatter undivided until they Know from Each of our Houses how Much each House has had, in order to make a final Division agreeable to the above Proportion. But in Case Either of us Should Receive any Headmatter From any other Person but only from the Factors aforesaid, Excepting only that seventy Barrels may be received By Naphtali Hart and Co from Caleb Russell of Dartmouth and thirty barrels by Rivera and Co from Jethro Haddway of Dartmouth which are to be considered as parts of their above Proportions, or should offer a Greater Price or Difference then afores'd for Headmatter: or larger Commissions than afores'd for Factorage: Or should refuse or neglect To Pay our Said Factors for the Headmatter to their Satisfaction. Then in either of these Four Cases our Said Factors shall Divide the Headmatter which would otherwise have belonged to such Houses (Who shall be deemed to have forfeited their Shares By such dishonorable conduct) among the other Houses in the aforesaid Proportions Near as they Can.

Fifth. That we will not Any of us, Manufacture either in whole or in part any Spermaciti for any other Person, But only For Ourselves respectively.

Sixth. Let our Factors be Directed to Transmit Acctts to Each of our Houses of the Headmatter sent to each House. And of any Breach of these Articles, and in the Month of December next They Shall Send compleat Acctt of all the Headmatter that has been sent to Each House, of all that has come to their Knowledge and how it has Been disposed of. They shall also Engage to Give us the Most Early Notice of any attempt to set up any other Spermaceeti Works, Because the Present Manufacturers are More than Sufficient to Manufacture All that is Ever caught in America. They shall Have Copies of These Articles and shall engage under Their Hands to Conform to the Plain Spirit and Entention of em on Their Part.

Seventh. That we will meet again here at Providence the First Tuesday, February Next (provided there has Not in the Mean time Ben any Manifest Breech of These Articles) in order to Continue this Union in such manner as May then be Agreed upon. And we will Then (Each House) deliver to the Chair Man for the Time Being Certificates under Oath or Solemn Affirmation of the Whole Quantity of Headmatter in Gallons received or Secured by Each House, After the Date hereof until each Day of Meeting, and of Whom received.

Eighth. That Messrs John Slocom, P. Rivera, Thom^s Robinson and M. Brown are hereby appointed to treat with the Said Factors at Newport and Nantuckett, and John Brown to treat with the said Factor at Providence, And Joseph Palmer to treat with the said Factor at Boston. And they are All To report their Proceedings with Sd Factors to Nicholas Brown and Co to be Communicated to The Other Manufacturers.

In Witness of our Free Consent to Every of the Foregoing Articles in Their Most Simple, Plain, and Obvious meaning and Declaring upon our Honour, that We will Not in the Least deviate from Either of em unless By Joint Consent; We Hereunto Subscribe our Names this 13th day of April, 1763.

     PALMER AND Co.
     NICHOLAS BROWN AND Co.
     ISAAC STELL AND COMPY, AND
     RIVERA AND Co
     AARON LOPEZ.
     THO ROBINSON AND Co
     NAPH'T HART AND COMP
     MOSES LOPEZ.

Thomas Collinson to Stephen Ayrault[1]

Esteemed Friend S. Ayrault,   London, September 23rd, 1763.

I REPLY in this to that part of yours of the 20th July, enquiring whether there was any intention of new Modeling the Provinces, by briefly observing there was an Intention to effect an ecclesiastical Change thro' out all the Provinces on the Continent. This was to be done by erecting one or more Bishopricks.[2] However I believe the general Design is at present suspended, and part of it only will be executed, in the new acquisition of Canada, where they seem determined to establish the Church of England upon the same Laws and basis as it is here, and one Smith[3] (now over in Ireland) it is said will be the first Bishop.

It will be well if this Erection of a Spiritual Prince prove virtually productive either of any moral, or political Good, in this late conquered District. In general, History and Experience evince the contrary, and frequently afford Instances that in proportion as Forms and external Orthodoxy are fix'd upon as Essentials, the Substance of Religion, and internal Rectitude of Mind gradually decay. Moreover a Bishop must have a See. this will call for the Allotment of a large Tract of Land, doubtless the best, and most fertile they can find; also all the Subordinate Officers of the Church, such as Deans, Deacons, etc., etc., etc., must be provided for in like manner.

To support all this the Property and Labour of the Laity must be taxed, and most probably (as it is here) their very Improvements will be taxed or tythed in measure with the Improvements. By degrees this new planted Church will become very powerful, and sooner or later the Party must submit to Laws fram'd by itself, in its own Spiritual Court, and however injured must wait the issue of an appeal from

---

[1] The original is in the Newport Historical Society.

[2] Cross, *The Anglican Episcopate and the American Colonies* (1902).

[3] Arthur Smyth was at this time Bishop of Down, and had been Dean of Derry to 1752, and Bishop of Cloufert for a few months in 1753. In 1765 he was translated to the archbishopric of Dublin.

England, etc., etc. Mark how those Colonies have most flourish'd, where they have most enjoyed spiritual Liberty, where all Religions that injured not the State went hand in hand with a peaceable Equality, — none set as superior, to Lord it over the rest.

If Inconveniences occur upon establishing a Hierarchy in Canada, how much more so if executed in Boston and the other Colonies, inhabited by the immediate Posterity of those very persons who fled from their native Land to avoid a Persecution inflicted upon them by this kind of Church Power. How unjust and (if I mistake not) contrary to Charter, to stretch forth this Spiritual Rod over their Inheritance now cultivated, populous and free, in a Country which their Fathers found a Desert.

I know not my worthy Friend whither these sentiments may concur with yours. Be that as it may, I always write with Freedom to those whose Person's or Characters I know to be worthy of Esteem. as such I now write to you, and conclude with my best wishes for your Welfare, Your respectful Friend,

Tho. Collinson

CHARLES WALKER TO CHRISTOPHER CHAMPLIN

Sir, Newprovidence, October 2d, 1763.

YOUR esteem'd favour I am duly honour'd with, and note the Contents. I observe your intention of sending a Vessill here, and if such a thing should have taken place, and arrives soon, doubt not but what she might arrive to a good markett, as this Island is at present much in want of such produce as you mention in your price currant. I long ere this thought to have been in Carolina, but payments are so dull, that I could not compleat my affairs; since which I am determin'd to try Providence for at least 3 years, and have enter'd in bussiness with Mr. Geo. McKinzie of So. Carolina, for settling a Store here. Mr. G. M. saild about three weeks ago for Carolina, for a fresh supply, so desire you would direct to Walker & McKinzie if you or any of your friends should adventure this way, and doubt not of their acting with as strict Justice and punctuality as in their power.

Our produce is at present very high, Madeira $3\frac{1}{2}$ In. plank at 20 ps. 100, Inch Boards 8 to 10, Braz^l at 22 ps. per Ton, Limis 8 per M.

Since you left Providence it is become very dolefull, little or know trade going on and what little there is, its centre'd in one or two hands which is certainly a great hurt to this Island. however I expect a compleat assortment of Goods, and shall then expect to partake with part of what trade is going on, if I am successfull with Industry, tho, one must have the patience of Jobe to live here, were there is no Society. I was this Morning at Church, being the 3d time for the space of Nine m[onths] and heard a very pretty Sermon, tho in my Judgment rather too seavere for a Criminal which is to be executed a friday.

by this time I expected to have had the pleasure of hearing of your Marriage, which I hope when ever happens that all the happiness that this Life can afford will attend.[1]

As to my part some months ago I had a great notion of trying the experiment, but can assure you that passion is much abated, and am proud to inform that I hope I shall wave all such thoughts till I go home where a certain one have the greate[st] right. Mr. John Baldwin married the fortune, Miss Boo Loone, with about One Thousand pound Sterling.

After you left this our old Logings became vacant, which has almost given me the hip. how I kill time, Champlin, would supprize you. You may remember I formerly con-

---

[1] Christopher Champlin was born in 1731 and died in 1805. See Mason, *Annals of Trinity Church, Newport*, 134 *n.*

verced with the fair Sex, but have dropt that agreeable Society, for fear that I should be too proud and taking of divers leaps that I may be the means of causing a [torn] and then I may be forced to doe that which would be very disagreeable to me and make me unhappy all my days. I am once a week at the New Guinea, where am a little diverted at a fandango.

As I purpose doeing Buissiness here hope you will write me by all oppertunitys and doubt not but what with a proper care that one may do somthing between your place and this.

Haveing nothing farther to add, but beg your acceptance of a Cag Limes I remain with unfeigned regard, Sir, Your most obedient Humble Servant,

CHARLES WALKER

Excuse haste and blunders, the Scooner being just ready for sailing.

THOMAS TALMAGE TO CHRISTOPHER CHAMPLIN

Sir,

I WAS consernd in a Sloop that was long since sold at St. Thomas to Henry Florence either of Marble Head or Salem for 1020 pieces 8, for which Payment Florence draws an Order on Lodwick Panet, which he excepts, promising to pay the same on demand in Merchantable Rum and Molases, but when Demand was made Panet was broke and unable to pay a farthin. I desire you would enquire after Florence and inform me where he is and his Circumstances, and I should be obligd to you for your Opinion whether he is not accountable for the above.

The Cargo the same time was sold to the Governor of said Island, for which he gave a Bill of £188 payable in Amsterdam, which is returnd protested. Since he is gone of, tis said home to Copenhagen. if Mr. Powell should go home to London and thinks there is any chance he could negotiate that Affair during his Stay in London, I would convey the Bill over to you, if I could have seasonable Notice.

My Vessell saild 3 weeks ago and is to touch at St. Martins to land 1 horse for a particular Gentleman there; thence to proceed to St. Eustatia there sell her Oxen and her Horses, with the rest of her Cargo; then to take a Load of Salt at St. Martins or Turks Island, and so down to Port Dauphine[1] and so return. Please to inform me your knowledge of such a Vioage.

If you have any cheap Rum French or New England, could send me a Cagg of ten or twelve gallons for the use of Laborers this Winter, and command Your Humble Servant,

THOMAS TALMAGE

Easthampton, November 28, 1763.

GEORGE CHAMPLIN TO CHRISTOPHER CHAMPLIN

Dear Brother, Thenerieffe, Novm: 27th, 1763.

I HAVE disposed of our adventure agreeable to the Price Current remitted you, all but the tobacoe, which I find Impposoble at any rate; however it will be a good Article to Leward. I have improved the proceeds of our Adventure in Wines and Unnions. Could not git above 1500 Bunches which I hope will answer very well, as they are very fine. I could git Credit, but the Wines are so high that I am afraid they will not answer. In regard to my small interes you may behave on account of Insurence as tho you ware in my Case, whilst I am with Regards, your Brother, etc.,

GEO. CHAMPLIN

JOHN TURNER & SON TO ANDREW HEATLY

Sir, Amsterdam, 31st January, 1764.

HAVING here to fore been favoured with your Commands we make free to tender our further Services unto you, hoping in case you should have occasion for any European Goods,

---
[1] On Santa Lucia.

or any West India Goods to ship for our market that you will favour us with the Preference of your Commission. we send you inclosed a list of Prices of our market for your Perusal. it is thought Sugars will keep at the Price they are at present. Rice is expected to go higher, unless there should be a large Crop this year and great Parcells arrive the next Spring. Tea is greatly lowerd since last fall, and probably will come down still more. there is at present with us little stir in Trade. we long to learn how it is in your Parts as to this Point, ever since the Cruisers from England are watching on your Coast for to intercept the Vessels bound from these parts for your Continent. We remain with perfect Esteem, Sir, Your most humble Servants
JOHN TURNER & SON

[Addressed,] To Mr. Andrew Heatly, Merchant at Newport, Rhode Island.

WILLIAM STEAD TO CHRISTOPHER CHAMPLIN

Sir, London, 10th February, 1764.

YOURS of the 22 November per *Sally* was Ladd [last] was fav'd with, and your order for Sundry Goods; but as of late Years have partly declin'd the N. America Business, therefore declin'd new Connections, so must beg to be excus'd executeing Your Order, of which thought proper to give you the earliest Information from, Sir, Your most Humble Servant, WILLIAM STEAD

[Endorsed,] Per *Hope*, Jacobson.

THOMAS COLLINSON TO STEPHEN AYRAULT[1]

London, March 20th, 1764.

MY worthy Friend Ayrault's Letter I now acknowledge the receipt of; almost within the same Hour that it came to hand, for as I always rather chuse to write from the Heart than the Head; no long Preparation is necessary.

---

[1] The original is in the Newport Historical Society.

Just at the time when the Question was asked: "Whether the Government intended new modeling the Colonies," the Scheme was in agitation for establishing Episcopacy, etc. Therefore your Question might as well be construed relative to the ecclesiastical, as to the civil new modeling, etc.

Supposing therefore as I did, that you meant the former, my Reply was to the former; and your Animadversions thereon corroborate an opinion I early entertained, of your sincere Integrity and Rectitude of Heart, and truly make me wish every member of the Church was equally happy in this essential of true Religion. You accuse me however of Partiallity, and to have demonstrated that; might perhaps have been speaking more to the Point, and more instructive to me (who always wish to be open to Conviction), than to have transmitted the Oriental Tale; that seems to me incapable of any steady Application. And trust me, my good Friend, I value more the sage Reflection of a sensible plain honest Man; than all the imitated Sublime of the East.

In relation to new modelling the Civil-Government of the Colonies; can only say it has long been a favourite Scheme with Lord Hallifax to purchase Proprietorship, and change them into Governments wholy under the Crown. The Execution of this plan; does not seem to make any Progress, being opposed by great Numbers respectable for their Judgment; Legislative Knowledge, and upright Characters.

What Man can gather either from ancient or modern History, a Colony that in the same space of Years from its Establishment; equalled or equals, Pensilvania, in Popularity; Improvement in Agriculture, Commerce and Riches.

None of the Phoenecian, Greek, Asiatick or Roman can boast the like. If I ask why, the reasons are too obvious to need mentioning, especially as I have already much exceeded the Limits I at first prescribed my self, and am in danger, nay more than in danger of incurring a repeated Censure for my long Detail. Very respectfully and sincerely yours,

THOS. COLLINSON

CONYNGHAM AND NESBITT TO CHRISTOPHER CHAMPLIN

Sir,   Philadelphia, 30th March, 1764.

WE have just received your favour 22d current from New York, and congratulate you on your Recovery from a disorder so fatal to many who have not had your resolution to try the experiment that kind providence has made known to his Creatures for abating the Virulance of the Small pox when taken in the Natural way.

To Capt. Gould [1] we have been obliged to return the Bills on Mr. Meradith which for want of Effects he would not accept. a vessell from Providence is, since we returned the Bills, arrived, and with some Effects and positive orders from the drawer of the last Bills to Mr. Meradith to honour them,

he still declines it, tho' as he has not enough to answer former engagements, and we have been able to do no more than to urge Captain Gould to secure himself from the drawer or Endorser, and to as speedy a Remittance as possible to prevent any ill consequences that may attend his affairs in Rhode Island, with the Best dispositions to discharge punctually his debts, no man has had worse luck than our Friend Gould, on whose account we shall gladely informe you whan any farther advices come to hand and in the mean time enquire of Mr. Stocker what the Bills were protested for we mean for what Sum, and the Interest and any other Charges that youl let us know we shall include in the first remittance we are enabled to make, damages on such Bills we have neither Law nor usage to authorise, they are on a footing with Inland Bills in England, and treated as such, to pay with interest and all charges from day of protest. we hope no ill consequences will attend the affair to Mr. Gould for some little time longer on this you may depend we would gladly serve him, and shall as soon as posible he can enable us, either to remitt you by Bill on N. York or to Rhode Island, If we can get it, or parmit your drawing on us immediately, or on our Friend

---

[1] James Gould, Jr.

in N. York for the Ballance due account of the returned Bills, which may be most agreeable to you. We are, Sir, Your obedit: Hble Servts.,

CONYNGHAM AND NESBITT

JAMES GOULD, JR. TO CHRISTOPHER CHAMPLIN

Sir, Newprovidence, May 10, 1764.

I HAVE been cruelly disappointed in the several attempts I have made to discharge the Bills I indors'd you. I have some time past, since my last disappointment fallen on three methods in hopes of discharging them Bills with the damages. the first is Bills on Virginia, ordering payment to Phila. the second is Two Sets of Bills I purchased, which is accepted by a Gent in Phila. and have sent Conyngham and Nesbitt. the third is by sending a vessle to Boston ordering payment of them Bills imediately, when as much of the Cargo is sold. if they all fail, I have the fourth reserve which is, that I shall be in Rhode Island my self sometime in June, if no accident befalls me, and will discharge them my self, if not done before that time. should all the methods I have mentioned fail, the posseser of the Bill will then have it in his power to pay himself with my Intrest in Rhode Island.

them Bills has lead me into a great Scrape by their not being presented in a reasonable time after their Arrival at the Northward, as they would undoubtedly [have] been paid. I have now by me protested Bills to the amount Eight Hundred and odd Pound Pensilv'a Currency, all protested, which I bought at three different times since I know'd your Bills was protested, and my greatest motive in the purchase of them was that either one or the other should discharge your Bills; but they have all failed, and I am now to seek for the Money I give for them. I am Your Humble Servant,

JAMES GOULD

Champion and Hayley to Christopher Champlin

Sir,   London, 14 July, 1764.

We reced your favours of 29 April and 18 May, covering two Orders for Goods which we shall provide and ship agreeable to your Instructions by the first opportunity, and you may depend upon us that the uttmost care shall be taken to comply with both as near as possible, and that they shall be purchaced upon the best terms. We hope this beginning of a Correspondence may be long continued to mutual advantage; to which end nothing shall be wanting on our parts, and we make no doubt but you will by punctuallity in your remittances render it equally agreeable to us. The Bill for £200 which you remitt us on your Colony Agent is accepted and will be to your Credit. Our time of Creditt with all our Friends in America is 9 Months from the date of their Invoices, within which time we should hope you will be able to send us what your present orders amount to, over and above the £200 bill, and that in your future orders, you will likewise be able to do the same; in which case you may depend upon your orders meeting punctual Execution upon the best terms. We write you by Packet agreeable to your desire to give you the best information we are able respecting the Refined Sperma Ceti, which article we apprehend can never answer; for it is chargeable here with a Duty of near a Shilling a pound and the price it sells for is only Eighteen or at most Twenty pence. as to introducing it in any manner to escape the Duty we think it impossible. that which Capt. All has brought is regularly paid and indeed it cannot be otherwise. The Master may smuggle a small Quantity, but not without great hazard; but it is impossible he should do that with any but a very small Quantity.

We have applied to Messrs. Battey and Cort in relation to Mr. Bell, and they tell us they have near Two thousand pounds of his Money in their hands, and that they shall have no objection to paying any Bills he may draw on them to that amount. We think you may therefore rely upon being safe in taking his bills on them, which we dare say will be punctually paid; but we should not choose to have the Money charged to our Account till we have rec'd it from them, as that would be making ourselves responsible for their payment, which is a thing we never do; but we dont say this as having any doubt of their being regularly paid, for we verily beleive they will be punctually so. We are very Respectfully.

Sir, 15 August, 1764.

ON the other side is Copy of our last respects. We now enclose you Invoices for the Goods you desired which we have shippd in the *London Packett*, Capt. Robert Calef, amounting to for the mark M £191.4.10, on which we have made £195. Insurance, premio, etc., being £5.19.3; and for the mark H £126.6.2, on which we have made £130 Insurance, premio, etc., being £4.0.3. We hope these Goods will upon arrival prove to satisfaction, and are very respectfully, Sir,

*Your most humble servants
Champion & Hayley*

[Endorsed,] Per Capt. Calef via Boston.

CHRISTOPHER CHAMPLIN, SEN. TO CHRISTOPHER CHAMPLIN, JR.

Charlestown, August 24th, 1764.

REC'D yours in which you informe me of your Buying 3 oxen of Nenigreat[1] at 4/6, and want to know if I will take 4/6 for my beer. I hop you don't think your agreeing with Thomas for 4/6 for oxen that wont be fit for a dog to eate by

---

[1] The Indian.

the Time you are to have them, for he hath brought them to me to keep, and I hant a working ox but is as good again beef as they are, and my beef will be fit for any Gentealmans Table. I shant have more than eight head to put of, and they will be good, so cant take 4/6 for them; but if you can give 5/ round for them, and pay the ferrag of them, you may have them and if that will sute shall be glad to know soon: for if I should keep them till fall, am in no doubt of fetching 6/. if you should feed the menawars Men [1] on such beef as that you have of Tom, you will have maney a Sevear Cuss. I have given an ordor on you in favour of Tom Nenigreat for £21:8:6¾, and if the beef wont sute, you shall take my chance with it and pay you in a nother way. This in hast from your father,

CHRISTOP. CHAMPLIN

---

[1] This is the first mention of participation in the supply of British naval vessels in New England waters, Newport being a central station. Of the harbor of Newport Robert Melville, governor of Grenada, wrote in 1763 or 1768: "The whole bay is an excellent man-of-wars harbour, affording good anchorage, sheltered in every direction, and capacious enough for the whole of his majesty's navy, were it increased four fold. There are no dangerous ledges or shoals within the Bay, or near its entrance, which is easy with all winds. Another advantage it possesses over any other harbour on the northern coast in the winter season, is, that it is very seldom obstructed by ice, and the tide is not sufficiently strong to render the drift ice dangerous to ships laying at anchor. The harbour has not been frozen up so as to prevent ships coming in to safe anchorage since the year 1740, and the oldest inhabitants do not recollect to have heard that it was ever so frozen up before since the settlement of the colony; It has other advantages which cannot be found elsewhere in America. A whole fleet may go out under way, and sail from three to five leagues on a tack; get the trim of the ships, and exercise the men within the bay, secure from attack by an enemy. The vicinity of the ocean is such that in one hour a fleet may be from their anchorage to sea, or from the sea to safe anchorage in one of the best natural harbours the world affords. Its central situation also, in his Majesty's North American Colonies, and its proximity to the West Indies, are advantages worthy of consideration, as it regards the protection of every part of his Majesty's widely extended possessions in this quarter." *Rhode Island Historical Magazine*, VI. 44.

Alexander Grant to Christopher Champlin.[1]

Sir, London, 12 Feb., 1765.

INCLOSED you have Invoice and bill of lading of sundry goods shipt (by order on Account and Risque of J: Powell, Esqr. Merchant in Boston) per the *Hope*, Captain Jacobson, for New York, amounting, together with a box of China per the *Edward Davis*, to £481.5.6. agreeable to your directions I have sent him bills of lading and addressed them to Mr. Gerard G. Beekman at New York, with orders to reship them to you by first good Opportunity. You'll please to observe that the Insurance is made only to New York, where the risque ends; that the Underwriters pay Average on any particular package, if the dammage thereon amounts to three per Cent, and in case of total loss to pay the whole of their Subscription, that is £100, instead of £98 as was formerly the Custom. In Trunk No. 5 you will find a piece of Cambrick marked D. C. No. 23 which pray send to Mrs. Cheesebrough. You'll also receive with the other goods, two Cases of China mark'd P. W. and M. H.; be kind enough to deliver the first to Mrs. Wilkinson and the other to Mrs. Heatly, who will pay you their respective proportions of the Cha[rge]s of which Mr. Beekman will advise you. It will be necessary, and I pray you'll immediately advise Mr. Powell,[2] or his brother in his absence of the circumstance of the Insurance, that if he chuses he may cover his Interest from New York to Rhode Island. The brass Kettles could not be got ready to go by this Vessel, but you'll have them by a Brigantine which sails next month for Newport. I hope the goods will arrive safe soon and to a good Market, and prove to your satisfaction.

They are all bought of good People and I have spared no

---

[1] The original is in the Newport Historical Society.

[2] Probably John Powell, son of Adam and Hester (Bernon) Powell. He married Jane Grant, who died in 1774, and he removed to England, living till 1800. His sister married Rev. Samuel Seabury.

pains to have them put up on the best terms. The discount for prompt pay you'll observe is deducted from the Amount of the several bills of Parcells. On one there is 2½ per Cent equal to six months Credit, another 3¾ to nine Months, and all the rest at 5 per Cent. If upon examination you find cause of complaint on any article, be particular in mentioning it, that I may procure redress or avoid dealing with such Person in future, at any rate let me hear from you on their Arrival and tell me how they turn out. I wish you health and Success in all your Undertakings, and am, Sir, Your obedient humble Servant,

JOHN SCOTT, JR. TO CHRISTOPHER CHAMPLIN

Sir, Cha's Town, So. Carolina, February 27, 1765.

YOUR favour of 22d ulto. per Capt. Winslow I have before me. I am surprized our Leather should stick ahand, when Mr. Russell sent some of the very same Leather and he inform'd Mr. Wilson that it was sold to some advantage; and he further says that ours might, on allowing short Creditt which we are not against, so they are but safe. as for selling at Vendue it will not turn to any account. however on the whole do with it as it was your own. Mr. Wilson don't know what was the quantity sent. I am not concern'd in the whole adventure, but in a 1000 li. wt. which is to be made up to me. Send me the Nt. Proceeds of all the Leather in good Sparma Citae Candles. I hope you will be able to remitt it by the first vessell, as I am in want of a few Boxes of that article. As for Mr. Jos. Atkinson, he is a man lately come from England to set up the Tallow Chandlering business, but quite a stranger to me. I happened to be in his company one day, and he was saying that he'd be glad to know where he could get any Sparma Citae, on which I made mention of your name, but told him at same time that he must send something to purchase it. that is all that passed between us, and as for his Circumstances know nothing about it. Mr. Wilson joins me with Compliments and am, Sir, Your most Humble Servant,

[Endorsed,] Per Capt. Winslow, Q. D. C.   JNO. SCOTT, JUN'R.

JOHN SCOTT, JR. TO CHRISTOPHER CHAMPLIN

Sir.   Cha's Town, So. Caro., March 22d, 1765.

I HAD the pleasure of writing you under the 27th ulto. per Capt. Winslow, since which am without any your favours. I should be obliged to you if you'd inform me what price you could get me a well built Schooner burthen about 60 Tons, at Marblehead, or at your place (but w'd give the perferance to the former as being in most esteem). If a good vessell, and well used, sh'd not care wether she was a year or two old. I am told in the fall, after the fishing season is over, such a one may be bo't pretty reasonable.[1] If so, sh'd likewise be further obliged to you in leting me know what of our produce will turn to account for to purchase one, as it will be better then sending Cash. I hope by the time this reaches you that you have disposed of our small adventure, and remit'd it in Sparma Citae Candles, as I formerly advized you. I am, Sir, Your most Humble Servant,

JNO. SCOTT, JUN'R.

Original per Capt. Pit via Boston.

---

[1] In April, 1765, John Rowe contracted with Eben. Lewis, for a schooner, forty-four foot keel, seventeen foot beam, and seven foot one-half in the hold, at £19. 10s. per ton. *Diary*, 80.

Nathaniel Greene To Aaron Lopez.[1]

Sir   Providence, April 10: 1765.

I RECEIVED by Mr. Lindsey fifteen 40 Gallon Cask, and am very much suppris'd att the same, as I never agreed to warrant any cask I should send you, but am more suppris'd that you should send them back, they being as good Cask as any made with you by any of your Coopers, as I have had as good a Cooper as any in this town to look at them since they come back, and he says they are very good bbl. I think you suffer yourself to be impos'd upon by the man that ajug'd them. I have ben credibilly inform'd that he cannot make so good a Cask to save his Life.

I have ben inform'd by two Gentemen then present that the barrils would have ben sent back likewise, if itt had not ben for some Whalemen from Nantuckett giveing there opinion that they ware as good barrills as they ever see, which I think is a grand imposition. I have sent by the boat thirty one barrills and eleven 40 Gallon Cask, which I expect you [to] take, as I have taken the utmost pains to gett them of the best sort. I shall send to make up the two hundred according to agreement as soon as I can gett them made, which will be soon. I have sent you four hundred feet and upwards of boards; shall send more as soon as I can gett them in, the ways being so very bad that the teams can not pass is the Reason that I have not sent more by this time. I remain,

Sir your most humble
Servt Nath: Greene

[Endorsed,] Per favour of Capt. Lindsay.

---

[1] Moses and Aaron Lopez owned and occupied a building on the corner of Duke Street.

An African Voyage

The Sloop *Betsey*, Nathaniel Briggs Master, Aaron Lopez and Jacob Rod. Rivera owners, for the Coast of Africa.
To Jacob Rod. Rivera.......................... Dr.

1765.
June 19.   To 11 Barrels pork . . . . at 60/ . . £33.—.—
           To 200 li. of Cheese . . . . . at 10/ O T. per li. . . 4. 5. 8¼
           To Cash for fish for the people . . . . . . 40/ . . 0. 1. 8½
           To 1389 Gallons Rum of Wyatt . . at 2/ L Mo. . . 138.18.—
           To Difference between Com. & Guinea hhd. 3/5½ . . 2.16.—
           To Cash for 10 li. Mutton . . . . at 8/ . . 0. 3. 5¼
           To Phil: Wanton bils for Medicines . . £140.5/ . . 6.—. 2½
           To Joseph Boss's Bill for a Boat . . . . 14.10.11.
           To 2 Doz. Razors . . . No. 50 . . . . . at 5/5 . . 0.10.10.
           To 2 Doz. Do. . . . . . .   51 . . . . 5/10 . . 0.11. 8.
           To 2 Doz. Do. . . . . . .   52 . . . . 7/6 . . 0.15.—
           To 2 Doz. Do . . . . .   53 . . . . 8/9 . . 0.17. 6.
           To 12 Doz. uncapt penkn's   22 . . . . 2/11 . . 1.15.—
           To 6 Doz. Capt Do. . .   23 . . . . 6/10½ . . 2. 1. 3.
           To Constant Wilbour's bill for packing
               10 1/2 bb. pork 0. 6. 5½
                                   Lawfull Mo. . . . . £206.13. 8½ [1]

Henry Cruger, Jr. to Aaron Lopez.[2]

Sir,   Bristol,[3] Sept. 4th, 1765.

My last Respects to you were under date of 2nd August per your Brigantine *Charlotte*, and Copy per *Two Brothers* via New York to which pray refer.

---

[1] The wages paid and time of voyage are known from the "portlage bill," in this collection. The master, mate, and one sailor received £60 each a month; two sailors, £45, one, £40, and one £30. The men were shipped in May, June and July, 1765, and discharged in May, 1766, for the most part. The total wages paid amounted to £2,385.15.6½.

[2] The original is in the Newport Historical Society.

[3] "Bristol is universally allowed to be the largest city in Great Britain, next after London. The anonymous author of England's Gazetteer, published in the year 1751, makes her to contain thirteen thousand houses and ninety-five thousand souls. When the author of this work was there in the year 1758, he perambulated it for two successive days, and from a near examination of the number of houses or new foundations, and even of entire new streets, erected since the said year 1751, he imagined he could not hesitate in concluding it to contain about one hun-

I have sent per the Bearer of this the Remainder of your Goods which could not be got in time for the *Charlotte* as per Invoice inclosed, amounting to £208.13.8 Sterling to your Debit. The Bill Lading I have inclosed to my Brother, Mr. John Harris Cruger,[1] at New York, and desir'd him to forward them per first Conveyance to you.

Last week after giving all the customary Notice I put your Ship *America* up to publick Auction, but not a single Bidder appear'd. Ships are so little in demand, I think you must lose a Deal of Money by her. I don't expect to make above 6 or £700 Sterling of her sell her when I will,— far short of your Valuation.

Her Plank, etc., I am with all possible dispatch getting measured and lotted out, and will sell as much of it as I can, but oh! it is bad Times. don't send any more Ships for sale till I give you Encouragement; confide in my Integrity, I will never deceive you, tho: indeed you are the best and only Judge what you can afford them at.

As to your Logwood[2] it has been a long time housed. I offer'd it for £7, and could not get it.

---

dred thousand souls, or to be about the magnitude of that part of London which is contained within her ancient walls. It is confessed, that London, within that limited compass, appears to be more populous, or to have more people appearing abroad in her streets; but that we apprehend to be occasioned chiefly by its communication with her vastly extended suburbs, her immense commerce and shipping, the greater resort of foreigners, and the near residence of the court, nobility, gentry and lawyers: whereas in the streets of Bristol, which are more remote from the harbour and shipping, the inhabitants are mostly either private families living on their means, or else manufacturers and workmen of various kinds employed altogether or mostly within doors." Anderson, *Origin of Commerce*, III. 324.

[1] See Sabine, *Loyalists of the American Revolution*, I. 343.

[2] Logwood was early used as a dye, being imported in the log which was afterwards chipped. It was introduced into England in the time of Queen Elizabeth; but the art of fixing the color was so imperfect that a law was passed prohibiting its use under severe penalties, and directing its destruction if found within the realm. The prohibition remained in force for nearly a century, though the wood was sold and used as "blackwood," and was removed only on the discovery of a means of fixing the dye. The tree is a native of America and in almost all commercial languages is known by the name of the principal region of supply — Campeachy — *Haematoxylon Campechianum*, Lin., *Bois de Campêche*, Fr., *Palo de Campeche*, Sp., etc. The privilege of cutting long constituted one of the diplomatic differences between Spain and Great Britain.

You perceive it is likely to be a long while before I can sell and be in Cash for these Goods, but, Sir, don't give yourself much uneasiness on that Account, for these are things that I suppose you could not foresee, and altho it is very trying times with we poor North American Merchants, yet we'll die hard, and honourable. Your Bills shall all, as before advised, meet due Respect.[1]

At present nothing further occurs. Inclosed is an Account of the Brigantine *Charlotte's* Disbursements, amounting to £54.6.3. Sterling to your Debit.

I am with Esteem, Sir, Your most Humble Servant,

HEN: CRUGER, JR.

P. S. Just upon closing the foregoing I received your esteemed favours of 18th June via New York and Dublin, and about an hour after received by the *Charming Fanny*, Capt. Osborne, your further favours of 17th July, ordering £2500. Sterling Insurance to be done on the *Friendship* Capt. Lindsay. as the Season is advanced, I shall be obliged to give 50/ per Cent. If it is effected before I dispatch the Bearer hereof, will send you an Account of the same.

As have already in the Begining of this Letter given you my candid Sentiments on the Sale of New Ships, and Lumbar Cargoes, will for the present say no more; they are certainly become a bad article, and the Ship you now value at £1500, if she fetches half the Money, you'll be well of.

At present, the vast Debts due to me from my American Correspondents are so distressing, and lay so heavey upon me, that I must beg you will be tender with me in drawing, don't over rate your Ships and Goods. I hope to see the times mend, when I shall take Pleasure in indulging you; but, bad as they are, be quite easy Sir, your Drafts shall all be duely honor'd by, Sir, Your much obliged Humble Servant

HEN: CRUGER, JR.

P. S. Since writing the above I have effected your In-

---

[1] The passage of the Stamp act was responsible for the depressed condition of trade with the American colonies.

surance as per Account at foot hereof, amount £75.16.0 Sterling to your Debit in Account Current.

Mr. Aaron Lopez
             To Henry Cruger Jr. Dr.

For £2500 Insurance made on the *Friendship*, David Lindsay, Master, at and from Rhode Island to Bristol, vizt.

On Ship	On Goods
£250.-.-. John Vaughan Jr.	£100.-.-. John Fowler.
100.-.-. Jas. Laroche, Jun'r.	100.-.-. Thos. Longden.
100.-.-. John Adlam.	100.-.-. Wm. Reeve.
100.-.-. Thos. Whitehead.	100.-.-. L. Schimmelpennig.
100.-.-. Edw'd Nicholas.	100.-.-. Rich'd Symes.
100.-.-. Sam'l Munckley.	100.-.-. Isaac Elton, Jun'r.
100.-.-. Thos. Griffiths.	100.-.-. H'y Bright.
100.-.-. John Curtis.	100.-.-. Jas. Bannister.
100.-.-. Edw'd Neufville.	100.-.-. Jno. Humphrys.
100.-.-. Chas. Harford.	100.-.-. Thos. Jones.
100.-.-. Geo: Champion.	£ 1000. on Goods at 50/ per Ct.
100.-.-. John Anderson.	and new policy 8/ . . . . . £25. 8.—
150.-.-. Rob't Gordon.	

£1500. On Ship at 50/ per Ct. and new Policy 8/ £37.18.0
                                                                £63. 6.—
To Commission on £2500. at 1/2 per Ct. . . . . 12.10.—
To the Debit of Mr. Aaron Lopez . . . . £75.16.—

John Williams to Christopher Champlin

Dear Sir,   *Maidstone*[1] at Halifax, 5th September, 1765.

Captain Allen of one of the King's Schooners sailing for Boston this evening gives me an oppertunity to acquaint you of our safe arrival at this place on Sunday last, after a tedious but pleasant passage of twelve days.

The *Squirrel* has been gone from hence about a Month ago for Louisburg and Canso, and is expected to return again in about three weeks time. I therefore have opened your Letter to Mr. Bell, and therein find that you had rather he should give you Bills on his Agent in London for the 38 pounds drawn on Mr. Lyle, or bring the money with him in case he returns to Rhode Island, than sending it by any other person, which is the reason I have not sent it by the

---
[1] The name of a king's vessel.

way of Boston, and particularly as we are at present quite sure of returning to Newport again.

We are at present in a very great hurry getting the ship ready for cleaning and believe shall be ready to sail from here again in 5 weeks time at farthest; I suppose Mr. Bell will take a passage in the *Maidstone*, in case no sooner oppertunity should offer of his getting to Newport. I am sorry to inform you that most of the Bread now remaining on board will be condemned, as it has proved quite musty and very bad; but at present cannot ascertain the quantity as it must all be taken out tomorrow or next day; there will be also some Butter which must be condemned, but the reports I shall not send to the Victualing Board as we are to return to Rhode Island again.

All my Messmates joins with me in our best Compliments to Mrs. Champlin and yourself, and hope you will believe that I shall ever retain a thankful remembrance of the many Civilities received from you and Mrs. Champlin when at Newport, and shall always (where ever I am) be extreamly glad to hear of your good family's health and success, who am with great truth and esteem, Dear Sir,

Your Obliged & very hum. Servant
John Williams

P. S. I must desire the favor of Mrs. Champlin to present my Compliments to Mrs. Bell, Mrs. Hunter, Miss Cowley, Miss Stell, and all the other dear little Girls of our acquaintance that she may happen to be in company with.

The report we heard at Rhoad Island just before we sailed

of Captain Smith's Lady being drown'd is not true, for she is at present with him at Canso.

[Endorsed,] To the Care of Mr. William Powell Merchant at Boston.

ROBERT MEARNS TO CHRISTOPHER CHAMPLIN

Glasgow, 12 September, 1765.

Invoice of Seven Casks Bottled Snuff shipt at Grennock on board the *Peggie*, Capt. Craig, Master, for Boston on Account and risque Mr. Christopher Champlain, Merchant in Newport, Rhode Island, to the Care of Mr. James Warden,[1] Merchant in Boston.

C.C. No. 1, qt. Snuff . . 110 at 14d	£6. 8. 4			
15 Dozen Bottles . . at 28	1.15.			
Cask	3. 9	8. 7. 1		
No. 2, Contains as above		8. 7. 1		
No. 3, qt. Do.		8. 7. 1		
No. 4, qt. Do.		8. 7. 1		
No. 5, qt. Do.		8. 7. 1		
No. 6, qt. Do.		8. 7. 1		
No. 7, qt. . . . . 117 at 14d £6.16.6				
16 Doz. Bottles . . . at 28 . . . . . . 1.17.4				
Cask 3.9	£8.17. 7			
	59. 0. 1			
Cartage Lightrage and Shiping Charges	14.—			
Freight to Boston at 3 per Cent upon £59 is	1.15.—			
Insurance upon £62 at 2 1/2 per Cent	1.11.—			
	£63. 0. 1			

Sir, Your favours of 24 June covering Bill upon the Commissioners of the Neavy for fifty Pounds Sterling cam dewly to hand, and is past to the credite of your Account, and according to ordor have shipt you as above.

But as Mr. Tillock[2] is not at home have not ventred to send the Carpet; but by the nex opertunity you may expected it, and he will write you more fully himself in the meantime I am, for Mr. Tillock, Sir, Your most Humble Servant,

ROBERT MEARNS

---

[1] James Warden, afterwards an addresser of Hutchinson (1774), had a store on Green's Wharf. He was not a native of America. *Mass. Hist. Soc. Proceedings*, XI. 393.

[2] In shipping twelve casks of bottled snuff in September, 1764, John Tilloch wrote: "I will take it very kind your discountenancing the sale of other snuff under my name; it is a mean low fraud. Surely the doers of it are men of no integrity."

Henry Cruger, Jr. to Aaron Lopez

Sir, Bristol, 13th September, 1765.

SINCE my last Respects to you, have received sundry Copys already answer'd; also your esteemed favour of 26th July ordering £500. additional Insurance on the *Friendship*, Capt. Lindsey, (who does not yet appear). Cost of the same you have herewith, £15 to the Debit of your Account.

After reading your Letter over with proper attention, I determined to give 3 days notice, and put your Ship *America* again up at Auction, but it proved all to no purpose. She would not fetch above £700., and your Limits are 750 Gs. Several Vessels are now ready to sail for New York not half loaded, as no Goods are going. this determined me to give Orders to get the *America* ready to sail for Newport without loss of Time, accordingly have order'd all the Goods you desire in your Letter, vizt. about 60 Tons Coal, 10 Tons Anchors, 2 of Oakum, 3 of Junk, 4 of Cordage, ½ bolt Rope, 6 Cables, 100 Bolts Russia, 60 Ditto English Duck, and Hemp.

The Goods that were shiped for you on board the *Minerva* shall be taken out, and put in the *America*. I shall insure the whole Cargo, and £800. Sterling on the Ship valued, at and from Bristol to Newport, for your guidance.

I expect shall be able to dispatch the *America* in about 3 Weeks from this Date.

Your Drafts to the Amount of £2200 are all accepted, and the greatest Part are paid. The Lumber by the *America* lays still unsold, no body offering to buy an Inch. Money is so scarce in the Kingdom, and trade of all sorts so dull, and the English Markets over done with North American Produce, especially Lumbar — nothing bearing the name of the least affinity of Wood will sell for any tolerable Price — and Lumbar Buyers in general are a Parcell of Poor Dogs, who must have Credit.

Oil, naval Stores, etc., will do very well, and as it's your

Method, or Conveniency, to draw, may better answer your Purpose, as the Sale of these Articles are not so tedious. Carolina produce generally answers very well. have great grounds to hope you'll soon be granted a free Trade to the foreign West Indie Islands. I think America hath seen its worst day — times must soon mend, but at present they are realy distressing.

By the *America* shall do myself the Pleasure to write you more fully. Interim and always I remain with Regard most Respectfully, Sir, your most Obedient Humble Servant,

HEN: CRUGER, JR.

[Endorsed,] Via New York. Rec'd and forwarded this 18th November, 1765, in New York, by, Sir, your obedient Humble Servant, JNO: HARRIS CRUGER.

HENRY CRUGER, JR. TO AARON LOPEZ

Dear Sir, Bristol, 4th October, 1765.

I HAVE paid due Attention to the Import of your esteemed favour of 12th August. I entirely concur with you that a wide distinction ought to be preserved between Persons of Consequence and established in a Trade, and Interlopers who too often through Ignorance, at the same time ruin both Markets and themselves. these latter Sir, you may rest satisfied shall meet little Encouragement from me.

Herewith is an Account of £1800. Insurance on the *Newport Packet*, Cost £54.16. to your Debit.

Before I proceed any farther in this Letter, it may not be improper to mention Capt. Osborne,[1] whom I have made Master of the Ship *America:* he appears to me an intelligent good kind of man, hope you may find him such. It seems as if Capt: Osborne was desirous to be in this Trade, and would be glad to hold a small Share in a Vessel with you, but, I chose to say nothing more to him on this subject, than that I would hint it to you. he has taken a good deal of pains to inform himself of the State and

---

[1] Jeremiah Osborne, of whom not a little will be found in this correspondence.

Situation of our Market; indeed it would not be amiss were you to confer with him.

The *America's* Cargo of Lumbar lies still unsold save the 34 Ps. Cedar, which have disposed of at 3 Months Credit for 3/ per foot. advise you to send no more Anchor Stocks; what have of late been sold, were used not as such, but as Timber; wherefore, to the Proprietor all is lost that is cut off the Ends to model them. When you consider the use of them, it must naturally occur the consumption can not be great, seeing one hundred would serve this City a year.

Your Logwood I have at last sold at £7 per Ton. one Tun of it was full of Tar, which were obliged to pick out and sell at only £6. Sales you have inclosed, Net Proceeds being £163.13.4 Sterling to your Credit. Last week I had a Cargo (arrived) of about 100 Tons fine Honduras Logwood, it is the best I ever saw; my orders are to sell it as soon as landed (for the most it will fetch), which I have done at £6.15. per Ton. this for your government.

The *Friendship* is not arrived yet. I wish I could give you any Hopes of a Sale of her. Trade is as much at a stand in England as in America; my Friends in London write me, they know not what to do with their Ships; here also is the same stagnation; which is the only Cause why there is no Sale for Ships.

I am in great Hopes 'ere long things will mend. I am very cautious how I interfere, and very unwilling to discourage Gentlemen in the progress of their Plan, or Business. it is certainly a delicate point; but still, Sir, as a mutual Confidence and Indulgence between two People so connected as are your good self and myself, must hope you will excuse the Liberty my attention to your Interest prompts me to take, in saying, I think you realy might do better than by sending New Ships and Lumbar to Market. it so happens now and then, that such an adventure turns out well, but it will not do to be extended. it appears to me, (for Reasons I fear too obvious to your good self) that you must sink Money by every Ship you build: the Time may come when the Demand for Ships will be great, then it may do, but not untill then.

Suppose, Sir, you was to keep one, or more Ships in this trade, load them with the most valuable Cargo Rhode Island produced, send them some times to Carolina, or the West Indies, etc., etc., the Produce of these places always meet a ready sale here. If the Cargo now on board the *America* meets a good sale with you, (and I think Hemp must) you never need be at a loss what to load your Vessels back with. I for my part am ready and willing to promote any of your Schemes, as far as it can be done by giving you the most extensive Credit for Goods you can desire, by which means you may monopolize all the best trade of your place. thus have I under the Sanction of a most sincere Regard taken the freedom to offer a few Hints, which you may improve to your own advantage.

It hurts me to read over my Letters to you, as not one that I have yet written but what is filled with discourageing circumstances; Those calamities are now become general. God grant we may soon be releived. I like to let you know the worst of things, tho: am ready to lend all the aid in my power to make the best of 'em.

Inclosed Sir is Bill Lading and Invoice of the *America's* Cargo, amounting with Cost of Insurance made thereon to £2452.2.6 Sterling to your Debit in A/C.

We had not time to get the whole ten Tons of Anchors made. Junk and Oakum were scarce; have shiped as much as could get; have sent 20 Tons of the best, and 20 Tons of the 2d Hemp call'd out shott; it is the method of the Rope Makers here to mix it, and pass it all for the 1st, by way of hint for your guideance.

The English Duck is from *two different* Makers, the Bales No. 1 to 7, is called Parliament Cloth, No. 8 to 12, is of an inferior Quallity. let me know which best suits your Purpose and I shall in future know which to send.

We have lately discover'd one Barrel of the Oil per the *Charlotte* to be Blubber, as per particulars inclosed.

I have endeavoured to be as frugall as possible in fitting

out the *America*, tho: were obliged to give her a few new Ropes and pay her uper Works. the Sailors are to work for their Passage; to 3 or 4 of the poor Dogs we are obliged to advance a little Money to get a few Cloths, they are to work it out. Capt. Osborne is shiped at 5£ Sterling per Month, his Mate at £3. the latter has had from Osborne one Months Advance. their Wages commence from the 16th September. I have paid Capt. Osborne £24.3.0 (as per his Receipt inclosed) for which he will account with you, it being for the use of the Ship *America*. an account of her Disbursements will send per my next. inclosed are the Plantation Certificates for canceling your Bonds.

Night is come, and as the Wind has been flattering all day, worked very hard to clear and dispatch the Ship, for which purpose Capt. Osborne will leave us in about half an Hour; I heartily wish you a quick sight of him, being in all your Commands with my usual Esteem and Regard, Dear Sir, Your most Obedient Humble Servant,

HEN: CRUGER, JUN.

P. S. It is necessary you send me two Certificates to cancel two Bonds given here for the Coal, one for 20 Chaldron and one for ten.[1]

H. C., JR.

HENRY CRUGER, JR. TO AARON LOPEZ

Sir, Bristol, 11th October, 1765.

I'VE already had the pleasure of writing you by the *America*, who is detained by contrary Winds and blowing Weather.

---

[1] An export duty on coal was granted from August 2, 1714, for thirty-two years by 12 Ann, c. ix, § 11, and by 6 George I, c. iv, § 1, was continued for ever. The duty per chalder, Newcastle measure, was five shillings in foreign bottoms, and three in British bottoms, but the duty was not collected on coal sent to the British plantations or Ireland. In this later act the proceeds were appropriated to the increased and additional fund of the South Sea Company, and for paying so much of the lottery orders of 1714 as were subscribed into the capital of the said Company. After 1729 they were applied to the payment of interest on £1,250,000 advanced by the Bank.

I have now to congratulate you on the safe arrival of the *Friendship*, Capt. Lindsay, who delivered me your most esteemed favours of 22d August, covering Invoice and Bill Lading of her Cargo, not being able to meet a Birth at our Key to my liking, have orderd her not to come up for a day or two. Your Drafts amounting to £1400. Stg. that you advise of, shall all meet due Honor, and your account charged accordingly. I wish to God we may have better Success in the Sale of this Ship, than we had with the *America*, tho I much doubt if we shall, as at present Trade, when compared to its usual State, is realy stagnated; no manner of demand for Ships. Times must mend, when they do, you may depend on the earliest advice and encouragement.

Oyl is as high as I beleive it will be this year, especially if the Importations should be large, which a little Time will determine. Vitious or Spermaceti Oil none at this Market; at London it sells from £21 to £22 per ton, and a dull article; Newfoundland £18 to £20, little at Market; New England £17; Whale £18. Please to observe all these prices are just now rather nominal than real, as the Dealers won't break a price untill they are well ascertained what Quantitys will arrive. Mahogony is become a mere Drugg all over the Kingdom, three entire Cargoes of it arrived lately in London. Tar is just now quite down, tho I imagine will get up towards Spring, and the price of Turpentine is likely to hold. Sugars are very high and a rising article, but alas, I fear *they* are out of your reach, The Marketts in England you must be convinced from experience are very fluctuating; in the course of a Month, they often rise or fall 20 per Cent, which every now and then inclines me to think it quite needless sending even the Prices Current. it is impossible to be informed what Quantitys of Goods may be expected, so many are the Ports in America from whence they come; frequently, when we think any articles are likely to be scarce, drop in Cargoes from all Quarters, when of course down goes the price again, and so vice versa; I have taken a good deal of pains to inform Capt. Osborne by word of mouth of the State of this Market the year round; I would not take the Liberty, Sir, to refer you to him, but that I think him both an intelligent and an honest Man. never is a long while, but my beleif of Logwood is, that during our natural Lives it will never exceed £7. per ton. Inclosed is an exact Price Current.

Yesterday my Broker told me he expected soon, a large Cargo of Vitious Oil from London, as that Market was likely to be over stocked; the conveyances of Goods from that Port to this, and from this to that, are so easy, the difference of the Market seldom continues long, or material, the Price of the London Market generally regulates this. You may depend I shall ever do every thing in my power for your best advantage, avoiding as much as possible writing any Intelligence but what may with safety be rely'd upon.

Capt. Lindsay being very desirous to embrace this so favourable an opportunity of returning home, I could not refuse indulging him with his Discharge, seeing no loss can accrue to the Ship in consequence thereof. I shall pay him and take his Receipt accordingly. the Sailors have also called for their Pay agreable to the Portledge Bill.

Capt. Lindsay is pleased to receive all the Passage Money for the Two Gentlemen he brought over. I think the Ship ought to have Credit for at least a Moiety. he says you chose to allow him the whole, so I've done on that Head; but, as you have allowed him £18:15:0 Stg. to bring him home, and as I have (for you) been so indulgent already to give him his Discharge, he ought to pay his Passage home (which is 5 Gs. to the Capt. and 5 Gs. to the Ship) or at least refund to you some of the £18:15:0 I have paid him; if it was my Case he should do one, or the other, as I think it is nothing but right, — this rests with you.

I shall not fail to send you the few articles you are pleased to order, and having some knowledge of these things, will be curious in collecting them.

We omitted in the Invoice per the *America* to charge 12

doz. Matts, amounting as per account herewith to £5.10.8. Capt. Osborne had occasion for 3 Gs. more, which I paid him (as per his Receipt) and your Account debited for the same.

Time will not admit of my saying more than that I am, with great Integrity and Regard, Your most assured Humble Servant

HEN: CRUGER, JUNIOR

JOHN POWELL TO CHRISTOPHER CHAMPLIN

Dear Sir, London, 28 October, 1765.

I WROTE you by Captain Bruce advising of my safe arrival here, since which received yours by the Bristol ship, that brought over Dr. Moffat and Mr. Howard.[1] The latter is under Inoculation. I saw him yesterday is well. But a little too low spirited. You have not mentioned the prices of provisions with you. I find Beef much fallen in Boston, and Grain rather dearer at Philadelphia and N. York than when left Boston. hope you'l improve a cheap time to lay in, for the winter supply. Sir A. G.[2] and myself have been to the persons who sold the Brass Kettles. The Principal is not in Town, but has promised to make good any loss. Their excuse I have endeavoured to set aside. I wonder much you did not mention it before to me. Mr. Grant I find took great pains to buy the goods sent you. But the Tradesmen now in London require a strict scrutiny into their Wares for exportation. Whatever recompence I can obtain you shall have credit for. I lost 6 per Cent difference in stock in six months only, and will be higher. Belchier paid your bill, also Captain Antrobus on his Brother in Ireland is accepted. Provisions are again dear in Ireland. I should think the Stoppage of Trade and scarcity of mony must reduce the Prices with

---

[1] Dr. Thomas Moffat, a Scotch physician, and Martin Howard, Jr., appointed officers under the stamp act, were burned in effigy before the Court House, and sought refuge in England after their houses had been rifled by the mob.

[2] Alexander Grant?

you, and all over the Continent. Tea, Hemp, and Duck, and all large Comodities, continue very high. That have ventured to ship nothing this fall, and am more confirmed have done right since the Riots took place. I hope Master Sullivan and you may be able to make out right, for if Williams returns, sayd the *Maidstone*,[1] the *Cygnet* will return to her Winter Station at N. London. Admiral Amherst is to succeed Lord Colvill.[2] I have heard of poor Bob's Death in the W. Indies; hope you will not be a sufferer. my Love to Peggy and Little one, Madam Bell, pray where is he — and all friends. I rest, Dear Sir, Your very Affectionate Servant

J. POWELL

I find nothing can be done i[n] regard to American Affairs till the Parliament meets.[3] God knows in what Temper that may be. There is many ill advisers here, who pretend to know much. Their views are to gain posts of office, etc.

[Endorsed,] Per Captain Hamilton.

GEORGE CHAMPLIN TO CHRISTOPHER CHAMPLIN

Dear Brother,   Baltimore Town, Novm: 12th, 1765.

I WROTE you a long letter 29th October by way of Philadelphia and orderd it in the Post office, which make no doubt has come to hand by this. When I wrote you I expected to be loaded by this time but its the most unluckiest time we posobly coud have come here on all accounts, in the first place the quantitis of Rum and Molosses that has lately been imported here from Boston, and the Nessessity the Vessells ware under of dispatch, has

---

[1] The *Maidstone*, man of war, Captain Antrobus, arrived at Nantasket, September 23, 1764. *Letters and Diary of John Rowe*, 63.

[2] Alexander, 8th baron Colville, a naval officer, who attained in 1770 the rank of vice-admiral of the White. He married Lady Elizabeth Macfarlane, daughter of Alexander, 6th Earl of Kellie, and relict of Walter Macfarlane. He died May 21, 1770, without issue.

[3] The King's speech was read in Parliament December 17, 1765.

nock'd the Markitts down to nothing; notwithstanding they are very high in Philadelphia. the Merchants here are shiping Rum and Molosses there for a Markit and Flour likewise. Flour is at 13/ and rising principally occation'd by the drouth the Mills stand still for want of water here's Vessells here loading for Lisbon which will purchase 30,000 Bushels of Wheat and 4,000 Barr[el]s Flour and at present have not the 1/4 part purchased. Cap. Willcocks is here. he has not got his Quantity of Flour as yet. I have agreed Punctually for all mine at 12/6, and am now ataking in as fast as I can git it from the Mills; having it pack'd light detains me some time, as I am obliged to have the Barr[el]s made on purpose. I hope to be loaded in 8 days without disappointment, then shall proceed over to Chaptank[1] in my way down to Patuxent to take in some Stock as its not to be had here. I have agreed with a man there to by me my stock again[st] I arrive there so hope not to be detain'd there long.

Custom House fees are exceeding high here. mine with the duties of 5 hhds Rum will amount to 18£ Currencey, so after paying that and purchaseing Provisions for my Vessell, shall not be able to put in for Cargoe to exceed the Memo. I shall give you at the Conclution of my letter by a ruf Calcolation.

The Stamp Act makes great Confution here.[2] the *Hornit* Sloop cruises of the Capes and overhawles every thing that passes. however hope we have no reason to fear him as we shall have a proper Clearance before the first of Novm: Cap: Willcocks has been down at Patuxent[3] to clear out since I came here, and the Collector gave him his Word and Honnour that we shoud be both cleard the 28th of October, which I have no reason to doubt; I have wrote the Colonel severall letters requesting him to se me cleard in Season which I am sure he will no[t] faile [doi]ng.

---

[1] Choptank River rises in Kent County, Delaware, and empties into Chesapeake Bay.
[2] *Correspondence of Horatio Sharpe*, III. 226, 229.
[3] In Ann Arundel County, about twenty-one miles southwest of Baltimore.

I beg you'll write me by all oppertunities to the Windard Islands. When I have compleated my Purchase at Chaptank will send you Invoice and B[ill of] Lading of my Cargoe, if I have oppertunity; if not you must govern yourself in regard to Insuranc by the memorandum at the bottom, which will be near the Contents and Amount of my Cargoe I shall take in. I have some Coffey and Cheese on hand.

Inclosed you have sales of Mr. Clark's Molosses, by which you'll find a ballance due to me, which beg you'll recover and give to my Wife, and you'll much oblige your Brother,

GEO: CHAMPLIN

Price sold at viz.

9 hhd. Rum	at 2/2 d
5 ditto	2/3 d
Molasses	19 1/2
Cheese	7
Coffee	11 d and 12

P. S. had considerable of Leakage 28 Galls. out of one hhd. through Wormholes. if I shud put in a little more flour than I have mentiond must lesson the Quantity of Stock etc.

Memo. of Sundry Merchdz. I propose to take on board for Cargoe viz.

180 Barrels Light Flour	at 22/	£198.
20 Barrels Bread	20/	20.
3M Staves and heading		13.10
50 Shoats . . . 1500	at 2 d	13.
200 Gees.	18 d	15.
Corn for the Stock		6.10
Provitions, port Charges, etc.		34.
		300.

will be the Neat Sales of our Cargoe or thereabouts.

GEORGE CHAMPLIN TO CHRISTOPHER CHAMPLIN

Dear Brother, Baltimore, November 24d, 1765.

I HOURLY expect the last Flour on board that I shall take in here, and in a fiew hours shall sale for Chaptank to take in some Stock, as I am inform'd by the Gentlem[a]n I imploy there to purchase it for me that its ready; so hope not to tarry long there. I have not time to make out an Invoice of my Flour, etc., as I have not yet collected the originall ones from the different People, and the post is now agoing out; but if I have oppertunity will forward you sales invoices, etc., from Chaptank if not must refer you to the Memo. in my last of 12 Inst., which will bee near the Amount I have and shall take on board for Cargoe.

I have delt here principally with Mr. William Lux[1] a very principall Merchant here who is fond of a Voyage to Newport; I have given him some Encoragement that a Cargoe of Flour, Bread, and some Barr Iron, may do there tollorable well in the opening of the Spring, to take N. E. Rum, West India Goods, etc., in return, which will suit him very well. I have left him a memorandum how to direct to you, as he tells me he will absolutely send a Vessell as soon as the Season will admitt, to Newport and to your address, which he desird me to mention you in my letters; and I make no doubt but you may depend upon his sending you one, as he is a very searious worthy Gentleman, and a Corospondance with him I am persuadid will not be out of your Way. beg you'll write me by all oppertunities. shall toutch at Dominica, and from thence if it does not suit to the Granord,[2] whin you write be kind enough to accquaint my Wife, and you'll oblige your Brother,

GEORGE CHAMPLIN

P. S. our Schoone[r] makes a good deel Water.

JOHN AND WILLIAM POWELL TO CHRISTOPHER CHAMPLIN

Sir, Boston, 25 November, 1765.

WEE have your Favour 22 Instant and find the mistake in the Newport Mail hindered your having our letter of the 11th, to which refer you for what relates to Williams the

---
[1] See p. 150, *infra*.
[2] Granada?

Purser. have wrote J. Powell fully about it by last Ships to London; and the more wee think of it the more wee find the necessity of making a stand with Williams about his intended incroachment, which if he is allowed in, the Contract will not be worth keeping.

Mr. Warden expects 2 Vessells from Glasgow every day; if any thing on board for you shall take care that you know it timely for to get it on board Langworthy; also some Oatmeal, if to be had, its 2 months since expected some from a Back Town, and our stations ships has had none this 12 months, nor is there any even at Hall'll,[1] from whence wee have an order to send some if to be had. Mr. Pain tells us this morning that his wine will be in the first East wind. wee have had 2 Letters from J. P[owell] of the 15. and 17 September. he had a fine Passage of 6 weeks. in regard to our Custom House wee are as far of now as 3 weeks ago; they only want the Surveyor to give them the least encouragement, or even to let them know he is indifferent about it, and they would give Clearances imediately. But so it is, he, the Surveyor, is afraid to give the Colector the least Sanction. Wee have got a Vessell gone to Phila. (one Whitmarsh) for Wheat and Flour, and have got a Letter from Capt. Bishop to the Phila. Gaurd le Coast to let him pass, he being loaded with Provisions for the Contractor; but how it will answer are afraid. The Macrell Catchers have brock and sold all their Macrell off at 21/4 per Br., and we have allowed so for all wee have sent to Philadelphia tho' not without great Reluctance and Scolding — so that Mr. Gibb's Bill parelley from us stands viz.

130 Brs. Macrell at 21/4	£138.13.4
Branding and Nailing 3d. each	1.12.6
Trucking the last Brs. on board	6. 6.0
	£140.11.10

Your M. H. Servants

JNO. & WM. POWELL

---

[1] Halifax?

George Hayley [1] to Christopher Champlin

London, 3 January, 1766.

Sir,

I MAKE no doubt but before you receive this letter you will have heard of the dissolution of the partnership between Mr. Champion and myself, which took place on the 31st of last Month; This event makes me think it necessary to address a few lines to you to acquaint you with my resolution to carry on business in my own name, and to make you an offer of my services in the execution of your future commands, assuring you that whatever you may think proper to entrust me with shall be attended to with the utmost punctuality and executed with the strictest fidelity, and that I will in every instance endeavour to approve myself worthy of your regards. I have no doubt but you must be well acquainted that the business of the House has been long conducted entirely by me, and that every part of it has been done either with my own hands, or under my immediate inspection (Mr. Champion's health having for several years past been so indifferent as to cause him to reside altogether in the Country); so that the dissolution of the partnership will make no sort of difference in the manner of my conducting the business; but I shall for the future labour in my own name to do everything in the best manner for the service of my friends, as I have hitherto done the like in the names of C. & H. I hope and flatter myself that such part of your business as you have hitherto entrusted me with has been executed to your satisfaction, and I shall rejoyce in future opportunities of shewing how much I am, Sir, Your most humble Servant,

GEO. HAYLEY

Copy. Original per Calef.
[Endorsed,] Per Capt. Shand.

---

[1] A merchant and alderman of London, who married a sister of John Wilkes.

Spermaceti Agreement[1]

This Indenture of Covenant made the fourteenth day of January in the Year of our Lord One thousand seven hundred and Sixty six — Between Peter R. Livingston of the City of New York, Esqr, of the one part and Robert Jenkins of Rhode Island of the other part. Witnesseth. that the said parties to these presents have agreed and by these presents Do agree to enter into a Partnership in the Business of Manufacturing Spermaceti Candles for the Term of Five years next ensuing. And for that end it is mutually covenanted and agreed by and between the Parties to these presents. That a convenient place for that Business shall be hired or purchased at the equal expense of both Parties, and a Square building erected of Thirty feet by thirty, with fourteen feet post, to which there shall be added a shed Thirty feet by twenty four foot with eight feet posts. the charge whereof is in like manner to be defrayed at the joint expense of both parties. And the said Peter R. Livingston doth hereby grant and agree to and with the said Robert Jenkins that he will annually advance for carrying on the said works so much money as will be sufficient to perchase six hundred Barrels of head matter every year, and cause the same to be delivered at the said works. And he the said Robert Jenkins doth by these presents covenant and grant to and with the said Peter R. Livingston That he, the said Robert Jenkins shall and will faithfully work up the said Spermaceti Candles from the said head matter in a masterly manner, and in all things conduct and manage the said works to the best profit and advantage. And it is mutually agreed between the said Parties that all the Utensils which are necessary for carrying on the said works and which are comprised in the schedule hereunto annexed, shall be purchased at the joint expense of both the said parties according to the computation therein set down. And Further, that all expenses attending the leasing or

---

[1] Original in the possession of George C. Mason, in *Reminiscences*, I. 44.

purchasing the ground necessary for the said works and for erecting and Building the same and also for perchasing the said utensils as well as the money to be advanced by the said Peter R. Livingston for the said supply of head matter shall in the first place be fully repaid from the proceeds to arrise from the said works and Business. And that the Residue of the said proceeds shall be divided between the said Peter R. Livingston and Robert Jenkins. That is to say. Two full one third parts equally divided shall be had and received by the said Peter R. Livingston in consideration of the moneys to be advanced by him for the carrying on the said works; And the remaining one third part thereof shall be had and received by the said Robert Jenkins in consideration of his labour and care thereon. And it is mutually agreed between the saide parties that each of them shall at all times have free recourse to the said works and liberty and authority to inspect the same and all Books and accounts relating thereto. In Witness whereof the parties to these presents have hereunto interchangeably set their hands and seals the day and year above written.

PETER A. LIVINGSTON

Witness
HUGH RIDER
HANNAH FERRIS

CALCULATION OF THE UTENSILS.

```
1 large yron screw with a false collar abt. 457 lb @  £20.12.11
2 long round Barrs 2 guid Barrs & 40 Iron Plates  }
    abt. 2233 lb. — . . . . . . . . 5            }  46.10. 5
1 Brass Box for the screw 187 lb — 16ᵈ   £12. 9. 4
    For boring the box to fit the screw       6
                                         18. 9. 4
    Deduct for 33 lb Brass out of the box 3ᵈ  1  2
                                         17. 7. 4

    Charges.
    Commisions. at 2½ pt       £5. 1. 5
    Insurance & Commss. @ do.   1
    Charges for shipping.      1.13. 9      7.15. 6
                                           £92.12. 2
```

Sterling cost of the above at 4/6 p Dollars. is	412 –
Timbers for a Large strong Press 50 dls. } Workmanship for Ditto. near. 50 "	100 –
Wooden Press with 4 screws & Plates sufficient.	70 –
21 doz. Candle Molds. 18 p doz. — 5 5/8 do.	118 –
1 Copper mill cost.	50 –
1 smaller "	15 –
50 barskets for Drainers. @ 1 1/2 Dols.	75 –
10 large tubs	5 –
7 sets of Working tubs.	14 –
6 Troughs & Drainers with sheet lead &.	20 –
1 large copper of 530 gals.	130 –
Sundry small articles.	20 –
	1029 –

HENRY CRUGER, JR. TO HIS FATHER

Honored Sir, Bristol, February 14th, 1766.

THE Debates in Parliament lasting so long on the Stamp-Act determin'd me to return to my Business ere it was terminated. I was three Weeks in London, and every Day with some one Member of Parliament, talking as it were for my own Life. it is surprising how ignorant some of them are of *Trade* and *America*. The House at last came to a Resolution to examine only *one* person from each place, that brought Petitions. Mr. William Reeve, being the *Senior* of us who went from Bristol, was put in the Votes. Upon hearing of this Resolve, I set out, and arriv'd here late last Night; it is now Afternoon, and not untill this Moment wou'd Mr. Penington let me know his Vessel was bound to New York. he assures me no Man in Bristol knows it but Mr. Hayes and myself. I will employ what little time I have in scribling as much News to you as I can, supposing every Body (on your side) are impatient for the Stamp-Act; Tuesday the 11th Instant Mr. Trecothick was order'd to the Barr of the House of Commons, where he was examined, and X examined 3½ Hours; the last Question Lord Strange[1] (your Enemy) asked, was this: if *he* did not *think* the Americans wou'd *rather* submit to the S[tamp] Act than *remain* in the Confusion they are in?

---
[1] James Smith Stanley, commonly called Lord Strange, a representative of Lancashire and Chancellor of the Duchy of Lancaster.

It was not a proper Question. Mr. Trecothick was order'd to withdraw: some Debates ensued: he was recalled to the Barr, and told the House had altered the Question to this, if it was not *his Opinion* the Americans wou'd acquiesce with the Stamp Act provided it was mitigated? Mr. Trecothick answer'd, it was his Opinion, that no Modification of the Act wou'd reconcile it and that the Americans wou'd be contented with nothing less than a *Total Repeal*.

This inflamed Grenville's Party. they called you, insolent Rebells. I dread his Party coming into Power before the Act is repeal'd. if they do, they'll certainly scourge you, altho, *some English Merchants* are ruined by it.

We have proved the Debt from the Continent of America, to England is *five Millions* Sterling. this Grenville attempted to disprove, and is what makes the Examinations at the Barr so tedious.

All the principal Manufacturing Towns have sent Petitions for a Repeal of the Stamp Act. A Manufacturer from Leeds was order'd to the Barr, who said, since the Stagnation of the American Trade he has been constrained to turn off 300 Families out of 600 he constantly employ'd. this fact will have great weight when added to many more evidences of the like kind. The Country Members are somewhat alarmed at so many People losing Employ, if anything repeals the Act, it must be this. the Present Ministry see and have declared the *Expediency* of repealing on *this ground*. if the late Ministers come in again, and enforce the Act, they will have 20,000 unemployed Poor in a suppliant manner petitioning a Repeal of the S: Act, otherwise they must starve, or; so I think there is no doubt but it must be repeal'd on some grounds, or some Cause or other, especially if you stick to your engagements of having no English Goods untill it is effectuated. this Resolution I hope you'll abide by, nay! it is my Opinion this tiresome Procrastination wou'd never have happen'd, if you had sent no Ships away 'till it was decided, for Mr. Grenville has declared he will try to keep it off this 6 Weeks in hopes you will at last submit, saying it is a Proof you are tired by venturing to send your Ships away, and that he has no Doubt you will also soon be tired of the *Lawless* State you are in. retrospect to the Question Lord Strange put to Mr. Trecothick, I attended the House of Commons all day Tuesday the 11th Inst. in the Evening, a Member (who is in the Administration) told me, things were doubtfull, and went vastly hard with them, that the K— was not staunch to his Ministers; that altho' he assur'd them he would support them, yet he had deceived them, that they dayly and hourly experience Lord Bute's dreadfull Influence, that the K— had empower'd Lord Bute and Lord Strange to say, his private wish was not for a Repeal of the Stamp Act; as it wou'd be derogatory to the Honor of his Crown, and Dignity of his Parliament to be compell'd to repeal an Act that had been so disrespectfully treated without first exercising their Authority by enforcing it. he further told me that the K— acted with great Duplicity — it is amazing what Power Lord Bute continues to have over him! my friend further said, he thought notwithstanding all this, they would yet have a Repeal of the Stamp Act. At one time the present Ministry were bent upon resigning, on finding the Duke of York and Duke of Gloster were against them, also all the K—'s *immediate* Servants, such as the Lords of the Bed Chamber, and nine Bishops, they were for carrying Fire and Sword to America, with this Argument, that since you snarle and begin to shew your Teeth, they ought to be knocked out before you are able to bite.

inclosed is a Minute or two I made the Days they happen'd. by them you'll see the Sentiments of the Great.

You also have an exact Copy of Mr. Grenville's Motion in the House which I had address enough to get, he little thinking what use was to be made of it; tho' if he knew I don't suppose it wou'd give him any Concern. he was backed upon a Division (after debating till 11 o'clock at Night) by 134 tho' lost it by a Majority of 140. I saw the List of the Minority in it were Sir Charles Hardy[1] and

---

[1] Sir Charles Hardy (1716?-1780) had been governor of New York, and was at the siege of Louisburg. He was elected to Parliament from Rochester, Kent Co.

General Abercrombie.[1] these are the Thanks for the Old Madeira you have given them. O! Curse them! about 10 o'clock when the House were almost wearied out, Old General Howard [2] stood up. at his Martial Appearance a profound Silence ensued. he spoke (I don't pretend to give you his Words, only the Substance) to this Effect: that he shudder'd at the unnatural Motion, he hoped in God it wou'd not succeed, for in all likelyhood he might be order'd to execute it, and before he wou'd imbrue his hands in the Blood of his Countrymen who were contending for *English* Liberty, he wou'd, if order'd, draw his Sword, but wou'd soon after sheathe it in his own Body. Secretary Conway said (tho' not at the same time) that he wou'd sooner cut off his Right Arm, than sign an Order for Soldiers to enforce the Act. the Majority against it in the House of Commons were 274; yet, when you reflect that 134 were for it, it is enough to make you tremble. When I left London the 12th Inst. it was about three to One the Act *wou'd be repeal'd;* but for three Weeks past there has been no dependance on any thing we hear — neither King nor Parliament knew. today the Ministry wou'd have the best of it, and things wou'd look well; tomorrow Grenville and his Party wou'd gain the Power, and then of course *no* Repeal. the Vox Populi now begins to gain ground, and I think since the Legality of Taxation is allowed, the Act will be repeal'd upon the Grounds of *Expediency*.

These Particulars, few and inconclusive as they are, I thought wou'd still be agreable, for the authenticity of them I will answer.

As so much Politic's may confound Business, I will do myself the Honor to write you a few lines on the latter Subject in another Epistle. I remain with all due Respect in Haste my Dear Sir Your Most Dutifull Son etc.

H. C. JR.

---

[1] Ralph Abercromby (1734–1801) is doubtless intended, but he did not enter Parliament until 1774. James Abercromby was a member in this year, from Clackmannanshire.

[2] Sir George Howard (1720?–1796), representing Lostwithiel Borough, Cornwall.

P. S. The Parliament have not yet done any thing about the Sugar Act and other destructive restraints on your trade. it will come as soon as ever the Stamp Act is settled. I imagine they will rescind all the restrictive clauses, and grant you everything you ask. their Eyes are at last open'd and they seem convinc'd what vast Benefit will accrue to this Kingdom by giving you almost an unlimitted trade, so farr as doth not interfere with British Manufactures. The West Indians are collecting all their Force to oppose us; I have reason to say they will at length be defeated.

'Tis said French Sugars Coffee, Cotton, etc., the Produce of foreign Islands, will have the Indulgence of being imported in our Colonies duty free, but must be put in King's Warehouses, and the Proprietors constrained to ship them off again (to any part of the World they please) in a stipulated time.

The Duty on Melasses will be reduced to 1d per Gallon.

GEORGE CHAMPLIN TO CHRISTOPHER CHAMPLIN

Dear Brother, St. Eustatia, February 17th, 1766.

THIS is the first oppertunity I have had to write you since I arrivd at the Islands. I had 6 weeks passage to Dominica, lost the half of my Stock the remainder was forst to sell to the first purchaser, as I had not 3 Bushells Corn left at my arrivall and none to be had there. I sold my cargo there at the price noted at the bottom, and finding Suggars very high at English Islands, ingaged with a French man to mett me with what Suggars I coud purchase under the Leey of Marygalant,[1] and accordingly he met me at the time but with only 22 hhds. thats good, the remainder he got seasd, acomeing out of Guardalupe, and I dare not wait there any longer therefore proceeded her, where I

---

[1] Marie-Galante, one of the French West India Islands, and a dependency of Guadeloupe. It has no good harbor, but offered opportunity for illegal trading with the larger island.

arriv'd this day and this moment met your favour of 23 Novm: as to proceeding to Carolina I did not think it prudent as by Accounts from two Vessell from thence theirs two hundred Sale imbargod there and as for Capt. Wanton's Scheme, it woud doe very well two months hence, but at present theirs no Molosses to be had at Guardalupe nor Martinicoe; besides there's two hundred Sale of Northern Vessells there waiting for Molosses. Sug: at St. Citts 45/ and at Antugua, not much less; add the dutty paying the Cask and takeing the Sug: at Short C[wt?] and very green will make them turn out very high. I shall this night proceed to Sant Cruse to lay out the remainder of my Money, as I am informd you may pick your Sugars there for the Cash at 5 ps. 4 cts. if so I hope not to be detaind there long Iaword [in a word]; I think I coud have done nothing more for our Interest, considering every different circumstance which time will not permit me to mention. We shall have about 1400. ps to improve for Cargoe after deducting all Charges, etc., which will purchase about 28 thousand Sug: at the price I am informd it is at St. Cruise. I got mine of the Frenchman at 5 ps. The same quality here is at 6¾. I have cleard from Dominica in Balast for Rhode Island and therefore if we can tu[r]n it we can enter our Vessell with a good face. as for selling the Vessell I dont expect it as every man that has a Vessell here has one to sell. as to stamps ther's none passes in the Island except at Barbados and Granads. I have proper Certificates from the Collector that theirs no stamps to be had. I am in much haist. Your Brother,

GEO. CHAMPLIN

P. S. I have been much unwell since I left Baltimore but am a little better.

Flour	43/ 6 per Barr.	Coffee	15 Souse.
Bread	24/ . . . C.	Coccoe	12 do.
Shoats	14½d.	the duty here and but Cask	
Staves	7£M.	will not doe to ship.	

HENRY CRUGER, JR. TO AARON LOPEZ

Dear Sir,   Bristol, 1st March, 1766.

THE Confusion of American Affairs hath affected us equally. I have been very deeply involved in them, and think myself amply rewarded with the bare Aspect, which now abounds with Looks and Promises of Success to America. the Stamp Act is not *yet* repeal'd, but it is as good as done. a Motion was made in the House of Commons for a Bill to be brought in for a Repeal and was carried by 275 against 167; the latter were only for a Modification of the Act. the Debates pro and con have been very warm and serious. As I have not time now to be particular, will trouble you with a copy of my last Letter to my Father just for your Amusement. there is little doubt but the affairs will be finish'd in a few days and the Act *repealed;* You'll be informed that the Parliament have settled their *Right* of taxing you. when that was done they proceeded to the *Expediency* of repealing the Act, which never wou'd have come to pass had it not been for the Merchants and Manufacturers of *England*. Trade here was totally stagnated, not one American Merchant gave out a *single order* for Goods, on purpose to compell all Manufacturers to engage with us in petitioning Parliament for a Repeal of the Stamp Act, by which thousands were out of employ, and in a starving condition. You, Dear Sir, shared in the common calamity I hope and persuade myself you will not murmur at this Momentary Disapointment when so much Good will come out of it. I hugg myself the Parliament will never trouble America again. I cou'd not think of giving out any of your orders untill I saw which way this Momentous Affair wou'd turn, and terminate. I congratulate you on our Success, and with redoubled Joy — as the contrary was at one time much dreaded. the Letter I shall inclose you, will give you a great insight into the Actions and Sentiments of our British Senators.

Immediately upon hearing, by Express, that a Bill was

to be brought in the House of Commons for a total Repeal, I set about providing your orders, all which I hope to have shiped on board the *Charlotte*, Captain Brown, by the latter end of this month. no doubt you'll wonder at not hearing from me oftener of late. I have the best excuse that ever I had for not writing, even a serving my Country, which I have been doing day and night. I am *no Politician,* but in this matter of America, and its Trade, I embarked Body and Soul. I have been in London with all the great Men in the Kingdom. The Stamp and Sugar Acts were my two objects. I think you American Gentlemen will have all your wishes gratified, but more of this in my next. I only claim a share of the merit, if all comes to pass that I expect. see the P. S. of the Letter to my Father. I will be very punctual in future to make amends for my past silence; have patience, and you'll reap the advantages.

Dear Sir, I have now before me your esteem'd favours of 4th September, 25th and 31st October, 8th November and 2d December, with their several copies, which I will not attempt to reply to this present writing, my time being in great demand, but have read them over frequently with much pleasure and attention; and shall be very full and explicit by the *Charlotte*, Brown, whom I hope to dispatch by the latter end of this month with all your Goods. Brown had a tedious passage, put into Ireland by contrary winds, and did not arrive here untill the 1st February, one while I gave her over for lost; he is now discharged. if the Oak Boards by him had been $1\frac{1}{4}$ In. thick, shou'd have rec'd on them a Bounty of 20/ per Hundred Boards, as they were not, got nothing. this for your future guidance. London is glutted with Oil, and so is this Market.

Yesterday I sold about 160 Barrels of your's to be taken to, in ten days, the White at £22, the Brown at £20 per ton. it is very low, yet nothing but its being of an Extra Quality got it a preference to some other Parcells which wou'd fetch only £21 and £19 per ton. The Logwood per *Charlotte* I sold at £6 per ton, in my next I shall be more particular.

All the *Friendship's* Cargo is sold but the Mahogany and Oak Boards. the *Newport Packet's* Logwood is sold at £8 per ton the Whale fins for £265 per ton.

I feel hurt when I tell you how small a sum I sold the *Friendship* for, after putting her up three or four times in vain to Auction, it was for only seven hundred Guineas, say £735 Stg, and the Person who bought her told me, he had done me a favour, as he might buy several other Vessels quite as cheap. her Sails were much against her, they were mildued and rotted, the Purchasers were at the Expence of a new suit, the Canvas is of a bad quality, too much *Paste* or *Flour and Water* in it, in order to make them feel thick and look shining to the eye.

Your two Sloops are arrived at Cork, and I suppose will be with you long before this. inclosed is an account of Insurance on them, also an account of £500 additional on the *Newport Packet* and !£900 and £250 on the *Charlotte*, cost of which being £110.13.0 is to your Debit in A/C.

Messrs. Lane & Co. of Cork wrote to know if I wou'd honor their Draft on me (Your Account) for £200 Stg. I wrote them I would and shall debit your Account for the same.

I cannot get £500 for the *Newport Packet*, her Masts are two foot too short, Rigging Sails etc. in proportion, which depreciates her at least £100 on that account, and I will say £50 more, because People conclude she is crank, and that you were *obliged* to undermast her more of this in my next.

Thus have I given you, Dear Sir, a diffusive and pretty perfect account of the state of your affairs in my hands which are entitled to a great share of my attention, and never shall suffer for want of *that*; notwithstanding this letter is wrote in so great a hurry, not so particular as I cou'd wish it to be, but the Confusion of the times now begins to be rectified and like Mud in troubled Waters to subside. I hope soon to see things fall into order, and their old channel of Regularity; of late all seems to have been floating on an Ocean of Scepticism. two days ago the Owner of this vessel assured me she wou'd not sail this 3 weeks, to day he told me, she wou'd certainly sail to morrow which precipitates me to conclude, tho' with the utmost Respect and Regard, Dear Sir, Yours etc.

HEN: CRUGER, JR.

When you send any more Plank let the Quality be as follows 2 and ½ Inch Plank, full sawed and square edged; 2 Inch Ditto, all the length above 20 feet, and 12 Inches wide.

White Oak, — *Red Oak* don't answer.

I just now reced a letter from Messrs. Lane, Bensons & Vaughan, of Cork, abstract of which you have herewith.

Cork, 18th February, 1766.

Sir,

We are now to advise you that the *3 Sallys*, Capt. Peters, is cleared out and ready to sail. The Cargo we have ship'd on her amounts to £598.10.7 Irish and the Disbursements on the Sloop to £59.2.7 which sums with the Value of the Sloop, you will please to have insured, at and from Cork to Rhode Island, for account of our said Friend. we cou'd not obtain within £100 of the price limitted for the *Industry*, therefore she is also to return, but what the amount of her Cargo will be cannot yet say, but you shall have timely notice thereof.

6 March 1766. This Bearer being detained longer than was expected gives me an opportunity of rendering you Account of Insurance on the *Three Sallys* cost as per account £26.16.0 to your Debit.

MR. AARON LOPEZ   Bristol, Xber 13th, 1765.
To HENRY CRUGER JR. Dr.
For Sundry Insurances vizt.

£500 added on Goods per *Newport Packet*, John Heffernan, Master } from Rhode Island to Bristol . . . . . at £3.—.— per Ct. } 15. 0. 0

£100 William Reeve   £100 John Gordon Jr.
50 Lambert Schimmelpennig £150 Edward Johns
100 Thomas Griffiths

£900 on the *Charlotte*, Thomas Brown, Master, at and from Rhode } Island to Bristol (£400 on Ship £500 on Goods) at £3 per Ct. and two } 27.16. 0
             Policys 16/ }

  Ship   £50 Lambert Schimmelpennig
£100 William Reeve   £50 George Champion
£ 50 Samuel Davies   £50 Thomas Easton, Junior

£100 Thomas Griffiths	£50 Edward Nicholas
£150 James Laroche Jr.	£50 Samuel Munckley
Goods	£50 Robert Gordon
£100 Thomas Whitehead	£50 John Thompson
£50 John Gordon, Junior	

£850 on the *Industry*, John Peters, Master, at and from Rhode Island to Cork (£350 on Ship and £500 on Goods) at £3 per Ct. and two Policys 16/ 26. 6. 0

Ship	£50 Lambert Schimmelpennig
£100 William Reeve	£50 George Champion
£50 Samuel Davies	£50 Thomas Easton Junior
£100 Thomas Griffiths	£50 Edward Nicholas
£100 James Laroche Junior	£50 Samuel Munckley
Goods	£50 Robert Gordon
£100 Thomas Whitehead	£50 John Thomas

£850 on the 3 *Sallys* from Rhode Island to Cork (£350 on Ship £500 on Goods) at £3 per Ct. and two Policys 16/ . . 26. 6. 0

Underwrote per the same Person's as the *Industry*

                  £ 95. 8. 0
To Comm. on £3100 at 1/2 per Ct. 15.10. 0
To the Debit of Mr. Aaron Lopez £110.18. 0

Also, Cost of £250 additional on the *Charlotte* from Rhode Island to Bristol . . . . . at £3 per Ct. and Comm £1.5.0 . . . . 8.15. 0

£50 William Gayner	£50 John Watkins
£50 Isaac Elton Junior	£100 John Gill

          Total   £119.13. 0

WILLIAM LUX[1] TO CHRISTOPHER CHAMPLIN

Sir,   Maryland, Baltimore, 24 March, 1766.

CAPT. SEARS deliverd me your favor of the 24 ulto. for which I am obliged. he is at present uncertain whether or not he loads here. if he does, I shall send you the 30 Bbs. Midlings agreeable to your Order. I had some conversation with your Brother Capt. George on the subject of sending a Vessell, and did propose doing it this Spring, but our demand for Flour has been so constant that I have not yet had it in my Power. I shoud have been glad you had men-

---

[1] William Lux, son of Darby Lux, had been long prominent in public affairs of Baltimore, a leading merchant, and later a member of the Committee of Correspondence, 1774, and vice chairman of the Committee of Observation, 1775. During the War of Independence he was concerned in privateers.

tioned the Prices of Flour, Midlings, Bread Stuff, Bread, Pork, Rum, Sugar, Molasses, Loaf Sugar, Train Oil, and any other articles that you generally send this way. And I now request you'l do it by the very first Post, as it may be a guidance to me, as I shall probably send a small Vessell when your Markets are encourageing. I shoud also be glad to know whether you coud not remit Cash or Bills of Exchange, as your Commodities will not always answer. I am lately concerned in a small Rope Walk. woud Cordage suit you, and of what size, and the price. Our produce is at this time high, and consequently scarce. I am very respectfully,

Sir Your most hble Sert.
Willm Lucas

JOHN AND WILLIAM POWELL TO CHRISTOPHER CHAMPLIN [1]

Dear Sir, Boston, 31 March, 1766.

WEE have your favors of the 14th per Mr. Bell and 27. per Post. The *Hall'x Packet* sailed from hence the day Mr. Bell got here. The Vessell he goes in may sail in all this week. wee have passed to your C[redit] Williams £20 Bill, and paid Mr. Bell your order for the same sum. wee are greatly obliged to you for your continued good offices, especially in keeping of the Beer affair. wee have not heard from Mr. Mumford sometime since, tho' expect Certificates for the Provisions bo't for her on her first arrival there. wee expect Butter from Hall'x by the Packet, (tho' will cost 6*d* Sterling per *li.*) and shall send you 20 firkins, with 1 Cask Oatmeal which is all there is on the Continent by what learn from Hall'x and New York. its a vexatious thing to want that article as the Pursers are so

---
[1] The original is in the Newport Historical Society.

fond of it, but in lieu thereof Rice must be issued, and indeed wee are obliged by Contract to furnish one half the Quantity of Oatmeal demanded in Rice, and paid accordingly only for Rice, even tho Oatmeal alone is issued. Your Most Humble Servants,

JNO. & WM. POWELL

in regard to Salt Provisions, they certainly must be cheaper with you than paying freight and risque from hence. But if not to be had must go from hence.

HENRY CRUGER, JR. TO AARON LOPEZ

Dear Sir,   Bristol, 9th April, 1766.

HEREWITH is Copy of my last Respects to you, under date of 1st March which I now confirm, and am since favour'd with your agreable Letters of 21st January and 18th February.

It is an invariable rule with me, never to deviate from the Words of an Order for Goods; but some times the Stupid Tradesmen, will put one thing when they have not the other, and are never candid enough to own it; you may assure yourself I am always as exact on my part as tis possible to be; when you order'd Shaggs,[1] you did not call them Shagg Duffles, nor even give me the *Wedths*. The dull Sale of Ships at present all over this Kingdom discourages me from telling you the large Ship you mention of 240 Tons will sell here even at £1300, low as the Price is, recollect what we dayly experience with the Ships you have sent here. The *Newport Packet*, lies still on hands, she will not fetch £500.

A small Quantity of proper sized White Oak Plank square Edge'd may sell, see my last Letter, tho' Sir, it is not an object worth your Notice, a little by way of filling up now and then will do, but at present the Carpenters are all glutted with it. the time approaches when I hope to see your Ships loaded with Foreign Sugars Coffee and all the

---

[1] A cloth having a velvet nap on one side, usually of worsted.

Enumerated Products of the West India Islands; then we shall do Business with Pleasure, the Present seems like endeavouring to sail against a head Wind, tedious Sales, difficulty in collecting Money, and many more disagreable Circumstances prove quite disheartning: I congratulate you on the *Certain Prospect* of an Amendment.

When I finish the Sales of Mr. Lucena's Oil and Fins, the Net Proceeds shall be to your Credit according to his Orders, I have written to Mr. Lucena by this conveyance. Your Whale Fins with Mr. Lucena's were properly managed. enclosed is a Copy of their Sales, Net Proceeds £154.4.9 Stg to your Credit.

As I was in hopes of selling the Brigantine cou'd not discharge Captain Heffernan[1] untill that was decided, which was not untill 28th February, when I determined to return the Brigantine, for her I cou'd not get £250 Stg.; Captain Heffernan was necessitated to receive his Wages here, and £15 on discharging him, having nothing else to subsist upon. his receipts, and Account of his Disbursements you have herewith. I made the best bargain I cou'd for your Interest to get rid of the Sailors, what I advanc'd on these Accounts will appear in the Ships Disbursments.

Heffernan's Passenger ran away and gave us all the Bagg to hold. he will more fully explain that matter to you.

The Bill you inclosed me for £55 Stg. drawn by R'd Crucher of Jamaica on James Bonbonous is refused acceptance to, if it is not paid when due, the 7th May, it shall be protested for Non Payment and returned you.

The Copper Pans and 6 doz Pannel Squares, which you returned, your Account has Credit for their Amount. I have taken care to omit sending the Goods you were pleased to counter order in yours of 31st October on account of the cargo sent per America.

I wish your Cooper to be more particular in his *distinguishing* the White and Brown Oil. it gives me uneasiness to write you any turns out *Brown* that you imagined was white, our Cooper who guages them seems to be very

[1] Of the *Newport Packet*.

exact, I obliged him to examine them twice over, and he assures me 13 Casks of the *Friendship's* Cargo, that was denominated white, proves to be brown.

'tis very odd no Buyers offer for the Cedar. the Man that bought the last sent it to London for sale, but tells me he can get no Chap to take it off his Hands. 1 ps. Heffernan says was washed overboard. Captain Osborne was quite mistaken in his intelligence of the *Friendship's* Mahogany. I have sold none of it yet, the quality is not liked, the purchasers won't give by 1*d* ½ per foot as much for it, as for that sent by the *Newport Packet*, of the latter parcell I have sold only two or three lotts.

I am sorry so much more Mahogany is coming by the *America*. I can't tell what I shall do with it. I have halled about a quarter of the *Newport Packet's* away, in order to lessen the quantity in the Eyes of the Buyers, as well as to make room on our Keys. the great piles that now remain on the Key get me a rap over the Nuckles every time I fall in company with our Mayor, but I laugh it off, saying it will soon be removed and so forth. if you can meet with some fine Jamaica Mahogany of proper lengths and good breadths, it will sell from 10*d* to 1/ per foot.

Am sorry you are disapointed in your notion that but little Oil wou'd be at market on account of the "indifferent Success of your Fishery last Season." you'll perceive, Sir, by the price, here is no Scarcity. I don't know where it came from, but this Kingdom was never more glutted with Spermaceti Oil than it has been all the Winter, and now.

Hemp is risen since my last, and Cordage of course. the Cordage now ship'd is of a very good quality for the price. I observe with some concern you have already drawn £600 Stg. towards the Cargo now on board the *America*. I must be frank and say, this is unexpected, I flatter'd myself you wou'd have thought it but equitable that as I am in advance £1300 Stg on the *Ship America*, you ought not to continue drawing untill that was *first discharged*. when you overvalued her, and your other ships, you *might* not have known how little ships were in demand, but upon being informed, and *fully convinced* the *America* wou'd fetch here, *not more* than £700, surely you ought to have had a little Compassion, and left the £600 you have now drawn for, to reimburse the £1300 I have paid; in breif, Sir, if I am £1300 Stg in advance for the *Ship America* and she will not sell for more than £600, if you draw the Value of her cargo out of my hands, how am I to be reimbursed the other £700? I will say no more on this subject than barely to reiterate the distresses brought on me by the vast Debts due from my Friends in America, who are ever declaring their Inability to pay occasion'd by the late calamities of their Country. I share with them equally, therefore must again intreat of you *at this Crisis* to have Mercy; after saying thus much, let us be silent on the disagreable part of our Business, and begin with another.

I am now, Dear Sir, at the 12th and altho' I did not expect to get Captain Brown away this 4 or 5 days, yet as the Wind is fair will not run the risque of his losing it by detaining him for Trifles, and letting Essentials suffer. his cargo is nigh compleated; therefore am determined to give him his Dispatches this Evening that he may embrace the fine Wind that blows. if in our hurry we have committed any mistakes in the number of papers herewith, I dare say Sir you'll excuse us, and point them out, that with you we may rectify them.

In the first place is the Sales of part the Cargo per the *America*, Captain Pope, Net Proceeds £544.11.2. Secondly are two Sales of the Cargo per the *Friendship*, that of the Oil Net Proceeds £566.3.0 Stg that of Naval Stores £318.9.4 Stg. also an Account Sales of the Ship *Friendship* Net Proceeds being £714.8.6 Stg. the Disbursements on said Ship is with Sales, amounting to £142.3.6 Stg.

Thirdly is the Disbursements and additional Disbursements on the Ship *America*, her Insett from and Outsett to Newport, the first amounting to £279.12.6, the latter to £6.4.3, with them is an Account of £1500 Insurance on said Vessel from Newport to this, cost £39.16.0 Stg.

Fourthly is the Disbursements on the *Newport Packet* Captain Heffernan amounting to £112.16.2 Stg. I can as yet render you Sales of no Part of her Cargo but the Logwood, which you have herewith, Net Proceeds £151.14.10 Stg. fifthly comes an account of what part of the *Charlotte*, Captain Brown's Cargo is disposed of vizt. all your Oil, as per the Sales Net Proceeds £220.4.9 Stg. Oak Boards and Staves, Net Proceeds £55.12.5 Stg. also the Logwood Net Proceeds £119.18.3 Stg. you'll find with the *Charlotte's* Sales an account of £400 Stg. Insurance effected on her this present Voyage to New Port, Cost £10.16.0 Stg. to your Debit, as is likewise an additional account of Disbursements on her, when Captain Bowers was Master, amounting to £4.8.10 Stg.

Inclosed is an Account of Insurance done on the Sloop *Industry* from Cork to Rhode Island Cost £24.4.0 Stg. also an Account of Insurance on *3 Sallys* cost £26.16.0 Stg. to your Debit.

I have returned you the *Newport Packet's* Portlidge[1] Bill with all Heffernan's Papers, his receipt for the Money I advanc'd him.

Herewith is Captain Brown's Receipt for the several sums of money advanced him amounting to £111.18.5 Stg. I made some words at letting him have so much, but he promises to make that satisfactory to you, which is all I aim at.

Dear Sir, I have just for your Government, drawn out a Sketch of your Account Current Ballance whereof in my favour being £10,784.8.4 Stg. to your Debit in a new Account. if on examination you find it right please to note the same in conformity with me, if any errors please to point them out, and they shall be adjusted accordingly: what Interest may be due on your Bills paid before I was in Cash for the Goods sold, shall be calculated when I am a little more at Leisure, and an Account thereof sent you perhaps

---

[1] According to Murray, an Americanism, now obsolete, corrupted from *portage*, perhaps in confusion with the sometimes synonymous *privilege*. He gives a use as early as 1636.

per my next, if not must crave your kind Patience a little longer.

I now inclose Bill Lading and Invoice for the Cargo of Goods now on board the *Charlotte* amounting to £2510.9.2 Stg. to your Debit. I heartily wish them safe to your hands and to satisfaction having taken a good deal of care in laying them in.

I fancey if you had known that Malt not made for Exportation did not get a Drawback, you wou'd not have order'd any.[1] I was loth to send it, but Brown told me it was designed for a Present, that you wou'd be disapointed unless you had it. the difference between Malt made for home Consumption, and that for Exportation, is at least 9/ per Quarter.

I must, Dear Sir, make use of your Friendship to favour me in the most Private and Expeditious Manner what your opinion is of Mr. Robert Crooke[2] of your place. I am sensible how delicate a thing it is either to ask or grant a favour of this sort, but these are occurrences that will happen in Trade. my reason for this enquiry is that I *have sent* Mr. Crook out by way of New York a pretty large Cargo of Goods, without knowing any thing of his Circumstances therefore must trespass upon your Goodness for your Private Opinion of him which shall be kept by me as an inviolate Secret.

N. B. for your Gouvernment in the Disposal of your *Hemp*, I have sent Mr. Crook 4 Tons.

Your Account it credited £9.2.2. Sterling for freight now on board the *Charlotte;* the freight made by her and the *New Port Packet* from Rhode Island to this place shall be carried to your Credit as soon as I make out Sales of Goods that pay it. To my Concern the Wind is got about to the Westward, still shall give Brown his Dispatches in ten

---

[1] The bounty on such malt was 2/6 per quarter. 1 Will. and Mar. cap. 12. § 2. Malt from wheat received twice that amount. In estimating the bounty thirty quarters of malt were allowed for every twenty quarters of grain.

[2] Robert Crooke came to Newport from Kingston, New York, and was a merchant of good standing. In May, 1747, he married Ann Wickham.

Minutes. he promises to go aboard immediately and endeavour to sail as the Weather is moderate; I heartily wish you a quick Sight of him, being with perfect Esteem, Respect and Sincerity in all your Commands, Dear Sir, Your most Obedient Humble Servant

HEN: CRUGER, JR.[1]

JEREMIAH OSBORNE TO AARON LOPEZ

Bristoll, April 29, 1766.

Sir,

SINCE my last per the *mine head* and Captain Kennedy, Mr. Cruger has returned from London. the affair of the Sugar Account was adjourned for ten days and will be brot to Determination this week. They will reduce the duty upon Molosses to one penny, with Liberty to import Wine, Lemons, etc., from Spain and Portugall without touching in England; Ships here are an extreeme dull Sail. I dont belive if the *Amerrica* in her present Condition was up for sail she would sell for 450 Sterling, which would be greatly short of her Value   in case she does not come back shall be with you in two or three months at furthest, and as the Streights Trade is opened, in case you are disposed to engage that way shall be glad to serve you. I wrote you per Kennedy the Entelligence I have procured respecting Lumber, and am glad to find the Cargo procured will answer. Scantling of various denomination is in continuall demand. little emported from Norway or made here. at present have no material news other then the papers afford. Your Humble Servant

JEREMIAH OSBORNE[2]

---

[1] April 8, 1766, an invoice of three casks of pewter shipped by Thomas Swanson, on board the *Boston Packet*, Captain John Marshall.

[2] "This Evening a Letter arrived from Mr. Nugent, Member of Parliament for this City, acquainting his Constituents that it was Determined in Parliament that Dominico should be a Free Port." *Osborne to Lopez*, May 12, 1766.

Estate Robert Jenkins Dec.d for
Funeral Charges to Chris: Champlin Dr.

1766
May. 2d
1 4/8 Black Taffety	24/	1.. 10..
1/2 y.d Black Gauze	6/	3.. ..
1 y.d Alamode		.. 12.. ..
1 Fan		1.. 15..
1 p.r Black Gloves		3.. 10..
2 y.d Load Ribbin	20/	2.. ..
2 7/8 y.d Black Satten ditto	10/	1.. 16..
1 hank Silk		1.. 2..
½ y.d Gauze		.. 15..
1 p.r Black Russell Shoes		0.. 10..
8 p.r Mens Gloves White	60/	24.. ..
1 p.r Best Lamb for M.rs Brown		3.. 15..
1 p.r Black Buckles		1.. 16..
1 Loaf Sugar &c	30/	13.. 10..
3/8 y.d Black Gauze	6/	2.. 5.. 6
Cash p.d Men bearing the body to the Grave		24.. ..
ditto the Saxton for his Bill		.. 26..
To Cash p.d M.rs Whalen for assisting at the func.l		0.. ..
To Edmond Townsend for Coffin		64.. ..
To Cash p.d Jonathan Wilson for p.r Gloves (say) Shaving M.r Jenkins		3.. 10..
		£218..14..6
To: Advertisements &c the Printer		16.. ..
		£234:14:6

Henry Cruger, Jr. to Aaron Lopez

Dear Sir,   Bristol, May 20th, 1766.

PER the Ship *America* I rec'd your esteem'd favours of 3rd and 7th March with their Copys via New York.

I cannot conceive what shou'd make the sudden demand for Oil you speak of, unless People wanted it to freight their Ships, having nothing else; it is at present exceeding low all over this Kingdom.

I have settled with Mr. Stevens to pay Freight for his Mahogany agreable to the Bill Lading without any Deduction for Shakes,[1] etc. an allowance of that sort wou'd be absurd. does not a bad piece of Wood take up the same room in a Ship as a good piece? such Wood as cou'd not bear the Freight aught not to have been shiped.

The Bills amounting to £600. on account of the Adventure per the *America*, shall all meet due honor. the Oak Bark *wont* answer, *dont* send any more, particulars in my next. the 1 M Pine Plank on the *America's* deck were all washed overboard in bad weather.

Pray present my Respects to Mr. Collector Robinson,[2] will do myself the pleasure of writing him per the *America*, Osborne, and send what he is pleased to write me for. the 3 Guineas Osborne thinks I advanc'd him, I fancey he is mistaken in. I cannot recollect any money advanc'd that is not charged.

I shall be glad, Sir, to do any thing in my power, respecting the Estate you are pleased to write about, but cannot proceed untill I have proper Papers of the Claiments pretensions, such as his Origin, etc., etc., attested, upon receipt of such, will without delay, try what can be done.

I have had the *America's* Cargo housed, no demand for Oil, don't send any more Cedar, Whale Fins have sold as per Account Sales herewith, Net Proceeds £125.13.10 to

---

[1] A crack or split in wood.
[2] Later a Commissioner of Customs, and the assailant of James Otis.

your Credit. I hear 2,000 Barrels of Oil are expected from London to this place, so great is the Quantity there.

I am now to inform you of the Sales of the Ship *Newport Packet* for the miserable price of £475 Stg. what was to be done? I cou'd not get more; the Gentleman who bought her asured he wou'd have given £150 more for her had she been properly masted. the Account Sales of the Vessel you shall have per my next.

The *America* I cannot get £600 for, and rather than sell her at the Wretched price I did the *Newport Packet*, determin'd to send her back immediately to you with your Goods, which with some Freight will nigh fill her. am in hopes of dispatching her by the last of June. if you can get a tolerable price for your Oil in Newport, do advise your selling of it there, for this Kingdom is overdone. had any advance on Oil (as you imagined) or the least prospect of it been in *England*, I wou'd have advised you.

After a deal of trouble and doubt, I think we are at last pretty *safe* in our hopes of having a free Port — Dominica — and a free Importation of Foreign Sugars in America, no Duty to be paid on them, but to be warehoused for re-exportation to *England only*. I think Rhode-Island must reap great advantages from this Regulation.

I here return you R'd Cruchers Bill on James Bonbonous with protest for non payment, cost of Noting and Protesting 8/6 to your Debit.

By the *America* will do myself the Pleasure to write you more at large. Interim I remain, Sir, etc.,

HEN: CRUGER JR.[1]

---

[1] "Here is a Brigt. from Falmouth loaded with Lumber her Plank are 2 and 2 1/2 and some 1 1/4 youl take notice it is established at London and practised here no Plank or Bords of any Thickness whatsoever Receives any Bounty for what is above 10 Inches wide; so that the Cargo of the Brig will loose half her Bounty, as her Lumber mostly is from 14 to 20 Inches Broad which is a thing in the Opinion of Every one unreasonable. But such is the Determination of the Customs. for your Regulation: your Long Plank from 26 to 36, 2, 2 1/2 and 3 is much more valuable than that of 10 and 15 feet Long: as plenty of this comes from Norway. But the other sort is scarce, and fetches 6d per foot 3 Inch and in proportion." *Jeremiah Osborne to Aaron Lopez*, Bristoll, June 24, 1766.

The Estate of Roberts Jenkins Jun'r Dr.

To 85/ P'o't Office at Newport Dr.

To Postage of Letters &c. from the
26 September 1760 to 5 July 1766
Sterling £ 1. 15. 2

P. Farnum

Sailing Orders of Captain Thomas Brown

Newport, July 2d, 1766.

Sir,

The Brig *Charlotte* now under your Command being ready fitted for the Seas you are to embrace the first fair Wind and proceed directly to Bristol where upon your arrival you are to deliver the Inclosed to Mr. Henry Cruger, Junior, of Bristol and follow his directions. I am not able to determine whether you are to return directly here, or to Cork in Ireland, and from thence to Jamaica; If Mr. Cruger directs you to come back to this place without first going to Ireland and Jamaica I would recommend you to use the utmost dispatch and endeavour to be here in the Month of November. But in case you proceed to Cork you are to apply to Messrs. Lane, Bensons & Vaughan, Merchants there, and follow their directions, using the same dispatch there as I recommended you at Bristol, from thence they will dispatch you with a Freight for the West Indies, probable to Jamaica. But should you go to any other Island you are to get discharged soon as possible and proceed directly for Savannah La Mar at Jamaica, where you are to apply to Mr. Abraham Lopez, Merchant there, where I shall lodge farther Instructions for you. In case Mr. Cruger has disposed of my Two Ships and remitted some effects I order'd before your arrival to Bristol there will then be a Chance of his putting up the Brig to sale; if so, and she goes off, I will provide you another more suitable Vessel for the Trade upon your return.

I conclude recommending you in the Strictest Manner to make the best dispatch you can from Bristol, and wishing you a prosperous Voyage conclude with perfect esteem, Sir, Your most hble Servant

Aaron Lopez

Acknowledge the above to be an exact Copy of my Instructions which I promise to execute to the utmost of my Ability. Thos. Brown.

WILLIAM LUX TO CHRISTOPHER CHAMPLIN

Sir,   Maryland, Baltimore, 15 July, 1766.

I AM glad to find by your favor of the 16 ultimo the arrival of Captain [John] Westgate[1] with you. It was lucky I only sent you so little of the midling Bread. we distinguish it here in three sorts vizt. Ship, Midling, and White.[2] as I imagined you were acquainted with each sort, I thought you meant to have had the Midling, and I shoud have sent all of that sort, if I coud have procured it.

I now inclose your Account Sales of Captain Westgate's Cargo, Nett Proceeds being £453.11.11 to your Credit, and I doubt not will please. I shall not be in Cash for some of it these 2 Months. I also send your Account Current Balance due to me £39.4.2 which I doubt not you'l find right. Our Harvest is now geting in and promises well; it will relieve us greatly, for our Exportation had so drained us that we were near starving ourselves.

Inclosed is Wm. Russell's Bill for £5.5. Stg. on Mr. George Mill at New Haven which I must beg you to negociate, and if paid remit it in Loaf Sugar. I gave Mr. Samuel Chew your Name, and woud have wrote by him, had I known when he sailed but he lives at some distance from me. he is a Gentleman of considerable Estate. Our distillery was disappointed in several Cargos of Molasses, which occasions Rum to be scarce and the price rose, but it will now be down.

I am respectfully, Sir, Your most hble Servant,

WILLIAM LUX

Flour	14/6		Sugars	50/ to 60/
Bread	14/6		Loaf Sugar	15d.
N. E. Rum	2/9	falling	Pork	90/.
W. I. Rum	3/3			

---

[1] Master of the schooner *Adventure*.

[2] This commerce marked the change which was taking place in Maryland and Virginia, away from tobacco culture and into grain and its products, flour, bread, and ships biscuits. John Beale Bordley was a leader of the movement in Maryland, and Washington attempted it in Virginia, in competition with the grain interests of Pennsylvania.

Henry Cruger, Jr. to Aaron Lopez

Bristol, 28th July, 1766.

Dear Sir,

It is now a long while since I've had the Pleasure of hearing from you, hope shall soon with an account of the *Charlotte's* arrival.

I am now writing my last Letter per the *America*, Captain Osborne, who has lain here too long for your Profit, had I known on her arrival that she wou'd return, it would not have been the case; for as I endeavour'd agreable to your Instructions to sell her, I cou'd not send out your Orders for Goods untill I found that impossible and determin'd to load her for Newport.

I suppose, Sir, you are impatient to know how stand your several Adventures in my hands; it is with pleasure I inform you *every thing is sold.*

The Mahogany Plank formerly recd by the *Friendship* no Body offer'd to buy, the quality is so soft and spungy; I found nothing was to be done but at publick sale, and letting it go at the Buyers' own prices; it is all sold as per Sales herewith, Net Proceeds £370.17.10 Stg. to your Credit; likewise is Sales of her Oak Boards and Anchor Stocks, etc., Net Proceeds £128.11.1. had the Oak Boards been square edged, they wou'd have sold much better. inclosed is also Sales of 4 Baggs of Pimento [1] and the Mahogany per *Charlotte*, Net Proceeds £148.14.0 Stg. to your Credit. I have at last sold at one stroke all the *Newport Packett's* Mahogany that remained. it is very cheap but it wou'd not do better by keeping, such large quantitys are dayly arriving and expected. Net Proceeds of the Sales herewith is £726.15.8 Sterling to your Credit. inclosed you'll find Sales of the Ship *Newport Packet*, Net Proceeds £461.0.0 Sterling to the Credit of your Account.

As I wrote you in some of my late Letters the buyers of

---

[1] *Myrtus pimenta,* or Jamaica pepper. A single tree would yield in a favorable year one hundred pounds of the dried spice. It was used for seasoning or for medicine.

Oil all having their Warehouses full, we cou'd not sell, which was rather melancholly this hot weather, there being such a continual and great waste in that article; a few days ago an offer was made me for all I had; after mature Consideration and Consultation I concluded to accept it; it is very low, yet I cou'd not at present sell another Parcell at so good a price, at least not untill cold weather approaches, by which time one quarter of the Oil wou'd have been lost. I sold two other Parcells with your's; The price of Oil may rise a little towards winter, but I never expect to see it again so high as it has been, so many are got into the Trade in consequence, *vast* is the *Increase* of our Importations.

I must beg you will please to order your People to be correct and exact, in the assorting, character and denomination of your Oil. it wou'd be of great help to us in the selling of it, and wou'd save us much cavelling here; let the Brown Oil be call'd Brown, and the White, White; and please to let Whale Oil be distinguish'd from the other; some *kinds* of your Oil has been called by the name of another Kind; I hope, Dear Sir, you'll excuse this Freedom and take my Observations in a friendly Light.

The Account Sales of your different parcells of Oil is herewith viz. *Newport Packet*, Net Proceeds, £367. 4. Stg. *America* . Do. Do. . . £323.13.3 Stg. to your Credit. your Account is credited £63.6. Stg., the Net Proceeds of Mr. Lucena's 37 Casks of Oil rec'd per *Newport Packet*.

Inclosed is an Account of the *America's* Freight inwards, amounting to £351.12.3 Stg., also an Account of her present Freight outward, £ [blank], both to your Credit.

You'll find here Account of the Brigantine *Charlotte's* Disbursements £254.18.5 Stg.; likewise additional Disbursements on *Newport Packet* £24.2.8. to the Debit of your Account. If possible will make out the Disbursements on the *America* before she goes and send you, if not will send them by next Opportunity. Osborne can tell pretty near what they will be. I am afraid her outfitt will come high; for Reason he will give you, she required great repairs.

Inclosed is Osborne's receipts for money advanc'd him amounting to £151.6.11 Stg., which he will account with you for.

I have sent your Collector the Beer he desired as per Bill Lading and Invoice herewith, the Amount £14.6.6 Stg. is (according to your Orders) to your Debit. the Taunton Ale is charg'd at the usual price. the Bridgenorth Beer I am unacquainted with the Price of, I believe none was ever before sent to America. the maker of it declares he cannot afford it cheaper. it will render me much pleasure to hear it pleases Mr. Robinson.

I now inclose you Invoice of most, if not all of your last Order for Goods, amounting to £1578.13.9, to your Debit. you'll observe some things advanc'd in price, especially Ruggs, Duffles and Blankets, occasion'd by a very great and sudden demand for them. you may be assured, Sir, yours is laid in on as good terms as any bodys. Lead and Shott is also advanc'd 5/ per ton. you'll observe tho' Ravens Duck use to be bought at 28/ I cou'd not get any under 32/ this advance is so large I was afraid it wou'd not answer to you, therefore have sent no Ravens Duck.

Please to send me Certificates to cancell the Bonds given on Account of Coal now on Board the *America*.

Inclosed is Account of £800 Insurance on Ship *America*, which I got effected at £2, being a fine time in the year. Cost £20.8.0 to your debit.

Your Account is credited £17.0.9 for Inward Freight on *Charlotte* last Voyage, and £13.8.8 for Ditto of *Newport Packet*, also £16.19.10 Sales of a few Staves per Osborne.

I was encouraged to send your Cedar round to London. Sales is inclosed £19.15.2 Stg. to your Credit.

Besides your own Goods, the Freight the *America* makes out is £74.17.2 Stg. to your Credit.

You'll receive (Mortality excepted) by Osborne, five Game Fowls of which I beg your Acceptance. I suppose they will prove very welcome to your Friends who love Cocking. the two Cocks with their Combs and Gils on are said to be Super Excellent altho' rather small; they are but one year old. was I to advise, it wou'd be to have a brood of Chickens out of them before they are fought, they'll be much abler at 2 years old. they were given to me by a Gentleman who assures me they are choice.

Mr. Steevens thinks ten Guineas for his Passage too much, rather than take less I left him to settle with you, not chusing to make a bad Precedent, for absolutely 5 Gs. to the Ship and 5 Gs. to the Captain is as little as any Cabbin Passenger ought to pay. I have rec'd from two other Passengers ten Guineas which have credited your Account with.

Thus much for the present, adieu!

Dear Sir, That you may be happy and prosperous is the sincere wish of Your most Obedient humble Servant,

HEN: CRUGER, JR.

NB. Proper Sizes for all kinds of Boards vizt.
2 Inch ten to 20 ft. long, ten to 12 Inches broad
2 $\frac{1}{2}$ Do. . . .   Do. . . . .
1 $\frac{1}{3}$ Do. . . .   Do. . . . .

P. S. Since writing the above find the two Passengers cannot pay their Passage Money here, but have lodged a sufficient Quantity of Plate in Captain Osborne's Hands to answer it in Rhode Island. was obliged to comply with this method of settling it which now rests with you.

GEORGE CHAMPLIN TO CHRISTOPHER CHAMPLIN

Dear Brother,   St. Christophers, July 28th, 1766.

WE arriv'd at Domineca after a tegious Passage of 32 days. it has been very tegious to me as I have not had a well Hour since I left Newport. my disorder has follow'd me very close and have had a great Cold followed with a prodigious pain in my head. in a word I have been very illy able to keep about, but have got something the better of it.

I sold all my Flour at Domineca at 47/ my sheep was in excessive bad order when we arriv'd, being very scant of hay. was obliged to sell them at 26/ the half wou'd have dy'd in 3 days. I can't git any more for my Candles than 2/6d; the Islands are full. I woud have carried them to St. Cruix if had been well; but I am so much to the contrary that I shall endeavour to git home as soon as possible. I have the pork on hand yet by reason of its being but very indifferent.

I have been here 48 hours have taken in 18 hhds. Rum, and shall take in 8 or 10 more for Cargoe, which shall, if the wether holds good, compleat in 3 days, then shall proceed to Eustatia, there dispose of my Pork at some rate or other and fill up with any thing I can find to our Advantage. I am your Brother,

GEO: CHAMPLIN

Price Current: Sugar 38/ to 42/; Rum 2/ ariseing.
[Endorsed,] Per Capt. Bannit, via Philadelphia.

HENRY CRUGER, JR. TO AARON LOPEZ

Dear Sir, Bristol, July 30th, 1766.

I HAVE had the pleasure of writing you very fully by your Ship *America* still here, tho' the Captain shou'd have had his Dispatches a week ago, had not the wind been adverse and the weather very unsettled and bad, which yet continues, and gives me an Opportunity of acknowledgeing receipt of your favours of 2nd June (with two Copys) and of 13th June.

I am particularly obliged to you, Sir, for what you say respecting the Nantucket Whale Fishery.[1] it will always afford me the utmost satisfaction to assist or contribute to your Interest. I wou'd chearfully lengthen my usual

---

[1] In 1764 Grenville encouraged the American whale fishery by abolishing the bounties paid to British fishermen, and relieved the American of all discriminating duties save an old subsidy of less than one per cent. In 1763 the quantity of American oil imported at London was more than three thousand tons, and forty tons of whale fins, valued at about £350 a ton, paid a duty of £31. 10s. a ton. The range of the fishery tended to more distant regions, and while the principal fishing grounds were still to the northward, the coast of Brazil offered a good adventure.

Time of Credit, cou'd I possibly do it; why I cannot *at present* is for this reason; the late Confusion in America stop'd the Circulation of Commerce, deprived the Americans of the means to pay their Debts due to England, and by that means, render the Debts of their Factors here *enormous*, this makes us very cautious how we extend our Trafick in that Country for a time, especially by *lengthening* the time of payment. I hope in the course of a Year or two, Trade will be of a better Constitution, and that we poor Devils shall be eased of our Load of Debt, when, Dear Sir, I know nothing to the Contrary but I shall be able to comply with what you propose. if so, and it shou'd then be agreable to you, we will revive the subject; at present I fear it would be quite inconvenient to me.

Inclosed is Account of £1000 Insurance, on the *Charlotte*, Brown, Cost £26.16.0 to your Debit.

I am sorry, Sir, I shou'd give you so much trouble in pointing out the Reasons for your Drawing on me more than I thought right. I wou'd not have complain'd, but my Spirits were quite broke down with Disapointments from abroad, close and perpetual Dunns here, and no Remittances from there, which alas! is yet too much the case. I hope you'll excuse my Necessities and think no more about it.

Your extreme kindness in favouring me with your Sentiments of a certain person I am much obliged for and shall keep to myself secret and inviolate.

If any thing further shou'd occur before the sealing of this will add it by way of P. S. I am with much regard, Dear Sir, Your most humble Servant

HEN: CRUGER, JUNIOR

HENRY CRUGER, JR. TO AARON LOPEZ

Dear Sir, Bristol, August 24th, 1766.

BY this bearer I have sent you Duplicates of all your Papers that went by the *America* who sail'd with a fair

Wind about the 8th Instant. I hope she will be with you long before this.

I have now the Pleasure of acknowledgeing receipt of your esteem'd favour of 1st July receiv'd per the *Charlotte*, Captain Brown. it cover'd Bill Lading and Invoice for her Cargo.

The Joists will turn out to as great a Profit as so small a parcell possibly can. I have advertised it for sale, and expect £5 Sterling per Thousand feet, the Boards will also turn out well. The Cam Wood I have sold after the rate of £39 per ton. Sugars are just now exceeding low, the Crops in the West Indies have been so great: this being a better Market than London, they are pouring vast Quantities upon us; I have had yours drawn, and low as the price is I expect to get for them about 35/ per Cent. Mahogany continues very low and in vast Plenty, but as you bought yours so very cheap, I have no doubt but it will pay the *Charlotte* a good Freight; The Lignum Vitae turns out but of a second Quality, — pithy.

As the Demand for Oil was very dull, the day the *Charlotte* arrivd, I sold all her Brown Oil at £16.10. per ton, in order to avoid the Expence of Warehouse Waste, etc. two days after which we had an account of Orders arriving from abroad for Oil and that the price was advanc'd 30/ per ton. I then of course repented my having sold your's, but it was too late; if I cry my Eyes out it can't be help'd. Trade will take such turns. immediately I advertised the White Oil by the *Charlotte* to be sold. I put it up in 4 Lotts — two sold at £22.10.0 and two at £22.7.6., to pay for in a Month; per my next you shall have the Sales of what is or then may be sold. The rise of Oil will depend greatly on the Success of your Fishery and the Quantities imported from America.

Such large Quantities of Turpentine have lately arriv'd the price is fallen from 15/ per Ct. to 7/ indeed no Buyers appear. I housed yours with about 2 or 300 more under my care. it will do better towards fall.

As no Freight offer'd hence to the West Indies, have adopted your last plan for the *Charlotte*, *she sails* to morrow in Ballast *for Cork*, to Messrs. Lane & Co., to whom I wrote as per the inclosed Copy of my letter.

The Bark the *Charlotte* brought I wou'd not have landed. I enter'd it at our Custom house as Dennage[1] and Firewood, in Cork it may answer.

If the Vessels that are up for New York are likely to sail soon will ship the goods you order agreable to *your Letter;* if not, will keep them for the return of the *America*.

You shall hear from me in future more punctually for the present I remain with Regard and Integrity, Dear Sir, Your most Obedient humble Servant,

HEN: CRUGER, JR.

I just now sold the Sugars at 35/ per Cent.

[Endorsed,] Per *Minerva* via New York.

WILLIAM LUX TO CHRISTOPHER CHAMPLIN

Sir, Maryland, Baltimore, 6 October, 1766.

CAPTAIN SEARS arrived here yesterday and on enquiry after your Health, and Captain George [Champlin], he told me of his arrival and that you talked of sending Captain Westgate in the Schooner here. I am this day favord with yours of the 23d ultimo, and am glad to hear you made so good a Voyage, and that he has recovered his Health. Flour at present is in great demand 13/6, and only Cash will procure it. we have not had so little Wheat in for severall years at this Season, the Farmers keep it back in expectation of the Price being higher, altho it is 4/6, which we never expected it to rise to this Fall, and as severall Vessells are now here loading both Wheat and Flour I am doubtful the Price will continue high. N. E. Rum is 2/3 and 2/4, Lo[af] Sugar 14*d*., Musc[ovad]o Sugar 45/ to 55/, W. I. Rum 3/, Molasses 22*d*, Cheese 6*d* to 7*d*, Bread 13/6. Please to send me a Box of Sperma Ceti Candles, if they do not exceed 2/3 our Curr[ency], about 20 li. will do.

---

[1] Dunnage, *i.e.* fagots of loose wood laid in the hold of a vessel to raise heavy goods above the bottom and prevent injury from water.

With Compliments to Your Brother, I am respectfully, Sir, Your most humble Servant,

WILLIAM LUX

HENRY CRUGER, JR. TO AARON LOPEZ

Dear Sir, Bristol, 9th October, 1766.

THE last time I had the Pleasure of addressing you was the 24th August via New York and via Philadelphia. I am since favored with your agreeable Letter of 4th August.

The Maker of the Sieves says he is sure they were packed and shiped, my Warehouse keeper has an Account in his Book of receiving the Shovells, also of halling them down to the Brigantine *Charlotte*. still Sir, as I dayly experience the Blunders of those folks, I can easily believe they may have committed another, shall therefore make Profitt and Loss Debtor to your Account for these Deficiencies £1.19.6 Stg.

I am sorry to find Brown is not like to get a freight; herewith are Copies of Mess. Lane & Co: his and my Letters.

The Mahogany by Brown turned out very narrow short Pieces, which renders it of very little Value. I was glad to get 3d per foot for it: the Turpentine is not yet sold. all besides of the *Charlottes* last Cargo is, as per Account Sales herewith. Net Proceeds £592.8.4 Sterling to your Credit.

Altho: there is a Vessel now up for New York yet, she loads so very slow, (owing to the unwillingness and backwardness of Merchants here trusting any more Goods to America where their Debts are already too enormous to venture much more) that I think her Departure too uncertain to put your last orderd Goods on board of her, as I realy expect the *America* back before this Vessel will sail, so have determined not to give a Stranger the freight that your own Vessel is entitled to; and I fancy this Delay can be no great Disapointment, as it will afford you an Opportunity of selling off your sundry Cargoes and by that Means enable you to bring our Accounts *nigher* a Ballance which am persuaded will give you equal Pleasure with myself.

At present we have very little doing in the Oil way. I can't tell for certain how it will sell, tho: believe at the following Prices — Brown Sperm: £20, White £22 to £23, Newfoundland £21, N: England £18, W Whale £18 to £19 per Ton. every other article at our Markets remain pretty much the same as per my last, save Sugars, which have taken a Start of 4/ or 5/ per Cent.

I remain with my usual Regard and sincerity, Dear Sir, Your most assured Humble Servant,

HEN: CRUGER, JUNIOR

LANE BENSONS & VAUGHANS TO CRUGER

Cork, 23d September, 1766.

Sir,

YESTERDAY we rec'd your esteemed favor of 26th ulto. by Captain Brown of the *Charlotte*, belonging to our mutual good Friend Mr. Aaron Lopez of Rhode Island. We are sorry to tell you that Freights for the West Indies were never so scarce and it is a doubt with us whether we shall be able to get anything worth while for the Vessel, but you may be assured of our best Endeavours to serve our friend. Captain Brown tells us the Vessell will want some little Repairs and she must have Provisions for the Voyage. pray advise in course whether you will accept our Bills for what she may want at 90 days d[iscoun]t.

We are with very great Respect, etc.

LANE BENSONS & VAUGHANS

P. S. Provisions broke extravagantly high but must soon fall 2/ to 3/ per Barrell.

Best Cargo Beef now 38/ per Ct.

Tallow expected to break about 42/ per Ct.

Abraham Lopez to Aaron Lopez[1]

Sir, Savanna La mar, Jamaica, November 16, 1766.

I AM now to answer your esteem'd Favour of the 30th of June per the Sloop *Industry*, Captain John Hyer, which for want of an Opportunity, had it not in my power to answer before. Immediately on receipt of your Favour, I advis'd Captain Hyer to dispose of every thing he could, at Kingston, as our Markett here was very dead, and indeed glutted, with most of the articles he had imported, except Sperma Cetae Candles, which if thro' having too large a Quantity, to dispose of there, he would send the remainder to me, would receive them, with pleasure, and dispose of them on your Account, to the best in my power for your Interest, but on not having been favour'd with an Answer from him, presume he had dispos'd of them there.

I am greatly oblig'd to you for the good Opinion you entertain of me, and at same time am sorry to acquaint you, notwithstanding the Justness of your plans, the Connections you propose would never answer in this place; for as I have large dealings with the Planters, myself, they would look on any Goods consign'd me, as my own (which has hitherto been the case with all Consignments sent me) and pay me for them, the same as they pay me for mine, in one or two years, and sometimes not for seven, therefore would not for the sake of the Commissions thereon, disappoint you in any remittances you might expect to make thro' this Channell, as their punctuality is by no means to be depended on. I am very sensible of the reciprocal advantages accruing on the different methods of Trade you propose, but without a punctuality in the payments (which I am sorry I cannot give any Assurances of) it would never answer your purposes. therefore would not chuse for any advantage I might receive, lead you into any Concern which could not fail of being attended with a series of disappointments you might not perhaps expect. Should any of your

---
[1] The original is in the Newport Historical Society.

Vessells arrive in this place before this reaches your hands, so as not to have time to alter your plans may depend on any Services to them in my power to render. It is with great Concern I note your being a Sufferer by your African Trade at Kingston last year. I wish you better success for the future. I have had many offers of this kind from Europe, but they are such fatiguing concerns and abstract me so much from my own business, besides the trouble in collecting the Remittances which is attended with much Labour, that it will never answer to any but those who make it their whole Employment. I am extremely sorry I can give you no better Encouragement to trade in this part. was it in my power to do you that Justice you have a right to expect in the remittances, from the Cargoes you propos'd sending I should not hesitate in receiving your Consignments; but these parts are so distress'd in general and so deeply involv'd, that there would be no putting any dependance on the payments, which if disappointed in, your Schemes must of course be render'd abortive; was there the least probability of succeeding should very readily embrace your Consignments and should be proud of having the Honour of your concerns, as I am no Stranger to your Honour and Probity of which have receiv'd many Intimations, and tho' am a Stranger to your person, am not a Stranger to your good Name which is equal if not superior to the kind Compliments you was pleas'd to pay to mine. I hope from this candid account you'll not misconstrue my Intentions, of refusing your Connections, for I assure you on my honour what I have wrote you, is a true State of these parts, and it would be impossible for me to render you such Accounts of your Consignments as I could wish or would be any ways agreable and rather than not give the Content my Heart could wish I had rather be without them altogether.

This I hope may not prevent our corresponding or my rendering you any Services here, you may put it in my power to execute, and as an Opening for a further Correspondence, I must request the favour of you to acquaint me the lowest price at which you could annually supply me with Fifty or Sixty boxes of the best Sperma Ceti Candles to be deliver'd at this place, and if the Terms are such as admit a living profitt, the Payment or Remittance shall be made in the most agreable manner to you you'll please advise.

Am extremely sorry it is not in my power to give you a better Prospect of our being nearer connected, but am with a further Tender of any Services in my power, which must desire you'll freely command and hope you'll believe me to be with the utmost Respect, Sir, Your very humble Servant,

Abraham Lopez

[Endorsed,] Per *Mercury*, Capt. Ashmead.

ISRAEL BRAYTON TO CHRISTOPHER AND GEORGE CHAMPLIN

Charlestown, South Carolina, December 6th, 1766.

Gentlemen,

THIS oppertunity offers per way of Phillidelphia to acquaint you of my proceedings here. I have sold one half of my Rum at 12/6 the most that any is sold for, butt all of it by one and two Casks at a time. here is two Vessells from Boston with Rum and more expecktd dayly, that keeps people from purchasing. Cheese sells at 3/ per the Single Chese, Potatoes very dull. I miss know oppurtunety of selling, but cant force people to bye. I shall make all the Dispatch in my Power. Rice 50/ and a great many Purchaseers for the Lisbon markets and the west indies, that I am afeard I shant be able to purchase under. I expeckt to begin to load in a weaks time: wee have know

News, so conclude with doing all in my power for your Intrest, you may depend on Your most Humble Servant,

ISRAEL BRAYTON

Prices Current of Nothr'd Goods.

Rum 12/6
Chese 3/
Dry fish £20 per hd. Scarce.
Flour £6 per Ct.

Spermcett Cand. 10/6 to 11/.
Unyons 2/6 Scarce.
Lamp oil £20 but no grate demand.

Prices Current here.

Rice 50
Corn 15

Peas 15
Shingles £5.

Capt. Durfee not arrived. We are all well on bord.

[Endorsed,] Via Phillidelphia.
Received (Philad'a 21 December 1766) under Cover and forwarded by Your Friend,

JOSIAH HEWES.

Forwarded from Newyork, 29th December, 1766, per your Friend,

THOS. FRANKLIN, JUN.

JEREMIAH OSBORNE TO AARON LOPEZ

Sir, Bristol, January 30, 1767.[1]

I NOTIFYED you from Cork, via Nantucket and Lisbon, to which place I arrived in 30 days. should I enter into a perticular Datail respecting the methods taken to dispose of the Rum it would be tedious, for you may well conclud considering the difficulty of the Season, as well as the Negotiation I was obliged to act with the gretest Caution from Cork we were obliged to put into Milford, which is an exeding good place for the Business. I wish I had 100 hhs on board. what made me more sollisitus if possable to gett it of was, in case we had landed it it would all have ben

---

[1] "We saw Mr. Redwood's Garden — one of the finest gardens I ever saw in my life. In it grows all sorts of West India Fruit, viz: Oranges, Lemons, Limes, Pine-Apples, Tamarinds, and other sorts. It has also West India Flowers — very pretty ones — and a fine Summer House.

"It was told my Father by a credible person, that the Garden was worth 40,000 Pounds, and that the man that took care of the Garden has above One Hundred Dollars per annum. It has Hot Houses, where things that are tender are put in the winter, and Hot Beds for the West India Fruit." Journal of Solomon Drowne, 1767, in *Newport Historical Magazine*, I. 67.

sunk. it neeted deducting 5 per Cent Commission £245.5.9, and had I have ben more acquainted it might have ben advansd 50 per Cent more. have only to say I have don the best I could, but hope our next adventure this way will answer better. I am sorry I am obligd to take Charge of the *Pitt*, as it will prevent an advantagus Plan I have concerted with a Number of Gentlemen at Milford for Disposall of 80 hhd. N. E., 20 hhd. West India, with Ten Thousand Weight Coffe, which I could have executed per returne of the Ship, yet am in hope to be round timely with the *Pitt*. Last Saterday wrote Mr. Stead; receiving no answer, repeted my Letter have received none as yet. it will be a disagreable Business to me yet will do my best. not 10 Barrell Oyl to sell here. we have mised it. Your Humble Servant,

JEREMIAH OSBORNE

ISRAEL BRAYTON TO CHRISTOPHER AND GEORGE CHAMPLIN

Gentlemen, Kingston, Jamaica, February 8th, 1767.

THIS is to acquaint you of my misfortune of being here. Two days after I left Charlestown I carry'd away my main Boom, and mett with constant Gales of wind at NE and ENE, that the fardest I fecht to wind was the Carcases, and was obliged to come here very much against my will I assure you in such a Vessell. my Vessell proves very bad and leakey in any thing of hard weather. I find the markets here very dull. I have know sold 60 Casks Rice at 13/9, all by Retail, which makes but about 3 Dollars Fraight per Cask: I am know bound to Savanalar-mar, with the Remainder in hopes of a better Price, for cant sell the Remainder here, being very plenty. with the Badness of my Vessell and Bad markets I am almost beat out; I am determind to sell at Savanalamar and purchase new Rum if reasonable with part if not all my cargo, and proceed to Charlestown, in South Carolina, if can git along, being a bad Season for the Gulf, and threw the Passage is imposable for this Vessell. I propose at Charlestown to load for the windward Islands once more, if agreable to you; which you may send me a Letter and lodge in Mr. Russell's hands weather you would have me come home; with what I bring from Jamaica, or sell in Charlestown and proceed, as I propos'd. you may always git a Letter to Charlestown the most ready way by Philadelphia. if I had a good Vessell to sail I should try hard to make you some before I came home: but this Vessel is a Nough to discourage any man. Rice altho very cheap here dont pay a very bad fraight if a Vessell carry'd any thing: but this Vessell is Nothing but a Pickpocket, this the dulest place at present I ever was in, and a purpetuall Cry for money. Nothing sells at any Profitt worth a speaking of: I am under a Nesasaty of laying out some of the Cargo, for the money here is so light, and I cant git it chang'd in Dollars That it wont do to carry of: Rum here in town at 2/9 that wont do to purchase. I am in hopes in the Cuntry to git Rum reasonable. Shall due all in my Power for your Intrest, you may depend on. I referr you to Capt. Simmons, who comes Passenger in the Vessell; for News. I wrote to you the 1st Instant by way of Mounte Christo, which I hope came safe to hand. So conclude

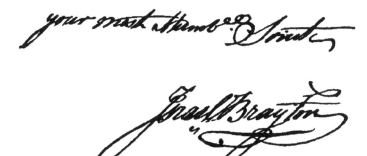

P. S. I shall sail for Savanalamar in two or the days. I have sold my Pork at £3.5 and £3.10. Shingles at 45/M

Jeremiah Osborne to Aaron Lopez

Sir, London, February 8, 1767.

I ARRIVED here last night. As yet have not sean Mr. Stead: but am informed there are up 20 Sail for Amerrica, Shall endevor to get 25 Tons of Hemp [and] 5 Tons Anchors for your account, as I understand the *Amerrica* will have none on board. Mrs. Cruger died and was enterred thre days past to our great Sorrow and which belive has prevented. the Captain is now weighting. therefore you must excuse Brevity shall write you largely in two or three days. Your Humble Servant

JEREMIAH OSBORNE

Jeremiah Osborne to Aaron Lopez

Sir, London, February 13th, 1767.

I AM now here. upon my arrival I apply'd to Mr. Stead for delivery of the Ship, which he readily complyed with, I then requested his Assistance to compleat your Orders, which he declined, further than lending me £150 upon Bottom, including premium, insurance, etc., which as yet have not accepted; being in hopes otherwise to accomodate my self; I next applyed to Messrs. Barkly and sons who have given their Interest in America to Messrs. Harford & Powell, to whom they recomended me. as yet I have not their Determination. they mentioned that if I had gott a line of Recomen[dations] from Messrs. J. & W Wanton Cuzens,[1] etc.; it made me smile and was something grateing to me considering the Difference of your Carracter and theirs. But wish we had taken this precaution. yet you may depend I will execut[e you]r Lisbon Plan. There are 14 sail for Bosto[n here.] Therefore you must conclude my Application fruteless: I am endevouring if possable to procure you 20 Tons Hemp, which as you have none shipd

---

[1] Probably Joseph Wanton and Matthew Cozzens.

from Bristoll I think you will want. the Rum I have disposed of. have retained £100 in my hand and paid the Remainder to Mr. Cruger, acct. of which have transmitted you per the *America*. had I ben more fully acquainted could have secured 50 per Ct. more. Trade her is exceeding dull and difficult   no price for Ships. I have ben on board the *Pitt*   find she has suffered greatly and will take at least £350 to fitt. I shall use all prudence and dispatch in getting her away and shall write you fully in three or fore days.

According to your Promise I expect the Ship *America* upon my return to execute the Plan I have settled at Milford, for which you may procure me 60 hhds N. E. from 60 to 100 Gal. each, and 20 hhd. of W. India, Iron Bound, with 10 Thousand Coffey — hold filled with pine Plank and Scantling for Bristoll.   Your Humble Servant,

JEREMIAH OSBORNE

JEREMIAH OSBORNE TO AARON LOPEZ

Sir, London, February 14, 1767.

SINCE my last to you via Boston and New York, through the Recommendation of our good Friend Mr. Lee of Boston, to the House of Mr. George Haley, as eminent and worthy a man as is in the Citty, I have found the assistance necessary. shall procede to New Castle according to your order and from thence to Lisbon. understanding you would have no hemp from Bristoll, Mr. Haley will ship you 10 Tons Hemp per the *Susanna*, Gardner, bound to your place. I have likewise orderd 5 Tons Anchors, from one hundred and three quarter to ten hundred via Boston in a ship of Mr. Hayleys to the Cair of your Friend H. Lloyd. this is some thing out of the way I am sensible, but it was a small Concession in favour of his Ship which is up for freight. Therefore hope youl excuse, for assure you I was put to difficulty before I meet with this Gentleman. your friend Stead was for making something out of us by his Bottom

Rea[1] which have avoided. I shall write you fully per Gardner and loose no time in getting round to you again. Mr. Haley offered me the 25 Tons with any thing else necessary; but Gardner could not take it in, and I did not choos to ship it via Boston as it pays a considerable Freight. Your Humble Servant,
JEREMIAH OSBORNE

ISAAC PEREIRA MENDES TO AARON LOPEZ

Jamaica, Kingston, 15 February, 1767

Sir,

YOUR kind favours of 9 and 12 December last per Captain Bradfield[2] I now have before me, covering Invoice and Bill of Loading for sundrys shipt per *Swansey* to my Address.

The choice of my Brother Abraham to your daughter Miss Sally, for his Consort, has merritted much our Aprobation, as also that of my honourd Mother. The Ameableness of your daughter, the Bright Carrecter and honour of yours and familys, as much in these parts, as those of ancient, in Portugal, cannot butt give us in generall the greatest Sattisfaction; that my Brother has united himself with; (which is doeing honour to the Memory of our Worthy and honourd Father.) From my Brother repeated Expressions of their reciprocal Love, must make them happy, and pleasing to you, and beg leave to return my Congratulating you and all your good family, on this joyfull Occasion, wishing them all the Happiness they can wish for, and pray the Almighty may crown them with his Blessings and make you a happy Father, and my tender Embraces to the Young Lady, with that of my spouse and family. I make no doubt, you have found in my Brother, such Bright Qualitys, which few of his Age are endowed with, particular from the Education of Youths, in these parts, he has those of Nature so strongly, I am sure with cultivating in your good Advice must make him a Bright Man.

[1] Bottomry.
[2] Of the *Swansey*.

I am sorry the *Swansey's* Arrivall to this place should be at a time when the Marketts are so supply'd, and the present scarcity of Currency. It gives me some concern our first Connextion's should not prove to more Advantage. was it not oweing for the Credit I have given for what Sales have made, as per enclosed Account, you inevitable must have been a great Losser, tho' I could wish I had been in Town at her Arrivall, Intirely oweing to my Brother Abrahams advices to me you had alterd your Resolution, in sending the Vessell to me, otherwise I should have taken care to have left proper Instructions. I have engaged Captain Bradfields load of Melosses for the middle of March, which I hope she will then be able to sail with 120 to 140 hhds for your Government tho' I am sure I shall not be in Cash for half her load. in order she might embrace the earliest opportunity I shall supply her.

I received a letter from Mr. Abraham Lopez of Sav. lamarr who gives a meloncholy account of the Brig *Charrlota,* as at large you have enclosed his letter. In order to serve you, I have answ[ere]d Mr. Lopez, if said Brig *Charlotta* should be oblidged to stay, till May, I would assist hir with 40 or 50 hhds Melosses, which expect his Answer. The Brig you advice me, intended for the Bay of hondorus, as yett we have no News of her; (I wish her safte,) at her Arrivall shall do the Needfull, and give you a full Account per Captain Bradfield of all Proceedings. Your Spermeceti Candles, I am sorry to say are inferior to any at this Markett. I have experience myself and burnt one, which does not answer the Quality. those I have seen from Boston etc. are very clear, and well prist free from Oyle. The Shadds have offerd at 12/6 and no Buyers; am afraid they will lay on hand. I was oblige to send the horses to the Country for Sale, as was not possiable to sell in Town at £15. Captain Bradfield was an Eye Witness, from New England what q'ty arrived to this port and was offerd the choice of one horse in 40 at £22.10. Im sorry to acquaint you the loss of Three horses in the Voyage, as Eight only landed, and those in bad order, poor and much brused, occasiond by the Captain's information of bad weather. I can't but recomend to you Captain Bradfield Assiduity sence his arrivall, and to be short in generall so.

My Brother advices me of comeing to this place in May or June, (with your Concurrence), I think will answer his purpose, provided its with such a Cargo, I have describe to him, in a Brig. 230 to 250 hhds, will answer much better then a small Vessell, as I can undertake her sales and Remittances. I make no doubt he will communicate to you the particulars for your Goverment. I can make Sale of 60 M Red, 10 M White Phild. Oake Staves, 30 M Common, and 10 M pitch pine-boards. I give this Advice; youll act as you shall think most conducive to your interest. If he arrives here in May or June, if in November or December, you may double the Quantity of Staves, as most Estates at Withywood will engage with me. Youll be please to give me Advice on Rect. of this your Intentions and what q[uanti]ty you can ship, for my Goverment, as I might engage in time. By Captain Bradfield I shall enlarge. Beg leave to conclude, assuring you of my best Endeavours with Zeal and friendship to serve you, allways ready at any of your Commands, with Love and Respects to you Spouse and good family, as mine joyns me Sincerely, from, Sir, Your Assurd and very humble Servant,

Isaac Pr. Mendes

Henry Cruger, Jr. to Aaron Lopez

Mr. Aaron Lopez
                To Henry Cruger, Junior Dr.

For over Credit given on Freight of Mahogany per *America*, 2nd Voyage. ½ of a Ton and 18 feet at 48/ per ton	£1.17. 9
Deduct Commission 2 per Ct.	0. 0. 9
To the Debit of Mr. Aaron Lopez	£1.17. 0

Account of Inward Freight per *Charlotte*, Thos. Brown, Master from Rhode Island.
By Robert Stevens Frt. 1 Cask Furrs	0. 3. 6
2.1.10 Elephants Teeth 2/	0. 4. 8
Average	0. 1. 0
	0. 9. 2

By Jacob Rod. Rivera Frt. 7.1.4 Cam Wood } 0.18. 3
        at 2/6
     Average 3/ per Ton . . . 0. 1. 0
Freight 19.1.4 Turpentine at 2/6 . . . . 2. 8. 8
     Average 4½ d per Bll. . . . 0. 3. 0   3.10.11
                  £4. 0. 1
To Commission on £4.0.1 at 2 per Ct. 0. 1. 7
To the Credit of Mr. Aaron Lopez £3.18. 6

Errors Excepted
Bristol, December 31st, 1766.

                 Bristol, February 5th, 1767.
Mr. Aaron Lopez,
     To Henry Cruger, Junior, Dr.
For Cost of Sundry Insurances vizt.
On the *Swansea*, Francis Bradfield, Master, at and from Rhode Island to Jamaica vizt.

On Goods	On Ship	
£100 Rich'd Gildart	100 Peter Thelluson	
100 Gilb't Harrison	100 John Clarke	
50 Geo: Johnston	50 George Ward	
100 Thos. Gildart	250 at 50/ per Ct. and Policy 8/	£6.13.0
100 Robt. Cowan Kellet		
100 A. Champion		
100 John Craven		
100 Rich'd Neave		
100 John Bradstreet		

£850 at 50/ per Ct. and Policy 8/ £21.13.0
                   £28. 6.0

On the *Heart*, John Newdigate, Master, at and from Rhode Island to Jamaica.
£850 on Goods at 50/ per Ct. and Policy 8/ £21.13.0
250 on Ship at Do. 6.13.0   £28. 6.0
   Subscriptions the same as on the *Swansea*.

On the *Diana*, James Potter, Master, at and from Rhode Island to Jamaica.

On Goods	On Ship		
£100 Robert Cowan Kellet	£100 Rich'd Gildart		
100 Rich'd Neave	100 Gilb't Harrison		
200 John Bradshaw	100 Thos. Gildart		
100 Peter Thelluson	100 Geo: Johnston		
100 John Clark	100 Al'r Champion		
100 George Ward	100 John Craven		
100 A. Hake	150 Cal't Bewicke		
100 Wm. Black	£750 at 50/ per Ct. }	19.3.0	
100 John Townson	and Policy 8/		
£1000 at 50/ per Ct. and Policy 8/	£25.8.0		44.11.0

                   £101. 3. 0
To Commission on £3950 at 1/2 per Ct. 19.15. 0
To the Debit of Mr. Aaron Lopez £120.18. 0

HENRY CRUGER, JR. TO AARON LOPEZ

Dear Sir, Bristol, 20th February, 1767.

By this conveyance I send Copy of my last Respects January 11th.

The 25th January was favour'd with your agreeable Letters of 14th and 18th November and 1st December by the *America*. we made all the dispatch in our power to discharge her. she is now taking in Goods for New York, and will be ready to sail in 10 or 12 days, but before I enter into the Reasons etc. of this unexpected Voyage, let me agreeable to Rule answer your Favours.

The Pine Plank looks very well, but *still* remains the great *Deficiency* of squaring the Edges; this will depriciate them some Shillings per Ct. I am advertising them for public sale next week. if the intended bearer of this should be detain'd untill then, will let you know how they sold, if not, you will of course be advised by the *America;* please to observe you have unluckily omitted to send the Certificate for the Lumber, pray do per first opportunity, as cannot receive the Bounty till we do it.

N. B. Pot Ash receives no Bounty. I expect to get £27 per Ton for these 5 Tons per *America*. in this, as well as all other articles, the price will depend *wholly* on the Quantities imported. I am firmly of opinion, nothing but a War can affect the price of Logwood, make your calculations about £5 per ton and you won't be hurt. never send any but good. I am about selling this by the *America* at £5.5.0 per ton, the Lignumvitae is also advertised to be sold. you shall soon hear more about it.

The T P Hob Nails have wrote to the Maker about, have not yet had his answer.

I will take care your Invoices in future shall be made out as you desire and direct, also the Goods pack'd and mark'd in the manner mention'd.

I oblig'd the Maker to allow a Discount on the Kerseys No. oo per *America* last Voyage of 5 per Ct. which is carried to the Credit of your Account, say 13/6 Sterling.

You are pleased to write me you saw a Sales of *Brown* Oil from Liverpool, made out about the same time yours per *Charlotte* were, that sold at £23, when yours sold at only £16. I cannot presume, Sir, to contradict what you saw, but, *this Fact I know*, the Current Price of Brown Oil was then in Liverpoole only £17 per ton.

I beg Liberty just to observe, Oil may be carried from hence to Liverpoole for less than 20/ per ton. Vessels are continually going backward and forward. would not the *certain* Profit of £6 per ton have induced people to send it thither from hence.

Inclosed, Sir, is Account of sundry Insurances vizt. on the *Swansea*, the *Heart*, and the *Diana*, cost £120.18.0 Stg. to your Debit.

Herewith you'll find Account Sales of 49 Blls. Turpentine Nt. £28.18.11 Stg. to your Credit. likewise Disbursements on the *America* last Voyage £425.16.2 Stg., also Disbursements on *Charlotte* £89.8.0 Stg. to your Debit, also additional Disbursements on the *America* £16.2.9 to your Debit.

Osborne is fitting out the *Pitt*, as I suppose he writes you. he has sent you Ten Tons of Hemp from London, we have none at present in this City. Osborne paid me £100 as about half the proceeds of the Rum sold in the Channel. I desired him to let me have the particulars, but he declines it. I must therefore refer you to him, he seems fond of the plan. I do not much like it, not from Conscientious Scruples, but fear, if he repeats it too often or too *extensively* some trap will be laid for him and Ship and Cargo exchequer'd. I do not speak of *Probability* but *Possibility*.

Your account has Credit for £3.18.6 Inward Freight per *Charlotte* as per particulars, and debited £1.17.0 as per particulars, Capt. Brown when he was at Cork drew on me £6.6.8 Stg. which I paid for your Account and debited it accordingly.

Dear Sir, it seems as if Heaven and Earth were combin'd to afflict me at the same time: Heaven, in depriving me of the best of Women — my Wife; Earth, in tormenting me with the next greatest distress *close Dunning* from necessitous Manufacturers and Tradesmen. one I sigh bitterly to bring back, the others as heartily to get rid of, such is the present melancholy situation of my mind and affairs. one I trust in God the lenient hand of Time will at least mitigate if not release, the other I must rely on the Justness and Consideration of my American Correspondents to remove. indeed, at present it is as much as I can do to support myself, and nothing but a great share of Natural Fortitude of Mind keeps me from sinking under my present Calamities.

It gives me vast concern to omit the execution of your last Orders, but really, Sir, I am so deeply involved, that it will be the height of imprudence to continue sending Goods untill my Debts in America are a little reduced, and I do assure you, nothing but the fair Character I bear amongst my fellow Citizens saves me from Bankruptcy, which Heaven avert; I do not indeed apprehend it, but yet it is a heartbreaking reflection to find myself *liable* and owing wholly and solely to Impunctuallity and Disappointments from America. If I am not paid how can I pay? I do not upon my Word, Dear Sir, doubt of your abilities, nor am I under the least apprehension for the Foundation of your Credit, but I repeat, if I am not paid, how can I pay?

I will just make a few remarks on the state of your Account. last July was due an Invoice per *Charlotte* amount £2530.14.9 Stg. only about half of which is paid. then to the remainder is to be added £2457.13.2 Stg. amount of Invoice due last September, and the 20th of next month will be due another Invoice, amount £2510.9.2 Stg., and before the *America* can well be back another Invoice will be due, amount £1593.0.3 Stg. to all these let me add the Cost of sundry Insurances, amounting to £626.6.6. Stg. the greatest part of which Sum I have paid long since. again, the Money advanced to Captains and Sailors say Disbursements on all your Ships (which is so much Cash down) amount £1409.19.6 Stg.

I shall not, Sir, animadvert on the foregoing, what must necessarily be the Consequence, will, I am sure very naturally occur to your goodself.

Inclosed is for *your Government.* your Account Current Ballance in my favour £10,514.10.5 Stg. is carried to your Debit in a new Account.

Thus, Sir, have I in a plain honest Manner endeavour'd to give you an ample and satisfactory Reason for my not sending you any more Goods untill your Account is a little reduced, and I throw myself on your Candour for the Validity of my Arguments, not doubting, but from the Justness of your Character and Good Sense, but I shall still retain every favourable Sentiment you ever had towards me: when, Sir, you think it prudent to send to me for any more Goods, I wou'd advise, in order to prevent Mistakes, that you make out a *fresh Memorandum* and direct all that are now subsisting *to be totally supprest.*

I come now, Sir, to give you my Reason for sending the *America* to New York, it is an incessant Attention to your Interest having Goods in a Warehouse ready to ship for New York, as soon as she was ready to take them in, concluded the Freight of them would defray her Expenses out, and knowing her going there or direct to Newport wou'd make only a day or two odds, this determined me on the Plan I have adopted, and as it's meant solely for your Interest, hope my conduct will secure your approbation.

The *America,* Capt. Peters, shall sail (wind and weather permitting) in a fortnight. by her will write you more circumstantially relative to Trade in general, which my late Misfortune disqualifies me from doing now. I remain with sincere Regard and Respect, etc.

HENRY CRUGER, JR.

P. S. The sundry Errors you point out in Casks No. 1, 2 and 3, per the *America* last Voyage, the person they were bought of has looked into, and inclosed you his answer on that subject.

Have debited your Account £1.4.0 paid Alexander Henderixon's Shiping note per *Charlotte* last Voyage. the reason it did not appear in the Disbursements was because Capt. Brown omitted to inform me whether the man was on board or not, but have made the Holders of the Note liable to refund the Money, if it shou'd appear the Man did not proceed the Voyage: of which please to inform me. The Maker of the T P Hob Nails cannot by any means take them back, as he says he never before or since had an Order for such, and as he exactly comply'd with your Order, shall therefore send them back per *America* agreeable to your Directions.

Your esteem'd favour of 19th December is at hand. the Error in Sail Cloth shall be look'd into, and per the *America* you shall have an answer thereto, and also be inform'd the amount of Brimstone Debenture per *Charlotte*. shall cause the Insurance to be struck off and Credit your Account for return Premio.

JEREMIAH OSBORNE TO AARON LOPEZ

Sir, London, February 20, 1767.

YOURS of December 19th I received and observe the Contents. I have left no stone unturned to obtain a freight for the Ship *Pitt*, but they have prooved abortive the only expedient is to proceede emediately for Lisbon and take in a load of Salt, upon Enquiry of the best hands find Coal wont fetch the prime Cost, and to be at extreordanary Insurance from hence to N Castle and back to the Downs, with Wages, provisions, and port charges, will be thrown away: the Ship is now in Dock wants a great Repair, but you may depend I shall use the utmost Frugallity and Dispatch in getting round, and hope to sail in 20 days. per this you will receive Advise from Mr. George Haley respecting the Outsett of Ship, and 10 Tons Hemp and 5 Tons Anchors ship'd for your Account. I should not have ship'd the Hemp and 5 Tons Anchors, but I understood there was none from Bristoll. Indead when I was there it was Cash, but find per Mr. Haley it is 6 m[onth]s here. I assure you we are extremely obliged to Mr. Haley for his Assistance and as I have given him the strongest Assurance of your

Honour dont doubt of your Complyance with his propositions. Your Humble Servant
                                    JEREMIAH OSBORNE
Shall write you fully before I sail.

JEREMIAH OSBORNE TO AARON LOPEZ

Sir,   London, February 25, 1767.

THE Ship is almost compleated, and ready to come out of Dock, as she was only spiked and treeniled [treenail]; and to take in a load of Salt which is a weighty loading I thought propper to butt boalt her: I have used every Endevour to obtain Freight some way of other, but fruteless. Never was such times here before: therefore the only expediant is to dispatch away for Lisbon as quick as possable. shall obtain my men upon a reasonable Lay: there are 100 Sail new Ships for sail from 150 to 250 Tons butt will not sell: doubtless you have hered of the Death of Mrs. Cruger, which am affraid is a Detriment to Mr. Cruger; Mr. Haley, the Gent who has ben so good as to honour your Credit, is a Gentleman ben a long time in the American Trade, extreeme good Carracter [and] a large Cappitall they say £100 Thousands pos[sibly.] May be introductory to further dealings he is a Corespondent of Benj. Mason.[1] I shall order £800 Insurance upon the Ship from here to Lisbon, and £1200 from thence to R Island, of which I shall before sailing give you notice. Compliments to Mrs. Lopez. Concludes me Your Humble Servant
                                    JEREMIAH OSBORNE

ISAAC PEREIRA MENDES TO AARON LOPEZ

Sir,   Kingston, 26 Feb., 1767.

MY last to you was by Captain Simmons. I therein wrote you at large, in particular on all subject, to which I must

---
[1] Benjamin Mason (1728–1775), a merchant of Newport, who married in 1754, Mary, daughter of Daniel Ayrault, Jr.

referr. Since I am to give you the agreeable and joyfull news the Arrivall of the Brig *Little Hart*, Captain Newdegate, after a long Voyage of 37 days. I assure you we where under great Aprehensions for her Saftey. I expected a Confirmation of your favour, per said Brig, to have lighten her of part of hir Cargoe that might have proved saleable in this port, butt finding Captain Newdegate orders so positive to be deld [to] Mr. Ab. Lopez of Sav. lamarr, I thought would not have been prudent to land any part in this port, (tho' some articles could have commanded Cash,) and wish you good Success therein. All the Advice in my power to serve Captain Newdegate to your Interest have assisted him with. tho' his Pasage was long he lost butt some of his turkeys and sheep, the horses where landed safle, tho' poor in flesh. Captain Newdegate will sail for Sav. lamarr in two days. at his stay in this port, he made sale of the frame, etc., that was intended (for Handorus) for £100 this Currency, occasion'd by Two Vessill arrived from the bay and gave Captain Newdegate and myself infomation of that article being out of demand, as there where now three frames for sale cheap on Credit. on this Consideration he sold at a lower price, and had for Payment Two fine Nigroes to be sold for Mr. Is. Rod da Costa on his Account and Risque, and the Proceeds to be paid in Jam[aica] to him, with the Sale of said frame, I assisted in my Advice to Captain Newdegate as I am sure will be to your Interest. Considering Three Carpenters Maint[en]ance and Wagess till arrived at your port would run high, and make a difference of more then £20, as I find your orders to sell said frame in this place for £120, the Captain will get a discharge from the Carpenters, which I shall take care be done properly.

Captain Bradfield is now at Withywood with the *Swansey* takin her Load of Molasses. I hope she will sail 20 March next, except any Rains should prevent. by him I shall write you at large, with a particular Account of Sales of her Cargoe, etc. Youll excuse this, as wrote in a hurry, not having time, from the knowledge of this vessell departing. Accept my best Respects to you and good family, and Love to my Brother Abraham and Miss Sally, as all my family joyns me, from, Sir,

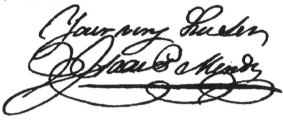

HENRY CRUGER, JR. TO AARON LOPEZ

Bristol, March 23rd, 1767.

Dear Sir,

BY this conveyance of your Ship *America*, go duplicates of my last Respects to you.

none of the Pine Plank would pass for 2½ inches, was oblig'd therefore to mingle all together and sell them for 2 inches only. this have done at 18/ per 100 feet. 2½ inches would have sold for 3 or 4/ per Ct. higher. pray attend to the inclosed hints touching Plank; they will prove of advantage. the Oak Quarter is sold for 12/6 per 100 ft., the 29 Oak Plank of 4 inches, are sold at 47/ per 100 ft., 8 Do. of 3 inches, at 39/ per Ct. the Logwood is sold at £5.5 per ton. the Lignum vita was put up at Public Sale, but no body bid, have since sold it at 6 mos. Credit, for only £3.10. it is very plenty. don't send any more, it won't answer. this was very small poor trash. the Barrell Staves are sold at the same Credit for £3.5 per m   by my next will render account Sales of these articles. The sale for Pott Ash is at present very slow. People have a notion large Quantities will be sent home, and the Price fall a good deal. I have sold only 2 or 3 Casks of yours yet, by way of Trial and at 27/ per Ct. Bristol lying so handy to Ireland (where so much is consumed) will always command as good a Price as any Port in England. Just now people are cautious how they buy, waiting to see how much will come home, and wanting it down at £25 per ton. White Oil sold here last week at £26 per ton, Brown £24. Mahogany continues as per my last. should you incline to speculate in Corn, Wheat is 8/ to 9/ per Bushell, flour from 18/ to 20/ per Ct. and certainly will not be lower untill next Harvest is gather'd in.

Inclosed is Bill Lading and Invoice for a few articles I thought you'd stand in immediate need of, amounting to £73.13.10 Stg. also Cost of £600 on *America* to your Port, £16, both to your Debit. you are credited £18.17.9 as per particulars herewith. The Sail Cloth you write of, the person I bought it from seems positive it was parliament Cloth. do look it over again, for, if you persist that it is not, he shall make an Allowance of $\frac{1}{2}d$ per yard. you have Capt. Peters Rect. for £25.4. advanc'd for Ships Use. the Disbursements shall be sent with my next Respects; they will be very small. the frt. the Ship makes to New York, £633.4.7 Currency, will be paid there. I have insur'd on it £300 Stg. for fear of accidents, Cost £7.16 to your Debit. the freight to Rhode Island is paid here £56.8.7 Stg. to your Credit.

Capt. Osborne must account with you for £10.6 Stg. being for freight of Beer and Syder now on Board the *America*, belonging to him. I have consign'd the Ship to my Brother, John Harris Cruger, with whom hope it will be perfectly agreeable to you to correspond. this is all that at present occurs, save to wish the America a quick passage, and to assure you I am with hearty and unfeigned Regard, Dear Sir, Yours, etc.,

HENRY CRUGER, JR.

P. S. I have advanc'd to P. Ackland, a Sailor, 2 Gs. which please to stop out of his Wages, as it will be charg'd in the Disbursements.

[Memo.] rec'd per Jersey via N yk.

JEREMIAH OSBORNE TO AARON LOPEZ

Graves End, March 31, 1767.

Sir,

AFTER my utmost Endevour I am obliged to go to Lisbon in ballast. Coal from New Castle there would not produce the prime cost. There are Number of Cargoes unsold, a Freight back was not possable to obtain, a number of Vessells to Boston obligd to go away half loaded and some in ballast. there are above 100 Sails new Ships from America to sell no Buyers. when I heard of the Loss of Captain Cuzens Ship thinking there might be large Orders I applyd to Messrs Herford and Powell, but as no Letters were saved and no duplicates arrived could do nothing. had the Ship layd one six months more she would not have fetched 350 pounds. she is in very good order for sail or otherways as you shall judge necessary to employ her. the Shippers of Oyle have sunk a great deal of money as Mr. Haley enformed me, who him[self] has sold 5 hundred Tons. in expectation of seaing you I remain Your Humble Servant,

J. OSBORNE

a sett of candle stick worth her £36 pounds I have on board from Enocks Mother for the Sinegoge.[1]

ABRAHAM LOPEZ TO AARON LOPEZ

Jamaica, April 7th, 1767.

Sir,

MY last to you was per the *Sally* Brighton to which I confirm and to which must at present beg reference. Neither time nor my present melancholy Situation will admit of my enlarging farther than to acquaint you, your Brig *Charlotte*, Captain Newdigate, sail'd for the Bay the 12th last Month. The Amount of the Cargo supply'd him from me with

---

[1] "As to what you mention of Newport being a station for the men of war, it arose from some chit-chat of the local advantage of the harbor last summer in England; but as so much money has been expended at Halifax for docks etc., will not take place." *J. Powell to Christopher Champion*, April 6, 1767.

Expences, including some Articles of your Cargo, is £151. 7.1¼, the particulars of which must beg refer you for 'till next Conveyance. With Grief I acquaint you the Heavy Loss I have met with in the Death of my Beloved Wife whom God was pleas'd to take to himself the 26th last month after a lingering Illness of three months. the Physicians flatter'd me with Hopes six days before her Death, as she was then deliver'd of a fine Girl (which is still alive), but to my great Grief is turn'd out the reverse, and I am in disconsolate Condition being left with nine small Children. I must endeavour to bear this Shock with Patience and hope the Lord will endue me with Fortitude so to do. I am afraid this unhappy Affair will occasion your Brig *Little Hart* a fortnight's longer detention than I propos'd, as I cannot go out to forward the Melasses on board of her, which I am heartily sorry for, but I shall use every Method I can fall on for her Dispatch. I have dispos'd of every article of your Cargo except the Shingles, Bricks, and Oyle, which are very dull articles at present. the Oyle is in such bad order that it takes 4 of the BBs to fill up two, and am afraid you'll be a considerable Sufferer thereby. this last article and the Horses will make but an indifferent figure in your sales but every thing else will I hope give content. must beg youll excuse my not having time to enlarge and believe me to be with the Utmost Respect, Sir, Your most Obedient Humble Servant,

A. L.

Westmorland, Jamaica, April 14, 1767.

Sir,

The beforegoing is Copy of my last via Philadelphia per Captain Hasleton. This hope may come safe to hand per the *Swansey*, Captain Bradfield, who is now laying too of this Harbour and has sent his Boat in for my Commands to you. I have only time to acquaint you your Brig *Little Hart* is gone round to Green Island to take in the best part of her Cargo of Melasses, and on her return shall [have] every thing ready to compleat her Load here and hope she will sail on Sunday Sevennight at farthest. The above unhappy Loss has been the occasion of her Detention longer than I could have wish'd, but my best Endeavours shall be us'd for her dispatch. I have not time to add as our Holydays are coming on and am with best Respect, Sir, Your most humbler Servant,

ABRAHAM LOPEZ

Please excuse Haste.

ISAAC PEREIRA MENDES TO AARON LOPEZ

Sir,   Withywood, Jamaica, 10 Aprill, 1767.

ABOVE is Coppy of what wrote you per favor of Mr. Simmons, which hope gott to your hands in due time. Since my last per via Boston, to give you the agreeable News the arrivall of Brig *Little Hart*, Capt. Newdigate, therein mentiond to you, could have disposed some part of her Cargo; butt the Captain not being willing, and his instructions were such, as I thought he could not have answerd landing any part of her Cargoe, prevented the same. I gave all the advice to Capt. Newdigate that was needfull to your interest. I hope he may succeed in his Voyage to the Bay. the bad accounts he had from thence, by two vessells that frames were a bad article, induced the Capt. with my concurrence to sell at Kingston for £100, to be compleated, to my Brother in Law Mr. Ab. of Jacob P. Mendes, for which he had two fine Creole Negroe for sale on Commission on the proper account and risque of the Shipper, Mr. Isaac Rodr. da Costa, the Proceeds to go on Pay't of said frame, as I make no doubt the Capt. has wrote you fully on this subject must referr to him. This will be handed you by Capt. Bradfield covering bill of Loading and Invoice for 100 hhds Molasses, shipt on board the *Swansey* on your Account and Risque, amounting to £437.16/, as also account of Sales of Cargo per *Swansey* amounting to £700.6.3¼. the Shads remaining, many have lost their Pickle and will turn out butt poorly. You may be assured my endeavours shall not be wanting to recive what outstanding debts of said Sales, and when in Cash shall procure good Bills of Exchange and remitt for London on your Account to Wm. Stead Esqr. agreeable to your derections. The Molasses on board the *Swansey* I can recommend to be the best on this Island and bought of the best hands at the lowest prices, am very sure its three pence better then the Northside Molasses.

I must acknowledge the receipt of your favour per Capt. Potter's of 13 feb. last, with the Beefs Tongues and Chorisas, all landed at Kingston, and have given directions for the sale. butt no Success. at my arrivall there, which (please God) will be in two days, shall do the needfull. We have had such large importations lately of Caser beef from Cork and London prevents the sales of yours, and am sorry at present cannot recommend any from your place. Agreeable to your directions the Captain has cleared 75 hhds Molasses. I do not send the particular Gage of each Caskfull, as they were oblidge to fill the want aboard. The Capt. can give particulars. The advantage youll recive thereby I hope will ad for other Losses. My Bussiness lays so much in the Country am oblidged to attend there nine months in the year; which prevents me from doing that Justice to my friends as I otherwise wish for, as you'll be please to observe the arrival of Capt. Bradfield and Capt. Potter's Mate, I was from Kingston, which may be of great prejudice to a cargoe and your interest. Therefore cannot think to undertake your Business with Justice, as am sure cannot give that due attendence thats Neccesary, and I injoy very indifferent state of health. I flatter myself you'll excuse my being so free as its my Obligation in Justice to myself and your Interest, tho' allways ready to serve you in any of your Recomendations, with my Interest, Advice, etc. If my Brother Abraham should resolve for this Island, depend on my exserting all in my power to serve him, free from any other Views, butt with Zeal and brotherly Love.

I must again recomend to you Capt. Bradfield's assiduity and attendence, deserving any preferments. I have sent my Brother Abraham by Capt. Bradfield a few articles, the produce of this poor country, beg your acceptance in partaking with your good family of part thereof.

Give me leave Sir to conclude with my best Respects and Love to you and Lady as my family joins me most senserly, and am with Esteem, Sir, Your assured and very humble Servant,
ISAAC PR. MENDES

JEREMIAH OSBORNE TO AARON LOPEZ

Sir, Lisbon, April 17, 1767.

I ARRIVED her in ten days from London: Expect my last on board next Wednesday: and hope to sail from hence in ten days from this date at furthest, if not before: I understand per Mr. Mayn your friend out of the Cuntry wrote him, some time past respecting a Passage to your place: we shall endeavour to conduct that Affair with discression: if Stevens has his Cargo of Lumber ready: and should want freight, that with Assortment of Rum Coffey and some Madeira Wine, made with mixing a good pipe of Tenerief and one of Madeiras would do for Milford. Your Humble Servant,
JEREMIAH OSBORNE

JOHN POWELL TO CHRISTOPHER CHAMPLIN

Dear Sir, Boston, 29th April, 1767.

BY my Letters from London the Commissioners of the Victualing have refused paying for the Water Casks you supplyed The *Maidstone*, as the Demand and Receipts should have seperate Certificates and Vouchers from the provisions. I must beg of you to get the Cooper that made the Casks to make Affadavit before a Justice that he made 27 Butts of thick white oak staves free from sap, and put 8 iron hoops on each Butt, by your orders for his majesty's Ship *Maidstone*, and that the Butts were delivered on board empty; and one from you that agreeable to the Captain's and Officer's demand you caused Mr. [blank] Cooper to make so many Butts and purchased such a Quantity of Iron Hoops to hoop them and that they were delivered aboard his majesty's Ship *Maidstone* empty as they came out of the Cooper's Shop. Williams imposed monstrously on you in many Things. If ever get the mony for the Casks will be 25 per cent. Loss or more.

I have often wrote Wantons and Sam Brenton about my demand for the Owner of *The Golden Grove;* his demand was 150£ Stg. When you see Samuel Brenton beg him to let me know what Sum they paid Captain Chitty, and if have Letters from his father, allowing it out of their Bond to the Admiralty, and when they will be ready to settle it with me or with you, for me, as it may now be uncertain when I shall see Newport I should be glad those Gentlemen would be in readyness to settle the matter. In as much as I told Mr. Sam. Brenton when here I would give them time to hear from Captain Chitty's father, in regard to what they supplyed his Son. You have not sent me the Survey of the damaged Hemp to transmit Home. I refer you to the Bearer for perticular matter relating my little family, etc. and from Mr. Harrison what occurs in public, being with great regard, Dear Sir, Your A. and H. Servant,

J. POWELL

JEREMIAH OSBORNE TO AARON LOPEZ

Lisbon, May 7th, 1767.

Sir,

WE have on board 350 moy last and lay ready to sail which should do this day, was it not for want of propper Entelligence from your Brother which hope to here this Evening. Marketts here are low. a Virginia man arrived here three days past could obtain no more then 2/8 per Bushel for his Corn. I have ordred on bord for your account 2 Boxes Lemon, 1 Cask Lisbon Wine 8 Jars Oyle 5 Fl Figgs 5 do. Raisons. and I ordred Mr. Haley in London to make Insurance from here to your place £1000 on Ship and Cargo. I understand per a Brig from Marblehead and Cape Ann salt is much wanted: there is none at Cales they come here for it. Your Humble Servant,

JEREMIAH OSBORNE

JOHN POWELL TO CHRISTOPHER CHAMPLIN

Dear Sir,   Boston, 12th June, 1767.

BY Mrs. Powell I expected to have received the Survey on the hemp and the needful documents in regard to the *Maidstone's* Casks, to recover that money. It was not at first done right to put them in the provission Voucher, as the Commissioners are perticular careful the ships are not supplyed with Casks except the greatest Necessity, and strongest Proofs they do not make use of the Kings Hoops, etc.

I now do purpose to pay you a visit next week. If no thing very material should intervene to hinder and shall hope to have the pleasure to see Mrs. Grant before she goes to Long Island. I intend to bring with me little Jack, as he wants the air and a ride after his long Illness, to see his Grand mama, and Relations at Newport to whom our kind regards being Dear Sir Your most Ob. Servant,

J. POWELL

WILLIAM LUX AND BOWLY[1] TO CHRISTOPHER CHAMPLIN

Sir,   Baltimore, 31 August, 1767.

YOUR favour of the 18th Inst. reached us by this days Post. we shall be very glad to see Captain George here. We requested you to remit our Balance in Loaf Sugar, but that Article is become so plenty here on large Importations from London that it now wont answer. We therefore request you to send it in good bright Muscovado, or if that shoud be scarce and Molasses low, send it in Molasses. Our

---
[1] Daniel Bowly.

Crops of Wheat are shorter than formerly owing to a great drought early in the year, but the grain never was so good. very little comes to Market yet, what does sells at 4/9. Flour 15/, but as this days Post brings advices of the Harvest failing in Europe and that large Orders are expected to be sent out to America, we expect the Price will be high here. We are glad you have received the Cash for Mr. Mills Bill of £5.5. Stg. which remit as the other. We are, Sir, Your very hble Servants,

WILLIAM LUX & BOWLY

W. I. Rum	3/6	Molasses	1/9
Country	2/4	Flour	15/.
Muscov. Sugar	45 to 55/.	Bread	15/.
Loaf	12½		

ABRAHAM PEREIRA MENDES TO AARON LOPEZ

Kingston, 28th September, 1767.

Hon[ore]d Sir,

I MUST now acquaint you of my safe arrival in this place Saturday night after a passage of 33 days. I cant say agreeable, being sick all the passage, and was reduced very low, at my landing I could hardly keep my Legs, but hope in a few days to recover.

I found all my Relations, I must leave you to consider their Situation. My Hon'd Mother is reduced very low, owing to the great Losses she has meet with. I assure you, Dear Sir, the Condition I found her in shock'd me to the heighest degree.

I found Marketts very low, my Alewives I shall gett 23/9 a bbl. Dryd fish in great plenty; the current price is 12/6. I shall send all my fish and monhaden round the County in 2 or 3 days, as the latter likewise will not answer. I cannot give you an explicit Account being busy at present in entering and this opportunity will be ready to sail in 2 hours, but may depend of Occurans by all Opportunity. The Schooner arrived here Yesterday. Capt. Pyner handed me your kind Letter with that of my Dear

Sally which was great Satisfaction to receve. as yett have not received the Sweet Meets. this Opportunity being short shall omit writing my Dear Spouse, but beg youll embrace her in my behalf with all the Love of a Loving Husband, and assure her of my embracing all Opportunities. To my great Surprize I found Captain All in the Brig *Africa* which gave me great Satisfaction, as you seem'd to have been dubious of him. he waited on me at my arrival but being entertain'd with all my friends who did me the Honour to wait on me, could not enlarge with him, but understand he sold 11 Slaves at 15£ Stg. he told me they are the Refuse. I suppose he wrote you of the Transactions. You may rest assured, Dear Sir, that nothing in my power shall be wanting in assisting and forwarding his Business and hope with the Blessing of God to dispatch him in 2 weeks if wind and weather will permit. as I have not seen his Negroes cannot form any Idea how theyll turn out, but by his Account I make no doubt of procuring £25 Stg. for the remainder. the Small Pox at present being very brief [rife] have desired him to lay off with the Brig. He was offerd at his first arrival by one Mendes Pereira £30 this Currency round in Cash, and am informed he has lost 3 or 4 Slaves since in Harbour, this I had from a friend of mine. I receive my Dear Mr. Rivera's kind Compliments and am sorry could not embrace this Opportunity in writing of him particular; but beg you'll tender my best Love to him and Dear Mrs. Rivera and Little Abraham. as yett have not seen Mr. Livingston he being out of Town. I dont imagine I shall proceed to Sav. Lamar so soon as I expected, occasioned by my Weakness and the Holydays approaching; but directly after the Holidays will proceed and write of all Transactions. I must close my short Epistle with Assurances of all my Care and Means in your Business and all possible Means to render it agreeable to you. I wish from my Heart I could have given you a favourable account of Marketts, but assure you they are discouraging; but hope will mend, as its the Consequence of this place, either a feast or a fast.

My Love to your Dear Spouse and beg youll embrace my Dear Little Jacob and Hannah with many kisses. I was very sorry to hear of his ill turn but finding he was better gave me great satisfaction. My Love to my Sister and Brother Joseph and hope they are well. Youll be pleased to tender my kind Compliments to your Worthy Brother as all his family, Mrs. Rebecca Ropes and her family, as likewise your Brother David. please to present my kind Respects to Mr. Jacob Hart and all enquiring friends and accept of my warmest Love, Dear Sir,

My Hands with Weakness tremble in such a manner I can hardly write. I beg youll desist from procuring the Fishing Boat. My Hon'd Mother and the Rest of my Family tender their best Love to the family in generall. My Compliments to Myer Polock and desire he'll send me by first opportunity a full power, as there is a house in being and in the hands of one Flamengo a young fellow of no Credit. Mr. Salsadas was here 5 months since and has left him Atty. it seems Mr. Salsadas has likewise a house, and if Mr. Rivera will send an authentick account of Mr. Salsadas Debt likely I may recover something.

I could now despence with 1000 bbl. Alewives lett them be with Roes. by no means any more Monhayden, as it will not answer att all and at no price. I do not imagin I should gett 12/6 a bb. for them.

Common Board £5 to £5.10; Pine Do. £7 to £8; Sper. Candles 2/4 to 2/6. Oyl in no demand.

We lost 10 Sheep on the Passage. I imagine shall gett 18/ to 20/. The Black Horse looks very bad. I beg youll send me a Copy of my dead Brothers account sales and all his papers.

ABRAHAM PEREIRA MENDES TO AARON LOPEZ

Hond Sir,   Kingston, 29th September, 1767.

I WROTE you last per Capt. Jauncey via N York since having meet this good opportunity of Capt. Isaac All, would not slip writing a few Lines in giveing you all the inform in my power.

I tenderd your Letter to Mr. Livingston, and I assure you meet with a good prospect of settleing all matters agreeable. We have appointed next Thursday the 31 instant for a Settlement, when make no doubt but matters will be settled to my satisfaction. at Capt. All[s] arrival in this place, he waited on Mr. Livingston for the gold dust which was dld. to him, the amount was 3½ oz.

I stept on Board Capt. All in order to view the Slaves. I must now leave you to consider the Quality of them when there is not a Guinea Man in the harbour, the Guinea Houses most empty and the Contractors with the french are in want of Slaves, all this favorable Circumstance and Capt. All cannot dispose of his Slaves: the Reason is because the major part of them are small things, and those that are large has Age on their Side. But may depend my Assiduity shall not be wanting in assisting Capt. All in any thing that lays in my power. I assure you was the Slaves good prime Slaves, I make no doubt of his getting £40. Stg. round, as by all accounts there has not been for a long time such a favorable opportunity as the present.

Capt. All waits on me every day, and we consult and shall doe every thing that is most expediant.

Since I wrote my last, Thanks be to God, I advance bravely in gathering my lost flesh, and hope to be mending every day. I must now give you a more favorable account of our Marketts. there was a Vessell from Boston with 70 hhd. fish and the Capt. and myself have come to an Agreement not to sell our dryd fish under 22/6 by the Quantity. there was some fish sold at 12/6 but that was some old fish that the fitches had on their hands and was desirous of getting it off. my Alewives I make no doubt of getting from 22/6 to 23/9 or perhaps more. by no meens the Monhayden will not answer. Candles from 2/4 to 2/6, Onions at 12*d* per Bunch but slow, Oil in no demand as its not the Season, but what is sold at present goes at £6 per bb. White Staves at £9, Pine Boards at £7.10 to £8, Common do. £5.10 to £6. a Cargo of Carolina Shingles will answer, as they are now at £4 per thousand. flour of all sorts are very low at present. Mackrells at 9 dollars per bb., your North Carolina Herrings at 6 dollars per bbl. Hoops in very great demand. the Soap I broutt I sold at £5 per Ct. had we was luckly as to have come but 2 weeks sooner, Castele Soap was at £15 per Ct., but has fell to £7. I have sold a few of my Sheep at 23/9 each, not above 4 or 5, but the major part of whats left are in good order, and the holdays approaching shall send the Sailors to Markett with what I can, and make no doubt but will turn out pretty well.

By the next opportunity I hope shall be more at Leasure and will write you every occurance.

As for familys Buisness its out of my power to inform you. all I can say is, that the Death of my poor Brother will prove very fatal to me. I hope god of his Infinit Mercy will give me Health and Life to labour and doe as well as I can with my little I shall have. I am very sorry, Dear Sir, to fill your Letter with family's Buisness, but looking upon you as in the Room of my decesd father hope youll over look it.

My Love to my Dear Sally and hope she's well and beg she'll write by all opportunity. You'll be pleased to make my kind Love acceptable to all the family, particularly Dear Mr. Rivera and his good family, and conclude,

Dear Sir, with profound Respects Your Affectionate Well Wisher,

ABR'M PEREIRA MENDES

P. S. I beg youll not neglect giving my Littel Jacob many Kisses at the Recet of this.

Having the opportunity of Capt. Jauncey have preferd him. he was to have saild this morning early and has been detaind.

[Endorsed,] Per favor Capt. Jauncey via att N York, and to the Care of Mess. Gomez.

ABRAHAM PEREIRA MENDES TO AARON LOPEZ

Hon[ore]d Sir,   Kingston, 1st November, 1767.

My last to you was per Capt. Jauncey N York where I wrote you two different letters. I must now acquaint you of the safe arrival of the Brig *Industry*, Capt. Peters, after a passage of 31 days. he had the misfortune in loosing one of his Men two days after his departure, who fell from the topmast head struck on the Harning and fell overboard and there was no more to be seen of him. All the Horses are in pritty good order particular the Stalion; we lost 11 Sheep on the passage and 5 Geese. I make no doubt but she will meet a very good market, which will be determined by the Quality of the fish, as good fish is now at 23/9 per Ct. The disagreeable News I had of my Dear Sally made great Impression on me, but having that satisfaction to think she's under your Care, and finding by your letter and confirmed by dear Mr. Rivera's of her being recover'd, has been of great satisfaction to me. I wish in God my Business and the Season would allow my being a passenger on Board this Brig, should with all my Heart embrace this Opportunity, as my dear Sally's Indisposition has laid me under the greatest Concern, any thing in this world could have done. I must only wish the Almighty God may grant her health and life, that we may embrace each other, which I hope will be shortly. Capts. Newdigate and Pyner took their departure from this place 15th Ultimo. their detention has been longer that I expected occasioned by the many Holydays we had succeeding. the fish we brought prove very bad it was salt burnt occasioned it to be very black, and the Monhayden would not fetch 12/6 was oblige to dispatch the Schooner with 50 bbls Monh. and 5 hhds fish to Black River, where she sold the former at 20/ per bb. and latter at 22/6 per Ct. which I think was pretty well sold as he got the Cash. The Rest of the Monhayden and fish I sent to Sav. La Mar in the Brig, and have had Advise from Capt. Newdigate of his disposing them at 18/9 per bbl. and 20/ per Ct. for fish, being obliged to attend the Sales of the Brig *Charlotte* and in daily expectation of the *Industry* prevented my Journey to Sav. La Mar. At my arrival here I wrote a letter to Mr. Lopez and this's a paragraph in his Letter, "With respect to Mr. Lopez Outstanding Debts I am afraid the Season at present will not admit their being collected, but doubt not receiving the Whole in this Crop;" At my disposing this Cargoe which I hope will not take me above 3 or 4 weeks will immediately sett out for Sav. La Mar and will write you more on that head. To my great Surprize my Alewives per the *Charlotte* prove bad, and was oblige to sell the Major part at 21/3 and 50 bbls at 23/9 had they prove good should have got 23/9 for the Whole. I sold 50 Boxes Candles at 2/3½ and the rest at 2/4 per lb, which I think is a Saving prise. After loosing 22 Sheep the rest neated me £45, that's a very pricarious article and think will never answer. The onions of Brig *C:* prove bad. I sold at 10d per Bunch; the Schooner's I sold at 1/ per Bunch. at present there is no Oyl in Town. it being not the Season there is no great call for it. I sold 1 bbl. at £5.10. What I sold was to good people and will have my Money soon. I approve very much of your Scheeme in sending to Georgia. I believe will answer very well. Instead of Horses and Stock lett me advise to send for Lumber or Rice, for those articles seem to be in great demand.

I cant but think that a Vessell with 200 bbls good Alewives, good Codfish, Candles, and oyl will answer, as those articles are in demand; particular the Alewives as it takes very much here. I waited on Mr. Livingston for a Settlement he spoke in a very submisive manner, and related to me of his being out of his Money and will loose 4 or 500£ by those Sales. I told him that was but little Satisfaction to my friends, however a propose to give me his Bond p[aya]ble in 4 or 5 months and to allow Interest from the time the Money was due, and I absolutely think we cannot settle on better Terms: as for going to extreem's its very expence[ive] and perhaps may keep me 8 or 12 months, as the Lawers and Marshall's are very uncertain, his Absence from this place this 4 or 5 weeks obstruck my Settlement; but as he will be in Town in 4 or 5 days will settle with him on those Terms, which I hope will meet your Approbation and that of Dear Mr. Rivera. I consulted with my friend Mr. Banch and he thinks me very prudent in the Settlement, as his Bond is not inferior to the best in Town and dare say will be punctual to the time of payment. I shipped on board Capt. Newdigate 2 prime Slaves, a Man and Wench, which costed me £72 for both. they are young Negroes and very able. I ordered Capt. Newdigate to take one punch[eon] Rum at Sav. La Mar, but he finding it at 2/6 took 3 punch[eon]s. I thought it was more than was necessary, but hope he will make it answer his Expectation. I shall take care to be moderate in advansing his Cargoe, untill I see the proceedings of the first Voyage, But Logwood at present is £6 in this place. if we could be so lucky as to obtain that Prise, will give me Infinite pleasure.

I must now give you a Narrative of my Transactions with Capt. All. At my arrival in this place I heard of Capt. All being here, which gave me great Satisfaction, more so as I heard Negroes was in great demand. he paid me a visit the first day, but being very weak and obliged to receive company could not talk over matters. at the third day, I waited on Capt. All on board his Brig and to my great Surprise, I found the Negroes nothing to what I expected. However I laid down to Capt. All the consequence of his being detain'd, the great Expence his Negroes must be att, his portlage bill running up, and the Vessell receiving damage every day and the approaching Winter, and desired he would deliver the Negroes in my hands and would use all means to procure him 20 or 30 punch[eon]s Rum. He absolutely told me he could not answer the same as it was against his Orders. I made for answer that nothing but Mr. Lopez and Mr. Rivera's Interest which I have so much at Heart would have prompt[ed] me to purpose that Question. I dare say had he delivered the Negroes to me I could have sold them to good planters for a very good prise. All my means was not wanting in helping to dispose the Negroes but as his orders mentions Cash or Rum could not obtain it. I imagine he must att last yield to my proposition and you may rest yourself contented, that my utmost endeavours shall not be wanting, and hope very soon to give you good Tidings on this head. upon the whole I cannot totally blame Capt. All as his Instructions was so particular. But he knowing the great friendship I had contracted with the family, might have induced him to yield to my proposition. I have already in my last desired you would desist in building the Well Boat as the gentleman is now off this Island. I hope Capt. Potter's Voyage has answered our expectation which beg youll acquaint me.

My hon[ore]d Mother is now somewhat better than she has been. as for my part, I injoy a perfect State of Health and hope to hear the same from you and all the family, as nothing will give me greater Pleasure. Youll be pleased to make my Compliments acceptable to your Worthy Brother, and his Wife and Children, your Brother David, Tea Reaca [Rebecca?], and the Rest of the family, and conclude with my hearty wishes for you and Dear Mrs. Lopez Health, not forgetting my Dear little Jacob and Hannah, whom I so long to see. My Love to Josey and the rest of my Sisters and remain, Dear Mr. Lopez, Your Affectionate Well Wisher

ABRAHAM PEREIRA MENDES

P. S. Youll be pleased to make my Compliments acceptable to all friends.

Kingston, 8 November, 1767.

The preceding is Copy of my last per Capt. Sewel via Philadelphia who sailed 6 days past. as this opportunity of Capt. Dotee for Boston offers would not slip acquainting you of Occurances. I had all the Horses landed. they are in good order. I was offerd for the Stalion £35. I hope to gett £40 or £45 [and] to turn the Rest out at £30. as yett have not sold any. [th]e Sheep are as yet unsold as there is no Buyers. I sold most of my Geese at 5/7½ and but few of my Turkeys at 8/9. The Codfish proved very good but to my Misfortune two days after my Vessell arrived, there came in 2 fish Vessells from Boston, but I have the Satisfaction to say my fish are so good, that I make no manner of doubt, if we have not many Vessels from Boston to sell all at 23/9. I have sold 10 hhds. at 23/9. I must now observe to you of the Mistake you now labour under in regard to the Weights of those 37 hhds you mentions to contain 9 Quintals. a Gentleman desired I would weigh one of those hhds and to my great surprize it contain'd with the hhd 8½ Quintals, and suppose shall find a vast many more short of Weight, which will be attended with a great Loss and a vast deal of Trouble. I sold 12 bbl Alewives at 24/4½ and if the Rest proves good shall obtain the same. I sold 300 Wt. Cheese at 9d had they been of smaller size would have sold the whole.

I must beg youll send me per first Opportunity if the Season will permit 6 or 8 large Caser Cheese, 12 half bbls Tongues, and some pickle Geese as they will answer. I hope in 3 or 4 days to dispatch Peters for the Bay. Your Negro Boy I assure you behaves extreem well. I had 2 of our Sailors prest from on board our Brig. I made all the Application and Interest I could with the Admiral but prove ineffectual, more so as the Capt. had forgott his portlage Bill behind. May depend I shall note to you all my Transactions, and conclude with the profound's Esteem and due Regard, Dear Mr. Lopez Your friend and affectionate Well Wisher,

ABRAHAM PEREIRA MENDES

P. S. There is no demand for Naval Stores.

Youll be pleased to give my kind Complements [to] Our Domine and hope he's well and beg youll acquaint him of my making application to Mr. Cordova for what Money was due to him, and Mr. Cordova told me he paid his father and did not owe him a Copper. therefore I belive he must put this Debt amongst his Other Debts, that is to say, amongst his Bad Debts.

Poor Samuel Hathway is now dangerously ill with the Small Pox and belive will not survive. the Small Pox is very brief [rife] in Town, every week there is 5 or 6 Children buried with that terrible disorder.

[Endorsed,] Per Captain Dotee via Boston to the Care of Mr. Nathaniel Wheatly, Merchant, in Boston. Please to send this immediately.

ABRAHAM PEREIRA MENDES TO AARON LOPEZ[1]

Kingston, 18 November, 1767.

Hon'd Sir,

THE Preceeding is Copy of my last per Cap'n Dote via Boston, who saild 10 days hense as this good Oppertunity of Cap'n All offers would not slip writing, I have made mention to you concerning the weights of the fish which I must again repeat. I have sold 15 hhds and was obliged to weight the major part, which was deficient in there weights, some one Quintall and others more, which I make no doubt but youl be made good. I have got a particular account of them; if in case an Affidavit from me is requird will immediately send it, as I am sure the loss will amount to £40. as Cap'n All was obliged to depart he deliverd me Negroes as per inclosed Memorandum, which are in very poor order, and make no doubt but he'll Certifie and may depend on my utmost endeavours to dispose of them

---
[1] The original is in the Newport Historical Society.

to your best advantage. I will not mention any more concerning Cap'n All, as I wrote very particular in my last but yett think the whole of his Transaction might have been better transacted. however I must leive to your own Inspection. Seven days ago arrived here Cap'n Vernon from Rh'd Island and to my great soprise he brought me no letters, but gave me the greable news of all the family being well which I assure you it was great Sattisfaction to me. Cap'n Petters will sail from hense tomorrow; the westerly wind we have had for this 7 days past prevented him. as yett have sold but one horse, which was the poorest, and got £22 Cash for him. the rest I have sent down to W[ithy] Wood and dare say will answer. by next Oppertunity will close the sails of both Cargoe per *Charlotte* and Schooner. I must entreat your favour to write me by all Oppertunitys if its only a single line. I have at last made a Settlement with Livingston as per inclosed account and hope will meet with your approbation and that of Mr. Rivera. I just reced a letter from Mr. Gomes in answer to mine per Cap'n Jauncey and conclude, Dear Sir, Your Affectionate Well Wisher,

ABRAHAM PEREIRA MENDES

ABRAHAM PEREIRA MENDES TO AARON LOPEZ

Kingston, November 29, 1767.

Dear Sir,

THE above was wrote 11 days agoe was the time appointed for Cap'n All sailing, but his indisposition has caused his delay. the negroes which All deliverd me was in such poor order, occasioned by their being consignd on board his small Brig, that I was oblige to sell 8 boy and girls at £27, 2 do. at £45, 2 Women £35 each. I gott the Cash for the Boys; but the Vessell having poor Rigging and going on the Winter's Coast would not venture to rimitt by him the money, but shall wait for your forther Orders. Could I got Insurance made here would have rimitted.

The poor Success I had in receiving your Outs[tandin]g Debts and not gitting Cash for the Cargoes have not enabled me to rimitt untill March, when hope to send £14 or £1500 Sterling. I dare say you'l have your part of the negroes shiped home which shall not do until your Orders. I received your dear letter per Cap'n Bordene from the Eastward, who arrived after 24 days Pasage. I assure you it gave me great Joy to here all the family in general are well. Cap'n Cuningham arrived here after 23 day Pasage. I had the pleasure of seeing him. he likewise gave me the agreable news of the family injoying health. I have sold all my fish to 4 hhds. there came in a Vessell from Salem with 90 hhds fish which brought it down to 20/ per Cent. it caught me with 14 hhds, and the rest I sold at 23/9 and 25/. Cap'n Peters sailed 10 days sence for the Bay.

Having no more at present to impart must conclude with my Wishes for your good Health in Co. of all your family, particular dear Mrs. Lopez. have sent a Cag Olives which beg she'll except, and am, D. Sir, Your Affect. Well Wisher,

ABRAHAM PEREIRA MENDES

P. S. Youll excuse the Writing being oblige to gett a Young Cousin to scrible over.

GILBERT DEBLOIS TO CHRISTOPHER CHAMPLIN

Boston, Nov. 30th, 1767.

Sir,

I'M favour'd with yours per post and am sorry to find the Chest of Tea proves ordinary, but think you can by no means lay the Blame on me as it was the very same Chest you tasted yourself and mark't. therefore you must have been a better judge of the quality of the Tea then I who never had tasted it, and had no reason to think it was not good, have since sold five or six Chests of the same Teas you chose that out of; had I recommended said

Tea to you on my own judgment without your tasting of it, think it would greatly [have] alter'd the Case. I cannot therefore consent to take the Tea back again on the Terms you mention for this reason, that since you bout said Tea of me there has been large quantitys imported from London and Holland, which has reduced the price to ¾ L. My. per pound, and have been lately selling at that price which is really less than what mine cost me.

It is very like you have only try'd the top of the Chest which offen proves but indifferent when lower down proves very good, think therefore you better make farther Tryal of it, should be very glad to accomodate this matter [*an entire line missing*] for the most you can get for it altogether which method would save me a great deal Trouble in my present hurry of Business. I'm very conscious to my self that there can't be the least Appearance of Fraud on my part in this Affair. I am in great haste, Sir, Your most hble Servant, GILBERT DEBLOIS

CHRISTOPHER CHAMPLIN TO GEORGE CHAMPLIN[1]

Newport, 1st December, 1767.

Dear Brother,

I WROTE you a few lines by last post since which I have had no further news. by last Advice Flour at Philad'a 18/ and N. York 20 to 21/ that I fear you must give 17/ at least. however the great price at those places will occasion less to be shiped, that you may hope for 45 or 50/ per Barr. in the Islands. Capt. Durfey informs me if you tarry at Baltimore there is some danger of being froze in by 20th this month. I mention this that shoud any disapointment detain, it wou'd not be imprudent to fall down below the Town 2: miles at a place which Durfey says it does not so soon freeze.

Robinson the Colector is gone to Boston to take his seat at the Board of Commissioners who set twice a week at the

---

[1] The original is in the Rhode Island Historical Society.

Concert Hall.. you'll find the moon changes 20th Dec. at the same time comes to opposition of Saturn which may occasion some blowing Weather. it is not good to weigh anchor for the last time, the day before nor the day after. Write from Baltimore when you expect to sail and a short scetch of your Cargo. The *Garland* Mann [of] Warr is here and sails for England tomorrow; that We shall have none here next Spring. Rum at So. Carolina 10 to 11/ and dull. 2000 li Coffee will command the cash here at 24/, if not 25/, any time by the middle of April; it now retails at 32/ and none at market, tho' many will be upon the same plan that woud not run too much on it   1500 li Cocoa may answer   it's high in Boston, tho' small quantity may sell in the Spring to some advantage. Windward Island Rum at N York now sells at 3/7 to 3/9 quick, if you are early may command 3/6. Geo: Sears is returned; his whole Expense to git his Sloop, etc., cost 550 Dollars. This is the last letter I shall write as you may be gone 'ere another can reach you. Write from the Island by every oppertunity. I wish you success and safety. Your Brother,

CHRIS. CHAMPLIN

BENJAMIN WRIGHT TO AARON LOPEZ AND CO.

Savanna Lamarr, Jamaica, 2d January, 1768.

Gentlemen,

THIS serves to advise and acquaint you of my safe Arrival. I made this Island in Nineteen days, and were Seven days in sight of the Land, before I got into this Harbour, being almost calm. Have the Pleasure of acquainting you of getting my Horses in safe, and in very good order, notwithstanding, the terrible Gales of Wind I met with, before I could well clear the Land, which destroy'd the greater part of my small Stock, and had enough to do to keep the Ship off the Land, were obliged to carry Sail 'till the Seas broke entirely over me in order to keep myself from driving on Shore. Our Schooner *Ranger* arriv'd safe, and by all accounts had a blowing time off our Coast, has damaged no Goods. Captain Bardin has raised me better than Two hundred Pounds Cash, and as many Goods remaining on board as may amount to Eighty Pounds. Captain Charles Cunningham arriv'd here about Ten days before me, he disposed of all his Fish and Candles before I arriv'd, and in short almost all his Cargo, his Dry Fish at 23/9 per Ct., Spt'y Candles from 2/6 to 2/9. I have disposed of all my Dry Fish except about 20 hhds. have sold none under 25/ per Ct. have disposed of about 34 barrels Lamp Oil f'm £6 to 7£ Spt'y Candles I have sold from 2/6 to 2/9, have about 25 Boxes on hand at present. Could have disposed of every Box the first day I arrivd, if I would have taken 2/6. they seem determined here to go upon the prudent lay. I have been obligd to open two accounts for one box Candles, they are of opinion that Spt'y Candles will be plenty and cheap this latter part of the Crop, but for my part I see no likelihood of it, but the Reverse. My Shad am selling at 18/9 per bll., Sup. flour 35/, Tarr at 25/, Philadelphia Staves at 12£ per M, Rh'd Isl'd Staves at 9£ per M, Egg harbour Shingles at 40/ M, Boston Boards f'm 6 to 7£ M. All the Ports on the North Side are glutted with Northern Goods. I can't give any encouragement to send any more Vessels to this Island this Year, am afraid that Produce will break very high this Year, by the Accounts from Europe that Rum sold well last year in England, and if Rum should break high Molosses will be high likewise. In regard to Jno. Bours's order on Mr. Abraham Lopez in your favour, I have deliverd to said Lopez, and have received the Bonds to amount of said Order, which Bonds am sensible are very good. Shall not be able to raise any Cash or Bills with the Bonds, must take them in produce and glad to get that timely. I find the greatest part of those Bonds not payable 'till some time in May and some till June. I have taken the shortest Dates, I have bespoke good Bills to the amount of Five hundred Sterling, and can have Two hundred Pounds Sterling more, if I can raise Cash to purchase them; but never see Cash so scarce in this Isl'd since I knew it. I cannot get Bills for any Part of Cargo. Shall be much put to it to raise five hundred Pounds Sterling in Cash to purchase those Bills.

You may depend I shall not let any Opportunity slip may turn to Advantage. hope you'l not fail sending the Remainder the Ships Provisions, with the white Oak Staves and heading to make our Puncheons, and if you please to send per Captain Potter 40 Boxes Spt'y Candles, shall be able to dispose of them. Mr. Abraham Per: Mendez informs me he has acquainted you of my arrival which hope came safe to hand.

Nothing remarkable to acquaint you with. You may depend on hearing from me per all opportunities. hope I shall be better able to acquaint you in my next what Quantity of Bills I shall be able to purchase.

The Wine will not sell here at any Rate, my Dry Fish do not turn out to my expectation. Osburn did not give close Attention enough when they were putt up. If the Fish had been such as we desired him to get I should have sold them all before this Time. Am Gentlemen, with Great Esteem, Your most Obedient humble Servant,

BENJ. WRIGHT

JOSEPH AND WILLIAM RUSSELL TO AARON LOPEZ

Providence, 19th January, 1768.

Sir,

ACCORDING to our promise when at Newport we now write you conserning our Brigantine. the Indigo we talkt with you about find we shant have occasion for, as we bought some here while our W. R. was at Newport, which, with that we had of you on account of the Ship, beleive will be enough to last us the Season. The Brigantine is at your servise for three quarters in such English Goods as you have or can get that we want, and the remainder out of those you expect to arrive at the same advance we gave you on a/c of the Ship, the Iron to be replaced and the remainder in West India Goods at the markett price.

The Brigantine, Sir, as well as the Ship is a nice likely well built Vessell and very proffitable Vessell for the Buyer she being of the following Dementions: 52 feet Keel, 20 feet Beam, 9½ feet hold, and 4 feet between Decks, long floor, and tho' paying for but 110 Ton is judged to cary 125 or 130 Ton. she's all finnished except about ten days Joyners work. she is a very nice Vessell and fit for most any Trade. you'l let us have your answer by the last of this week.

We think it best and most prudent for you to send the master or some carefull person to go down in the ship. there is wanting some sheet lead for to put under the Catt heads as we have none at present and there's none in this place, wou'd have you send some up as its proper the Catt heads shoud be leaded and bolted, in case she shoud drop anchor in going down.

We remain Most Respectfully, Sir, Your Most Obedient Servants,
       Jos. & William Russell

P. S. if agreeable you may have the Sloop on the same Terms as we offer you the Brig. she is a pritty Vessell and faithfully built.

Henry Cruger, Jr. to Aaron Lopez

Bristol, February 13th, 1768.[1]

Dear Sir,

I HAVE now before me of your esteem'd favours those of 27th August with duplicate and triplicate 25th October and 7th December, and fully observe the Contents.

Herewith is an Account of the sundry Insurances order'd in the above mention'd Letters, Cost £303.15.6 Sterling to your Debit. these Accounts wou'd have been sent you sooner, but I postponed writing you from day to day in hopes of, nay! almost sure of advising you the arrival of the *Pitt;* but no *Pitt* yet appears, that I am tired of expect-

---
[1] Trecothick and Apthorp wrote from London, February 5, 1768, that the frost had been so severe as to shut up the Thames since the end of December.

ing. Disappointments throughout seems my Lott. did the Gods consider my pressing Necessities, they would certainly have granted Osborne more favourable Gales, and er'e now have safely wafted him to his destined Port.

I also hand you here inclos'd the Account Sales of your Pott Ash, net Proceeds, £126.7.0 Sterling to your Credit, please to observe one Cask upon using turned out so bad a Quality the man returned the remainder of it, say £1.3.9, which I think of returning to you for your Government, 'tis mark'd Jesse Baker No. 22.

Your Account has Credit for the Bounty on Deals per *America* last Voyage, £14.12.6, say on 14 hund. 3 qrs. and 9 deals at 20/ per Ct. less 4/ Expences on receiving it; also has Credit for £8.16 Sterling receiv'd from the *Underwriters* on the *America* last Voyage, for *Damage* her Cargo sustain'd which the Ship, alias yourself, was obligd to pay Mr. D. Phoenix on some Nails.

In your favor of 26th June you own receipt of an Account sent you in mine of 23rd March last, £18.17.9 which you say you had debited me with, as that account went away in our hurry uncopied, will be much oblig'd to you to *send me an exact Copy of it.*

I am the more impatient for the *Pitt's* Arrival because of her Logwood, which is every day tumbling down lower and lower; within these three Weeks 'tis fallen 15/ per ton. I have sold this last fortnight about two hundred Tons at only £4.10; and in London it is selling at £4, at which wretched price 'twill soon be here.

Pott Ash is mending, I think, and is in more demand than Pearl Ashes; Oil is selling, Brown at £22 per ton, White £24, not much at Market, Cotton Wool very low say 10d to 14d per lb.

As (I flatter myself) it now cannot be much longer before Osborne arrives, when hope to have some of your further agreeable Letters to answer, will for the present conclude with respectful Regard and sincere Esteem, Dear Sir, Yours, etc.

HEN: CRUGER, JR.

Abraham Pereira Mendes to Henry Cruger, Jr.

Kingston, Jam'a, 18 February, 1768.

Sir,

In consequence of a desire of my Father-in-Law Mr. Aaron Lopez of Rhode Island, I am to inform you that his Brigantine *Charlotte*, Capt. John Newdigate, is safe arriv'd here from the Bay of Hunduras, and as said Vessell is now bound a second Voyage there, I beg you would get Insurance made on her to the Value of £400 Stg. on the Hull from Kingston to the Bay of Hunduras, at or before the 20th Instant, and at and from the Bay to Kingston, the Value of £400 on the Hull and £300 Stg. on the Cargoe.

The Brigantine *Industry*, Capt. Peters, is safe arriv'd at the Bay and I expect her every day. as soon as she arrives I shall acquaint you thereof of further Insurance.

I shall in a little time make you a Remittance per Bill of about a Thousand pounds Stg. more. I would have done it before but this time of the year commands no produce which being the only Channell that Commerce is drove thro'.

I have not further to add but conclude with my Compliments and remain, Dear Sir, your very humble Servant,

ABRAHAM PER. MENDES

N. B. You are to observe that Capt. Jno. Peters now commands the Brigantine *Charlotte* from Kingston to the Bay. this is for your Government in regard to the Insurance.

John Powell to Christopher Champlin [1]

Boston, 19 February, 1768.

Dear Sir,

I HAVE to acknowledge the receipt of your Letters of the 8 and 17 Instant, with the Documents regarding the fresh Beef supplyed the *Garland*. Wilson's behaviour is extra.,

---
[1] The original is in the Newport Historical Society.

tho' I have met with some that would as willingly leave me the bagg as he did you. The Expence is great, Two Dollars and heavy postage. I fear if he may not skulk when he gets home and make excuses he was not with the Ship, and lay pon the Steward, etc. however shall send them forward to Mr. Law; wrote him long since to lay in a Caveat against passing his accounts. If ever receive it, will be attended with Loss and Charge. all Steps to over oblige these People meets with ill returns.

Freeman of Connecticut talks of sailing next week, takes in freight for Newport, by whom shall ship the Beef Pork and Butter. Please to write Mr. Joseph Richardson to ship you only Thirty Barr's Bread note are small, or as much as you judge will serve both Vessells till go to Hallifax. I judge the *Senegal* will stop here in her way to Hallifax, which you may hint to the Capt. for your Goverment in the Supplys.

If you think best to supply Loaf Bread, which never did, write Mr. Richardson for as much Flour and Cunals as may be needfull. It is impossible to know what turn Bread and flour may take, till May I judge will not advance. It may be lowest on the first opening the River, before any demand for Newfoundland, etc. If you can buy as cheap at Newport as can be imported, it will not answer to lay in more than really want to be at the charge of storage, etc., especially while so high. I have not ben able to get the Blank Certificates struck off, shall by the time you may want them, to send you. . . .

I am with great Regard, Dear Sir, Yours,

J. POWELL

JOSEPH AND WILLIAM RUSSELL TO RIVERA AND LOPEZ

Providence, 23d Feb., 1768.

Gentlemen,

YOUR favor per Capt. Brigs of the 19th inst. we received. We concieve a like Sattisfaction in cultivating a Commerce between us and are willing to improve every opportunity that offers for our mutual advantage.

We observe you consent to take our Brigantine on the Terms we offerd her to you the 19th ulto. and as the Captain approves of her we agree to lett you have her, and agreeable to your desire have deliver'd her to him and Mr. Hacker now takes her down to Newport as he order'd him with a Cable and Anchor. we wish her safe to your hands and likeing. As to the several articles you mention at the foot of your letter, we agree to take the amount of Ten pounds Sterling in H & H hinges, Fifty pounds of the same Indigo as we had last of you, the half Cask of Hobb Nails. as to the T Nails the seal of your letter happen'd to cover the Quantity, but we will take eight or Ten Thousand of 'em and not more, as we shou'd not know what to do with 'em, having Six Thousand now by us which will last us some years. As Mr. Ingraham the Joyner is not quite finnisht his work which he undertook by the job, he consents to go from home to compleat it on condision his board is paid; and as he has done the job very reasonable we have told him it shall be paid, which doubt not you'l comply with as it will not be but about a week.

We here inclose you the Brigantine Bill amounting too £619.5.0¾ Silv'r L. Mo., which you'l please to pass to the credit of our Account. We remain Gentlemen your most Humble Servants,
Jos. & Wm. Russell

Benjamin Wright to Rivera and Lopez

Savana la Marr, the 29th February, 1768.

Gentlemen,

Yours per *Betsey Ann* is now before me. find inclosed Captain Thomas Tillinghast's bill of Ladeing with an Invoice of sundries shipped on the joint Account of Owners of the Ship *America*, agreeable to Memorandum left with you, all which you have complied with the greatest Exactness, which layeth me under the greatest obligations to return the Complement as nearly as posable in complying with your Orders, and fulfiling every Incoragement I gave you in regard to remitting good sterling bills to Bristol. it is not in my power to acquaint you the Amount of Bills I remitt for your Account, as our Payments are so precarious in regard to what we shall receive them in; but am in hopes shall be able to remitt six hundred Sterling   you may rely on the goodness of those bills. in regard to John Bours Order flatter my self shall be able to gitt them discharged by close application and carrying the matter on ezey. find it will not answer at any rate to be harsh; they rather be sued then not, as it would gaive them longer time. shall spare no pains to serve Mr. Bours as I no his Necesity. att the Schooners arrivall at Kingston Mr. Mendez forwarded your letters, at the same time acquainted me of a mistake that happned he hoped would not fall under my Censure   he had bartred away twenty eight boxes my Candles for Coffee and sold four Boxes for Cash at 2/6 per lb. I thoat the above mistake ware verry extroadnearry as I know that you are verry particular in transacting your busness   could not amagine that you had made two Invoices for one percel Candles. the Captain likewise must be a novice to sign one bill of Loadeing to deliver the Candles to two different people. I rote them both on the subject in the plain language. Yesterday the schooner arrived here from black River. Mendez is here likewise. They now inform me they have twenty-five boxes for me so there is twelve boxes deficent. Those Candles had ingauged all at 2/9 per lb. You may rest asured the twenty-five boxes they are pleased to deliver me will go at the 2/9 per lb. had you sent 50 boxes more could have disposed of them at 2/9 per lb. Notwithstanding I have been obliged to sell Candles at 2/6 to raise little Cash. In my first via Georgie hope you have received dated the 2 January, wherein informed you the Prices I had sold att. I have now no Cargo on hand which came in the Ship except a few Hogsheads Codfish   am under no Apprehention but shall dispose of them soon   have sold sum dry fish sence

I rote you via Georgie at 23/9, as I found sum part of my fish not to answer our expectations, at any rate the last four bbls. Lamp Oyl I disposed of at 100/ hope shall be able to give you as good account of Oyl as any you ever sent this way, notwithstanding have suffered sum by Leekage. shall by next opertunity forward you Account Sales. shall willingly comply with your request in assisting Mendez in despatching the *Betsey Ann*. the schooner arrived here in a unlocky time, just as the produce begins to come to marquett. the price of produce is not yet broke to our likeing, and if we push hard for rum and molasses, am afraid it will be detremental and be the means of brakeing the price of Produce high, which will make a greate differance in the ship's Cargo. notwithstanding there has been one hundred and fifty Puncheons Rum purchased on the North side this Island at 2/6 per Gallon, yet we on the south side are striving to gitt Rum at 2/3 per Gallon. we do not chose the north side shall be a presedent for us; but wheather we shall accomplish our designs is yet unceartain. you may rest assured the *Betsey Ann* shall not wait for me. Mendez requests me to putt fifteen Casks Rum on board shall comply to his request timely. have now on board the Ship *America* sixty two hhds Mollases am takeing daly altho the price is not yet broak am afraid it will go at twelve pence per Gallon, as am sure Rum will be high the planters are not willing to part with there Molasses, espetally those that have Convenancy for destilling. Markets here is low and the Island much glotted with all most every article. Captain Potter being late will be to your advantage. shall spair no pains to make despatch am in hopes shall leave little or no mony behind me. if you determine that the ship shall come to this port next fall, I will lay before you what I think rally necessary to have provided timely, as the Ship may be here at least three weeks sooner: seven thousand hoops, five thousand white staves, six thousand reed oak staves, teen thousand Jersey boards, two thousand white oak heading, three hundred bbls splitt shads — those caught in the fall — fifty bbl Lamp Oyl, one hundred and twenty boxes spermcita Candles, sixty hhds best Codfish, fifteen bbls Tarr, teen half bbls Tallow, thirty thousand Eggharbour Shingles, 20 bbl pork, fifty barrels superfine flour, fifty bbls common Do. all the above articles procured timely so as the ship could sail one month sooner then she did last year. those articles procured timely would turn to advantage. it is fully my opinion that a Early Vessell to the north side would answer verry well with dry and pickled fish, and Candles, comon and fine flour. should you have a Vessel to bestoe on any poor young fellow would beg it as a favour to bestoe it on William Bardine, who I can recomend raly worthey your notice, and is verry capeable of disposeing of a Cargoe in this Island. his Industry this Voyage has given me a greate oppinion of him. we are all well on board have perfect harmony subsisting among us. Your kind assistance in getting my small part of the affects per the *Betsey Ann* insured at Bristol layes me under the greatest obligation, and greatly adds to the many favours all ready received. it [is] imposable to give you any information what time I shall sale. have nothing remarkeable to acquaint you with. Am Your Most Obliged humble Servant and Tenders of service,

BENJAMIN WRIGHT

N. B. I have exprest above that every thing of the Ships Cargo ware sold except 4 hhd fish, but I am mistaken; there is the wine on hand and eight thousand shingles.

B. W.

HENRY CRUGER, JR. TO AARON LOPEZ

Bristol, March 2nd, 1768.

Dear Sir,

THE *Sudden* Departure of this Ship, as the Wind is sprung up fair, will prevent my enlarging, but I have detained the Captain untill I can inform you that Yesterday Evening the Ship *Pitt* arrived safe at our Key after a very tedious and dangerous Passage. As no Goods are left for New

York, she shall be immediately dispatched for the Isle of May and Rhode Island.

I have received all your late favors, and have perused them with much Attention. the Contents will be observed; but 'tis impossible for me to reply to them by this Opportunity, as the intended Bearer cant stay any longer. next Week I shall dispatch two Ships for New York by them will do myself the Pleasure of addressing you again. in the meantime I remain with much deference and Regard, Dear Sir, your obedient and faithful Servant

HEN: CRUGER, JR.

[Endorsed,] Via New York. Per *Grace*.

March 9, 1768.

Dear Sir,

ABOVE is Copy of a few lines wrote you per the *Grace* in a hurry. the Ship *Pitt* makes a great dispatch in unloading. her Oil turns out excessive fine and good, tho' as Summer approaches, it lessens in Value and *demand*, we have so little night in Summer, the consumption by *Lamps*, compared to what it is in Winter, may be called nothing; and then Hot Weather is very destructive. I mention these particulars to point out the necessity of having Oil at Market early in the Winter. however, it will fetch a good price even now, because very little is at Market, save what is dayly brought from London, this market having been all the year, till now, above 30/ per ton higher than that, but the great Quantitys lately arrived there and brought round to this place, have nearly reduced our Market to a level with that.

The 6 hogsheads of Jamaica Sugar must be sold for Exportation agreeable to the late Act of Parliament, that all Sugars *from the North American Collonies* shall be *deemed foreign*. Osborne has brought 6 hogsheads of Rum, if they are tolerable they will pay at least a *good Freight*, as Rums are very high. the Pot Ash will sell for about £25 per ton; the Pimento about $7\frac{1}{2}d$ or perhaps $\frac{1}{8}$ more; the Logwood for about £5.10 to £6; the Oil, Elephants Teeth, Cotton, etc., I cant say exactly, but the inclosed Price Current will shew whereabout they are; you may depend on this, no pains shall be wanting on my part to obtain the utmost farthing for every thing.

As few Goods will be left for New York this Spring, except what are order'd by the *Owners* of the Vessels that are now loading for that place, Capt. Osborne will sail, without loss of time, for the Isle of May for a load of Salt, for the purchase of which he is preparing his Cargo, to the amount of about £120 Stg agreeable to your Orders. I shall take the Liberty to insure as usual £800 on Ship *Pitt* the Voyage round, having no doubt but it is your Intention and that you have forgot to order it. I hope you'll approve my cautious conduct.

Dear Sir, as you are very sensible of and seem deeply affected for the many *Inconveniences* and *Distresses*, your *great* and *long* standing Ballance hath for a good while past, heaped upon me; I will not recapitulate any of 'em, nor dwell much upon the disagreeable subject; for I flatter myself from the generous Steps you have taken, the period is not remote when our Correspondence will be carried on with more Satisfaction and advantage to both parties; the time, in my Mind, already dawns upon us,   but yet Sir, *'till the day is come*, can you be displeased with me for guarding against a return of those distresses in which your disapointments involved me, and out of which your Justice and Friendship are now with their united endeavours about extricating me? to get money by the execution of Orders is my Business, but yet I must pay some Attention to the reproaches of People, whom I cannot pay in a reasonable time; and a little too is due to my own peace of Mind. for these Considerations forgive me, Sir, for not executing your Orders. the Ballance of your Account must be reduced before I can be happy; and what remittances *are come to hand* have not greatly exceeded the *increase* of your Debt, as you'll perceive by your Account Current which I shall have time to make out by my next; you are so kind as to promise remittances from Jamaica. *they are not yet come.*

these are the unaccountable delays and woeful disapointments I so much dread.

Perhaps, Dear Sir, I say too much upon this subject. I would gladly say less, but am in pain lest I offend you, therefore thus candidly and explicitly impart to you the Honest Sentiments of my heart, that you may the better reconcile my Conduct.

The Ballance of your Account *is now* above £11,000 Sterling, the Net Proceeds of this Cargo will not be above £2,000. there then still remains £9,000.

I hope the course of this year will nearly if not quite reduce the Ballance, which will restore joy to the Soul of him who is now much distressed, tho' with *unabating Friendship* and sincere Regard, Dear Sir, Your faithfull humble Servant,
HEN: CRUGER, JR.

P. S. here inclosed is Account of £400. Insurance on the *Betsey Ann*. Cost £12.8.0 to your debit in Account Current. The few pressing Cloths you order for your Works shall be sent by Osborne.

[Endorsed,] Via New York Per *Ellis*.

BENJAMIN WRIGHT TO AARON LOPEZ

Sir,
Savana La Marr, the 9 March, 1768.

YOURS of the 16 January is now before me, have strictly complyed with your request. have shipped on board the schooner *Betsey Ann*, Thomas Tillinghast, Master, sixteen puncheons Jamaica Rum, for your own private Account and Resque, which hope safe to your hands and to a good marquett. the price of produce here is at last broke, and can assure you my heart is allmost broke with it, Rum at the extravagant price 2/6 per Gallon, Mollases at 12*d* per Gallon. if it had been in my power to have purchaced produce at the price it went at last year should have done sumthing worthy your notice, which might have united our new acquaintance more closely. Altho I have let no thing slip that might have served the Voyage, but as I am sensible you do not judge from Consequences only but from Real Causes, keeps me in spirits and pushes me hard to remedy the grevance by Despatch as much as lyeth in my power. hope my Actions will express that plainer then my words. Mr. Mendez luckely was here at Captain Andrews arrivall here, which was a great happyness for me, as I had just drawn out my accounts and began to dun the people which is a task soficent for one person. if Mendez had not been here, should have complyed with your request and dun every thing in my power to serve your Interest. Mr. Mendez sence Captain Andrews arrivall has reimbursed me with the Candles which he disposed of mine through a mistake, so every thing is set to rites of that affair. I have made use of my best Endeavours with those of my friends to gitt your Sloop away with as little Expence as posable did not let the Sloop come in to the harbour, got in with Collector to give me a permitt to land the Goods. the Sloop anchored at bluefield, sent all my boats with the schooner and onloaded her. Gave the Collector 23/9 for the permitt and cancelling certificate, gave the land waiter four bitts, and that was the whole of the Expence. am verry sure if Capt. Andrews had the conducting the affair you must have paid the pilotage in and out, which would have been four pounds entering, and clearing twelve pounds more. Mr. Mendez favourable accounts of the Marketts in this Island is a Mistery to me. I have sent our Tender to allmost every Port in this Island, found the marketts no ways inviteing, and many of the ports every thing dull and much glotted. I should be exceeding glad to be the Author of good news, but not ironically. We have now on board the *America* eighty-six hhds Molosses, and shall to morrow send to be filld forty more. Should have been one of the first Ships for home, had not Mr. Bours' order prevented. Have nothing more to add. Shall advise you per every Opportunity of my Proceedings. I am, Sir, With Great Esteem Your Assured Friend and humble Servant,

BENJAMIN WRIGHT

Abraham Pereira Mendes to Aaron Lopez

Sav la Mar, 11th March, 1768.

Dear Mr. Lopez,

I RECD your severall favors per Johnson, Tillinghast, Coddington, Andrews, and Brayton (with duplicates) all which gave me infinit pleasure to hear of your being in perfect Health in company of all our family to whom youll be pleased to make my best Love. Capt. Andrews meet me at Sav La Mar, which handed yours with Invoice and Bill Lading of Sundries to my address. We gott her clear with a reasonble Charge of 26/3 for all Charges.

The Sheep are all in poor order, most of them having the Swelling under the throat and the running in the Nose which prevented my disposing them. The Horses are in poor order. Some can scarce walk being old, which is the case of Northward Horses. The Staves are so bad that I cannot gett half price for them. I wish instead of those articles you had send Split Shads, Candles, and fish, which would have turned out to great advantage. the Oysters has not a handfull in each Cag. I see no posibility of turning the Cargoe in Cash, as I assure you there is many here, that has not taken as much Cash as will defray their port Charges, such is the Scarsity of Cash, but may depend shall follow your Instruction as soon as the money is collected. The Backwardness of our Crops and the great Rains we have had prevented my sending Tillinghast with a full Load, as most planters has pree-ingaged their first Rum, which was the reason Capt. Wright procured so many. I used all Meens but prove inefectual. have wrote my friends at Bl'k River to try all Meens to procure me as much rum as they can to accomplish her Load. Have noted all your Instructions in regard to a due Remittance to Europe, and may depend it shall be my constant Study to accomplish your earnest desire in all particulars. I observed yours and Dr. Mr. Rivera second resolution, concerning Hyers, which I think very prudent, as Logwood bears no price at Home, and quite a drug here, which gives me utmost Concern, as

we are so deeply connected in it. As yett have had no
tidings of Capt. Hyers, which when arrives will follow your
Instructions. I am very sorry my Buisness will not allow
me to be in Town at his arrival, as my presence is very
requisit. Mr. Lopez has advised me to collect your outstanding debts my self, as there is a greater probability of
receiving them. I assure you, Dear Sir, the Job will be very
tedious, as most of the people lives 20 and 30 miles distant
from this and having buisness at Black River, Withywood,
and Kingston, and more so at this critical time, which is
the Crop and my presence required in all these places I
cannot think how its posible I can support it, as these places
are 100 and 150 miles from each other, but shall pick up
Resolution with your Interest at Heart, and pray to our
Maker for Health and Hope to accomplish the whole, which
I will use my utmost endeavours to leave no Debts in Jam'a.
I have had the bad luck of receiving your Cargoes before
your Advices, which happed bad, as I was always caught
unawares. I shall take care if Pyner's Craft is sold at the
Bay, to place in the room of King, and assure you is care
and assiduity deserves encouragement. As I am oblige to
attend on severall people in the Country, cannot answer
your severall Letters explicit, but may depend of my utmost
attention to every particular. Capt. Pyner has returned
from the Bay and have ordered him round to Lucea[1] and
Montego Bay, where there is a probability of disposing his
Load, tho' I believe low. You may gett best Jam'a Logwood at £5 per Ton by 10 Tons. I am heartly sorry to
hear of Lemuel Wyatts unhappy misfortune, more so as
our friend dear Mr. Rivera sustained a loss. I am very
proud to find you had escape from the jaws of the lyon, as
you was always a great Shipper with the Coasters. I return
you my hearty thanks for your kind present per Brayton,
and am sorry times will not permit my sending any thing
good. Youll be pleased to make my Love to Dear Mrs.
Lopez, my Sisters and Brs. more so [to] my Little Jacob

---

[1] A village on the northwest coast of Jamaica, seventeen miles west of Montego Bay.

whom youll embrace with 100 Kisses for me. I wish I could see that happy day of Returning to your dear Companies as I assure you I am heartly tired of Jam'a and hope in God, these Journeys will not lett me suffer. I must entreat your kind favor to over look any ommissions as I could now quarter myself and find sufficient Business for each. I shall procure the Vine Slips and send per first opportunity, as time will not permit sending that quantity.

Please make my Compliments to Mr. Polock and acquaint him have taken his house in posesion, but cannot dispose of it without an authentick Power, and beg he'll transmit per first opportunity.

Since Capt. Andrews sailed from thence sold a Box Candles and at the opening of it found 5 or 6 Candles short. shall take care to weigh the rest and make a proper Memo. so that the fellow may answer for the same. he would not dlr the horse larning he says it was his perquisit. Must conclude with my best Esteem and pray for a continuance of Health and am, Dear Mr. Lopez, Your Affect. Son,

ABRAHAM PEREIRA MENDES

JEREMIAH OSBORNE TO AARON LOPEZ

Bristoll, March 20th, 1768.

Sir,

THIS serves to acquaint you that Mr. Cruger is willing to stand 1/4 in a Ship of 160 Tons, more or less, to use the Bristoll Trade. I will stand 1/8 the Advantages arrising from here to you, I need not at present point out if agreable, as I think it will [be], you may make the necessary preperation if the Ship at Providence, whose dimentions you ware pleased to communicate to me, is not disposed of, I think she will do and may be gott ready upon my Return to take in a fall freight. I think by our Connections with Boston we shall always be ready to secure a Retreat: I shall sail from hence the 10 April. Your Humble Servant,

JEREMIAH OSBORNE

Henry Cruger, Jr. to Aaron Lopez

Bristol, March 23d, 1768.

Dear Sir,

Since my Respects of 9th Instant I remain without any of your favors.

I will now proceed to tell you what Progress have made in the Sale of the *Pitt's* Cargo. The Piemento is sold the Casks at 7½d and the Baggs at 7⅜d per lb.; the Oil, Elephants Teeth, Mahogany, and Logwood were put up at Public Sale. the Oil sold at £24 per ton, and a few Lotts we took in to keep the Sale up are since sold at same Price. the Elephants Teeth were deemed very *ragged* and bad; therefore sold for only £13.17.6 per Ct. Mahogany went at 4d and one Lott at 4½d; it was but small. the Logwood, about 60 tons, sold at £5.5. the rest we continued to take in, by now and then knocking down a Lott at a Crown and half a Crown more, but to my Concern not a Soul wou'd give higher than £5.5. I'v since offer'd it at £5.7.6 and been refused, so shall be obliged to let it go at £5.5 but upon my Life 'tis not the value of the Wood, and yet it will be a dangerous Attempt to house, for the Kingdom is as full as it can well be, thousands of tons are stored upon Speculation; but I'll be hanged if it is not lower before it's higher. the Purchasers of your Wood assure me it is not above half chiped — for my part, I know not what they'd have. The 6 Hogsheads of Sugar I have refused Money for, the offer being very low, occasion'd by markets abroad being so. had these Sugars come directly from the place of their Growth they wou'd have sold for at least 10/ per Cent higher than they will now. they cannot be consumed in England. Osborne has landed his Rum; it is devilish bad, have yet sold none of the Pott Ashes nor Cotton.

Captain Osborne has put the *Pitt* in dock; she much wanted it. she will be out in a day or two, and take in her Ballast, her Cargo being almost ready I know nothing that will prevent his sailing for the Isle of May by the 10th next

Month. Osborne informs me a freight is always to be had at *Rhode Island* for this place; if so, I wish you'd write my father, as imagine he'll be glad to send the *Pitt* back, if any body wou'd give her a good freight.

Dear Sir, Captain Osborne thinks it is your Inclination to establish a Vessel on this Trade and that it may be done to an Advantage. he thinks it will be agreeable to you for me to hold a part in her. if you approve the Plan, I'm very willing to hold a Quarter in any Vessel you chuse, and I have no Objection to being concerned in a like proportion of any Cargoes you may from Time to Time send home in said Vessel. Osborne wishes to hold a 1/8 in her, as to that, I have no Objection if you have none. what Advantage he promises to himself from it I can't find out, nor what Benefit he'll be of to the Ship. as you'll see him soon after you receive this, I'll say no more than that I shall be perfectly satisfied with any thing you do. I remain with much Esteem and Integrity, Dear Sir, Yours, etc.

Hen: Cruger, Jr.

P. S. No Remittances from the West Indies are receiv'd by yours, etc. H. C. Jr.

Tar 5/6 per B'll; in Liverpool only 4/6 per B'll.

Jeremiah Osborne to Aaron Lopez

Bristoll, April 1, 1768.

Sir,

This serves to acquaint you we are still here, have begun to take in and if wind permitts shall sail per the 10 Instant for the Isle of May. I have endevoured to procure what knowledge of the Trade I could. I was obliged to go into Dock to fix her Ruther one of the Gudgings being brook. I found her false Keele knocked of, which judge was done at the Long Whorfe before we sailed. the Iron bound Cask in which the Rum was put at Rhode Island were exceding fowle and have hurt the sail both at Milfood and here. They would not buy it att all at Milford, and in case it had been ordenary, at present it would have fetched 9/. Per Captain Holmes via Boston Mr. Cruger wrote you respecting his being concerned in a Ship 160 Tons more or less. in expectation of seaing you, I remain Your Humble Servant,

JEREMIAH OSBORNE

6 m [ ] Hams will do here in the Fall. if good will fetch from 6 to 8d per pound as many as you can send.

HENRY CRUGER, JR. TO AARON LOPEZ

Dear Sir, [Bristol,] April 6th, 1768.

PLEASE to be refer'd to the foregoing. the *Pitt* will be ready to sail by the 10th Instant, by the first Opportunity, after her Departure, will send you Invoice of her Cargo, also an Account of her Disbursements.

When the Purchasers took away their Oil and strictly examin'd it, they found, to use their own Expression "a good deal of foul Play," a mixture of Whale and Sperm   the good was as clear as Crystal; the adulterated was like melted *Butter*. Osborne was shewn the difference which he promises to point out to you. I am very glad there are not many Casks in this Condition, for they insist upon a Survey and an Abatement on the few that are bad. I have sold the remainder of the Logwood at £5.5; the Rum at 7/ per Gallon. had it not been very bad it would [have] sold for at least 9/. The Pott Ashes are sold at 25/ per Ct., 3 months Credit. in London it is 27/ per Ct. the other day this Market was 20/ higher than that. The 6 Hogsheads foreign Sugars are not yet sold, no Demand for Exportation. The Cotton, being a very dead Article, sold for only 10$\frac{1}{4}d$ per lb. some of the Plank is sold, some not; by my next hope to furnish you with Sales of every thing, and your Account Current up to the Day I send it. In the Interim I remain with immovable Regard, Dear Sir, Your most humble Servant,

HEN: CRUGER, JR.

P. S. Upon asking Capt. Osborne for the proceeds of what Rum he had sold in the Channel, he gave me for answer that he would settle with you but had no Money to pay me. This I mention for your Government.

[Endorsed,] Per Capt. Hull, Q. D. C.

Henry Cruger, Jr. to Aaron Lopez

Bristol, April 28th, 1768.

Dear Sir,

I HAVE before me your esteem'd favors of 15th and 29th February, the first cover'd my Father's draft for £61.0.1¾ Sterling in your favor, which is passed to your Credit in Account; the last order'd £1800 Insurance on the Brigantine *Diana*, Captain Potter. it is effected as per Account herewith, Cost £117.16. to your Debit.

Last week I rec'd a Letter from Mr. A. P. Mendez desiring me to make Insurance for your Account on the Brigantine *Charlotte* from Jamaica to the Bay and back again as per Particulars herewith. it is done and the Cost is £35.14.0 to your Debit, as is likewise £24.8. Premio on the Ship *Pitt*, as per Account herewith. her Cargo is insured you'll find by the Invoice inclosed, which amounts to £193.13.5 Sterling to your Debit. we have exceeded your Limits in this Cargo. 'tis Osborne's doings, who will give his Reasons. please to observe the Cargo by the *Pitt* is insur'd only to the Isle of May; what Cargo of Salt, etc. she takes in there, you are (if you please) to insure to Rhode Island. you have Bill Lading for the present Cargo to the Isle of May, and Osborne's Receipt for the pressing Cloths as per Invoice, amounting to £19.0.1 Sterling. you'll find here Plantation Certificates to cancell your last Bonds, on the *Pitt* who has been cleared and ready to sail this fortnight, but detained still by stormy adverse Winds.

For your future Guidance, let me inform you, it will not do to send North American Rum to England, because by the last Regulations no Rum imported here can *draw back the Duties* but what comes *direct* from the British West Indies, and Rum from North America (altho' it may be made in the West Indies) is deem'd North American Rum and may not *be exported.* of course it labors under too great Disadvantages to leave any Profit.

Am sorry 'tis yet out of my power to render you Account Sales of the *Pitt's* last Cargo, but the Sugar sticks on Hands because we have no demand from foreign Markets, where *only* they can be consumed as they came from North America. The Staves too remain unsold, this place is so full can get no body to buy them. the Boards are all sold. I have had some plague with the People who bought your Oil, concerning what I mention'd in my last. however have at last finally settled by letting little better than 4 Tons in the whole, go at £20 per ton. this I suppose will put you upon a more precise Examination of what you in future send.

"Sad Hours seem long." *no Remittances* yet from Mr. Mendez. these severe Disappointments make Trade, nay my very existen[ce,] a Burthen. I assured many of my Creditors they should be made easy by the month of March, relying on the flattering hopes Mr. Lopez gave me. they are angry, I am unhappy. your Ships go out full freighted, return in like manner, end a successful Voyage — but produce *nothing* to your friend Cruger, who endures the Heat of the Day. I do not envy you your Gains, but from a sincere and dejected Soul assure you, no Consideration, (could I but have foreseen what has happen'd) should have brought on me such heartfelt Misery as your large Ballance, or more properly the Consequences — I mean *close Dunnings.* oh God! at times it half kills me, but I'll say no more, as am sure it must hurt you. I heartily wish you, Dear Sir, Success in every undertaking you have employed our Money in, and that all your Ships may prove as profitable to you as they are otherwise to him who remains, with unremitting Regard and Deference, Yours etc., Humble Servant,

HEN: CRUGER, JR.

P. S. The Cask [of] Pott Ash Jesse Baker No. 2 which I advised you was bad and return'd on my Hands, I have put on board the *Pitt.* you will find it included in same Receipt as the Pressing Cloths. Inclosed is Osborne's Receipt for £50 Sterling advanc'd him on account Ship *Pitt,* for which he will account with you. 'tis a great deal of Money; however that you two are to settle.

H. C. JR.

HENRY CRUGER, JR. TO AARON LOPEZ

Dear Sir, Bristol, June 1st, 1768.

MY last Respects to you was the 28 April, since which am favour'd with your agreeable Letters of 25th March and 12th April, the first cover'd my Fathers Bill on me in your favour for £102.8.0 Stg. said Bill is passed to your Credit in account.

I have receiv'd from Capt. Benjamin Wright of your Ship *America,* four Bills at Sixty days sight amounting to £461.7.6 Sterling. they are all accepted, and when paid shall be to your Credit in Account Current with my thanks.

I now inclose you Sales of the *Pitts* Cargo, Net Proceeds £1869.11.2¼ Sterling to your Credit; also Sales of 10 Elephants Teeth, Net Proceeds £41.14.4 Sterling, 2/3rds of which, say £27.16.3, is to your Credit. you likewise will find herewith account of Disbursements on Ship *Pitt* amounting to £352.9.4 Sterling to your debit.

Inclosed is your Account Currant up to 20th Ultimo. Ballance in my favour (Interest included) is £9760. — .8 Sterling to your Debit in a new Account.

I expect to write you again before the Sailing of this bearer so will for the present conclude with Esteem, Dear Sir, Your most Obedient humble Servant,

HEN: CRUGER, JR.

I am now at 5th July. have receiv'd no more of your esteem'd favours, *nor any remittance from Jamaica.* I know not what to say of Markets. inclos'd is a price Current for your Guidance. Oil is likely to keep up all the summer, and in fall there is no Danger of its keeping up. I find 4 Inch Ash Plank (as long as possible) answers very well.

JOHN POWELL TO CHRISTOPHER CHAMPLIN [1]

Monday, 13 June, 1768.

Dear Sir,

I HAVE yours with the Certificates 2d Supply to the *Senegal.* Your ps. Silk was put in a package of Mr. Dublois, which desired him to tell you is now at my House, and shall be sent you by the first good Oppertunity. The Bale sent by Brown's Waggon am glad is got safe. I expect to hear from England in regard to the Essence, till then must have patience. It would have been better not to have disco[unted] any Oatmeal, as attended with a Loss, and 2 bushels could be no object to the Purser. You had better charge a Com[mission] on the Supplies, and what you judge proper on rect. and delivery of any article sent you, as God knows now when shall see you. Jenny is freer from pain than has been, but confined to her Chamber, and the Sons of Liberty have declared open Warr. The fatal consequences are obvious. The Com's have taken shelter aboard the *Romney* [2] and Mr. Harrison [3] and family at   .[4] I could wish my self and family at Newport. Jenny was much agitated a Friday night as the mob continued some time in King Street, with their usual Exclamations, and what is to come next God knows.[5]

---

[1] The original is in the Newport Historical Society.
[2] They landed at Castle William, where the Board held a session June 21.
[3] The collector of the port.
[4] A blank.
[5] "June 10. Some Damage to Mr. Harrison the Collector and his Boat Burnt." *Letters and Diary of John Rowe,* 165. "Last Friday Evening [10th] some Commotions happen'd in this Town, in which a few Windows were broke, and a Boat was drawn thro' the Streets and burnt on the Common; since which things have been tolerably quiet; it being expected that the Cause of this Disturbance will be speedily removed." *Boston Gazette,* June 13, 1768. "Last Friday evening, the officers of the customs for this port, made a seizure of a sloop lying at Hancock's

Please to tell Mr. Hyers the box or Cagg Sweetmeats were d'd out of Mr. Hughes Store with one sent Mr. Oliver of Cambridge last week. I wrote him about it but have received no answer that I fear has made use of it. Please to keep the Butter remaining in a cool Cellar, and sprinkle a little fine Salt on each head, when issue it. I am with kind regards to all friends, Dear Sir, Yours

J. POWELL

BILL OF EXCHANGE

St. Augustine, 24th June, 1768.

£30.17.5

THIRTY days after sight of this second Bill, first not paid, pay to the order of John Mason, thirty pounds seventeen shillings and five pence sterling, value of him, and place that sum which has been laid out for Lumbering and plaistering to the Contingent Account of His Majesty's province of East Florida, as per General Account and Vouchers herewith transmitted.

*Florida, as per —
James Grant*

To William Knox Esquire
Crown Agent for his Majesty's
Province of East Florida,
London.

---

wharf, and which they ordered to be carried off under the guns of his Majesty's ship, Romney. — This affair occasioned a dispute between the officers and some of the people who happened to be on the wharf; in which Mr. Harrison the Collector, Mr. Hallowell the Comptroller, and Mr. Harrison's son, were all pelted with stones and wounded. — Soon after which, a number of people assembled, went to the house of Mr. Williams inspector-general, broke some of the windows of his house; as also, of the houses of the Collector and Comptroller; but were prevented doing further Damage by some gentlemen of the town. — After which, they burned a pleasure boat belonging to the Collector in the Common. — Mr. Devine, Inspector of Exports and Imports, was also attacked the same night; he had his sword broke, and with some difficulty made his escape with the assistance of some of the people present." *The Boston Chronicle*, June 13, 1768.

JAMES LUCENA TO AARON LOPEZ

Savannah, in Georgia, 28 June, 1768.

Dear Sir,

THIS will be delivered to you by Captain Nathaniel Waldron. he is to proceed from this port to the Windward Islands there to procure a Cargo of Molasses, and other produce, and then he is to proceed to Rhode Island, and deliver to you what Cargo and money he may have belonging to me, to be invested in Rum, and what you think proper for the intended Voiage to the Coast of Affrica. If Captain Waldron proceeds the Voiage round, he is to have from the time he first takes in any part of the Cargo, the customary wages and privelege given in general from Rhode Island to a Master of a Vessell of the burthen of myne. The mate John Brown is also to have the customary wages and privelege of Rhode Island, to begein from the time the Molasses Cargo is delivered.

And neither of them are to receive of you any wages for the west India and Affrica Voiage being agreed the whole to be paid here. I desire of you to let me know the time when the alteration of their Wages takes place, as the wages they now go for are very high.

As this Letter will not come to hand this long while, I will take other opportunity to write more at large and Remain, Sir,

Your Affectioned Cozen
James Lucena

P. S. As we are not acquainted what are the customary wages and privelege to the Coast of Affrica is left to you to determine it.

ABRAHAM PEREIRA MENDES TO AARON LOPEZ

Savanna Lamar, 25th July, 1768.

Dear Mr. Lopez,

I RECEIVED your many kind favors, the last per Captain Potter, which gave me the agreeable News of Dear Mrs. Lopez safe delivery of a Boy, may the Almighty grant Health and Life to the New Born. I am very sorry had not the pleasure of being present on that happy Event. Capt. Potter came to bad Market, as he was late he sold his fish at 17/6 for Cash, and went to Northside 3 weeks since. As my Business required my presence here, was oblige to quit the Town. my second Voyage here as caused me a Surfeit and a fitt of the Gout, which has laid me up three weeks, and am now in a most deplorable Condition and cannot mount my horse, which has put my Business backward. Captain Hyers arrived in Town during my Absence. I never expected his Arrival as he was so long on the Voyage: my friend in Town have disposed of his Cargoe, and as I had not a particular Account of the Sales, must refer and by the Bearer, which I hope will not exceed 6 weeks, as I would glad by escape August. The Bay Voyage's has intirely disconserted all our desires as the Vessells made long trips. the Brig *Charlotte* have compleated her second Voyage 4 weeks since, as was oblige to send her back to the Bay for the Wood we have there, and have ordered from thence to Rhode Island. I engaged 120 Cask Molasses, which with 20 punch. Rum would have compleated the *Industry* Cargoe. as there was no Vent for her first Trip in Town, and being much afraid of Great Charges, was oblige to send her to Lucea and Montego bay, as I wrote you before, as the Weather was boistrous and her Sails bad, kept her on that trip a considerable time, and at her arrival at Withywood my Brother applyed to those people with which I engaged my Melasses, and to my Misfortune has disapointed me. there Reason was that I did [not] take their Melasses when it was ready, which I could not doe, as the Brig was not present, and for me to take Melasses to lay on the wharfe I should certainly loose the whole, as you are convinced [of] the precariousness of that article. I assure you, Sir, I would willingly give £100 than have been concerned in the Bay Voyage. the Vessells has been 55 days beatin up to Kingston, which has shattered all their sales, and Wood so discourageing that I could not gett any thing for it here, not even £3.10, which would have taken rather than ship which was my last shift. but as its on a reasonable freight, which is 25/ Stg., am in some hopes it may answer, as that article is at £5.10 Stg. per ton. I am at present in great Concern as I have the money by me and cannot procure a Load of Melasses; more so as I am so uncivell and cannot proceed to Withywood for fear of the Consequence, I am much afraid your Out-Standing Debts will not be collected, not for want of my caer, but the people being incapable. I have shipped on board Captain Hyers 12 punch. Rum, and have made bold to alter your Orders in sending her back to Georgia, which I am sure could not be your Intention did you know her detention in Georgia would be so long, and I should not be here to receive from Georgia, have thought proper to alter her Voyage, which hope will meet yours and D[ear] Mr. Rivara's Approbation. I was debating with myself to send her in Balast, but as there was Concerners have shipped Rum, which is very heigh, Captain Elliott have shipped 169 hides on board, the freight of which you'll settle.

Must conclude with my kind Love and Rigard to Dear Mrs. Lopez, Joseph, and my little Brothers and Sisters, as likewise your Dear Brothers, to whom youll give my kind regard, and am Your Well Wisher,

ABRAHAM PEREIRA MENDES

I have paid Capt. Hyers to 24 July for his Expences a shore, amounting to £14.16.3 this money .

HENRY CRUGER, JR. TO AARON LOPEZ

Bristol, 1st August, 1768.

Dear Sir,

SINCE my last am favored with your's of 20th May. it requires no particular Reply, further than to notice my father's Bill on me for £250.18.7 Sterling, which is passed to your Credit. I wish it had been twenty times as much; my Perplexities almost turn my Brain, from too frequently revolving my Disappointments I can't help often crying out, I hardly know whether Mr. Lopez is the innocent or intentional Cause; whether it is, or is not in his power to relieve me from all this Distress, provided he would a little distress himself; but the Cause you certainly are, Sir, of making me a most wretched Man, by living in perpetual fear that the Patience of my Creditors will be exhausted and my Affairs brought to a Crisis, good God avert it, a Crisis that am sure would kill me, and to tell you the Truth, I do not expect Indulgence after this year. you now know the whole, and if you are benevolent you will exert even a desperate Effort to save a young man from so early in life being obliged to unfold and expose the State of his Affairs — a State he seldom gets over. I do not let any body know it is you, Sir, that has brought me to this Precipice. I would not injure your Character nor Credit for the World; but yet, as a *categorical* Answer has been demanded of me to the following Question, "When do you expect any considerable Remittances from America?" I am under the Necessity to desire, (tho: with all Deference) from you, the same kind of Answer to this, What will you do for me by Christmas, that can be *depended upon?*

I beg of you, dear Sir, not to flatter yourself or me with Remittances from the West Indies, (Experience has evinced) they are not to be confided in. you have buoyed up my hopes with Expectations of a Remittance from Mr. Mendez, and I amused my friends with that Phantom above a twelvemonth — alas! the Dream is out, and none of us here the richer. cruel, hard fate, *not a line nor a Penny from Mr.*

Mendez, perhaps 'tis his Fault alone. however, Dear Sir, my Credit is now come to this pass as to admit of no longer Delay. I give you this previous Notice — much will depend upon your Answer. whilst I can keep my Creditors in Temper and forbearance, no doubt for *both* our Sakes I shall, for I sincerely am your hearty Well Wisher, and most Obedient Humble Servant,
HEN: CRUGER, JR.

P. S. After maturely weighing the matter, I would gladly be off holding the 1/4 of a Ship (mentioned a short time ago) in Company with your good self and Captain Osborne; my Circumstances in their present Posture won't admit of it.

Musqueto Mahogany I think is getting up again. a small Cargo sold the other day from 5d to 6d per foot. ut supra et semper,
H. CRUGER, JR.

JOHN POWELL TO CHRISTOPHER CHAMPLIN [1]

Boston, 23 August, 1768.

Dear Sir,

. . . .

THE Town is at present very quiet but God knows how long may continue. is Bohea Tea in any demand with you. I have had 10 Chests by me some time very good. Our wise Merchants have prohibited the Importation from Great Britain. Only, 100 Chests its said some months since, came thro' the Newport Turnpike to this Town.[2] Remember us to all the family. I am with Aff't Regards, Dear Sir, Yours,
J. POWELL

when did Mr. Grant hear from Jamaica? I have no Letters since 3d March. was then in hopes to have seen him by this.

---

[1] The original is in the Newport Historical Society.

[2] In June tea was freely advertised by merchants, but after the middle of the month offers ceased for some weeks. In August Bohea again appeared, "by the hundred, dozen, or less," in the advertisement of Joseph Barrell.

HENRY CRUGER, JR. TO AARON LOPEZ

Bristol, 19th September, 1768.

Dear Sir,

I AM favored with your exteemed Letter of 7th July, and duely note the Contents. Permit me to say, I am well pleased to be off holding a Share in the proposed Vessel, for the very Reasons you give — they are indeed a losing article.

I shew'd your Letter concerning the thick Oil, to the Purchasers. they persevere in saying it was not Sperma Caeti, because, *that* always subsides and leaves the Oil as clear as Water. I could not contradict them, but wished the next Cargo I receive from you may turn out *clear* as did the greatest Part of the Parcell in Question, with all the Sperm pitched to the Bottom, as such gave high Content.

In my Letter of 1st June, advised you of Capt. Wright's having remitted me on your Account Bills to the amount of £461.7.6 Stg. which are all paid; and have since received from him £195 Sterling that are accepted, and when paid will be passed to the Credit of your A/C.

not a Penny yet from Mr. Mendez, 'tis terrible! if he felt my Sufferings, imagine he'd find Means to make the Remittances, you promise, and my Distresses are so anxiously longing to receive.

to avoid the Repetition of unpleasing Words, must request your Reference to my last under date of 1st August, which Letter, I ardently hope, will meet the Weight and Attention the Sincerity and Exigency of its Contents so loudly call for.

please to see the State of our Market by the inclosed Price Current. I remain with unalterable Regard and Deference, Dear Sir, your most Obedient Humble Servant,

HEN: CRUGER, JR.

Henry Cruger, Jr. to Aaron Lopez

Dear Sir,   Bristol, October 3, 1768.

SINCE the above Copy of my last I remain without any of your late favors.

I have receiv'd a Letter from Mr. Jacob Melhado, Sr., Copy of which you have inclosed, ordering Insurance on the Brigantine *Charlotte*, Account of which you have herewith; Cost £ [blank] to your Debit. it gives me pain to write what am going to do, but your Remittances come so horridly, I must beg as a favor you will not increase your Debt, by ordering me to make any more Insurances for you, unless it be on Vessels or Goods bound to this Port, for which I stand a Chance of being paid; for really every now and then, Despair seizes me, and holds me in Torment untill I am for a little Interval releiv'd by the fair Contents of your Letters; how far they have been complyed with, the Ballance of your Account can fully answer; but for the present I'll say no more; 'twould be a Satisfaction to me, altho' a poor one, just to know how it happens that Mr. Mendez hath not yet remitted me one farthing out of the large Sum you expect he has; if he could not remit me £1500 or £2000 he surely might have made a beginning, by remitting me £300 or £600 or £700, where the fault lies I can't tell, but I must add, it don't look well.

Whatever Insurance is order'd on your Account before you receive this, you may depend upon it's being done in the best manner in my power, but after the receipt of this, hope you'll expect me to do no more for you (unless it be on what you may be sending to this Port) untill your Account is ballanc'd, an Account that has more than once nearly prov'd fatal to me; Wherefore, I must again and again implore you to pay due Attention to my Letter of 1st August. I remain, Sir, Yours, etc.

                                        HEN: CRUGER, JR.

P. S. Inclosed is additional Disbursements on the *Pitt* amounting to £22.17.9 Sterling to your debit.

[INCLOSURE]

Kingston, Jamaica, 4th July, 1768.

MR. HENRY CRUGER, JUNIOR.

Sir,

THIS is to acquaint you that the Brigantine *Charlotte* is arrived from the Bay of Honduras, and is ready to proceed another Voyage there. therefore I am desired by Mr. Abraham Pereira Mendes to inform you to get her insured, under the Command of John Piner who goes now Captain of her, from Kingston in Jamaica to the Bay, and from the Bay to Rhode Island (Newport), the sum of Four Hundred Pounds Sterling on the Hull, and three Hundred Pounds Sterling on the Cargo. have nothing farther to add. I remain, Sir, Your very humble Servant,

JACOB MELHADO, SENIOR

P. S. Mr. Mendes wou'd have given this advice himself, but his being out of Town prevents it.

HENRY CRUGER, JR. TO AARON LOPEZ

Bristol, October 18th, 1768.

Dear Sir,

I AM favor'd with your esteem'd Letter of 29th August. the Contents affects me a great Deal. I am heartily sorry that my Letters shou'd make you unhappy. I would not write in the manner I do, could I help it; but, Sir, if you knew the distress your great Ballance has plunged me in, you wou'd excuse almost any thing I cou'd say, for it was the Language of a greatly troubled mind. I will wound your Mind with no more Dunnings, if my Creditors (with theirs) will shew me Mercy; the contrary Behaviour in some of them, stings me to the Soul; how can I help complaining to the principal Cause — but I'v done, I'v said enough in late Letters, by adverting to which you'll discover my embarrassed Situation, and if I can command my Penn, will never again disturb your Quiet by a Communication of my feelings, or sentiments, or sufferings, I throw myself (entirely) into the Bosom of your Justice and Benevolence, whether it will glow with an ardent Desire to shew me a *Preference* to those of your Correspondents in London, whose Stars have been more propitious, Time will discover — their Funds and resources compar'd to mine are inexhaustible; in brief Sir, I repose unbounded Confidence in your Honour and Friendship and here I'll rest.

The Bill of £38.15.10¾ Sterling drawn by my Father that you remitted me, is to your Credit with Thanks.

I am sorry for the Death of poor Osborne, as a Man, but neither you nor myself will sustain any great Damage from it, he paid too much attention to his own Interest and too little to that of his Friends. *Dear Self* seem'd to be the Foundation of all his Words and Actions.

When Osborne last sail'd from hence, he desired me to send his Account Current to Messrs. Robert Stevens & Son of your Port, (as I had not time to draw it out when he was here). the Ballance in my favor is £80.1.6 Sterling. I mention this circumstance no way doubting if 'tis in your power to take care of me but you will do so, which will greatly oblige me. between two and three years ago, he persuaded me to buy a parcell of twice laid Cordage, which he took to Rhode Island to sell for me. he has never given me any other Account of it than that it is in his Brother's Hands, who he had left Orders with, to send me Account Sales of it, as soon as sold, and to remit me the Net Proceeds. I trouble you with these things as peradventure by knowing so much, you may have it in your power to serve me in them.

Permit me just to add, that I deliver'd Captain Osborne a Note of Hand drawn by Martha Lazarus on Enock Lyon for £4.4. Sterling, which he was to receive and remit me. I hope Mr. Lyon will see this Money repaid me. inclosed is Osborne's Receipt for it.

Inclosed is a Price Current for your Government. Oil is likely to keep up all the year, and if no very great Quantities arrive, am inform'd it will be scarce and dear towards the Spring.

I recollect nought else to add, but to assure you, I have a Respect and Esteem for you, and that I put ample Confidence in all you have said to me, no way doubting but a short time will dispel this Cloud of Uneasiness and Difficulty, and the chearful Sun once more smile upon us both, which that God may grant is the incessant and fervent Prayer of, Dear Sir, Yours, etc.

HEN: CRUGER, JR.

October 20. Altho' several Vessels are lately arriv'd from Jamaica, I have yet received not a penny from Mr. Mendez.

30th. Nothing further to add. no Remittance from Jamaica.

HAYLEY & HOPKINS TO CHRISTOPHER CHAMPLIN

London, 20 October, 1768.

Sir,

For the last three years during which I have carried on Business alone, I have devoted my whole time and attention to do it in such a manner as might give satisfaction to all my Friends in America, and as it has pleased God to bless me with un[in]terrupted health, I flatter myself not the most trifling disadvantage to any of them has arisen from my being without a partner; nevertheless it has all along been my intention (in order to add a Stability to the House) to engage in a new Partnership as soon as I could meet with an opportunity of doing so with a prospect of answering that valuable purpose. I am very happy in acquainting you that I have now contracted with my approved Friend Mr. Edmund Hopkins, a Gentleman whose more than common abilities for business has made me long wish to have this connection with him take place. I am sure I shall be happy with him, and I have not the least doubt but his conduct will be agreeable to all the

COMMERCE OF

Your most humble servant
Geo Hayley
Hayley & Hopkins
Hayley & Hopkins

The firm of "Your Hayley & Hopkins" is
The form of Your title line " " We wish the
Hayley & Hopkins

Gentlemen who may favour us with their commands. Our partnership is to commence the 31st day of December next, and you will please to address your future favours to the new Establishment of Hayley and Hopkins.

I beg leave to return my sincere acknowledgment for your past favours, and to assure you that the same care which I have hitherto taken of the Interest of my Friends shall still be exerted in the service of those who may favor the new establishment with their Commissions.

I am very respectfully, Sir, Your most humble Servant

GEO. HAYLEY

[Endorsed,] Per Capt. Hulme.

HENRY CRUGER, JR. TO AARON LOPEZ

[Bristol,] 31 October, 1768.

Dear Sir,

IN my Letter of 3d Instant I wrote you (in order to save Time and preserve Method) that "inclosed was an Account of £700 Stg. Insurance done on the *Charlotte*, Cost £......[1] to your Debit," thinking then that I should have been able to effect it before the sailing of the Vessel the Letter went by; but behold our Underwriters here would not do it, but at an inordinate Premio, for which Reason, I sent it up to London to be done by my Insurance Brokers there, and before I had their Answer the Vessels by which I wrote you were sailed, so I could not by those Opportunitys, give you the advice I now do. their answer was, the Underwriters in London had suffered so much by these Bay Risques, that they gladly would be excused writing at any rate, but to oblige me (who am a very good Customer) they would take it at an advanced Premium, — this was my Brokers answer. I then again tried every Office in this City, and to a Man they would have nothing to do with it, upon which I wrote my Brokers in London, and told them that I had orders to effect the £700, and it must be done, let the Premio be

---
[1] See next letter.

what it would, and to encourage them, and to shew I have not so bad an opinion of the Risque, I have taken £100 myself, at the Premio the rest is done at. If they do it at all, and I have an Account, before I'm obliged to seal this Letter, you shall be advised, with Cost of the same. Yours ut supra,

HEN: CRUGER, JR.

HENRY CRUGER, JR. TO AARON LOPEZ

Bristol, 3d November, 1768.

To HENRY CRUGER, JR., Dr.

For Cost of Insurance on the *Charlotte* John Piner Master from Jamaica to the Bay of Honduras and from thence to Rhode Island, vizt.

	On Ship Valued		On Goods.	
£150.	Timothy Bevan Junior	£100.	H. Cruger Jr.	
150.	William Trotter	200.	Jno. Sholbred	
100.	A. Hake	300.		
400.	on Ship			
300.	on Goods			
£700.	at 8 Guineas per Ct.			£58.16.
	Policy			0. 5.6
	To Commission on £700. at 1/2 per Ct.			3.10.–
	To the Debit of Mr. Aaron Lopez			£62.11.6

3d November, [1768.]

Dear Sir,

I HAVE already had the pleasure of addressing you per this Bearer, and since, have received your esteemed favor of 7th September, ordering Insurance on the *Jacob*, which (agreable to my promise of 3d October) shall get effected on the best Terms in my power,[1] and per my next hand you Account thereof, as I now do, of that per *Charlotte*, Cost £62.11.6 Stg. to your debit. the premio is high, but nothing save an advanced Premium would have induced the Underwriters to speculate, — the Bay Risques are become so hateful.

Having nothing further to communicate, I kiss your Hand and remain, Sir, Your most humble Servant,

HEN: CRUGER, JR.

---

[1] The insurance for £1200 cost £69.16.0, or at the rate of five guineas per cent.

BENJAMIN WRIGHT TO RIVERA OR LOPEZ

Savana La Marr, the 12th November, 1768.

Gentlemen,

THESE serves to acquaint you of my safe arrival had twenty three days Pasage had no blowing weather. I spook with a Briganteen in Lattitude Thirty six belonging to Conecticutt. he informed me that he sailed in company with Capt. James Potter, hope you have had the pleasure of seeing him before this time. my salt fish I disposed of the first day I arriv'd at 25/ per Ct. heartily wish I had broat double the quantity, as, that articule was in good demand which has been the meens of my getting my money in to good hands. Every other articule that my cargo consists off, seems dull by reason of sundry Vessels have been here this summer with the articuls of flour and Spermicita Candles I am under no concern; the remainder of my cargoe will come in play before the Croop is over. flatter my self I have Lodgick enough to vent or sell our Oil to as good advantage as last year. Am in hopes my Sails in general will not fall much short of those last year, except the artical of Sperm Cita Candles. the Island seems well stock'd with that artical.

Our friend Mr. A. P. M[endes] is now here, and has been this for or five weeks, as am informed; and in regard to his affairs am not able to give you any account, have had no time to sound in to the bottom of his misstereous proceedings. I am now about setting out into the Country to see my friend the planters where I expect to putt off or ingauge the greates part of my oil. You may rest asured I shall advise you of my proceeding by all opertunitys and every other occurance that may happen, whereby you may reep the best advantag am willing to convince you that I am truly sencible of the happy sittuation I poses by haveing the best of Employers therefore shall pay due Respect to any advice rec'd from you, or even any thing you please to committ to my care.

Am with greate Esteem your Most Obedient Humble Servant and Tenders of Service,

BENJAMIN WRIGHT

Hast had like to prevented my mentioning about our Schooner *Ranger*. She arrived safe at this Island with ninteen day passage broat every thing in with out any damage happening to the goods. at my arrivall found shee had not desposed of more then one third of her Cargoe the other two thirds on hand. I beleve the young fellow has taken all the pains in his power to sell his cargoe and has been verry carefull in getting his pay when ever he despos'd of any article, for which I commend him much. I have not rec'd Capt. Allen's account sales yet; therefore cannot advise you but you may depend on having the particulars per the first Opertunity. I still do not despair, but yankey dodle will do verry well here, notwithstanding times at present do not seem any thing inviting, and if you will please to call and see my little famely when ever convenency will admitt, will greatly add to the many favours allready conferred on your humble Servant

BENJAMIN WRIGHT

N. B. was obliged to open this letter after it was seled to mention the Schooner *Ranger*.

GEORGE CHAMPLIN TO CHRISTOPHER CHAMPLIN

Charlestown, December 8th, 1768.

Dear Brother,

THIS is the first oppertunity that presents to acquaint of our arrivall here 18th November. the same day arriv'd here a Ship and a Sloop from Boston laden with Rum and Scamme Home 8 days before us notwithstanding that quantity arriving at once have sold all ours at 14/6, Apples about 3£, Cheese 2/6, Soap and Wax candles at prime Cost Spermacatia Candles must carry to the West Indias, as I have not sold one Box nor had an offer for any. the loaf sugar is a very bad Comodity here at present, as their's such quantitys of Bristoll Sugar sold here at Vandue. I dont expect to make sale of half ours what I have sold got only 4/4, and here's a duty 4*d* per lb which had we known before we saild we might sav'd 7/8 of it. however what I cant sell shall leve with Russell who will advance me near the amount in Rice.

Produce here is extravagantly high. Rice broke at 70/, and large quantitys ship'd at that Price for the Foreign Markitts. it is now at 60/, and its redus'd to a certainty it will not be lower untill the 20 January. Therefor shall purchase as soon as I conveniently can and proceed to Jamaca, as theirs only one Vessell gone there, and she saild the day I arriv'd with 200 Bar: at 70 /. theirs 4 Sale gone to Windward, all of which have carr'd Rice more or less. Pork has not yet come to markit. shoud any arrive timely and at a proper Price will take 20 or 30 Barrs. on deck; otherwise shall fill my deck with Shingles, which I think will turn to more profit than Pork at the price they talk of: shall write you particular in my next in regard to my Purchas. I am in Health, your Brother,

Geo. Champlin

P. S. Since I closd the above I find two ships which enterd out for Europe are destind for Jamaca. They are allmost loaded at 70/ and will sale 10 days before I can. should they absolutely proceed to Jamaca, I think our best chanc to Windward, of that shall write you more particular in my next. Rice in 24 h[our]s has advanced from 60/ to 62/6, and very little at market; but make no doubt it will be at 60/ in 3 or 4 days.

G. C.

Dear Brother,   Charlestown, December 13th, 1768.

WHAT is containd on the other side is a Copy of my two last to you, since which have purchas'd my Cargoe of Rice at the extravagant price of 62/6, which is the Cash price and will continue so sometime. I expect to sale in 3 days if wind and wither permit, but am much at a loss to say whare, as think the Chance of a Markit according to what accounts I can get to be near equal at Jamaca or Windard therefore shall be guided in that respect by the wind when I am at Sea. if can goe to Windward without much beating shall give that the preference, otherwise shall proceed to Jamaca. at my arrivall at either place shall neglect no oppertunity to acquaint you thereof. I rec'd your letter by Burk, and hourly expect Durfey's Arrivall, which will nock Rum down to 12/6, as theirs 200 hhds. West India Rum enterd here within 4 days, and the greater part of my Rum and the Boston ships is now in store and the Merchants tell me they'd be very glad to take the money they gave us. The Still Houses have a stock 600 hhd. Molosses, and run of 6 hhd. a day. their's only 4 Barr's. Pork been at Markit yet, and that sold at 14£, and dont expect to git any therefore our Cargoe will consist in only four articles, One Hundred and forty three Tierces Rice, thirteen thousand Shingles, all our Spermacatia Candles, and about five Hundred dollars in cash; I am with wishing we may arrive safe to a good Markit, Your Brother, etc.

Geo: Champlin

P. S. shall git the start of the ships before mention'd in that case shall proceed to Jamaca without fail.

Henry Cruger, Jr. to Aaron Lopez

Bristol, December 22nd, 1768.

Sir,

I HAVE your favors of 28th September and 6th October, with Invoice, and Bill Lading, for some Pott Ash, and Spermacoeti Oil, receiv'd by the *Pitt*. fearing any more Oil may suddenly drop in, as this is the Season, and much expected, I sold yours, and the rest that came in her, at Public Auction immediately upon landing. two Lotts went at £26 per Ton, one at £26.5., and one Lott at £26.7.6 Sterling, a Sale that I hope will merit your Satisfaction.

the Pott Ashes I sold in like manner at £26 per Ton. as soon as these Articles are deliver'd will make out, and render you Sales. inclosed is an Account of £200 Sterling Insurance made on them, Cost £5.8.; likewise Account of £300 on the *Jacob*, cost £17.5., both Sums are to your Debit.

This Day's Post brought me a Letter from Mr. Mendez, covering on your Account only one poor Bill at 60 days for £150 Sterling. it is sent to London for Acceptance, and if paid shall be to the Credit of your Account Current. by our God, 'tis cruel! I am, Sir, Your humble Servant,

HEN: CRUGER, JR.

29th December. I just now receiv'd an Account of the Bill remitted me by Mr. Mendez being noted per Non-Acceptance, and don't expect 'twill be paid at Maturity.

H. C. JR.

HENRY CRUGER, JR. TO AARON LOPEZ

Bristol, December 31st, 1768.

Sir,

ON the other side is Copy of my last Respects via Boston, since which have receiv'd your esteem'd favor of 11th November covering my Father's draft on me for £100 Sterling, that when due shall be plac'd to your Credit. the Insurance noted in your said favor shall be effected and per my next you may expect Account thereof, and a more particular Reply than I have time at present to make.

I observe your Remark touching the Duty's on Rum and Piemento per *Pitt*, in which can discover no Error. at foot you have the particulars which hope may appear clear to you and cause you to note the same in Conformity.

Your Account is debited £7.9.2 Sterling for sundrys vizt.

Paid a note for dieting the *America's* People 2nd Voyage, which the woman brought in only a few days past. This happen'd a day or two before the Ship sail'd and the Crew being in Town went to this Person's House by Osborne's Order.	0.15.2
Pilottage of the *America*, 3rd Voyage, from Kingroad to Bristol.	6.14.–
	£7. 9.2

this last Note I paid the Pilott, but as there was some Concerns between Osborne and him, Osborne desir'd I wou'd not charge it to you saying he would repay me himself. his motives I am a stranger to; but still complyed with his request, but as he is now no more, am oblig'd to debit you for it, which I presume can make no difference to you, seeing you *never before* have been charg'd with said Pilottage. I remain with respectful regard, etc.

H. CRUGER, JR.

Musqueto Mahogany $4d$ to $4 1/2 d$ per foot. Pigg Iron £5 to £7.7 per ton, as in Quallity.

BENJAMIN WRIGHT TO AARON LOPEZ

Savanna la mar, 2 January, 1769.

Gentlemen,

THIS serves to advize this my third Letter, hope the other two came safe to your hands, which will acquaint you of the low marketts I arriv'd at. I have sold the greatest part of the *Jacob's* Cargo. what remains on hand consists of flour and Spermacety Candles, the former about 30 barrells the latter about 30 boxes. my oyl all dispos'd of except 4 barrells, none of this article has been sold under six pound per barrell. the pine boards receiv'd from Capt. Andrews sold at £10 per M, the Boston boards at £8 per M, White oak Staves and heading £12 per M, R[ed] O[ak] Staves at £10 per M. Spermaceti Candles from 2/6 to 2/9 per pound, but the greatest part at 2/6 per ℔. Shingles from

37/6 to 40/ per M. Ship Bread from 25/ to 26/3 per Ct. Supf. flour from 30/ to 35/ per Ct. Common ditto 25/ Spirits Turpentine 6/3 per Gall. Codfish at £1.5 per Ct. Tallow from 11*d* to 12*d* per pound. Axes 50/ per doz. Shads 18/9 Kegs biscuit 10/ Tarr 25/ per Barrell. dureing the time I have known this Island, never knew half so many vessells in this port from North America; I am sure there is five hundred bbs. flour in this harbour, when two hundred barrells would be enough for this parish. the masters of Philadelphia Vessells are selling their oyl at 95/ per Bbl and 100/ per Barrell, and think they do great matters. some of their Casks gauges 36 Gallons. Can assure [you] I have not sold five pounds worth of any article to any Scotchman. I am become a person of consequence; I am of the Court party. I belong entirely to the Creole Interest. I flatter myself shall be able to sell the remainder of my Goods on as good a lay as my neighbours.

Yours of the 3rd and 8th November is now before me, wherein you impart to me your intention of dispatching the Brigantine *Charlotte* to my address. all which I am ready to undertake, and shou'd she arrive timely shall be able to dispose of her Cargo, and notwithstanding the dullness of the times and badness of the marketts hope I shall be able to prevent your being a sufferer by your consignment to me, shall leave nothing unnoticed that may turn to your advantage. you likewise inform me of your intention of sending the Brig. *Industry*, Captain John Peter. it is fully my opinion that the *Industry* has better prospects of making a Voyage than the *Charlotte*, provided she brings her Decks full of good young horses, which is the only article inquir'd after.

Your request shall be strictly comply'd with in negotiating Robert Joseph Dunn, Esquire's, Bill of Exchange; likewise the small order on Samuel Ladisma shall receive and pass to your Credit.

Your directions in regard to the remittance to Bristol to your mutual friend Henry Cruger, Esqr., shall strictly observe, notwithstanding it will be attended with great difficulty on account of Cash being prodigious scarce and Bills of Exchange must be purchased with it, especially such Bills as may be depended on, but notwithstanding the difficulty I have pointed out, the thing may be done through different Channells, and by a round of Commerce, all which hope will be accomplished with Success. Your inclos'd letter for A. P. Mendez I deliver'd him with my own hands. in about two hours he desir'd to speak to me. I did myself the honour to wait on him. he sayeth with a ruffled Countenance, my father has desir'd me to put all my business into your hands, and desires me to come immediately home. he was surprised that you should imagine that I could do my own business and settle all his affairs when they was scatter'd, from one end of the Island to the other. my answer was as follows, our mutual friend your father wrote me on the same subject, and shou'd you be inclin'd to embrace your father's request, which I would advise you to comply with by all means, as I know they want to see you, as you have been absent a long time; and if you think proper to deliver your papers into my hands, and let me know the state of your affairs, shall willingly accept to effect, and shall be glad to release you from this place, as you may go and see your little agreeable family, which I shou'd think one of the greatest blessings in life. he tells me he shall come home in the spring and not before, and is determined to take his passage in the Ship *Jacob*. he has never given me any Encouragement that he will deliver his papers into my hands, so that Affair stands newter. till further Advice we are on extream good terms. I look on him to be a sensible genteel young man as any of his age. his judgment in business I do not meddle with; shall leave that part to my superiors my worthy owners; as I know their Abillity, shall say no more on that subject. You remind me to procure a Stock of patience in order to transact some further business in this place, all which can easily procure, and in regard to the other Stock, which I think full as necessray as that of Patience, you make no mention of suppose you imagine I am well supplied with, which is a Stock of Assurance. can assure you should that be your opinion you are not much out in your Calculation.

I now touch on a grand point you may rest assured that Rum will not be for less than 2/6 per Gallon this year, the price of Coffee and Molasses cannot give any account of yet. You will please to acquaint Captain Andrews, that in the Boards receiv'd from him, there was better than 2000 feet mistake. we have been very carefull in keeping Accounts and have taken the Wharfingers receipt, for all the Boards deliverd which agrees with the mate's account. Our new mate has given entire satisfaction as yet. am determined to dispatch the *Jacob* some time in April, and come myself in Captain John Peter should he come here. I belive Mr. Dunn will pay you a visit in the Spring. God bless you all. have no more room.

[Endorsed,] Per the *Eagle*, via Philadelphia, Q. D. C. Forwarded by Samuel and Jno. Morton.

GEORGE CHAMPLIN TO CHRISTOPHER CHAMPLIN

Granada, January 16, 1769.

Dear Brother,

I LEFT Charlestown the 15th december and met Cap. Durfey agoing in, by whom received your letter; in consequence of which and the Wind proveing favourable I proceed'd to these Islands. and arriv'd at Dominica the 7th Inst. and cou'd git only 17/ offerd for our Rice, and 2/3 for Candles, from whence proceeded here, but was to late. two Vessell from Georgia arriv'd 3 days before us with Rice. However have sold all ours at 22/, Shingles at 30/, 20 Boxes Candles at 2/8, payable in Cash the 20th Febry: with demurrage after that time. I have sold to two different

Men, call'd and recommended to me to be as good as any in the Island, which I don't in the least doubt. I am afraid I shall be puzl'd to obtain 2/6 for the Remainder of our Candles, as her's 400 Boxes arriv'd since I came; Rum will not be at Markit till the last of next month. some think it will brake at 2/6 others at 2/2. Coccoa is at 14 Souce, Coffe 20 So. I hope to get all my Money in hand to be one of the first purchasers of Rum when at Markit. You need not give your self any Concern about my bringing any contriband goods. It's a thing I shan't attempt these precarious times; I am now delivering our Cargoe as fast as possoble which comes out in very good order. I shall write you again in a fiew days. I am your Brother, etc.,

GEO: CHAMPLIN

P. S. Since I closd the above have sold 20 Boxes Candles at 2/7, and 7 ditto at 2/8. in case none of our Rice is damaged the gross sales of our cargoe, with the addition of the money brought from Carolina, will amount to thirteen hundred Pounds by a ruff Calculation.

G. C.

Granada, Jany. 29th, 1769.

Dear Brother,

THE above is a Copy of my last to you via Philadelphia, since which have Delivered all our Cargoe in good order. have 17 Box's of Candles on hand which cant sell at any rate at present, the Markit is intirely glutted with that article as well as with every other Commodity we can import from the Northard. Captain Whipple in Mawdsley's Sloop has been here, but could not sell one single article here except his small stock. he offer'd his Candles at 2/6 but cou'd not obtain it. theirs 20 Sale touch'd here with 10 d{ay]s and been obliged to go away; very lucky for us we sold our Cargo as we did, as theirs large quantitys arriv'd since, and will be retaild soon at a years Credit 22/ and 23/. this goes by Captain John Tanner, bound to Eustatia, to be forwarded by first oppertunity. I shall keep you duely advis'd of every circumstance relating our

Voyage as oppertunity serves. mean time am in Health Your Brother, etc.

GEO: CHAMPLIN.

[Under endorsement,] Groton, 28 March, 1769. forwarded by, Sir, Your most Humble Servant,

THOS. MUMFORD.[1]

GEORGE CHAMPLIN TO CHRISTOPHER CHAMPLIN

Granada, Feby: 8th, 1769.

Dear Brother,

I HAVE wrote you 4 Letters from this place of the particulars of the Sale of our Cargoe, some of which no doubt will come to hand; My paiment is due 20th Inst. and be that time I hope Rum will begin to come to Markit as the Mills begin to grind very fast this week past. Tho' am afraid Rum will brake high, as here are a Number of Vessells weighting for it. it's very uncertain what the Price will be, but am sure not under 2/4, and am much affraid higher, as the Planters ships large quantitys to Europe this Season, and are likewise well accquainted with the Price at N. York I don't imagineny a Vessell will sale with New Rum untill the Middle March, and I hope, if am blest with Health and met with no disappointment in my Payment, to be one of the first. I dont think it will answer to purchase any Coffe, as their's such large quantity's allready gone and so very high here, the Vessell by whom this goes has 25 thousand [pounds] on board. At the Bottom you have the price I sold our Cargoe at. I cant think of any thing more material at present, but shall write by all Occations. Your Brother, etc.

GEO: CHAMPLIN

Rice	22/ per ct.	Coffe	20/ Sous
Shingles	30/ M	Coccoa	14/ Sous
Candles	27Boxs 28/	Rum	2/9 Old
	20 ditto 2/7	Sug	38/ to 40/
	16 ditto on hand		

[Endorsed,] Per fav: Captain Wm. Brown.

[1] Groton, Connecticut. Mumford was a prominent merchant of that place, and took an active part in the War of Independence.

Henry Cruger, Jr. to Aaron Lopez

[Bristol,] 20th February, 1769.

Sir,

Above is Copy of my last, since which have not heard any thing further from you.

I now hand you an Account of Insurance effected on the *Charlotte* and *Diana*, Cost of both, £150.12. Sterling to your Debit; also Account Sales of Oil and Pot Ash rec'd per *Pitt* Net Proceeds £185.2. – Sterling to your Credit. you have likewise your Account Current made out up to the 31st December last. Ballance in my favour (Interest included) still is *£8366.16.9 Sterling* to your Debit, and to my *Grief* and almost distraction. believe me, Sir, it is not the Advantages I lose from the deprivation of so large a sum, nor is it the fear of suffering any thing by you in the End, that make me and have made me, so wretched; it is the grievous and intollerable dunnings brought on me by such an unexpected Disappointment, such a fatal Event. That you pay me but 5 per Cent Interest and that I *could*, if I had my Money out of your Hands, *have made ever since it hath been in, 10 to 15 per Cent of it*, is what I do not harp upon; I could and would *silently* put up with such *a Loss*, tho' I esteem it more than £500 or £600 a year; but I cannot bear the barbarous Treatment I dayly meet from the People I owe Money, without complaining to you, — unavailable as my Complaints have hitherto proved.

I will friendly avoid repeating to you that Asperity of Language which I have suffered on your Account, but 'tis well known you have rec'd large Cargoes of Goods from London. whither go the proceeds? who than myself has a juster claim to them? the List of remittances in your favour of 11th November affords but small relief, because not much above half is yet come to hand; and it is quite unsatisfactory, because it is quite inadequate. upon Receipt of it, I wrote to Messrs Ximenes & Lousada of London, that acknowledged to have received the Logwood and Mahogany you mention, but say they have no Orders to remit the proceeds to me; this is Odd enough! as I naturally concluded you might have sent Directions to them *by the same Opportunities* you wrote to me; inclosed you will find a Copy of their Letter to me. I beg of you to write to them. this concludes me for the present. Dear Sir, Your most humble Servant,

HEN: CRUGER, JR.

P. S. As you have dealt largely in Ship Building for Sale, it may not be amiss just to say they never were plentyer nor cheaper. the *Pitt* upon arrival here woud not sell for any thing like £500 Sterling. I mention this for your Government. there are several quite new American Built Vessels now in this place for sale, from 250 to 300 tons burthen, said to be well finish'd and well bolted, that may be purchased from 7 to £900 Stg. this you may rely on for a Matter of Fact. I hope this information may be of service to you.

[Endorsed,] Via New York per *Ellin*.

HENRY CRUGER, JR. TO AARON LOPEZ

Bristol, March 24th, 1769.

Sir,

ANNEX'D you have Copy of my last Respects.

The Bill of £150 Sterling Mr. Mendes remitted me on your Account is return'd under Protest to my Friend in Jamaica. the Charges on it amount to £1.17.5 Sterling to your Debit.

The Season for Oil (being winter) is now over, but 'twill be in demand again about October. a Cargo of mahogany wou'd sell well here, say from $4\frac{1}{2}d$ to $6d$ per foot, at which Prices am now selling. Jamaica Mahogany wou'd sell much higher. I flatter myself that you will soon give Messrs. Ximenes and Lousada *Orders* to pay me the net Proceeds of the Logwood and Mahogany in their hands, and likewise make me a considerable Remittance direct from New Port, which may prevent the much dreaded Necessity of *my coming to America.* Inclosed is a Price Current for your Guidance. I am Yours, etc.,

HEN: CRUGER, JR.

5th April. Since the above nothing material has occurred. I entreat you, Sir, to consider me. H. C.

BENJAMIN WRIGHT TO ABRAHAM PEREIRA MENDES

Sir, Savanna la Mar, 3d April, 1769.

YOURS of the 19th March by Captain Lovelace is now before me. Inclosed I find 2 Notes of hand from David Lopez, likewise John Fitz Gerald's Note, all which shall spare no pains to get discharged. the two former I think bids fair for Profit and Loss Account; the latter Note beleive I can get discharged by order on some person or other where I may be able to hook it in. Your Instructions in regard to Cope's Affairs I laid before him with a Discharge, provided he paid the Hundred pounds and give his Obligation for the Remainder, all which he approved of, and said he had given you his word that he would pay the Hundred pounds to me; but notwithstanding he found his Crop turn'd out so poorly that he could not comply with his Engagement with you, therefore would not do any thing with me about the Affair; but at the same time desired I would not advise you by this post, and for what reason I know not. and as it appears to me you have put some confidence in me, or you would not have sent me the Papers, therefore chuse to report any good opinion any person may please to entertain of me. So have sent you his Answer word for word timely, as you may conduct accordingly. You may depend I shall not omit answering any favour of yours let it be on what subject it will. The Ship will sail for Rhode Island in Eight Days with a good Cargoe on board, she is as deep as I could desire to have her. I think there is but one thing wanting to make our mutual friend intirely satisfied at the Arrival of the Ship *Jacob,* which would be my Freind A. P. M's Person to go in her,

which I find by your favour per Lovelace, will be wanting.
I expect by the 25th April to see you at Town or Withywood, where we must consult on Affairs in a Freindly
Manner about the Outstanding Debts of the several Consignments to you last year, which am informed in my last
Letter from home that there is now outstanding upwards
of Sixteen hundred pounds, which is a large Sum to collect
in this Crop. therefore where you can get good Produce
I advise you not to refuse. I will receive the Produce and
send it to my Friend. I am strictly commanded to take
the Affair in hand, am order'd to leave none of the Affairs
unsettled, and to receive produce in payment rather than
leave any thing behind in the Island. those Outstanding
Debts is the only thing that has prevented my going in the
Ship. have settled all my affairs here except a trifle, hope
you will push the People hard who stands indebted and let
us do every thing and settle the Affair intirely, as you are
sensible it is a Cruel Time to be out of so much money for
a Trading Man for more than two years before he gets it,
and perhaps some may stand over another year. however,
these are Accidents unforeseen and frequently happen,
but hope your being well acquainted in this Island hope
you have not got any Money into bad hands. Mr. Lopez
informs me he acquainted you that he sent me a Power of
Attorney, or should have acquainted you of it my self before you left this place, which power was sent for no
other reason only to release you from a long fatiguing
Voyage, as you might go to your Family and Freinds,
which would be more glad to see you than you can imagine.
without Ceremony and as you did not chuse to accept of
my Offer in taking your Affairs in hand and settling them
for you, I now make you an offer of my best Services on the
same Subject, either in assisting you or taking the whole
on me to collect the Outstanding Debts or get them secured
in a better manner than they appear to be at present, all
which must and shall be done before I leave this Island.
I am, Sir, Your Humble Servant,

BENJAMIN WRIGHT

BENJAMIN WRIGHT TO AARON LOPEZ[1]

Savanna La Marr, 8th April, 1769.

Gentlemen,

THESE per the *Jacob* hope safe to your hand. Inclos'd you'll receive a Sketch of my proceedings, likewise an Account of Sales of what is disposed of belonging to the Ships Cargoe. Am afraid you will find it not so correct as I could wish, as hurry often makes blunders. You have likewise Invoice of Sundrys shipt on the joint Account of the owners of Ship *Jacob*. Have sent you no Account Current (for this Reason) the Cargoe is not all disposed of. Neither was it in my power to collect the whole of the Disbursements being much hurried in dispatching the Ship. And at this time the Vestry is setting in order to tax us on Trade, and am obliged to attend the same in order that I may not be over-taxed. All which prevents my sending my papers in such order. Therefore if any thing appears misterious, hope I shall have the pleasure of clearing it up to sattisfaction.

The Schooner *Rangers* Cargoe still remain on hand; the Spermacaeti Candles and flour not all sold. Have not time to send you her Account Sales at this time, which please to excuse. I wrote you in my Letter of the 27th February that Captain John Newdigate told me he had two Hogsheads of Molasses and one Hdd. Sugar to be delivered to me for Sundrys sold for your Account at Withy Wood, all which acquainted you of; but he detained one Hdd. of the Molassos, so I received only one Hdd of Molassos and one Teirce of Sugar, which have carried to the Credit of your private Account, and debited the *Jacob* for the same. the Sugar he charged very high at 30/ per cwt. I think there is better Sugar on board our Ship at 28/ per Ct. I received a Letter from A. P. Mendez the 19th March, wherein he informes me that he cannot think of coming home in the Ship at any Rate, as he had Matters of Consequence

---
[1] The original is in the Newport Historical Society.

to settle for the Concerned as well as for his own Account, he even did not desire to be remember'd to you or family. "Horrid Ingratitude, the most heinous Crime A Man can be Guilty of." Inclosed you have a Copy of my Letter to him of the 3d April, wherein you will see my determination. Notwithstanding your Instructions per the *Charlotte* are (discretionary), when Absolute Orders in things of this Nature are most to be depended on, shall in a few days wait on the Young Man at Kingston, which is near Three Hundred Miles from this place, and lay my Commands on him. Am determined to have his affairs settled in a more secure manner than they appear to be at present. I was willing to entertain as favourable opinion of the Young Man as possible, and had much rather medigate matters than agravate them; but in justice to you shall not let the affair rest any longer, as I see no preparation either to settle his affairs or come home. he seems to be void of Thought on that subject. I expect it will detain me much longer than we imagined, but shall do every thing in my power to secure your Interest in the best manner, and if I should receive any of his Debts in produce, which is the most probable way to receive it, you have given no Orders to ship it to you, neither have you advised me that you will send a Vessell; I now acquaint you whatever I receive in payment for the Outstanding Debts contracted by Mendez shall ship it to you without further Advice, adviseing you timely to cover your Property, if you think proper, as I cannot give you any Encouragement for sending any more Vessells to this place this Year as the Season is farr advanced and no one thing in demand. I did much expect a Line from you before this time, as you wrote me per the *Charlotte* you should have an Opportunity in four weeks from the Date of yours per her. I now seem to stand my own Conducter. The Horses per the *Charlotte* are all sold, one at Thirty-Two Pounds, Two at Twenty-Six Pounds each, one at Twenty-Eight Pounds. They turned out on an average Twenty-Eight Pounds per Horse. Cap'n Nicholls from Connecticutt arriveing about six days before your Vessell with Forty four Horses on Board, which was great Determent to the Sales of your Horses. have sold about Forty Barrells of Shads at 18/9 the half barrells. Pork have sold the greatest part at 45/ per half bll. have sold about half the Candles, as they are much better in Quality than those per Schooner *Ranger*. the Boards and Shingles, have sold the Boards at £6, the Shingles at 40/ per m., as I advised you in my letter of the 27th February. The Plank belonging to the *Charlotte's* Cargoe, with the Paint, Oil, and seven Cheeses, I did not receive: the Corn I have sold at 5/ per Bushell, the Salt at 3/1½ per Bushell. Some Tallow sold at 11d per lb., some Tarr from 20/ to 25/ per Bll. have sold four Barrells of Lamp Oyl from £5 to £6 per Bll. have some of Potters oil by me, and am afraid shall not be able to sell it this year, as the Season is farr advanced. the Spirits of Turpentine per the *Charlotte* stick on hand with the vile New York Staves. the Philadelphia Red Oak Staves are on hand likewise. am afraid shall not sell them this year. and in regard to the Remittance to Bristol find it impossible to comply with, as Cash is so extreemly scarce, and nothing will purchase Bills except Cash. therefore shall endeavour as long as possible for Bills, and if I fail getting them, must ship you the Produce of the Neat Proceeds of the *Charlottes* Cargoe, adviseing you of the same timely as you may govern accordingly. My business here is fine and forward so can better attend on Mendez's affairs. Have not yet received your Bill of Exchange from Joseph Dunn. Expect to receive it in three or four days. Shall make him allow Interest on his Note, as it has been so long standing. Your Order on Samuel Ladisma is discharged and you are credited for the same. Whenever you [divi]de the Ships Cargoe you will please to deliver my 1/8 part to Captain Charles Bardin, who have desired to receive it, and you may rest assured that I shall do every thing in my power [to] secure your Property in this Island and send it to you as fast as I can. You shall be advised [by] every opportunity. have nothing more to add; only my best Respects and Sincere Regard for your self and family and am with Esteem, Your Humble Servant and Tenders of Service,

BENJAMIN WRIGHT

P. S. Have sent Mr. Revera a pott of Sweetmeats.

You'll receive 206 Hdds and 3 Teirces as appears by Bills of Lading the other 5 mentioned in the Invoice was started in order to fill the others. Likewise you'll receive Certificates for the canselling my Bonds and the Brigantine *Charlotte*.[1]

JOSEPH ROTCH & SON TO AARON LOPEZ

Bedford in Dartmouth, April 27, 1769.

Respected Friend, Aaron Lopez,

WE receiv'd thy esteem'd favour of yesterdays date the contents of which shall be duly notic'd. we are very glad thou did not send us the Rye and Flour, as we only wanted Rye, and wrote for the flour because we thought there was no probability of gitting the Rye. We have deliver'd Captain Devall a Cable of the size he wanted wt. 7.1.26 at 50/8 is £18.19.1, which please to credit our account. We are sorry to acquaint Thee that it is out of our Power to procure a Whale Boat either new or second hand that will do, neither do we know of a Master unship'd that we think capable of takeing charge of a Vessell. Whale Irons we can procure any Quantity, but are at a Loss how we shall forward them, as we are now loading our Sloop *Hope* for Boston, and was waiting an Oppertunity to desire thee to ship us the Remainder of the Mahogany per Greenman, if it was so much in the way that it could not wait her Return. it is not probable that the *Hope* can take the

---

[1] "Above is an Invoice of 50 hhds Granado Rum, which dispose of at New York in the best manner possible and return us the hard Money. Should it happen that by takeing some York Paper Money you can obtain more for the Rum and can buy Good Bills of Exchange drawn on Gentlemen at London at 30 days sight Indorsed by such men in N. York as are of Good Property, and not exceeding £175 N. York Currency for £100 Stg. then I wou'd have you bring me £400 Stg. and the Remainder in hard Money at your Return." *Christopher Champlin to Joshua T. D. St. Croix*, April 19, 1769.

Mahogany in less than three weeks from this time, therefore if it must be remov'd before that time must beg the favour of thee to ship it per Greenman. if he comes thou may send us 3 firkins Butter and 3 firkins Hogsfatt if any arrives.

shall not be able to procure the two other Boats thou mentions, which we are sorry for, as we should been glad to have supply'd thee with them; and if in future thou should want either Boats or whale Irons, and will let us know seasonably, we will procure them from the best workman. Boats will receive much Damage in laying by a Summer, therefore the Builders seldom build more than they engage in Winter. Having nothing further worth thy Detention at present,

and Remain very Respectfully thy assured Friends — Jo. Rotch. & Son

LAMAR HILL & BISSET TO ABRAHAM REDWOOD

Mad[eira], 22 May, 1769.

Sir,

IN consequence of your annual Order, established with us, we have shiped on board the Schooner *Chance*, commanded by Nathaniel Barnard, whose Bill of Loading goes inclosed, a pipe of fine, or particular wine, for your this Year's supply, for the Cost of which, as noted at bottom, £28.12/ Stg. we shall in a few days take our reimbursement on Messrs. Trecothick & Apthorp of London; We have recommended it to the care of our mutual Friend, Ralph Inman, Esquire, who we dare say will get it safely conveyed to you. We have not to add, but that we are with great regard, Sir, Your most Obedient humble Servants,

LAMAR HILL & BISSET

1. 1 pipe of fine wine at £26 Stg. of common gauge £26. 0.0
10 per Ct. for difference of gauge 2.12.0
£28.12.0

Joseph Rotch & Son to Aaron Lopez

Bedford in Dartmouth, 5 mo. [May] 5, 1769.

Respected Friend, Aaron Lopez,

THY esteem'd favours of 3rd and 4th Instant are now before us. Agreeable to thy request have now sent 12 whale Irons, at 4/ is 48/, per Anthony's boy which hope will come safe to hand and prove good.

Thou need not be at any further trouble about the Butter and hogsfat, as we have wrote to Boston for those Articles. We observe what thou says with respect to the Pork; which if it is most agreeable to let the Quantity thou mention'd stand charg'd to us thou may do it. This we will not consent to by any means without it is thy Choice, as it will make no manner of difference to us let it be settl'd either way. We are much oblig'd for thy care in delivering our Letter to Peter Mumford. we will endeavour to see T. Nye this day and deliver thy Letter to him, and shall apply for an answer which if we obtain, shall be forwarded per first conveyance. In the Interim remain very respectfully, Thy Assur'd Friends,

JOSEPH ROTCH & SON

P. S. we find no encouragement to continue the weekly Carrier, as no person this way will give anything towards it.[1] Therefore have wrote to our Friend Nathaniel Wheatley that at any time when there is a necessity of writing to us, and no opportunity presents from Boston for this place, then to inclose a Letter to thee, which must beg the favour of thee to deliver to Anthony as he can come at any time.

And if thou should have any letters address'd to thy care for us from other people, or should want to write us, if it

---

[1] "We are obliged for thy care in forwarding our Letters to Boston and have now taken liberty to order our Letters from Boston left in thy care and have engag'd William Anthony to ride to us weekly with our Letters. Please to deliver the inclosed to him. He is to wait on thee every week as soon as the Post is arrived from Boston. We don't intend to trouble thee in this Manner very long as we Intend to have a box fixed in Mumford's house on purpose for our Letters." *Rotch to Lopez,* March 8, 1769.

appears to be any thing of consequence, shall be oblig'd to thee to send Anthony if no other Opportunity presents.

BENJAMIN WRIGHT TO AARON LOPEZ

Savana la Marr, the 2 June, 1769.

Sir,

THESE serves to advise, my last regard to you was, by Captain Battan via Marble head, where you had a duplicate of the Ships Cargoe, hope safe to your hand. time will not admit of inlargeing on any subject as the gentleman is waiting who carrys this letter to Lucea to give it to Captain Warner timely, as it may not lose its intended Conveyance. your Brigenteen *Industry* is almost loaded, and if no unforeseen Accident happens she shall asueredly sail the Eleventh June. you may depend her bends shall the greates part be under water, notwithstanding it is attended with the utmost difeculty to get molasses at this time as the season of the year is far advanced, and what renders it still more disagreeable is the scearcety of Cash, there is not enough money in this parish for the Planters to bribe the Marshals, letting alone there paying there debts. I have pushed Edward and William Woollery so hard for payment of there protested bill, that all friendship is entirely at an End between us, notwithstanding I have applied in as decent a maner as my Capasity would admitt of. I see no Prospect of getting one farthing this year. They have not any Corespondance in England, therefore they cannot draw bills. they sell the greatest part of there Crop in this Country, and the Marshall seems to be the greatest Purchaser, which should think is against them. I observe in one of your letters to me a small tuch which seeams to carry sum face of Reflection, wherein you are fully of oppinion I will see Woollerys affair settled, as I began the work. you will please to observe, that them bills was no part of Busness transacted for you. Therefore whenever I am to be blaimed, I do not expect it from you. And if you happen to burn your fingers in Rhode Island,

I think it ungenerous to blame me for it in Jamaica. notwithstanding I shall do every thing in my power to secure the property, be it whose it will, even if I had not began the work. have two horses still on hand not sold; the other eight turn'd out on an average £30.1.2 per horse; the Candles and flour on hand; Common Bords sold from 6 to 7£ per m, Jersey Bords am seling from nine to ten pounds per m; Salt am selling at 3/9 per bushall; Tallow will not sell till next year. as the seasons are so far advanced am fraid shall not be able to get near all my pay this year, and the people begin to think me settled here for life, as a factor and treet me verry unkind in paying me my money. my being sumthing ambitious in despatching this Brig put it out of my power to wait on Mendez, by whome I now begin to fear you will be a Greate Sufferer. I have spaired no pains to informe my self how he conducted him self dureing his Tarry here am sorrey to inform you I have heard nothing in his favour, but shall not say any thing further on this subject, as I shall set out for Kingston in order to see what account he can give of him self as soon as the Brig is gone. I have applied to Abraham Lopez to see how he has setled your Consern with him. find they have setled it to there own likeing. have given him many of the Outstanding debts which I think precareous, and those which are any wa[y]s tolerable Lopez has taken to him self, and he has got Mendez's Receipt for five Shillings in full for your Account. I shall take accounts against the people for the out standing Debts, and youse my utmost Endeavours to save all I can for you. I have taken a Copey of the Account setled by Mendez and Lopez, wherein appeareth the Ballance due to Abraham Lopez was £24.6.4 Curency, and in the Account Mendez rendred you find you stand charged with £29.3.11 Curency, which must be cleared up to my satisfaction, as do not intend to let any thing escape close Examination through Mendez's hole Transactions during the time he has been here. time will not admit of any thing more only you shall have a particular account per the *Industry*. Could not let this oppertunity slip letting you no how I went on with the *Industry*. there has been ma[ny] oppertunities from the north side this Island to right to you, and the only thing that prevented my not righting was the distance from me and my being much hurri[ed.] you will please to excuse this Scrawl with the blotts and bad spelling. Am with Esteem Your humble Servant,

BENJAMIN WRIGHT

[Endorsed,] Per the Brigantine *Catharine*, Captain Warner, Q. D. C.

HENRY CRUGER, JR. TO AARON LOPEZ

Bristol, June 7th, 1769.

Dear Sir,

MY last to you was 24th March, am since favour'd with yours of 3rd, 14th and 15th March.

That of 14th cover'd my Fathers draft on me for £208.7.10½ Sterling, which you will find carried to the Credit of your Account Current.

The candid and explicit Manner in which you have vouchsafed to unbosom yourself, respecting your affairs in the Hands of Mr. Mendes is, I humbly think, an information that our Connexions entitled me to have; nor has it done you any injury in my Opinion; for to tell you the Truth, so much promising through that Channel, and so little performing, tended naturally to create unfavourable Ideas; but, the cruel usage I perceive you have suffered from Mr. Mendes greatly extenuates the injurious part of your Conduct towards me. to be sure, we have both of us had a terrible time of it; and may the great Director of all things soon relieve us! Heaven knows the sincerity of my declarations when I say, my Soul, on account of your vast, tremendous Debt, has known no repose these two Years and upwards, and as I esteem you a man of Justice and humanity, am sure you must have participated in my Affliction.

The first Oil at Market in the *fall* of the Year, never fails selling well and readily; this is the reason why I would encourage your sending to this place forty or fifty Tons. I am sure your sentiments are too enlarged and generous to conclude this Advice is given only to extract a Remittance out of your hands. no, upon my Life and Honour, it is calculated for your Interest: and I should be glad to be half concerned with you in the Adventure, suffering you, rather than fail, to draw on me for my Moiety, even if it was sixty Tons of Sperma: Oil between us, each half concern'd.

Suppose you pushed off one of your Vessels early in the fall, filled up with Mahogany, the Consumption of which is greater and greater every day. I think it will sell upon an Average for at least 5d per foot.

Captain Osborne's Death has proved him a sorry fellow. he teazed me untill I let him have, sorely against my inclination, Goods to the amount of above £130. Stg. for an Adventure, on his own private Account, to the Isle of May,[1] where he was sure of making an East India Voyage. he owes me between £200 and £300. Sterling. to be sure I have through good Nature, or perhaps folly, been finely soused by him and other Captains. *bought Experience* they say is the best sort.

Inclosed is a Price Current for your Government. I wish it may prove serviceable to you. adieu Sir, may the Supreme disposer of Events bless you with prosperity and Peace, and enable you to restore the same to Your most Obedient Humble Servant,

Hen: Cruger, Jr.

Benjamin Wright to Aaron Lopez

Savana la Marr, the 17 June, 1769.

Sir,

Inclosed you have an Invoice of Sundries shipped for your Account and Resque on bord the Brig *Industry*, Capt. John Peters, which hope safe to your hand, and to a good Markett. You will see the difference between the Invoice

---

[1] The Isle of May is a small islet at the mouth of the Firth of Forth.

and the bills Loding, which diffarence they tell me they have started in filling up the other Casks in the Invoice. you have the gauges of each Cask as I had them from the planters, and how they have shifted them since they have rec'd them on bord they may account with you. the account the Capt. rendred me when I went to clear the brig out and have the bills of Loding signed I have inclosed you, and should they have made any mistake and should have more Casks Molasses on bord then they say, it is only keeping a Lookout when unlodeing, for I am sure they have none of there own on bord, not as I have any reason to suspect any mans Varasity, butt for all that, when a person sees into matters him self then he has no room for suspition. the Brig is stowed most scandelous or could have got teen or twelve Hhds more in to her. I hartely wish the Cargoe may arrive safe to your place without any damage happining to it. I want to express my self in severall points, but why should I consern my self with affairs that is not my Concern. this day had, as I thoat, a fine oppertunity of selling all the superfine flour per *Industry* to sum Spanyards; but on opening it found it all musty and extreemly bad. therefore it must lie here. Am sure it never has been damaged on bord the Brig, and what can enduce you to send bad goods to this place canot tell, after my giving you my sincear oppinion on those matters that bad goods will not sell here at any Price and it is attended with as much expence to land those bad commodities as it would those of the best kind. shall forever stop my peen this subject. I have a favour to ask, which is to receive of Capt. John Peters forty-seven Dollars, for which have inclosed you his Recept. this money belongs to a poor young fellow who has a large famely in Cumberland. he desired I would assist him getting this money to his wife, as she is much in want of it, and it must be dun verry still and unbenoon to any person for this reason he is much in debt. You will be kind enough to forward this letter to John Dexter, Esqr., Cumberland, whom you will please to deliver this Cash or even to his order, takeing his or there

Receipt for the same. have nothing more to add only repeet my sincear Regards for my Owner.

BENJAMIN WRIGHT

N. B. there is a cooper come home in your brig I agreed to give him one Months pay, which is six dollars, at his arrivall at Rhode Island for many services dun by him in triming Casks and many other ways.

One [of] Captain Peters people had a pair shoes you will take notice of, wen pay day comes on his name aply for to said Peters, the price 10/.

I have let Peters have twelve pounds 6/10½ in Cash, which he will account with you for. Am your humble Servant

B. W.

N. B. have advanced Captain Peters £2.8.9 since the above in Cash.

HENRY CRUGER, JR. TO AARON LOPEZ

[Bristol,] 20 June [1769.]

Sir,

ANNEXED is Duplicate of my last Respects. This day came to hand your much esteemed favor of 24th April covering my Fathers draft on me £668.0.2½ Sterling, that when due shall place to your Credit, likewise a letter from Capt. Benjamin Wright, dtd Savannah la Marr, 19th April last, handing me a Bill of Exchange for £53.1.5½ Sterling, that goes this night for acceptance, and if paid, shall also be to the Credit side of your Account.

I repeat my sincere wishes for your Prosperity, and am with hearty Regard, Dr. Sir, Your most Humble Servant,

HEN: CRUGER, JR.

HAYLEY & HOPKINS TO CHRISTOPHER CHAMPLIN

London, 24th June, 1769.

Sir,

SINCE our last, of which the above is Copy, we have reced your favour of 5th April with an order for Goods which shall be complied with as punctually as we are able. We have exerted ourselves to gett as many as possible on board Captain Scott, for which we now enclose Invoice amounting to £1081.15.10, on which we have made £1100 Insurance premio, etc. being £28.17.9. The remainder shall be dispatched by the first Vessell when ready.

The 4 bills you remitt us are accepted and in due course shall be placed to your credit viz.

John Powell on Thomas Law	£100.-.-
G. Goodenough on Comm'rs of Victualling	23.10.-
J. Pattin on Thomas & William Maude	20.-.-
J. Bell on Henry Cort	50.-.-

We attend to your remarks upon the time of our charging Interest. We wish it was in our power to alter it. You may be very certain if we gave longer credit to any one of our friends in America we would have given it to you. We are very sensible Mr. Stead and some others here have given 12 months, but we are quite sure that upon comparing the prices of what we ship with those of many of the articles shippd by those who give 12 months you will find a much greater difference than the additional 3 mo. credit will compensate for. This is a matter which has in this House been very thoroughly considered and we have often wished to extend the credit to 12 months for the reasons mentioned in your Letter; but as we must in that case buy the Goods at 3 months longer Credit, which we could not do without paying more than the 3 months Interest would amount to, we have always considered it as more for the Interest of our friends not to alter. We can most seriously affirm that 9 months is the very utmost extent of the credit we purchase at one article with another, and that we are rather Loosers than Gainers by the article of Interest. These reasons we make no doubt will be satisfactory to you and convince you of the propriety of our present method and time of credit. We shall only add that you may most absolutely depend upon it that we will always give you every allowance that we give to any body else, as we have the greatest reason to be satisfied with your punctuality and honour. We are etc.

P. S. The bill you remitted us for £40 drawn by Jere. Bigg on David Greig being protested we now return it to you with the protest. The charges we have paid thereon is 6/9 for which you are debited. We hope you will recover the Amount with customary damages.

[HAYLEY AND HOPKINS]

Original per Scott.
[Endorsed,] Per Captain Bryant.

WILLIAM LADD TO CHRISTOPHER AND GEORGE CHAMPLIN

Mole St. Nichola, June 26th, 1769.

Gentlemen,

THESE by Captain Stanton serves to equaint you that have got ten thousand gallons of molasses on board, shall be ready to sail from here in six or eight days if am not detained longer by a sloop that is gon for molasses for Captain Toman and myself, but am in hops she will be here in a few days; have given 22/ per gallon for all have got and dont expect to git aney for less. The Candils have sold for 45/ have sold 22 barrels flour at 9 ps. 8/8, and 7 at 8 do., and have 15 still on hand that cant tell what shall git for them. there was above a thousand barrels brought in the day after I arived so that thea are prety well stockt with flour and is still coming in every day. there was upwards of twenty sail of English Vessels arived here in five days after I arived. there is about thirty five sail here in all so that cant expect molasses to fall; all kind of Northward produce is very low for the prizes of which I refer you to the price current, and am, Gentlemen, with Respect, Your most Humble Servant,

WM. LADD

price current

Codfish . . . . 3½ ps 8/8	flour . . . 6, 7 and 8	
shad 2¼	Candils . . 40s to 45 but in no demand	
Boards 16	oile . . . . 13 ps 8/8	
hoops if good 20		

[Endorsed,] per Captain N. Stanton.

HENRY CRUGER, JR. TO AARON LOPEZ

Bristol, July 6th, 1769.

Sir,

My last was a few lines dated 20th June, am not since favour'd with any of your Letters, nor any Remittances from the West Indies. this may occasion Brevity.

I fully depend on seeing a Vessel of yours the ensuing fall. you cannot wonder if my Patience is exhausted, and the faith of my *friendly* Creditors stagger'd. it's high time, Dear Sir, to bring matters to a Serious Issue. the Cord of Friendship and Indulgence is strained so tight, that it must absolutely break, unless greatly relaxed by a considerable Consignment next Fall. would to God it were in my power, even to forgive your Debt, I would do it rather than any longer torment you and myself about it; but alas! I am dayly stung to the very Soul by the Insinuations and Dunns of People to whom I owe Money, and have it not in my power to pay; so that with an aching Heart I must inform you, that if you do not next Winter greatly alleviate your Debt, I shall be impell'd to [*a few words are here heavily blotted out*] for I can no longer go on in the manner am now *indulged* to do. From my own poignant feelings and sufferings, am no Stranger to the effect this dunning ought to have, and naturally will, upon your Mind, but Lord God, Sir, whence springs all this tribulation! in fine, it must have an End, hurtfull thought! I implore you, do prevent it, and send Relief to the Wounded Mind of Your injured tho' Sincere friend,

HEN: CRUGER, JR.

P. S. If you conceive my taking a trip to America will by any means facilitate your discharging the whole of this Ballance, I will endeavour to embark sooner than I otherwise intended, as I must be here again next Spring. I am disposed to do any thing in my power to help you out.

H. C. JR.

25th July.

Dear Sir,

HAVE only to add to what precedes, that Mr. Lousada is now in this place, and has given me Liberty to value on his House (Ximenes & Lousada) for £296.6.8 Sterling on your Account, which have accordingly, and in course said Sum will be to your Credit. I am ever, Sir, Your most Humble Servant,

HEN: CRUGER, JR.

JOSEPH ROTCH & SON TO AARON LOPEZ

Bedford In Dartmouth, 7 mo. 25d, 1769.

Respected Friend, Aaron Lopez,

INCLOS'D is Bill Laden of 45 Casks Headmatter per the *Betsey*, Caleb Cory, Master which we wish safe to hand.

We receiv'd orders from our mutual Friend, Jacob Rod. Rivera, of the 14th Instant mentioning the Quantity and the price of Headmatter agreed on. The Quantity we shall endeavour to ship you if we have Success, but we have been oblig'd to engage a part to the Manufacturers here to prevent difficulty in purchasing. the Quantity that we have now ship'd will be at the Market price, but we dont apprehend that it can possibly be fix'd at your Limits, as £212.10/ is now given in Boston for all that can possibly be obtain'd.

We should not have shipd this parcel now had it not been to save Expence, as the greatest part of it was just tried and not stor'd, and Greenman here ready to take it. it is now soft as it has not had time to cool, but believe it will all be good, near 40 Bar[rel]s is from the Western Islands. Please to ship us per first Opportunity 3 Hogsheads N. E. Rum, 2 Hogsheads W. I. Rum, and 1 Pipe of best Western Island Wine. If any Malaga Wine is to be bought should like to have 1 or 2 Quarter Casks. Time not permitting to add, Remain very Respectfully Thy Assured Friends

Jos. Rotch & Son

P. S. have now return'd the Cask of last Invoice in good order and full of good Headmatter.

Jeremiah Bigg to Christopher Champlin

Sir,

I was thunder struck at seeing the Contents of your letter;[1] what am I to conclude from such extraordinary behavior in my Agent, who has above a Hundred Pounds of mine in his Hands, and must have had these eight Months. My fears tell me he will shortly be a Bankrupt: This affair must no doubt give you some uneasiness, as you have very little knowledge of me, or my circumstances. however, I will, as soon as I conveniently can, come on shore, and remove that uneasiness, by offering you such security, for your Money, as, I flatter myself you cant object to. Happy I am that it is in my Power so to do, otherwise I shou'd have been miserable indeed, as this Rascal's protesting my Bill wou'd not only have affected my Pocket but Reputation also: I shall wait with the utmost impatience and anxiety 'till I hear of the other Bill of 30 Pounds, my doubts will then be clear'd up, and I shall be able to judge what steps to take. If your correspondent has given you his Sentiments upon it, shou'd be pleas'd if you wou'd communicate

---

[1] Probably refers to protest of bill mentioned on p. 283, *supra*.

'em to me. I am, with best respects to Mrs. Champlin and Family, Your humble Servant,

JERE. BIGG

Senegal, August the 14th, /69.

HAYLEY & HOPKINS TO CHRISTOPHER CHAMPLIN

[London,] 20 September, 1769.

Sir,

SINCE our last of which the above is Copy we have rec'd your favour of 14th July and 4th August, with a bill on Lane, Son & Fraser for £524.8, which is accepted and in due course shall be placed to your credit. We have an Account of Scott's arrival at Boston by whom the chief of your Fall Goods went. We therefore are hoping to hear that they are arrived safe with you. We observe your remarks on the state of your trade and publick affairs. We impatiently wait the meeting of Parliament, till which time no true judgment can be formed of what will be done in those matters, which will be a great while first, as we dont expect they will meet till after Christmas,[1] so that it will probably be February or March before any thing can be done. We are very respectfully, Sir, Your most humble Servants,

HAYLEY & HOPKINS

The bill on D. Millagan for £23 will be protested but is not yet quite due.

[Endorsed,] Per Captain White, via Boston.

---

[1] Parliament met November 8. "Great stress was laid upon the conduct of the Americans; and the capital of one of the colonies was declared to be in a state of disobedience to all law and government; and to have proceeded to measures subversive of the constitution, and attended with circumstances that manifested a disposition to throw off their dependence on Great Britain." *Annual Register,* 1769, 64.

Joseph Rotch & Son to Aaron Lopez

Bedford in Dartmouth, 9th mo. 29th, 1769.

Respected Friend, Aaron Lopez,

We receiv'd thy esteem'd favour of 30th ult. per Capt. Cory, with the 3 Quarter Casks and 2 half Pipes Wine, also the 3 hhds. and Puncheon of Rum, all which we will keep if we can possibly dispose of them, but are fearfull shall be oblig'd to return one of the Casks Madeira wine, as we have no manner of use for it except in our family. This we should not offer to do did thou not mention it would be very agreeable to have one of them. We are much oblig'd for thy kind Intention of sending us a small case of sweet wines, and are very glad they happen'd to be omitted putting on board the Vessell, as we have a very good stock of that sort at present. Therefore beg thou will give thyself no further trouble about it.

We are also oblig'd for thy offer of the two sets Exchange for £275 Sterling which we have no Occasion for. If we could dispose of them to any of our Friends at the 4 per Cent under parr we would gladly do it; but we are oblig'd to sell our Bills at 5 per Cent Loss, some of which now lays in Boston unsold.

We are sorry to acquaint thee that we are in a most disagreeable situation with respect to purchasing Headmatter, as we are now well assurd that all the Agreements in the world will not prevent the Boston purchasers from exceeding the Limits agreed on. We have been offer'd £215/0 St. per Tun for 17 Tuns delivered here, and the same price for any Quantity delivered in Boston. The people knows the price in Boston and some have been so exasperated with us already for offering £200. that they have taken their shares out of Vessells which we were owners in, and others insist on our sending it to Boston except we advance the price.

At Nantucket it is generally sold at £210 and £212.10/.

Therefore should be glad to know whether the Manufactorers intend altering their Agreement or not.

We need not mention the Impossibility of purchasing at an inferior price as thou art sufficiently acquainted with Whalemen to know how hard they are to deal with.

We should be glad to hear from thee as soon as possible to know what is best to be done. In the Interim, We remain very Respectfully Thy Assur'd Friends

Jos. Rotch & Son

P. S. Inclos'd is an Order on Captain William Grinnell of your place for £6.0.0 L. Mo: we shall take it as a favour if thou'll receive the money of him and pass it to our Credit.

Isaac Werden to Aaron Lopez

Quebec, October the 14, 1769.

Exchange For 19£ H[alifa]x.

Sir,

AT sixty days sight of this my first of Exchange my second of equal Tennor and date not paid, pay unto Mr. Aaron Lopez or order Nineteen pounds Halifax Currency Value in account with him, and charge the same without further advice to account of, Sir, Your most humble Servant

I. Werden

To John Malcom Esqr., In his Majesties Customs at Newport, Rhode Island.

Mr. Lopez, Sir,

As the above named Malcom is a drole mortal perhaps the above method may have the best success with him which please to make first use of or indeed any other measures you may judge most probable to effect a payment in which you will much oblige, Sir, Your very humble Servant.

I. Werden

Henry Cruger, Jr. to Aaron Lopez

Bristol, October 18th, 1769.

Sir,

It is a pretty long time since I last had the pleasure of paying you my Respects, in which interval have been favour'd with sundry of your esteem'd Letters dated 29th June and 3rd August also with their Copies.

The polite and affecting assurances you give me of your disability to answer my pressing demands, at once fill me with every emotion of pity and regret, and has determin'd me to leave your Peace undisturb'd in future, by never dunning you again. Pardon, Sir, my past solicitations, they sprung not from a distrustful Mind, not from an avaricious or rapacious Heart, but from the fearful necessities to answer needy tradesmen, and, to say no worse of them, impatient Manufacturers. would to God, my distresses were at an End! but that they are not, altho greatly alleviated, is no less Melancholly than certain. I must confess, I have frequently thought myself neglected by you, when I have been informed of large Consignments of Oil, etc., going to London, when so large a Ballance was so long owing to me. surely, in right, I stood first upon the List. at other times, I have heard of your receiving large Cargoes of Dry Goods, etc., from London, when my natural hopes and flattering wishes would say, surely Mr. Lopez with the produce of this Cargo, or that, will send a little relief to his afflicted Correspondent and friend. you, Dear Sir, are the best Judge why my just and fond Expectations have (to my inexpressible disappointments) been hitherto blasted. I am disposed to put every generous Construction upon your past conduct, and I hope we shall live to see the day when, in turn, your generosity will stimulate you to make me ample recompence for all I've suffer'd on your Account.

Your favour of 29th June cover'd my Father's Bill on me for £668.-.2½ Sterling, which was in course passed to your Credit.

Mr. Lucena [1] of Georgia has consigned me for your seperate Account 13 pieces containing 3,600 ft. of Mahogany of the Musqueto shore kind, and all but one piece of so bad a Quallity that, take that piece away, I could not obtain $2\frac{1}{2}d$ per foot for the rest. for the whole have had an offer of $3d$ but ask $3\frac{1}{2}d$, and it is but just that I complain too of the Deer Skins rec'd from Mr. Lucena as being exceeding bad in Quality, and taken together were deemed $6d$ to $8d$ per lb. worse than other peoples, being greatly worm-eaten. the Quantity sent were 179 Skins in the Hair, for the joint account of you and our mutual friend Mr. Rivera. I have sold them as per Sales herewith (duplicate of which will be sent to Mr. Rivera). Net Proceeds £19.18 Sterling, a Moiety to each of your respective Credits. Mr. Lucena likewise remitted for account of you and Mr. Rivera a Bill of £80 Sterling that is paid and credited half to each of you.

I have lately heard from my friend Mr. Nathaniel Grant of Jamaica concerning the Bill of £150 formerly remitted me by Mr. A. P. Mendes of that place and returned thither. he writes as follows "Your most esteem'd favour of 6th March covering D[anie]l Moore's Bill for £150 Sterling under protest came duely to hand, I will use my endeavours to procure payment as soon as possible, but fear I shall not obtain it earlier than the next Year," so that we have reason to apprehend it will turn out a bad affair.

Agreeable to your wish I have procured a continuance of the Insurance on the *Diana*, Captain Potter, as per particulars herewith, cost £54.5.0 to your Debit; as is likewise the cost of £900 done on the Brigantine *Charlotte*, being £24.4, the Account whereof you'll find inclosed. the Brig doth not yet make her appearance nor am I over-eager to see her, the Cargo she brings being such a drug, Logwood £4. to £4.4. Last spring Mahogany got up to $5d$ and $6d$ per foot. this price sat all America at sending it and in such abundance too, that our City is now so full of it, it is once again reduced to it's old horrid price of $3d$ to

---

[1] James Lucena, from whom is a series of letters in this collection, in Portuguese.

4*d* per foot. I have sent, as a proof to confirm what I say, our presentments or Bill of Entries by which you'll perceive, we have imported into this place in less than twelve months near 400 thousand feet, and sufficient to lower the price to what I quote it; and the Devil of it is, we are in dayly expectation of three Cargoes to arrive consisting of one hundred thousand feet more. I will only add, rely upon my doing with yours the best I can, tho' you must expect the Sales will be excessive tedious.

Inclosed is a Price Current of our Market at present, its alteration depends entirely upon the greater or lesser Quantity of each Article that may arrive. this is all that now occurs.

I remain with sincere sentiments of goodwill and respect, Dear Sir, Your most Obedient Humble Servant,

HEN: CRUGER, JR.

P. S. I have since sold the Mahogany consigned me by Mr. Lucena at 3½ per foot.

[Endorsed,] Via Boston Per Jno. Gally.

JOSEPH ROTCH & SON TO AARON LOPEZ

Bedford in Dartmouth, 10 mo. 19, 1769.

Respected Friend, Aaron Lopez,

THY esteemd favours of 11th and 18th Instant came in course to hand on receipt of the former we had a conveyance for Nantucket by which we orderd the Corda[ge] made immediately and forwarded directly to Newport, if any Opportunity. If no Opportunity direct for that place, it was to be sent here. we doubt not but the Ropemaker will take care that no time is lost in making this parcel and to have it of the best Quality.

We are much oblig'd for thy Trouble of forwarding our Letters, and also for engaging Daniel the Rigger. he came very seasonably for our business.

When we wrote about Pig Iron we thought it could be obtain'd in Newport, but as it is up Country we dont imagine it can now be procurd seasonably. Therefore thou need not take any further Notice of it.

We observe that thou has orderd our mutual Friend Nathaniel Wheatley to credit us the Ballance of a Bill Exchange remitted him; also £150 paid him by Benjamin Alline is order'd to our credit. We should be glad if it was in our power consistent with thy Interest to have ten times those sums to receive. we have already wrote the Determination of the people here with respect to Headmatter, and they are of the same mind now. we are requested to advance the price within £6.0 T[eno]r of Boston price, or ship it to Boston, and as we will not comply with the former are oblig'd to do the latter, and in a few days expect to ship all we have on hand to that market. We have perus'd the Circular Letter from the Manufactorers to their factors and observe their just complaint of the low price of Oyl, Loss on Bills, and other Disadvantages they labour under by a slow sale, etc. But to what purpose, are all those Arguments made use of to people whose private Interest is all they are concernd for. We have told them the same before and have since read the Circular Letter to them, but it will be of as much service to speak to the wind as to endeavour to perswade them to sell at £200 when it is £220 in Boston. You are not the only sufferers by the Headmatters going to Boston, for we lose all our Commissions on all that goes in that Channell. Therefore as we see no probability of procuring any at your Limits it will be entirely needless for the money in N. Wheatley's hands to be orderd to our Credit, as we suppose that we have already received more than the Headmatter sent. We shall draw off thy accounts in a few days to see how it is, and if there is a balance due from us we will remit it immediately.

We have already got the displeasure of so many by endeavouring to keep the price at £200 that we never intend to give any other person encouragement for purchasing in future; but when we have any to dispose of we shall endeavour to give our old Friends the refusal. We are sensible we have a deficiency to make up for the Mahogany by not supplying Pork at the price agreed on, which with all other matters shall be settl'd to satisfaction, and at any time when we can be of any service only be kind enough to let us know in what manner and it shall be comply'd with. please to acquaint our Worthy Friend J: R. Rivera the Situation we are in with respect to Headmatter. We shall write him in a few days but time will not permit at present. Remain very respectfully, Thy Assurd Friends,

JOS. ROTCH & SON

P. S. We cannot find what became of the small case of wine, but we think ourselves equally indebted, as if it had come to our hands.

[Endorsed,] Per Post.

JOHN POWELL TO CHRISTOPHER CHAMPLIN [1]

Boston, 23d Octo., 1769.

Dear Sir,

NOT hearing from Jenny this Post makes me uneasy fearing she may not be well.

I hope you received your Box and bale shipt by Hubbell a Connecticut man.

a Subscription is on foot here, called a Self Denying Ordinance to starve one half of the Inhabitants of this good Town, and not to admit Scot's Goods, to build Ships, to employ the idle tradesmen.

I send you Mein's last advice to the Well Disposed Comittee.[2] my best Regards attend you and the family. I am, Dear Sir, Yours,

J. POWELL

I do not write Mrs. Powell. Please to tell her the Children and family are all well, and to give me Notice when intends to be at providence that I may meet her there. Tea is

---

[1] The original is in the Newport Historical Society.
[2] See *The Boston Chronicle*, October 19-23, 1769, with its "Catechism of the 'Well Disposed,'" which ran through several numbers.

advanced to 4/ none in Town except myne that is not lock't up by the Committee. If no Dutch should be smugled will fetch 6/.

HENRY CRUGER, JR. TO AARON LOPEZ

Bristol, November 1st, 1769.

Dear Sir,

ANNEX'D is duplicate of my last Respects. The 29th October the *Charlotte* arriv'd here, and is now unloading. she brought me your favor of 21st August, a former one of same date I before receiv'd, which cover'd my Father's draft value £350.5.10¾ Sterling, that at Maturity will of course be to your Credit. your last esteem'd Letter cover'd Bill of Lading and Invoice for the *Charlotte's* Cargo, that shall do my best with, and hope to obtain 3 to 3½d for the Mahogany, £4 for Logwood, and £5.12.6 per ton for the Pigg Iron, which is but an indifferent sort, as have proved by many Essays I got made out of a former Parcell consign'd me per Nicholas Brown & Co. on board your Brigantine the *Little Betsey*.

I am thankful for your kind endeavors to ease my Debt, and for that purpose permitting me to sell the *Charlotte* at £320 Sterling, but low as these limits are, don't think shall be able to sell at them; however, when she is discharg'd, I'll see about it. Freights are so very scarce, owing to the present stagnation of Trade in general, that fancy you may be looking for your Brigantine back again in Ballast. I say this, as I put it down for granted she won't fetch £320 having not long since sold as good a Vessel just arriv'd, and went to Sea again for a trifle, at only £250 Stg.

No doubt I shall prevent any unnecessary or extra Charges falling on your Vessel, owing to Capt. Newdigate's being unacquainted with the customs of our City, due care shall also be taken about your Mahogany, out of which nothing shall be taken save the Masters Priviledge of 1432 feet you mention.

I think it very probable that Mahogany will rise by the

time Newdigate can return here from the Bay. the present low price will discourage People in general from sending, and the few that do, will I really think, not be hurt by it.

Inclosed is Sales of the 13 pieces Mahogany ship'd me by Mr. Lucena of Georgia on your Account, neating £23.8. Sterling to your Credit.

I am oblig'd by your Friendly expressions and wishes for my Welfare. be assur'd Dear Sir, mine for you are as warm, and sincere, for I really am in every sence of the Word, Your sincerely attach'd Friend and most obedient humble Servant,

HEN: CRUGER, JR.

SAILING ORDERS TO CAPTAIN POTTER

Newport, November 3d, 1769.

Sir,

THE Ship *Jacob* now under your Command being ready fitted for the Seas you are to embrace the first fair Wind and proceed directly to St. Anns in the Island of Jamaica, where on your safe arrival dispose of your Cargo for the Most you can, and invest its proceeds chiefly in Molasses some Rum and Sugars; I desire you'll be carefull on examining the Quality of what Rum you may purchase for the Cargo, and to receive none, but what sinks Oil, as great difference is made at these Markets when it proves short of that Standard. I propose to dispatch very soon a small Vessell to North Carolina in order to load there, chiefly with Red Oak Hogshead Staves and some other produce, so as to enable you to supply your Customers with such articles, as are now dificient in your Cargo; Therefore you'll be pleased to preengage the Sale of them, previous to their Arrival.

As I shall order Insurance on the Ship, expect the underwriters will make it a Condition that she quits Jamaica, before the 26th July next, which desire you'll attend to in a particular manner, ordering your Bussiness and engagements with the Planters in such a way, as you may be able to effect it, without exposing my Interest to the intolerable disadvantage of leaving behind any part thereof; as it not only lays me to the risk, that attends debts contracted on that Island, but deprives me the Use of so much Capital; therefore in due attention to all these reasons, let me again reiterate my possitive instructions, both to quit Jamaica, before the above period, and to leave no Interest behind, which being all at present occurs; have only to add my sincere wishes for your safe return with a successful Voyage and am very truly,

Acknowledge the preceding to be a true Copy of my Instructions, which I promise to comply with.

JAMES POTTER

JOSEPH ROTCH & SON TO AARON LOPEZ

Boston, 11 mo. 20, 1769.

Respected Friend, Aaron Lopez,

OUR mutual Friend Nathaniel Wheatley acquainted us, the price thou could furnish us with a quantity of Molasses and Rum, say the former at 10/6 O. T. per Gallon, and the latter at 13/ O. T. we expect to have a Vessell at Newport soon, when we shall want some put on board her. The Price of all our Headmatter, is now fix'd at £215 per Ton here, which is £209 at Dartmouth; therefore as it exceeds the manufacturers agreement, shall not be able to ship any more to Newport, except a small parcell which we have promised our Friend J. R. Rivera, for a small ballance we have had in our hands some time. therefore the money left in our Friend N. Wheatley's hands by Benjamin Allen and for the bills Exchange, now waits thy order. time not permitting to add, have only to assure thee, that we are very respectfully Your assured Friends,

          Jos. Rotch & Son

Jno. Newdigate to Henry Cruger, Jr.

Sir,   Dublin, December 5th, 1769.

This will inform you that I arriv'd here on Tuesday, having as kind and favorable a Passage as in the Summer Season and moderate fine weather. I met with worthy Gentlemen here whom I was addressed to, and your Friend Mr. Dunn will do all that lies in his Power for getting me a Freight which at present I can't acquaint you whether or no, as I have but this day seen him; possibly I may as the Broker Mr. Fraser tells me. You may depend, Dr. Sir, of my using the utmost frugality in regard of the Vessel as I have but little to do to her, and shall make the utmost dispatch away if I do get no Freight. I shall write you as soon as I am unloaded how things will go on in regard of my Proceedings and am, Sir, Your humble Servant,

          John Newdigate

Henry Cruger, Jr. to Aaron Lopez

Dear Sir,   Bristol, December 6th, 1769.

The preceding is Copy of my last Respects. the Logwood by the *Charlotte* is sold at £4.4 per Ton, which is 4/ more than I can get for two Cargoes I have arriv'd since. the Mahogany all remains unsold. such Quantities have arriv'd within this last Month the Buyers are in hopes it will soon be to be bought at 3*d*. I will never sell so low untill others do before me. by letting Newdigate have some very good pieces he sold his small Parcell to a Countryman by good Luck for 4*d* per foot. I should be glad to have sold yours at the same Price. I have not yet met a Chap to my Mind for your Pigg Iron.

I tried hard to procure the *Charlotte* a Freight from hence to the West Indies but none was to be had. however a Gentleman of my Acquaintance offer'd to load her for Dublin. I could get from him no more than £70 Irish for the run, which I accepted, considering Newdigate was in no great hurry to get to the West Indies and I thought tho' a small Sum, yet she being so small a Vessell, it was doing something towards paying Port Charges; and then if she has any Luck, he is in a way to get a Freight thence to the West Indies, as from Ireland they are continually sending Provisions thither, and I have strongly recommended Newdigate to all my Friends in Dublin. for these reasons, and as I meant and studied to advance your Interest, hope you will be satisfied with what I have done. I enter'd into a Charter Party. the Brigantine is to be discharg'd at the expence of the Shippers, in 8 days after her arrival in Dublin, or they are to pay Demurrage. they are to advance Newdigate sufficient for his Port Charges taking his receipt for the same, and to order the Ballance to be paid to me here. the *Charlotte* could not carry as much as Captain Newdigate imagin'd and engag'd for. Newdigate says the Merchant quoted to him among other things only 40 hogsheads Sugar; the Merchant insists upon it he said 60 hogsheads. the Vessel left out of what she agreed to carry vizt. 54 Barrels Rice, and 9 Hogsheads Sugar, which the Shipper says he will deduct the usual Freight of out of the £70. then on our part we shall have a demand on him for the freight of some Iron and 51 boxes of Tin Plates, which he promises us he wou'd pay a seperate Freight for; when I come to make a final Settlement depend upon me for doing it as much to your Advantage as shall be in my power. I must beg your Patience on this head untill it's concluded. the *Charlotte* sail'd for Dublin with a fair Wind the 1st Instant, and hope she is safe arriv'd ere now. my next I suppose will convey you that agreeable News.

Since my last I am favor'd with your frank and much esteem'd Letter of 19th September. I will only add on that Subject may Providence prosper your endeavours and my Wishes, which will render Comfort to us both. if the present Cases were remov'd I have no doubt but our future Correspondence would be more advantageous and happy.

In the Article of Spermaceti Oil, some of my Friends in New York have disappointed me, and so has Mr. Lopez. what a strange thing it is that People will not strive to be the *first* at Market, *when they know* all depends upon that Circumstance. by the last two Ships from New York came 50 tons White Oil. the part that came to me was from Gentlemen from whom I had no reason to expect any, but to my Chagreen, not a drop from those from whom I did expect some, because I encourag'd it. I suppose when the Market is glutted, these Gentlemen will be sending in consequence of my former Advices and encouragements, and when their Goods come to a low Market they will think it very odd and with Wonder say, "the Price is always high untill our Goods arrive, and then, to our disappointment and loss it is fallen." Winter I have before said is the Season for Spermaceti Oil; after Christmas it begins to fall. therefore whose fault is it but their own, if People will not send their Goods to Market untill after the Fair is over? the Oil that came from New York was white Spermaceti, and sold tho' the Quantity was large, at near £27 per ton, since which one or two Parcells have arriv'd. Plenty in all things produces cheapness. You'll perceive by my Letter to you, Dear Sir, of 7th June, wherein I recommend your sending Oil, I beg'd you wou'd do it early in the Fall, that you wou'd for that Purpose push off a Vessel of your own. had it been convenient to have follow'd my Advice, you'd have clear'd a pretty Penny these bad times, which wou'd really have afforded me sincere Satisfaction. by the end of this Month the great Demand and high Prices will in all Probability be over. these things are rather mortifying. excuse my Freedom and Zeal. it springs from the warm Friendship of, Dear Sir, Yours, etc.

HEN: CRUGER, JR.

P. S. I had like to have forgot the Account of Insurance on the *Charlotte* to Dublin, which is underneath, amounting to £6.17.6 to your Debit. when Captain Newdigate informs me of his arrival at Dublin and further destination, will insure £300 on the Ship untill she shall arrive at the Bay; and should he get any Freight for the West Indies will of course cover that by Insurance to it's place of discharge.

November 25th, 1769.

MR. AARON LOPEZ
          To HENRY CRUGER, JUNIOR Dr.
For Cost of Insurance on the *Charlotte*, John Newdigate, Master, at and from Bristol to Dublin,

£300 . . . . on Ship	Valued	
70 . . . . on Freight		
£370 . . . . at 25/ per Cent		£4.12.6
	Policy	0. 8. -
Commission on £370 . . . . at 1/2 per Cent		1.17. -
To the Debit of Mr. Aaron Lopez		£6.17. 6

SAILING ORDERS FOR CAPTAIN HYER

Newport, December 12th, 1769.

Sir,

THE Sloop *Industry* now under your Command being ready fitted for the Seas you are to embrace the first fair wind and proceed to the Island of Tennerif, where on your Arrival deliver the inclosed to Mr. Solomon Townsend with your Cargo agreeable to Bills Lading; and in his absence keep the Letter I have addressed him and make use of the other Letter I have given you for Messrs. Mahony & Wolfe, to whom you may also deliver your Cargo and receive in return such Effects as either of those Gentlemen may deliver you, with which you are to return home making the best of your way and as you are sensible this is a Charter'd Vessell, I depend on your losing no time in improving every advantage to render the Voyage short. When you return from Tenneriff would be glad you would touch at St. Martins or Saltertudas, and take in about 10 or 1200 Bushells Salt and proceed here, but endeavour to avoid coming into the Harbour in the forenoon so as to prevent your entering the Sloop immediately on your Arrival; and if the Wind is fair that you could come in at the back part of the Island and send me an Express will be much safer. I have nothing to add save my best wishes for your safe return and am Your Humble Servant

AARON LOPEZ

P. S. I desire you'll procure me about one thousand good long Vine Slips, which please to see well put up in a Cask or Box with Earth, etc.

Acknowledge the above to be a true Copy of my Instructions which I promise to comply with to the best of my knowledge.

JNO. HYER

HENRY CRUGER, JR. TO AARON LOPEZ

23d December, 1769.

Dear Sir,

ANNEX'D is duplicate of my last Respects, and am since pleased by the Receipt of a Letter from Newdigate in Dublin, where he arrived 5th Instant. He was then dubious whether he could get a Freight, or not, to the West Indies. he promises again to write me as soon as his Vessel was discharged, but have not yet heard a second time from him. untill I do, can say no more about his further destination, or how shall settle with the Gentleman who charter'd her.

A person who makes Spermaceti Candles near this City, requested me to enquire what Quantity of *Head Matter* you could ship home annually, and at what price. If he approves of the Terms, and you chuse to send any, he may buy a good deal. to this, pray favor me with an answer as soon as convenient.

Have met a Chap for your Pigg Iron per *Charlotte* at £5.15.0 per Ton. the Mahogany by her, I put up to publick Auction, and was lucky enough to push it all off, at the Prices noted in the Sales inclosed of the Brigantine *Charlotte's* Cargo, for the net proceeds of which I credit your Account £465.6.9 Sterling.

Herewith is a Price Current for your Guidance. I am,

wishing you many Happy, and Prosperous New Years, Dear Sir, Your most Humble Servant,

HEN: CRUGER, JR.

P. S. You have herewith Account of disbursements on *Charlotte* amounting to £150.2.0. Stg. to your debit.

[Endorsed,] Via New York Per *Grace*.

LORENZO DE MERRA TO AARON LOPEZ

Bilbao, January 17th, 1770.

Mr. *Aaron Lopez*,

I HAD a Cargo of whale Oil from London this winter and being much in esteem here would now sell for £23 per Ton. I sold that for £21 per Ton. you have at foot the computation of an English Ton with the Measure here for your Government so that if you may think it encourageing to try this place which is in your way to London we consume annuly 600 Tons and upwards. Dry fish hath sold from 90 rrs to 100 per qql. I had one Cargo which neat'd clear of Charges 18s per qql. remittance with the ship in fourteen days.

Spermacatte Candles a few would sell being the nearest to madrid. Indian corn yellow grain is sildom under Twenty Rrs per Fanega. Bees wax wale bone good articles here. my Friends in London Messrs. Heyett & Bercly will give you my Character and anything I can serve you in shall be done with Dispatch and remittance or forwarded as you direct. I am sir your Humble Servant,

LORENZO DE MERRA

```
140 vellons make a Ton English 28 Dollars 32
    vells . . . . . . . . . . . . . . .  1837.16
Duties to the Consulado ½ . . .09.00 ⎫
New impost at 2 r[ei]s per 32 . .08.06 ⎪
Prebestado 2½ per Ct. . . . . .48.30 ⎬  . . . . 0073.22
Co[o]per . . . . . . . . . . . .10.00 ⎭
                                   R   1763.23
```

Sterling clear of all Charges £19.11s.8d.

John Newdigate to Henry Cruger, Jr.

Dublin, February 4th, 1770.

Sir,

This informs you that I am loaded and ready to sail for Jamaica and is to touch at the Island of Madeira, where I am to take in 30 Pipes of Wine, which will amount to in all Freight, when please God I arrive at Jamaica about £100 that Currency. there are no Freights to be had here. There is a Ship here from London of 300 tons bound for Jamaica, which offerd to take in Freight for 7/6 per ton but cannot get it. at the latter end of December was ready to sail in Ballast and was to go away the next day following after, but this Freight offer'd and I took out my Ballast and took it in, but could get no sooner dispatch'd than at present. I am heartily sorry to take up so much Money on your Account, but when I came to overhall the Vessell found her Transum all rotten and several of her Timbers, which put me to a great expence, and being oblig'd to buy Beef and Bread for the Voyage and other expences, it came to the amount I drew on you for.

Sir, I wrote you two letters one at my arrival here and at the 15th December, but has never heard from you, which I am sorry for. I am afraid you never got the Letters. at my arrival here I deliver'd the Letters from Mr. Weldon to Mr. Mahan and his Father. my Vessel lay at Pole Peg two miles from the Town, as I cou'd by no means get over the Barr she drew so much Water. the next day Mr. Mahan sent a Lighter down to me to load her, and desired I wou'd take care to keep the Lighter Men from pilfering the Goods, as they were great Rogues. I accordingly loaded the same and sent her up to him, and she lay ten days and nothing taken out of her. after that he sent two others and they took the whole out, and they lay at the Quay 10 or 12 days and did not unload, and the Men belonging to them aboard all the time, and it's likely they to steal his Sugars, for no such thing was done aboard my Vessel. after that I apply'd to Mr. Weldon to get out his Iron, and

Sperma-ceti Candles Warranted pure: are made by JOSEPH PALMER &Co. at Germantown near BOSTON to be Sold at their Store in Boston, New-England.

N.º 353.

lb.   Gr.
36¼   8¾
27½   18.

No.rr.l Candles
5 to the lb.

Chandelles ....
5 au lb.

Chandelles de Sperma-ceti garantues d'être sans aucun Melange sont Fabriquées par Joseph Palmer V.ca German town proche de Boston, & se vendent à leur Magazin en Boston, Nouvelle Angleterre.

in two days he gave an order to land it at the Iron Quay. immediately went to getting it out, and the people that was to receive it abused Mr. Weldon and repeated over sundry times that he never paid any Man for his Labour, and he and his Iron may be dam'd for they wou'd give themselves no trouble about it. I acquainted Mr. Weldon of this and he told me to land it and not mind them, and accordingly I put it all ashore, and it lay outside of the Gate 5 days. after that I got my Vessel into the Carpenter's hands and apply'd to Mr. Mahan for the 20 Pounds I was to receive of him, and he put me off from time to time, and a fortnight after that he told me there was no Money for me and that his Sugar was missing of near 24 ct. wt. knowing that no Embezzlement was done aboard my Vessel I was very uneasy and being a Stranger in the Place I know not what to do. I went to a Notary Public and all my people, and have done as you see. (say, they have made Affadavit that the Cargo was not diminish'd on board and likewise how landed). Mr. Patrick Weldon abused me much about his Iron, but the Character he bears here is very bad, for he never dealt with any Man that he had not Words with. When I sign'd Bills of Lading at Bristol for the Sugars there was no quantity mention'd, only 51 Hogsheads, and the same quantity was deliver'd here, and the quantity of Barrs of Iron.

I shall, Sir, you may depend remit the Freight to you from Jamaica, and I am very sorry to take up so much Money on your Account; but believe me I cou'd not do without it, and so conclude, Dr Sir, Your humble Servant,

JOHN NEWDIGATE

JOHN PETERS TO AARON LOPEZ

St. Nicola Mole, February 6, 1770.

Mr. Aaron Lopez,

I ARIVED here after a passage of Twenty Eight Days. the night after sailed from Rhode Island I had southley wind, two days after that a verry harde Gale at S S E in the above Gale I lost one horse and four Sheep. Mr. Manuel has sold the horses for three hundred and fifty Livers per head, and he has sold the sheep for twenty five Livers per head. Spermicit Candles at about 46; Souse pork sixteen pieces Eight per barrel. Beef is verry low. the Boards I belive will answer verry well. there is shad been sold for Twelve Bitts. Mr. Manuel has been oferd Twenty Five pistoles for the Two Chaise. Mellasses is at 23 Souse, and Sugar is very high. Mr. Serzadas tills Mr. Manuel he has shiped some of your Effects he had in his hands in a Vessele bound for Rhode Island, and the Remainder he will ship by me. Oil is verry lowe. I expect to be disspatched by the 20 of next month. as for any more perticulars I shall wright by the next oppertunity so no more at present, But remain

JOHN NEWDIGATE TO HENRY CRUGER, JR.

Dublin, February 8th, 1770.

Sir,

INCLOSED you have the Transactions of my Proceedings in this place and likewise the two Affidavits. I am heartily sorry I could not hear from you before I left this place for I have wrote at my arrival and in December, which makes me think you might have never receiv'd the Letters from me. I am really heartily sorry to take up so much Money on your Account, but buying of Beef and other Provisions and other Expences and my people having the Small Pox which cost me what I have receiv'd and more, so beg, Dr. Sir, you will not think it unfrugal for after 'twas unloaded

I put my Vessel up for Freight and tryed all manner of ways to procure a Freight, but could not untill I had got all my Ballast in and the Vessel ready for Sea and cleared out. then I was offerd 300 Barrels of Beef, and something in my way to call at Madeira, where I am to take in 30 Pipes of Wine, so that the whole Freight will amount to what Mr. Dunn will inform as I have gave him an account of every particular of what I have on board and by whom ship'd. If, Sir, I have gave you offence, as I am positive it cannot be pleasing to you when you see what Money I have taken up, you will be angry believe me, I am sorry altho' I do not feel it, for let any stranger come here and have no person to advise with, the people in this Country will take all advantage of him. they have rob'd me of all my new large rope I had out for fast, and cut both Cables and carried some part away, for such a place and villains I never saw, and I am sorry indeed I ever came into this Country. this is the first time and hope it will be the last unless I cannot help it, for really the best Merchant in the place will take advantage if it lies in their Power by any means. as for Mr. Patrick Weldon he has a most terrible bad Character. I need not give you a particular Account of what Money I have disburs'd, as I have deliver'd it to Mr. Dunn and he is to send it to you. I have been detain'd here, and several Vessels has been these 6 weeks for a fair wind to go down Channel.

Dr. Sir, if I have offended you I hope you will not intimate anything to Mr. Lopez, as my dependance is on my behaviour; I am positive you will not be pleased when you see the amount of what I took up as I have bought Provisions and every other article according to his orders for to last the Vessel untill she arrives in America, which was his orders to me when I left him. I am sorry I came this Voyage. I beg you may get the Vessel cover'd for Madeira and Jamaica and the Bay and Home, this, Sir, is at your own discretion, as I know not what Mr. Lopez has wrote you so conclude Dr Sir Your most humble Servant,

JOHN NEWDIGATE

JAMES DUNN TO HENRY CRUGER, JR.

Dublin, February [20], 1770.

Sir,

I was duely favor'd with yours of 20th November per Capt. Newdigate, requesting I wou'd use my endeavours in procuring him a Freight for the West Indies, and also that I wou'd give him any assistance which he might want, in answer to which his Vessel was in such bad order as to oblige him to put her in repair before he cou'd attempt to look for a Freight, or sail upon such a Voyage, and for which purpose I was oblig'd to advance him Money to the amount of £107.0.2, for which you have an Account inclosed and the Captain's receipt for what Money was paid to him to discharge several small accounts, of which you have his account, and tho' I used all my endeavors to procure him a Freight, it was not untill he was ready to sail and had taken in his Ballast that one offer'd for Madeira and Jamaica; and we thought it was better to accept of it than to let him go empty, as it wou'd in some measure help to pay the expences of his outfitt. Inclosed you have an Account of his Freight List. His being so long detain'd here by contrary winds was a great means of the Charge running so high, and it was not in his power untill Friday Evening the 16th Inst. to sail; but as the weather is very broken and the Insurance is not great I think you wou'd do well to insure her; of which you are the best Judge. therefore I submit my Will to yours. for the amount of my advance please to credit the Account of Messrs. Henry & John Cruger of which advise them, and as all their Mahogany is mostly disposed of I am in hopes of being able shortly to furnish them Sales of the same, which is all that at present offers from, Sir, Your very humble Servant,

JAMES DUNN

John Newdigate to Henry Cruger, Jr.

Sir, Whitehaven, February 19th, 1770.

THIS serves to inform you that I left Dublin on the 16th at 2 oClock with an intent to proceed to Madeira and Jamaica, but at 9 at night it began to blow extreme hard and at South. I endeavour'd to put into the Isle of Man but could not by reason of its blowing so extreme hard. I then attempted for Whitehaven. My Vessel could suffer no other Sail but her Foresail, which Place I obtain'd with great difficulty, and in coming inside of the Pier Head she struck very hard and beat untill the Tide left her, which caused her to make more Water than she ever did, and I cannot inform you what damage she has taken as yet but refer it 'till my next. This is as hard a Gale as ever was known in this Channel. there is a Vessel since I came in which struck and is lost, Vessel and Cargo, from the Streights bound for Belfast, and two others stove and receiv'd great damage. this unfortunate Voyage must be of dissatisfaction to you. really I am sorry and cannot help these misfortunes, for had we kept out two hours longer we should have lost our lives and Vessel. I wrote you from Dublin on my Sailing and where, desiring you would be pleased to insure the Vessel. if you have not as yet, beg you may, for I know not what damage she has receiv'd nor can I inform you, but shall in my next, for the Gale holds so hard there is no stirring in the Harbour. since I began to write this there are two Vessels arriv'd all tore to pieces with the Gale, so refer to my next and remain, Dr Sir, Your most obedient Servant,

JOHN NEWDIGATE

Benjamin Lyon to Aaron Lopez

Sir, Montreal, February 26th, 1770.

I SHOULD have wrote you before now had I not expected to see you myself, but affairs not turning out as I expected I must have recourse to the Pen. I carefully sent your letter to Isaac Werden by Post, but neither I nor Levy Salomons ever received any Instructions about the Contents, but found out since the Quantity of Beaver certainly haveing been ship'd for you, which if not turn'd out to your satisfaction neither I or Levy Salomons can be blam'd for it. I am also sorry to acquaint you that I am crediteably inform'd that Mr. Werden has purchased on your Account between 7 and 9 Hundred Pounds of Beaver Wool at 3/ Hallifax[1] per Pound, which is look'd upon here not be worth 2 pence a Pound nor in England. He also purchased on your Account a large Quantity of Beaver at 3/ and 9*d* per pound, which by what Levy Salomons informs me (as the Furrs were all received by him for the Person he purchased them off) are the greatest part what goes here two for one. This is in my opinion not your intention to trade in this Country. Therefore I give you this for your information, being fully convinced that this letter by comming into your hands will never be made use of, as our Circumstances will not permit us to be at Enmity with any person, and I heartily wish you may find it otherwise for your sake.

As we could not perform our agreement with our Creditors on account of not getting in our debts we are obliged to carry on the Bussiness some time longer, butt if you should chuse to have any Connections in this Country I would recommend to you to examine the following Proposals. That is to consign as much of your West India Goods to Levy Salomons in Montreal and Hayman Myars (in case he returns again to Quebec) or Mr. Stephen Moore, Marchant, in Quebec, as both places will answer much better, Levy Salomons knowing the difference of Peltries and the Markets for the different Ports so well that it undoubtedly will answer in this Manner to have your effects mostly

---

[1] Before 1765 the province authorized loans in anticipation of revenue or to meet a deficit, but issued notes only in large denomination, bearing interest at six per cent. per annum. In 1765 provision was made for the issue of small notes, as the circulation of large notes proved too inconvenient. *Nova Scotia Laws*, 5 Geo. III, c. ix.

turn'd into Furrs and have all the Fine Furr ship'd for your Correspondent in London and such as will answer your Markett and Philadelphia to be sent to your Port which will allways be equal to Cash. I make no doubt but your remittances would yield from 20 to 30 per cent, and I am certain the Profit on the Furrs will exceed those on your Goods; and the whole Profit in this Country on Furrs depends on the recept of them here, the greatest part of which is received by Levy Salomons, and who you may depend on will do all in his Power to promote your interest. Should you consider and think well of this plan you may flatter yourselves to be able to carry on a larger Trade to the West Indies then any man that ships here, and the Marchants who remit in species would not be eable either to buy or sell with you. If you should chuse to be connected in this or any other manner you shall think proper, please let me know by Post. As I cannot recommend any certain articles which would at present answer this Market better then others I leave the whole to the Bearer Mr. Myars. you may if you should chuse have some remittances in wheat. the price at present is from 4/ to 4/ and 6*d* Lawfull per Bushell. I am, Sir, Your most obedient and Humble Servant,

BENJAMIN LYON

[Endorsed,] Per favor of Mr. Hayman Myars.

SIMEON POTTER TO AARON LOPEZ

Bristol [R. I.], March 1st, 1770.

Sir,

YOUR favor of the 23 ult I received per Mr. Orr and observe you have received the 3 Blls. Indigo, and as to the Bill I sea you are onest. I have received no answer from Captain Whipple to my letter altho I know he has received it. as to the Money being advanced by your Corespondant on my Credit I cant say I know the Gentleman or he me, and was it advanced for my Youse I shuld not hesitate a moment. But so far to the Conterarey of that, when my Sloop put back to stop a Leak the hol Expence was not more then 50 ps. 8/8, and Captain Whipple sold three hhds. of my Molasis to defray that Expence. as to your detaning the 6 Dollars fraght its very well. But as to the 4 Dollars charged you as a present to the Water[1] was giuen in Newport to save the Duty, and out of my money I sent to pay the Dutes of my molases. Thearfore I shall think very hard if it's not repaid me again. I hope Captain Whipple will give you a satesfactuery account about the Bill. I shall due euery thing in my Power [to get] it settled. I am Your Humble [Servant]

SIMEON POTTER

CAPT. WILLIAM MINTURN TO AARON LOPEZ

Barbadoes, March 2, 1770.

Gentlemen,

I TAKE this my first oppertunity to inform you of my safe arrivall at this Island after a hard blowing Passage of 24 days, where I find the Markets to be very low for our Cargo and horses very dull sail at low prices. on inquirrey I am informed that the Markets is very low to Leward for fish and horses perticular. I waited on Mr. Jones and he told me that if I tarryd here that he would ship the Ballance of Mr. Lopez account by me, which I judge it would be most to our advantage to tarry here, as our horses was not sutuable to go to Leward with. and to make the best of a bad market I have sold as follows: Spermacitty Candles at 2/, Salt fish at 17/6, Munhadin at 12/6, Alewives at 18/9, hoops at £6, Staves at £10. the Oil I cant sell at any Price the Chess I have not sold but excep'd it will fetch from 6*d* to 7*d* per lb. the Price of Rum is not broke yet; it is thought the Price will be 20*d* or 22*d* per Gall. I cant inform you when I shall sail, as I have Six Hor[s]es on hand it is very uncertain when I shall sell the remainer part of my horses,

---

[1] Tide waiter, "a custom officer who awaited the arrival of ships (formerly coming in with the tide), and boarded them to prevent the evasion of the custom-house regulations." The term has passed out of use.

but if no Dissopointment I am in hopes to sail by the 10 of April.

P. S. I shall call at some the Leward islands to sell my Oil.

WATERS HANNARS TO AARON LOPEZ

NewBern, March 6th, 1770.

Sir,

I HOPE these few Lines may find you in a better health then when I left Newport. I am now loaded and shall sail this day for the Mould.¹ I have binn hear three or four weaks longer then Mr. Ellis or I expected when I arived, but ther is benn very bad weather hear sence I came, so that Mr. Ellis has benn greatley dissepinted or should have saild before. I am very sartin that Mr. Ellis has dun all lay in is Power to sarve your Intress. the Sault which I brought, Mr. Ellis sould biggest part to the Country men, and they came not according to prommas, and he could not get a Store in the place to put it in so we was ableag'd to make a Store of the Sloop.

Sir, I hartly wish your health and remain Your Most Obedient Humble Sarvant,

WATERS HANNARS

N. B. I hear incloes the Sirtifekats to cancel the Bonds at Newpor.

---
¹ Mole.

NATHANIEL BRIGGS TO A. AND A. LOPEZ

St. Nicklass Mole, March 6, 1770.

Gentel Men,

THIS is to leat you now of my safe ariuel heair after being at Dominica, and St. Kitts, and the other Island at St. Croix, have sold my Loumber and about 80 Boxes Spermaceti Candles, my hoops and whit Staves and heading at £9, Read oak Staves and Bords at £4.10/ St. Kitts Corrency delivered at St. Criox, and have taking one bord 20 hogsats of Rum and hope that it will anser well. I have got one bord 21 hogsets of Molases and shall make all the Dispach can. Molases at 23 1/2 Sous, fish sels from 21 to 22 Liver, Shads for 2 peses, Markrils 5 peces, Candles 48 Souses, pork at 16 peses eight, oil at 10 peses, Good Sugar from 6 to six and half times is dul hear. I have bin four days have sold and gave away and sould all the Shads and Mackles, most of the dry fish But hope you will not forgit the Ginney Voige, But to send Capt. English[1] away soon. I do intend to saill the last of this Mounth at all advens. Nothing more to ad from your to sarve,

NATHANIEL BRIGGS

HENRY CRUGER, JR. TO AARON LOPEZ

Bristol, March 7th, 1770.

Sir,

MY last was dated 23d December. am since favour'd with your agreeable Letter of 9th December per the *Aaron*, Capt. Holmes, who safely deliver'd his Cargo, in which was included 108 Barrels of Oil on our joint account, and with it came about 300 Casks more of same sort on my father's Account. 'tis lamentable, I had almost said wonderful, that people will not make a point to send their effects to Market when the season invites and when they are most likely to obtain the highest price. I will only add on this

---

[1] William English, then on his way to Newbern, N. C.

subject, had your Oil come to Market three Months ago, as I strongly recommended, *we should have got £4 or £5 a ton more for it.* Your Bill of £144. — .3 Sterling for my half of this Oil, in favour of Moses Levi has appeared and met due honor. Without Loss of time I caused the Oil by the *Aaron*, (in all about 70 tons) to be advertised and sold at public auction. it went much better (considering it's late arrival) than I expected; ours sold at £23.5 per ton. my next will furnish you with the sales, as it is not yet guaged and delivered.

The Bill of £1626.6.5 which my father drew on me for your account, being the Amount of Ship *Aaron* and a few things put on board her, will be pass'd to the Credit of your Account with me the 10th Inst. being the day it becomes due. I am sensible it was *at the request* of my father, Mr. Lopez provided him with this Ship. the only observation therefore that I would make is, that, were I to-morrow to sell the Ship to the highest bidder in this City, she would not fetch within £600 Sterling of her prime Cost. it is self-evident, that my father could have no other object in the purchase of this very dear (tho' good) Vessel, than to obviate, in some degree, the difficultys, you, Sir, complain of in your endeavours to liquidate this ponderous, tedious ruinous debt; suffice it to say, as no benefit hath, nor indeed was it *expected* that any benefit would, accrue to me; but, *bona fide*, the contrary, I hope the day will come when you, dear Sir, shall think of serving me in turn; what my sufferings merit, I leave the equity of your own bosom to determine. you have generosity, may Heaven give you power.

In some former Letter I wrote you that I had insured the *Charlotte* hence to Dublin; in my preceding one informed you of her safe arrival there, and that Newdigate promised to write me soon, another letter respecting his future destination for my guidance in making insurance, which advice have I been dayly expecting, with much impatience, to know *whither* he was bound from Dublin, or if he had a prospect of freight, or was to proceed in Ballast, or what, but unfortunately as you'll soon discover, I heard not a syllable from, nor of him, untill the 25th Ultimo, when received a Letter from him dated at Whitehaven, where he was drove (the day he sail'd from Dublin) by a violent gale of wind and there he writes he stuck, but could not tell what damage his Vessel had suffer'd; but hoped I had made insurance according to his Advices from Dublin, which Letter never came to hand, nor indeed *was the Post due* untill the day after vizt. 26th Ultimo in the Afternoon, so that of course *I had not done any Insurance* on his Vessel nor Freight; for before the receipt of those letters, I knew nothing about them. however, I immediately wrote to London to have effected £300 on his Vessel to the Bay and £90 on Freight to Jamaica, etc. *provided* the Vessel be fit to proceed her Voyage, which I hope to hear from Newdigate and wonder at his silence, it is one of his faults. my next or a P. S. will give you more particulars of him. inclosed are copies of all his letters and other papers concerning his Vessel, and also of Mr. Dunn's Accounts. it is to you, dear Sir, he ought to give a strict account of his Expences and doings *in Ireland.* he mentions in one of his Letters, that he wrote me from Dublin under date of 15th December. *if he did*, tis mysterious what became of the letter, for I never received it, nor its Copy.

If the Spirit of Prophesy be ever given to any man, who stands more in need of that advantage than a Merchant? Ambitious to advance your Interest, and pleased with the Appearance of having done it, I was happy in procuring the *Charlotte* a freight to Ireland. what a strange reverse of my flattering expectations, whether it be the extravagancies of the Captain, or the exigencies of an old Vessel, I know not, but this I know, that could I [have] forseen the great expences that have attended her in Ireland, she had not gone there, especially now we are likely to have great deductions from her Freight that she made from this place thither. the freighters bring a charge against the Captain and Crew of great embezzlement of Sugar and some Iron, etc., to the Value of near £40. this is intollerable, nor will I easily submit to it. I'll spend the remainder of the Freight in

Law rather than acquiesce; they have shewn me some proofs of their Loss which they intended to bring in support of their charge, but I soon convinced them they were too nugatory to proceed upon. they are in hourly expectation of Affidavits and the Lord knows what. I won't begrudge time nor pains to do you Justice, and must beg your Patience for the event. for the present, I respectfully take my leave; wishing you Health and Prosperity, that happiness may follow, and am with sincere Esteem, Dear Sir, Your most Obedient Humble Servant

HEN: CRUGER, JR.

P. S. No further news yet from Newdigate. I've insured the *Charlotte only to the Bay;* you will do what you chuse from thence.

Pray send my Father, to forward me, a *Certificate* (that it is of the growth, etc. of the Brit. Plants.) to enable me to receive the Bounty here on the Ash plank you put on board the *Aaron* for my Account, as Holmes brought no such paper with him. I kept this Letter open to the last moment, and to my great astonishment and concern have not heard from Newdigate. Herewith is certificate to cancell your Bond on *Charlotte*.

NATHANIEL BRIGGS TO A. AND A. LOPEZ

Gentelmen, St. Nicklass Mole, March 11, 1770.

THIS to infourm you that I have one bord Sixty hogsets of Molases and 19 hogsets of St. Crueax Rum, which I was ablige to tak in pay for Candlis sold thair. I have sold all but the oil and ten Boxes Candles. Sop I cant sel at now rate oil is at 9 peses Eight hear Candlis at 48 Sous. I sead my self [*illegible*] to sail in fifteen Days and if possbel can. I bag you wold not forgit Africa Voige, and send the teander away as soon as posbel can and git as much Rum for the Ship redy at my arivel, for I find that they will a grat meaney goin Capt. peater will sail in 2 Day. Shall write by him, from yous to sarve

NATHANIEL BRIGGS

WILLIAM ENGLISH TO A. AND A. LOPEZ

Newbern, March 16th, 1770.

Sir,

I ARRIVED att the Barr in Eight Days and on the Ninth att Newbern. I mett with noe accident on my passage but hard Gales of contrary winds which occation'd a tadious passage. Captain Hanners lay att the Barr when I arrived ready for Sea, Captain Ripley att Town, out of patience as I am att present. I wait for Mr. Ellis's motion. My small cargoe is nott all out as yett, nor neither have I taken any thing on board. the Slaves is in good order which I have spared now Labour to gett them in, tho are nott sold as yett. Mr. Ellis tells me I shall sail in a few days, but I fear not as there is but a poor prospect yett. as for Barrell Staves there is none to be had att present. But if any arrives before I sail Mr. Ellis tells me he will ship them. Rum and Salt is low att present but the rest of the Cargoe bares a midling price. Sir, I wish the Almighty God may prosper you and your Family, and am with Great Respect, Your most humble and most Obedient Servant,

WM. EINGLISH

NATHANIEL BRIGGS TO A. AND A. LOPEZ

Mold St. Nicklan, March 17, 1770.

Gentelmen,

THIS is to aquant by Capt. peaters's that I have one bord aleaven thousand Gallons Moloses and nineteen hogsets of St. Creas Rum and am in hopes to sail in teen days from this. the Molases that I have one bord cost 23 1/2 Sous per Gallon. I hope to purchis fifteen thousand Gallons Molases for Cargo this day hase com in 700 hogsets of Molases which I hope will loer the prise. I allso bag you wold not forgit the Ginne Voige and send the teander away [with] Captain English, for I don't lous any time hear. this day I have bin hear fifteen days. I also heard by a small

Sconer from St. Anns in Jameca that Captain potter was vere sick when he left that plase; also ses that Captain Heffend was arived their. so nothing more at pasent from your to Love

Nath^{el} Briggs

JOSEPH ANTHONY TO AARON LOPEZ

Philadelphia, March 21, 1770.

Worthy Sir,

I NOW take up my pen to say that Pork is like to be very high is now at £4 and rising Beef at 52/6 should be glad to hear from you before I purchace any except the 16 Barrels Beef sent you per the *Abigail*. I have sold your oil at 67/6, Candles part at 2/2. if you have any thing in the freighting way I should take it a particular favour if you would help to dispatch our Sloop, as I am oblidged to tarry here. I am antious for her speedy Return. there is nothing for you at Willing & Morris's. if you have Ocation for any thing from this way Please to command your Very Humble Servant,

JOSEPH ANTHONY

WILLIAM MINTURN TO A. AND A. LOPEZ

Barbadoes, March 23, 1770.

Gentlemen,

I WROUGHT you by the via of Boston informing you of the Badinness of the market and relating my proceeding on the Voage which I hope will come safe to hand. I have sold the remainer of the Horses since I wrought you my first, but cant not sell the Oil at any Price the Cheess I have sold from 6 to 7 per lb, but it fell short greatly in weight. I waitted on Mr. Jones a few days ago to know how much Rum he had to ship Mr. Lopez. he told me that about 20 hogsheads would settel the account which he says he will let me have in 10 days time. I am ingaged a full freight for the Sloop. I shall touch at the Granaders in order to sell my Oil, if possible, without paying port Charges. it is out of my Power to inform you when I shall sail from this Island as the People pay for horses at there Leisure, but I expeck'd to sail on or about the 10 of April. all kinds of Northerd Produce very low and dull, sail Hoops excepted. Hoops is worth her now £8 per M Hoops, at the Granader is £20 per M, and none at Market. for any further Perticulars I refer you to Captain Gardner relateing the Voage. I remain your to serve,

WM. MINTURN

The 14 Horses sold for £292 payable in Rum at 22d per G.

P. S. Pray acquant Mr. I. Bowers that I have setteled his affair. I shall ship his Rum on board of our Sloop *Grayhound*.

RICHARD GRINNELL TO AARON LOPEZ

Bay of Hondoray, Apriel the 1st, 1770.

Sir

I AM very sorry for your many misfortans which I suppose Capt. Potter has informd you of, yet I have still moore to inform you of that att that time I new nothing of in the Gail in which I lost your Horses your Bread got dammaged, likewise your flour, one Barrel Pease Stoofe; and as there is no news of Capt. Newdagate I no not what I shall do with your Intrest. the Plank I have landed tho not sold, but nothing that I have on board of yours will fetch Cash, Turtle Shell, or Sassopirella neither wood. if it would sell for wood and I could git paid in a reasonable time, I would dispose of it, as I could sell the[m] again for Cash which I could bring you home. But as I cannot I think best to bring you your Goods a gain. I have received all Capt. Newdegats Notes of Mr. Jones, which made the Sum mentioned in Mr. Joneses Recipt. Mr. Jones tells me that hee should have colected Capt. Newdegats Deats had you answered his Letter concerning the wood hee sent you by Newdagate. Neavertheless I am informd that Mr. Jones has endeavoured to git the wood in his own hands but could not. as soon as I received the Notes which is many, I demanded Payment, but most of them has some excuse to make. Some say Newdagate had cheated them, others say there is Error in the Account, and in all I dont expect to git only Eleaven Pound Bay, which is a Note Mr. Fits Gibbins gave Newdagate. Mr. Card says your Demand is very just and he will pay it. hee very much blames his Brothers Conduct. I hoope Newdegate will arive before I sail to take Care of your Intrest but I shall do the best I can for you and am your humble Servant,

RICHARD GRINNELL

HENRY AND CALEB BOWERS TO AARON LOPEZ

Swansey, April 23rd, 1770.

Mr. Aaron Lopas,

SIR, the Lowest that we can carry the Gentleman you sent to go pasenger with Captain Palmer is two Doble Loons, which if you give y[our] Note payable at his Return in case he fails we [are] ready to carry him.

HENRY AND CALEB BOWERS

MAHONY AND WOLFE TO AARON LOPEZ

Thenerife, 4th April, 1770.

Sir,

ON the 15th ultimo we were honour'd with your's 12th December last per Captain John Hyer of the Sloop *Industry*, who it seems has your orders to give us the refusal of his Cargo, a favour we were strongly inclined to acknowledge by taking the same at as high prices as the Market wou'd well bear, had not we discover'd a stronger inclination in the Captain of giving the preferance to Messrs. White Brothers (with whom it seems he had been formerly acquainted) which he accordingly effected; we therefore thought it needless, in such case, to make him any overtures, knowing that the other Gentlemen, thro' his influence, wou'd out bid us, offer what we wou'd; however lest you should imagine we slighted your kind intention of commencing a correspondence together, we did make him such offers as we thought no other House would venture to exceed, unless done thro' prejudice, which here happen'd to be the case. Indeed as this is a mode of transacting business we have hitherto been unacquainted with, were at a loss how to act, so as to cooperate with your kind intention, which we must say the Captain did at all events resolve to defeat. Let it be [as] it may, shall be glad his Negociation proves agreeable to the Concernds which is the main point.

Captain Story arrived here the 13th ultimo and brought with him the parcell Cacao he had been encouraged to by the person who lent Mr. Townsend the 1000 hard Dollars for that purpose, and expecting he wou'd take it at a reasonable price kept him in suspence some days 'till at length he came to offer him no more than one R[ ]p a p[oun]d which was exceeding low. As the quantity was rather large he cou'd scarce find any body that wou'd enter on it, the more so as he wanted part Money; however at last he succeeded and found a Chap to take the whole parcell at 25/ per faneg of 110 li. payable part wines, and part as much money as wou'd pay the Maltese the said 1000 dollars with the interest incurr'd 'till 1st January; and tho' this Man was paid at the rate of 15 per Ct. for 3 1/2 months, still he insistes upon a further Sum agreeable to Mr. Townsend's promissory Note, which Captain Story refused paying, not being allowable by Law, whereupon he desired of us to forward you said not and call to you for the deficiency. But as we think the demand unreasonable, shall only inclose said note, and leave the rest to your own determination; whatever this may be you'll please to acquaint us of it that we may shew it to him. Some thing more cou'd be obtain'd [for th]e Cacao p[torn]ines, but he was necessitated to give it to him [   ] pay as much Money as wou'd satisfy the forementioned [   ].

We have given Captain Story a small Commission for 2 Horses and a Mare provided he returns this way soon; shou'd he not, you'll be so good to call to him for it and forward them to us per very first conveyance.

Flour and all kind of grain are likely to be in demand during the course of the present year, but Lumber and Naval Stores are become a mere drugg, of which hints you'll please to avail your self in case it suits you to make further tryals this way. We remain very respectfully, Sir Your most obedient humble Servants,

MAHONY & WOULFE

Vid. wine £7:10 to £10, according to age and quality. Brandy £11 to £12 per pipe.

JOHN HEFFERNAN TO AARON LOPEZ

Montego-bay, 2d April, 1770.

Sir,

RECEIVED yours dated the 5th February, mentioning your good Caution being so sensible of your moracilous and mananimous Proceeding in mercantile afairs that your eable to give advice to the Great. there shall not want any asiduety in my Power to promote your Intrust, which I always have at heart. our Plan is fell throw the Gentlemen that Captain Potter expected to bee concearn'd with are suplyd with Vesel's before I arriv'd, which I make no doubt but Captain Potter has inform'd you of before this time. I am bound to Kingstown from here with flour, Lamp oyl, and Spermiceta Candles, which wee here is in demand there. I had a very good Passage from Carolina seventeen days into St. Anne, brought the Cargo in good order, loosing on my Passage Ezikiah Sanford, and my Cozzen John Wigneron died on board of mee after a long spell of Sickness. I left St. Anne the 27th march. Captain Potter has been very sick but know recovr'd very well. there are just began Cropp at St. Anne. I cant form any Idea when I shall sail from this part of the world. I shall lett you know in my next which will bee by the first oppertunity that offers this being the first Oppertunity I have had since my Arrival. Captain Grinal lost all his horses, and the remainer part of the cargo he landed at St. Anne which Captain Potter has wrote you via the mould by Captain Gassee to bee forwarded. I am very well and my Crew all well thank God. hoping these may find, Sir, you and yours in good helth, having nothing perticular to add, I Remain Sir Your Very Umble Servant to Serve,

JOHN HEFFERNAN

JOSEPH ANTHONY TO AARON LOPEZ

Philadelphia, April 11, 1770.

Worthy Sir,

YOUR favor per post requesting a Quantity of Salt and yours per whitman ordering a Quantity of Provisions, both came safe to hand. I purchasd and shiped by Captain whitman 800 Bushells of Salt at 17*d*, and shall bring you some more in my Sloop if I have room. I have also sent you 10 Reams of Wraping paper. as to the provisions they are very scarce and dear. Pork comes in very small Parcells and commands the Cash at 4£ to £4.2.6 as quick as it is landed. Beef scarce at 52/6. However I shall endeavour to get you all I can, while I have any money to pay for it, as nothing but cash will do, tho I dont expect the Quantity you want can be got for love nor money. However you may depend there shall be nothing wanting in my Power, to serve my worthy Friend Mr. Lopez, to whom I have gratitude enough to think my self under the greatest obligations. I am with all possible Respect your Very Humble Servant, JOSEPH ANTHONY

N. B. there is nothing for you at Messrs. Willing & Morrisis.

Nathaniel Russell to Samuel and William Vernon

Charlestown, 5th May, 1770.

Gentlemen,

I AM favored with yours of the 14th ult: covering Invoice and Bill Loading of 4 hhds and 36 Loaves Sugar, which have received in good order. the Market at present is very largely supplied with that article from Philadelphia and N. York, and the price reduc'd to 5/; but I expect it will be up again to 5/6 in a short time. I have not dispos'd of any of yours yet.

Inclosed you have Invoice and Bill Loading of 80 Barrels Rice shipped on board the Sloop *Charlestown* on yours and Mr. James Tanner's Account, amounting to £1005.13.4, with which have debited your Account Current. I have also inclosed you Account Sales of 4 hhds Rum received the last voyage, Neat Proceeds £153.19.3 have pass'd to your Credit. I am with Respect, Gentlemen, Your Most Humble Servant,

NATHANIEL RUSSELL

Price Current

Nor'd Rum	11/	Sp. C Candles	10/
W. I. Do.	12/6	Oil	£17.10/
Jamaica Do.	17/	Rice	45/
Loaf Sugar	5/	Hemp	£8 per Ct.
Brown Do.	£8 to £10 per C.	Pork	£14.

Zebadiah Story to A. and A. Lopez

St. Eustatia, the 14th May, 1770.

Gentlemen,

IN my last by Captain Hyer at Tennereffe I neglected the amount of the Cargo, which was ninety five pipes and 1/2. Captain Hyer expected to sail in 2 or 3 days after me directly for Rhodeisland, where I hope he hath ariv'd in Safety. I sail'd from Tennereffe the 8th April and ariv'd here the 4th inst. In my way down I went on shore at Barbadoes, St. Lucia, and Dominica, but could sell nothing. At my arivel here I found four Verssels with wine from Tennereffe and Medera, but their wine being of a bad Quality they did not sell a Pipe after, and are sence sail'd for Newyork and Philadelphia. I have sold 12 or 14 Pipes from 66 Ps. to 88 in Payment I have taken Bills which I shall sell here for Sugar and Cordage, which I shall ship if any oppertunity offers before I sail; if not I shall leave it with Mr. Mayers to effect. I have agreed to carry Mr. Pascall and family to Newport, whos Passage and freight will amount to near 300Ps., for which I shall tarry here 8 or 10 days longer, and in the meen time I am in hopes to barter away twenty [or] thirty Pipes more for Sugar, Duck, Ozenbriggs, Cordage, etc. I expect to see you in 30 days, and sincearly remain your Very humble Servant,

ZEBADIAH STORY

HENRY CRUGER, JR. TO AARON LOPEZ

Bristol, May 14, 1770.

Dear Sir,

FOR want of the pleasure of some of your late favors have but very little to add. I have at length brought the freighter of the little *Charlotte* to Dublin to a final settlement; after a deal of quib'ling and quarreling, from which sort of people in future pray God deliver us. Newdigate mistook the size of his Vessel egregiously when he agreed to take 54 barrels of Rice and 9 hhds of Sugar more than she could carry, for we enter'd into a Charter Party, which I was obliged to abide by. to be sure the whole has turned out an unprofitable affair. herewith is a State of the account, Ballance to your Credit being only £44:1:9 Stg.

Permit me dear sir, once more to recommend your sending a good parcell of Brown and White Spermaceti Oil here *early* next fall. I have very little doubt, if it come about November or before, of selling it from £25 to £28 per ton. after Christmas the Market falls apace. I will conclude by saying, I have two Motives in offering this Advice. the one mentioned, is because I am morally certain the adventure will turn out to your profit; the other is, that it will afford some relief and render a little Justice to, Sir, Your injured tho' unalterable friend and humble Servant, HEN: CRUGER, JR.

THOMAS GILBERT TO AARON LOPEZ

Freetown, 15th May, 1770.

Sir,

By Mr. Evins I am inform'd that you have sum Inclination to charter my Schooner which will be redy in a few Days (except Mainsaill and fore Saill which must be new), and if you are amind to charter pleas'd to lett me know by the Barer, and on what terms and what Voige, as otherwise I shall send her a whaleing (John Strange, Master) and as you gave me Incuragment by your Letter last to me that you would seply; if you are still of the same mind ples'd to right me. We shall wand Provisions and Duck for the afores'd Saills, if it sutes to let me have the Duck, ples'd to let Mr. Grafton have it, who I have here inclosd a Line too, that he make the Saills as soon as may be. if successfull you shall have the oyl if otherways pay as soon as I can. I am your obliged Humble Servant,

THOS. GILBERT

P. S. Ples'd to forward the inclosd to Mr. Grafton if you seply with the Duck.

[Endorsed,] Per John Samson.

ABRAHAM LOPEZ TO AARON LOPEZ

Savana La mar, June 1st, 1770.

Mr. Aaron Lopez,

I AM now to answer 2 of your most esteemd favours. In regard of what you desired to be acquainted with a protest'd Bill of Exchange was left to my care some time agoe; as I could not receve the same when demand'd, I put it in suite. at the last time poor John Coddington came to this Island he took every paper of his left in my Possession, in order to collect the same him self, while I deliverd him every thing I had, and do beleave he collected every thing, all to that bill of exchange, which I think at his going away he left the same to the care of Mr. Robert Moody. Therefore you may inform Messrs. Joseph and William Wanton to apply to said Gentlemen to know if that matter is setled or not. said estate is in my debt of 7 or 8 pounds to carry on the Law suite of the Drawer and endorser of said Bill. I received the Gudgeons, Coposes and Fruite plants, the amount of £25.18.7. with that account for Doctor Fraser Negroe. I shall settle the same with Captain Benjamin Wright and return you my sincere thanks for the trouble and care you have taken in sending me those things. I must sincerely request the favour of you per very first conveyance to send me attested with every proper step you can take that Account of Doctor Frasers Negroe, that I may recover the same here, as the Executors of said Estate will not allow said Account without my getting a Judgement on the same. It is a very hard case on me for my good nature, that I am obliged to pay this money to you, and now to be kept out of it for some months to come by said Executors, and likely a chance of looseing of it altogether.

I must farther request the favour of you by the very first Vessell that comes to this port or to Hanover, youll get made of the very best stuff six Steel Stepps to the Modell, and 1 dozen pair of Copusses to the Modell of the square of the Neck. The Copusses to be 3 inches long from the Neck and three inches and half deametor. pray let them be well steeld and be made of the very best stuff. when I know the expence of the same shall settle here with Captain Wright. Excuse all this trouble I give you. all my family joyns with me with our Regard and Compliments to self and all your good Family, wishing this may find you all joying your Health as we now remain at present, I remain with due esteem, Dear Sir, I am your very Hble Servant to Command,

ABRAHAM LOPEZ

Benjamin Wright to Aaron Lopez

Savana la Marr, the 2 June, 1770.

Dear Sir,

THESE covers an Invoice and bill of Ladeing of sundry Merchandise shipped for your account and resque on board the Brigenteen *Hannah*, Israil Ambrose, Master, which hope safe to your hands and to a good markett. I have been obliged to keep the Schooner *Ranger* much longer than I intended for this reason only, I found it imposable to go up and down the coast with out her. hope to despatch her in three or four days at furthest am afraid her detention has disobliged you. what ever comes in the Schooner *Ranger* will be on the joint concearn of Ship *Jacob* have sent you no Account Sales for this reason, nither Brig nor Sloops Cargoes all desposed of shall suffer much in the Codfish, they lyeing so long on hand they are perrishing fast, and new fish are soon expected therefore am afraid they will stick on hand my being so late out this Year the Island was filled with every Article, therefore could not get my Cargoe off any sooner. provisions of all kind now begins to be in demand. Bords of all kinds are in demand. I hope your Brig may arrive sooner then I rote for her to come, and should she arrive here by the beginning of July I think she will nick the Markett, should we be luckey enough to not have any Vessell arrive before her. hope you may have ordered Capt. Benjamin Allen this way early this summer. I think he [will] make you tollarable good voyage. I shall have sum produce to give him which I shall collect after the *Hannah's* Departure. I am in hoopes to receive one hundred and fifty Pound of Abraham and David Mendes Bond, which is only the one half of there Bond. Abraham Solomon's Bond for one hundred and seventy pounds sum od Shillings, shall receve the hole or at least am faithfuly promised that it shall be punctuly discharged. I have likewise received about fifty Pounds of the Outstanding debts contracted by Isaac P. Mendes, allso the ballance of Edw'd and Williams Bill of Exch[ange] shall receive, Richard Hugens Reeds Bond, and private Account shall not receive one farthing this Year the drouth has bee[n *torn*] he has scarcely putt his [*torn*]

I am verry sorrey for detaining your Brig and Schooner so long, can assure you that things has not gone on any ways kind this year every body that I have delt with this year has been verry backward in payeing me, and those old Sins of Mendes takes up a greate deal of Time, they are so scattered through the Island. your draught on Abraham Lopez will be discharged every Shilling of it. I was under the disagreeable necessity of takeing on bord the Brig four hhds sugar for an old friend of mine, oltho I think the freight of the suggar is full as much as can be made by purchaseing suggars at the extravigant price it now sells at. your Brig *Hannah* is a poor thing for this Traid; she will not carrey enough by one hundred hhds. I shall make greate dependance on your complyeing with my request in procureing the Lumber I rote for, and could you advance the quantity it would not be amiss. I can despose of near two hundred thousand Lumber, prevoideing I can have it here by the middle of December, and dressed out agreeable to the sample I sent you by Capt. Benjamin Allen. I have returned the Beavour hatts which I received from Brig *Industry*, Capt. Jno. Peters, likewise the Barrels Beef per Sloop *George*, for this Reason, it is in a perrishing Condition and will not keep here any longer. nothing more to add only wish you helth with every other Blessing this world afords is the sencear wishes of Your Most Obliged Humble Servant,

BENJAMIN WRIGHT

N. B. Should my little family call on you Pray be bountifull, which will greately add to the many favours allready conferred on Poor Old yankey dodle.

I have been under the disagreeable necessity of advanceing considerable for a mait for Capt. Ambrose, after takeing his mait to come in the Schooner. I have advanced William Kean sixteen pounds two shillings Jamaica Currency, not being able to get one on better Terms he is a man which belonges to newport should the Brig arrive safe make no doubt he will tarry in your Imploy till he works the whole, after deducting what wages he may have due. I did not think it safe to send the Brig home with Ambrose alone for reasons best none to myself. I have advanced Ephraim Smith one dollar which you will see entred on the Port'dge Bill. I likewise gave the Carpenter 1 hhd Mollases, he being a faithfull Servent and not haveing any time to do anything for him self, which hhd mollases have charged you with; and if you think I have been to free with your Intrest will give you Credit for the same. I never set down to write you sence I have been in your Imploy so confused as I now am the damned Custom house officers put one allmost mad with there extravigent demands. I am afraid this voyage will make me turn Mendes on your hands, for I shall really be afraid to see you again, and what steeps to take to remedy this bad Voyage I no not. I am with greate Esteem Your Most obdent humble Servt., BENJAMIN WRIGHT

N. B. I have sent the Remander of the Shoes by the *Hannah*.

JAMES HUNTER TO AARON LOPEZ

Fredericksburg, Virginia, 4th June, 1770.

Sir,

CAPTAIN SAMUEL HATCH the bearer hereof informing me, that you have it greatly in your power to dispose of large quantitys of Bar Iron and Flour, in the manufactory whereof I am deeply concerned, I beg leave to acquaint you, if you shoud at any time have occasion to forward to this market Rum, Molasses, and Sugar, that I am willing to take them in exchange, and supply you to a considerable amount annually. I refer you to Captain Hatch for particulars, and should be much obliged by a line on this head by Post at your leisure. meantime I am very Respectfully, Sir, Your most humble servant,

JAMES HUNTER

Sailing Orders for Captain Hammond

Newport, 6th June, 1770.

Capt. Nath'l Hammond,

WE order you to proceed directly to Gottenburg, with our Sloop *Dolphin*, and get the best information you possibly can, what house is the most likly to do your business the best, and give you the quickest dispatch, when you have determined what Merchant to adress your self too, deliver him our Letter, after directing it, together with the Invoice of your Cargo, and also the bills of Exchange for £187.10 Stg. drawn by S. & W. V[ernon] on Messrs. Hayley & Hopkins Merchants in London, which you must indorse as they are made payable to you. you may give the Gentlem'n to whom you adress your self too the greatest assurance that the bills will be punctually paid.

You well know that we have sent this small Vessil to Gottenburg with her load of Rice, some Sugar and Ginger, in order to make a tryal if an advantagious Trade may be carried on from hence there. therefore as our Vessil is very small, in order to have some Value return'd us in Goods, we have ship't 500 Spanish mill'd Dollars and the above Bill of Exchange for £187.10/, the whole amount of which we wou'd have laid out in good Bohea Tea, without you think some other Goods will answer better as good Shroud Junck,[1] if may be had at about Three Dollars per Ct. 4 or six Tons may answer, Duck equal in goodness to best Rushia at 6½ Dollars per bolt[2] about Twenty or Thirty bolts: and any other articles that you are well assured will turn to better profit then Bohea Tea, which we suppose can be bot at 1/4 or 1/6 Stg per li. or perhaps less.

You will also inform your self well what all kinds of goods from America are worth at Gottenburg, viz. Rice, Logwood, Indigo, Permento, Sassaperilla, Sassafras Roots; Cotton,

---

[1] Old or condemned cordage and cable, cut into small pieces, used when untwisted for making points, gaskets, swabs, mats, etc., and picked into fibers to make oakum for calking seams.

[2] Bailey (1721) defines a bolt of canvas as containing 28 ells.

Sugar, Cocoa, Chocolate, and Rum, etc., etc., and make your self acquainted with the prices of all kinds of Goods that are generally ship't from thence, particularly India Goods, Teas of all kinds, Spices, China and piece Goods, Duck stout and small.

You will take especial care that all your goods are ship't for St. Croix consigned to Mr. Cornels Durant, merchant there, Invoice and bills Loading made out agreeable thereto. when you have finished your business, may either proceed North about or down Channel, as the season is far advanced. when you come on this Coast avoid speaking with any Vessil, and go in at the East Side of the Island and let us know of your Arrival as soon as possible, and where you intend to anchor. we think best within the Point at the East End, under the Rhode Island Shore: send a man on shore too us, charge him not to let any one see him. the Negro will be the best, and we shall soon let you know how to proceed, by sending to you.

If you cannot be admitted to Trade at Gottenburg with the Cargo you have on board, proceed directly to Hamburgh, and adress your self to Mr. [blank] merchant there, and invest the whole of your Cargo in good Bohea Teas, observing the same directions in respect to shiping the goods as from Gottenburg. we wish you a good Voyage and safe return and are Your Friends and Owners.

[*Unsigned* [1]]

[Signed] Nath'l Hammond.

SAMUEL RATHBUN, JR. TO AARON LOPEZ

Sur,   New Shoreham, June the 7th, 1770.

I HAVE a percil of choyse pickled Codfish, which should be very glad if they would sute you. pray be so kind as to let me know by the bareer, and if they will, I'le bring them. I expect I shall have some small mackrel allso, which wont

---
[1] The ship was probably sent out by S. and W. Vernon, as the charges for the cost and outfit of the sloop, amounting to £24,719.14.11, were divided between S. and W. Vernon and James Tanner.

likely be ready til the first of next month. we jest begin now to cetch them. I shall take it very kind if you would take them, for money is not to be had, and I want to pay you as fast as posable. if it should sute you to trade further for fish, should be glad to know if you have any fish salt, and the price by the hundred bushel, which concludes your obliged friend,

SAMUEL RATHBUN, JUNIOR

DANIEL TILLINGHAST TO AARON LOPEZ

Providence, June 21st, 1770.

Sir,

YOURS of the 18th and 21st Instant have before me should have answered your first and sent you some [rum], but Hacker has been but one trip since, and I was then out of town. as to the wants of in one Hhd. of Rum per Hacker cant account for it, as it was filled up quite full when it went out of the Still House. it must be oweing to the Hhd. not being tight, as some of them I have now in the Still House, two of which Hhds. have been obliged to have a head taken out of each and new flag'd. they lost me several gallons before I found it out, as to the quality of the Rum I have been as carefull to make it all alike as possible, and as good as any I ever made up for Guinea. I ordered Hacker to have the Rum inspected on board the Boat, and if any under Proof to bring it back again, as any Distiller in Newport will condemn Rum that doth not come out of there Hands, or rather any that comes from Providence. I shall still Low wines tomorrow, will then send you down 12 gallons High wines to putt in the 3 Hhds. you mentioned. if you could confide in any person hear to se the Rum before it was shipt I would willingly pay the Expence of Inspection. as to any more Molasses I should be glad of a few Hhds. more if it be good, — some of that I had before was very poor. I had not time to examin the whole of it when I was there, and have distill but 5 Hhds. of it yett. I have now sent you 5 Hhds. of Rum, 528 gallons hope it will be full and to your Captains Likeing. I am, Sir, your most Humble Servant.

DANIEL TILLINGHAST

ALEXANDER WILSON TO AARON LOPEZ

Kingston, June 22, 1770.

Sir,

I SUPPOSE Capt. Newdigate has informed you of my leaving the Vessel, which I was obliged to do while in a Christian Country, for if I had not left him in the Bay he would have left me. he is not the man you take him for, if you please to enquire of the people they can tell [you] what he is. I dare say you have heard of Mr. Crudger, of his second Marrige in Dublin, and leaving his Wife sick of the foul desease, which if caught will pay for it. he has used me very ill and all people can say the same, for he is a Rogue and I should be glad to have the pleasure of seing him and you together. ask the people about the Mahogany they pick't up last Voyage and you paid for it. Out of seventeen hundred weight of Beef bougt in Dublin he only sold in Madeira 20 Bullocks of it, and very often obliged his Whores with a roasting piece, and a few Coals, and great many other things which I dare say you will find out. he flung the Merchant at Bristol out one tierce of Rice, and intends to charge the Brigg with it. he has stoped from me the Order of 14 Dollars and 15 Days pay that I was at London, tho' he has got a Receipt for the Whole he owes me money yet, and I cannot [get it,] but I have sent Captain Richarson the order, and you will pay him or keep the Money in you hands. after hurting me all he could, when he went away he gave me the Character of an Informer, which I never deserved. he loves to broach his Cargoes so well that [no one who] knows him will ship any thing with him. So, Sir, I hope you will pardon my Boldness in accquainting you of a few things that was necessary for you to know, and if his mate and people speakes the truth, will tell you the same. From Your Most Obedient and Most Humble Servant,

ALEXANDER WILSON

I dare say he will lay me out to be a great Rascal but the people knowes better.

JAMES BRASIER TO AARON LOPEZ

Sir,

I HAD the pleasure to write you the 1st ultimo. Since which I have paid your draft in favour of Captain Benjamin Wright for £110.10½ Cy. and advanced for Captain Jno. Newdigate £16.12.6, which I apprehended was very necessary upon the following Account: said Newdigate having taken upon freight at Madeira some Wines for Savanna la Marr. He put into Bluefields, and very imprudently loaded his Boat with part of the said Wines the same evening (without reporting at the Custom House) with an Intention to land them here.

But the Officers of the Customs having private information of this kept a Look out for him, and very unluckily one of them happened to be upon the Wharf when Newdigate's Boat loaded with the Wines arriv'd. The consequence was the Wines were immediately seiz'd, and a Custom House Officer dispatch'd to Bluefields to rummage the Brig in order if possible to proceed to extremities. But upon my Application to the Collector in his favour he was for releasing him, but the Comptroller, I understood, wanted a fee before he wou'd come into it. Newdigate hereupon apply'd to me for advice, and assistance, which upon your Account I very readily granted him, and supplied him upon the occasion with the beforemention'd Sum of £16.12.6. But the Officers of the Customs hearing that it was publickly said, and generally believ'd, that Newdigate had brib'd them, they very strenuously deny'd their having receiv'd a Bitt from him. You'l please to enquire into the Truth of this affair and I shall be glad to know Issue thereof, as the Comptroller in particular, to whom Newdigate protested he paid the Money, positively denys it. I therefore repeat my request that you'l enquire strictly into the affair before you suffer him to charge you with it. I am With Compliments to self and Family, Sir, Your most Humble Servant (for Mr. Abraham Lopez)

JAS. BRASIER

Savanna la Marr, July 2d 1770.

WILLIAM PARKER TO AARON LOPEZ

Shrewsbury, July 4, 1770.

friend Lopus,

THIS comes to acquaint you of my Proecedings. We arrived at Newyork and met with some Difficulties in landing the wines. we landed 10 pipes of your wines the rest I was obliged to bring to the Jerses; but shall send them up in the first boat. Your rum sold at 3/4 per Gallon, and Molases at 1/10, and Spirits at 4/3. I have shipt by the Shooner *Hopestill* 11 bbr. pork and 3 of Beef, pork at 85/. and beef I judge will be 45/. which was all I could buy here. the remmainder I will have ready, by the Schooner return. from thy friend to serve,

WILLIAM PARKER

P. S. flower in York is rising very fast. it is 17/ and very scarce. the hhd. of Brandy I have sent to York.

W. PARKER

ROBERT GRIFFITH TO ———

Sir,

I SHALL be glad your self and Mr. George Gibbs will inform me how I shall proceed with your Goods I have on board the Sloop *Hope*. Let me here from you, as I must deliver them in Boston Goverment shall proceed to the North end of your Island or Howlands ferry. my Compliments to Mr. Revera. from yours

ROBERT GRIFFITH

July 8th, 1770.

HENRY ISREALL TO AARON LOPEZ

Jamaica, St. Anns, July 8th, 1770.

Sir,

MEETING with this favourable Opportunity have embraced it. I am hopefull you'll excuse my taking the Liberty in troubling of you in this Letter. I live in the Country and we are obliged to live very hard as we cant gitt such sort of provisions as is suitable to our Religion without sending to the Towns in Jamaica. it is then a great Length and chargeable and what we gett is very poor Stuff and dear. I would therefore be kindly oblige to you if you would be so kind as to take the Trouble found in sending by the Return of Captain Potter for Saint Anns, Two good large Barrell of good בשר Beeff (fatt and prime pieces) and will send you the Payment by the Return of the same Vessell. I must also beg you'll send me it as reasonable as possible, as I have a large Family, and I have enough to do to support 'em genteelly. If you'll please enquire of Capt. James Potter, of me or of Captain Hefferron, they will tell you, or of any other of the Captains that trades here. I have been in this Parish going on forty-two years. Captain John Freebody, Jun'r, who was here in the year Fifty-Three at a Circumcission of one of my Sons, can tell you. I am onacquainted with your Person or Family but I hope they enjoy their Health. I am with Esteem, Sir, Your most obedient Servant

HENRY ISREALL

N. B. If you can, or if it would be agreeable, I would be much [obliged] to you to have packed up in one of the Barrells a few Tongues.

DAVID BEEKMAN TO AARON LOPEZ

St. Croix, 12 July, 1770.

Sir,

I ARRIV'D here after a tedious passage of 40 Days and founds Times at present prety low owing to the Crops being near off since last fall they have had two or three Guineamen in and they sold from £30 to £34 Ster'g per head. the last Cargo sold at £33. they will always I think fetch the prices above, provided the Negroes be good and Gold Cost slaves are taught [thought] to be best. you may depend that shou'd you or any of your friends have any Command this way no one will serve them on Better Terms then I shall, and take more care of their Interest. you have at foot the prices of Goods that will sell at present. Excuse the Liberty I have taken in sending you this. I am with offers off Service,

Sir,
Your most Humd Sert
David Beekman

Rice	5 to 6 ps. Ct.	Codfish	6 ps. per Ct.
Pork	20 Barl.	Tobaco	6 to 8 ps. Ct.
Flour	8 Do.	Spermacity Candles 4 to 4½ Bitts li.	
Bread	10 Teirce.	16th August. Markitts the same.	

JOSEPH HOLMS TO AARON LOPEZ

New York, July the 10th, 1770.

Mr. Aaron Lopis,

YOULL recive this from the Hands of Mr. John Fergus, whome I onderstand is well aquanted with the Guinea Trade, and duering a passage from the Cape Devards St. Iago on board my Ship as a passengar behaved himself as a sober honaste Man: and so remains with Due Respect to all Your Famly, Your Most obedient Humble Servant,

JOSEPH HOLMS

Isaac Guion to Aaron Lopez

New Rochell, July 23d, 1770.

Dear Sir,

I AM this moment arriv'd at this place, on my way to New York having a tedious passage; am inform'd the Price of tea is greatly fallen since I left New York. therefore desire you'll please to inform Mr. Levy, not to send the two Boxes tea 'till further orders, if he has not already sent them, as I suppose there must be a considerable Loss from what Intelligence I have receiv'd, upon tea at 6/ per li. hope Mr. Levy will not be any ways injur'd by my not having the tea. if I find on my arrival at New York I can dispose of the tea to save myself, shall imediately send word to have it sent.

I am with Compliments to Mrs. Lopez, Sir, Your most Obedient Humble Servant,

ISAAC GUION [1]

Leah Mendes to Aaron Lopez

Kingston, 6th August, 1770.

Honourable Sir,

THIS hope will find you and family in perfect state of health, as I enjoy, and the rest of the family, and which hope will continue with a great deal of felicity and happiness for inumerable years. It is with great pleasure and joy I now write you acquainting of the dutifulness of my Son Abraham in complying to our request to return home, he has insured me of never disobliging, nor never to cause you and his wife any more griveance, and will always be bound to your obedience, and he has acknowledged his fault of being so long absent, and it is with no doubt it gives him great concern in reflecting of his folleys, but you are fully sensible that youthness and bad advisers is always of great prejudice, and much so when they wont be rule[d]. but

---

[1] The will of Isaac Guion, gentleman, of New Rochelle, Westchester County, New York, is in *N. Y. Hist. Soc. Collections*, 1903, 104.

all his transgression will be an example for his better amendment, and I make no doubt that he will fullfill his promises to me, and he goes overjoy'd to your feet to crave pardon, and which I hope you'l grant for the sake of a poor widow'd mother, who will always receive great satisfaction and contentment in knowing of his good proceedings and dutifullness to you, and as God, (the best exampler of the hole world) forgives mankind, so I hope you'l be so please as to pardon him, and in granting me this favour I shall forever acknowledge.

If, please God, nothing interposes next year I shall resolve to go and enjoy yours and my loving Daughter's company, for a hole twelve months. no more to enlarge but remain, craving you a great deal of happiness, from, Sir, Your Most humble Servant,

LEA MENDES

Loving Daughter,

IT is with great pleasure I now acquaint you of Abraham compling to our request in returning to enjoy your sweet company, and I beg of you that you'l forgive him of his misbehaveing and his absence from so good a Wife as you, but he has promised of never causing any more grieveance, but always to be the instrument of seeking for to give you pleasure and content, and therefore hope all will be forgotten, and shall always be please to know of both your happiness, and remain craveing you health and prosperity from, Your Loving Mother,

LEA MENDES

Per Favour of Captain Wright W. G. P.

ANTHONY STOCKER TO AARON LOPEZ

Philadelphia, the 14th August, 1770.

Sir,

YOUR favour of the 24th Ultimo I duly receiv'd and note the Contents, and agreable to your directions therein I shall wait your orders before I do any thing farther in the attachment on Mr. Cozzens effects, which I shall be glad to receive as soon as convenient, as the Courts comes on the first Week in the next Month. I take this oppertunity of adviseing you that on the 9th July I enterd into a Copartnership with Mr. Thomas Wharton, Junior, of this City, a Gentleman of Fortune, of known Integerity and Punctuality. I shall be greatly oblig'd to you for your favours and Interest among your friends for our new house, the firm of which is Stocker & Wharton, and you may depend when you or they shall favour us with your Commands we shall study yours and their Interest as our own. I am with great respect, Sir, Your most humble Servant,

ANTHONY STOCKER

STITES AND BRASHER TO AARON LOPEZ

Sir, we advised by the Post, that if the Nailes were given up by the Committe and not suffer'd to be sent here; that you should sell them on our Acct: and take Commissions for Sale, as it is likely they will sell well with you now as they are scarce (we sold ours here for 1/1 per li.) if they will but pay the Commisions, we chose you should have that; and ship us for the balance you will have in hand Cotton Checks, small figures, and dark, if you have them; if you have not a sufficiency of them, some Nutmegs and Mace, a few peaces of your best Buckram, some Lawn [or] Cambricks, from 30/ to 40/ Sterling. Accomodate this order in the easyest manner for yourself, as any of the articles will do here. if the Nailes do not come to your hand, then the balance of Cash as above directed; with the Amount of Mr. Polox Draught on us, £11:17:9 3/4 York Money, which you was so kind as to offer to see paid; for which with other favors, we remain, Sir, your Much Obliged and very Humble Servants,

STITES & BRASHER

New York, 18th August, 1770.

P. S. We rec'd the Trunk with all the Contents by Mr. Jacobs.

Thomas Lanwarn to Aaron Lopez

Crutched Friars, 12th January, 1770.

Sir,

In consequence of the application of Mr. Robert Sorsbie to us for that purpose, we hereby engage that any Agreement that Messrs. Lovell Morson & Co. of Dominica may come to with any person, for Negroes consigned to them for sale by Messrs. James Clark & Co., shall be punctually performed; and we hereby undertake also to accept and pay any and all Bills they may draw on us in pursuance of such Consignments, in all cases but that of the Island wherein such sale shall be made, or they reside, being invaded by an Enemy.

We are respectfully, Sir, Your Most Humble Servants,

KENDER, MASON & Co.

Messrs. Lovell & Morson sell as well to the French and Spaniards, for whom they have large orders to execute, as to our Planters of B. Bs. Antigua and Dominica; so that under these circumstances, Dominica seems to bid fairer to render you advantageous sales, than any other Island.

London, 29th Aug., 1770.

We agree that the withinmentioned Guaranty shall subsist not only for such Negroes as may be consigned Messrs. Lovell Morson & Co. by Messrs. James Clark & Co., but also for such Negroes as may be consigned to them by Messrs. Butler and Brown or Robert Brown Esqr.

KENDER, MASON & Co.

Sir,

ABOVE I send you a Copy of the Guaranty for Messrs. Lovell Morson & Cos. House at Dominica which you will please pay proper attention to: You will immediately after the close of your sales remit to Mr. Brown an Account thereof, and all such Bills as you receive on Account of such Sales. I am (in Mr. Browne's Absence), Sir, Your Most Obedient Humble Servant,

THOS. LANWARN

Abingdon Street, 29th Aug., 1770.

[Endorsed,] To Captain Jno. Clark, Captain Sam'l Haycraft or Captain Mich'l Dove of the *Mary*, at Messrs. Lovell Morson & Co., Dominica.

[Memo.,] N. B. recd from Capt. James Clark at Newport, March 6th, 1772.

JOHN WRIGHT TO THOMAS WRIGHT

The Bay of Handras, Sept. 9th Day, 1770.

Loving Wife and Honored Parents,

I TAKE this Oportunity to acquaint you that I am in good health at present throu the Blesings of God and hope that these may find you all in the same. I roate you a Leattor jest aftor our Arival hear which I hope you have received with sundrey othors. this is to aquaint you that I am a coming hoam mastor of the Brigg, for Capt. Newdigate is not a coming home in the Vesel this Voige. I expect that we shall sail in 10 days or a fortinate at the furthist. I hope by the Blesing of God to sea you all by the first of December. I shall not past the Island without seing some of you if posible I can avoaid it. I shall lift the in sign at the main Top Galant mast head at my Pasing the Island, which may easily be discovred from some Bodey. Pray dont for git mee to my Litel babeys and sistors and brothors and all my frinds. I should be glad if you would send me of if you have aney oportunetey som Shurts and Jackits and Stockins which at present I am vearey naked of to ware in Company having all my Cloaths stoale away from mee. this from your Loving husband and Dutiful Sun untill Dearth.

JOHN WRIGHT

[Endorsed,] To Mr. Thomas Wright Living on Blockisland to be left at Mr. Samual, Care F Carey in Newpoart, Rhodisland. Per Favor Capt. Benson.

SAMUEL GORTON TO AARON LOPEZ

Warwick, September the 10 Day, A.D. 1770.

Mr. Lopos, Sir, you may depend upon fifty Half Barrals in three or four weeks time or less with paying three quarters of the pay to be in Rum Sugar and Molases at the market price, and the other quarter in Dry Goods as they are mark'd in your Shop, and the half Barrals to be at three Pound ten Shillings a Peace. I think this is according to our tolk last week when I was in town. I expect you will have the Pay redy at the Delevery of the Cask, and if you give me a good chance in these I see nothing to hender me from makeing you as many as you will want. I would be glad if you wood be so good as to rite me a few lines in answer to this, and to let me know how soon you will want more and how many more, and by so doing you will oblige your friend

Samuel Gorton

Isaac Werden to Aaron Lopez

Granada, September 12, 1770.

Good Sir,

BEFORE I left Quebec our house wrote you of my proceeding to Dominica, where I have called and where I shall speedily return to. The greatest part of the cargo on hand is common flour, which by no means answers Dominica market, as most of it goes to the french, who at any price will have superfine flour. I could [have] sold any Quantity of that sort there, for 50/ york C[urrenc]y per Barrel, but having common, it has brought me here to do the best I can with it.

You no doubt have e're this our letter which inform'd you of the Terms we would do your own Business at Dominica, and which this confirms for the same time. If Cargoes be suited to the place it far exceeds any province I have seen for Business, and I hope to receive some of your concerns. what I would now advise is salt fish in hhds. as near of a weight as can be, Spermacita Candles, rale boards, Scantling Timber, 4 inch by 4, 4 by 5, 4 by 6. I shall have constant intelligence from this place, and when any cargo better suits here then at dominica, it shall be sent here and beg you'l direct your master accordingly.

gold Coast slaves sell from 35 to £38 Ster. and bring the Cash imediately, as mertinico, gordilupe, and grand Torre, and many to the Leward french Islands are supply'd at that Isle, being a free port, where numerous Cargoes of Slaves and superfine flour and salt fish is yearly sold and if it could suite you to order the foregoing articles, I am well persuaded you'l find your Interest in it. the flour must be the best and from philadelphia.

as we had not the honor of any of your late favours I am doubtful whither you persued the voyage to that place you had proposed, and hope you did not as nothing could sell there to a profit.

If you did not, must desire you'l ship the beaver sent you in bags to London, to your own friend to do the best he can with it, and if any loss on it it shall be ours. they must know better what to do with it, as Comte & Co from Quebec sends it yearly and never sold it for less then 5/6 Ster. beg my hast may excuse blending self and Co. so odly together. Mr. mercier is closing with all possible speed our Quebec concerns, and after may likely joyne me in these Isles. Permit me to subscribe with all possible Respect, Sir, your most Obedient and most humble Servant,

I. WERDEN

Sup'r F Flour at Dom. 50/ Salt fish 25/ Sperm Candles 3/6 Lumber £6. dollar worth 8/3.

P. S. one Vessel lately so[ld] Sperm'ta Candles for near £1000. value, and know of no p[lace] where so many might sell. I beg my gratefu[l Com]pliments may be made to Mr. Rivera and your self, and hope [you wi]ll remember me when you write to your Correspondants in [Eur]ope or America, as I expect to be some years at dominica, faithfully to execute the Command of my friends, and where I shall surely meet with every Indulgence in the power of the Civil majestrates to admit.

[Endorsed,] Favor of Capt. howland.

HAYLEY AND HOPKINS TO CHRISTOPHER CHAMPLIN

London, 22d September, 1770.

Sir,

SINCE our last of which the above is Copy, we have rec'd your favours of 24th July, 2d and 8th August, by which have the following Bills vizt.
Christopher Hargill . . on Joseph Sherwood . . £ 22.10.
Hays & Polock . . . . " ourselves . . . . . 35.
Nicholas Lechmere. . . " Lane & Co. . . . . 45.
which are all accepted, and when in Cash shall be placed to your credit.

We observe your final determination is not to import any Goods 'till Spring, in which we believe you judge right. We hope before that time Trade will be upon a more agreeable footing. We are, etc.

HAYLEY AND HOPKINS

Original per Hathaway.

THOMAS POTTER, JR. TO AARON LOPEZ

So. Kingstown, 1th October, 1770.

Sir,

WEE are out of Salt and want some more over as soon as possible. I have taken in uperds of 30 Casks of Seed. the Forty Bushels Salt that came over last did not last 4 howers. if the Bote cant come to Newport on Monday I desire you would git some frait Bote that belongs somewhare up the River to bring over a 100 or 150 Busheles untill franklins Bote can come over. pray let the Salt be as large as possible. I have likewise sent the Hors I spoke with you about by the barrer, which I think there ant a better Shipping Hors in the Goverment you, Sir, will have no Commissions or Charge on this Hors; the prime Cost is all which I did not mean to be out of the way in, and am, Sir, your Humble Servant,

THOMAS POTTER, JR.

N. B. I dare venter to expect 100 Casks of Seed at least, if can be suplied with Salt of equil quallity with the other. T. P.[1]

CHARLES DUDLEY TO AARON LOPEZ

MR. DUDLEY presents his Compliments to Mr. Lopez, will be glad to know if Mr. Lopez is in Cash for the Negro Wench sold in Carolina; if he is, then Mr. Dudley will be glad to know if he may value himself on Mr. Lopez in favour of Mr. Riviera for £50 Sterling on Account.

Wednesday, 17 October, 1770.

SAMUEL CHAMBERLAIN TO AARON LOPEZ

Swansey, October the 27, 1770.

Sir,

I HOPE you will excuse my not waiting on you before this to settle the freight of my Goods that was brought from Jamaica. my absence has bin oweing to my haveing a very severe fitt of the Gout which has lasted me this four weeks, that I am not able to walk. otherwise I should have waited on you in Person. I have a Bill of Exchange for £200 Sterling drawn by one Mr. Jarrett in Jamaica, which is as good a Bill as can be drawn and will comand the money in Jamaica at any time you please. I beleave Capt. Potter can inform you of the Drawer, wheather he thinks the Bills are good or not. If it be agreeable to you I will let you have these Bills in part of Payment for the freight, and their is one Mr. Peter weaver who has a small Sloop for sail, and I have some thoughts of becomeing a Purchaser from him. he tells me that he is in Dept to you some money, which I

---

[1] The confusion in the currency of Rhode Island is shown by the following proposition, made October 2, by Daniel Tillinghast: "Since I came up have spoke with my Brother about the Bills but your terms will not answer, we can gett more for them than you offered. I will let you have fifty Pounds Sterling at Par and about one Hundred Dollars in treasurers notes and take Malasses to the amount at 36/ old tenor per gallon, if you'l take both Bills and Notes."

will also alow, with a Proviso you will take any Part of said Sloop with me, and, Sir, if you can supply me with such artickels for Cargo as I shall want for Barbadoes, I should be glad to lay out what money I have to spare with you. Please to favour me with your Answer per Beairer and you will much oblidge, Sir, Your very humble Servant,

SAMUEL CHAMBERLAIN

P. S. The Bills are drawn upon Mr. David Ximenes in London.

WILLIAM HALL TO AARON LOPEZ

North Kingstown, October 30th, 1770.

Respected friend,

I RECEIVED yours of the 24th and am very sorry it has not ben in my power as yet to make you easey. I expect to receive a Sum next week and I will come and see you next week. Dont be on easey I shall pay you all I owe you next month I hope.

the Lottery is not yet drawed, as the Tickets are not all sold. the town is about to take the Remainder they expect twill be drawn soon. I remain your friend to serve,

WILLIAM HALL

RALPH INMAN[1] TO AARON LOPEZ

Sir,

I HAVE taken the Liberty of Recommending my Friend Mr. William Pollard to your notice. He is a Partner in the House of Messrs. Green, Ford & Curtys, of Barcelona, that has large Consignments from the Southard, and he takes this Tour to pay his Friends a Visitt, is the Reason of my Introducing him to your Acquaintance; should you,

---

[1] Of Cambridge, later a loyalist, but did not leave Massachusetts. He died in Cambridge in 1788. Frequent mention of him is found in Rowe's *Diary*. A daughter married Captain Linzee of the British Navy.

or Friends, have any concerns that way, and your Civilities to him shall esteem a favour done,

Sir Your most Hble Sert
Ralph Inman.

HENRY CRUGER, JR. TO AARON LOPEZ

Bristol, November 10th, 1770.

Sir,

I HAVE your favor of 31st August, covering a 2nd Bill per £421.3.10 Stg., drawn by my Father on me, for Rum, etc., rec'd from you. as I before advised you, the first of same Set was rec'd from him, and from that I credited your Account 31st October, when it became due.

I am sorry you were prevented putting your intentions of sending me some Oil in execution, by the *Aaron's* departing before your Fishing Vessels came in. I dare say you are well inform'd when you say that article sells highest in London when the Season is anything advanced, but I confess I do not agree with you. for some time Oil has been cheaper in London than here, so as to encourage our Buyers to go there, and pay Freight round; and it is not expected but it will remain under our Market, which is now at £30 per Ton for White, and £25 for Brown.

I lately received from Jamaica £100 Stg. in part of the £150 Bill I sent there to be recovered of the Drawer on your Account. this remise is unfortunately noted for non acceptance; I shall do the needful if not honor'd at Maturity, and advise you. the drawer of the Bill sent to Jamaica, requests some further Indulgence of time for the remaining £50 and Charges. I have declined giving it, and urged a speedy settlement.

I did flatter myself I should this fall have had the consignment of a Ship and Cargo from you, imagining you'd be led from Motives of Generosity and Justice to make me such a Remittance, when you consider'd what a loser I must, and have been, by all the Quebec Adventure, and Candles, and by the Ship *Aaron*, which has sunk me Money ever since I had her, and now lies an Incumbrance on my Hands, and all this done by my Father, (who well knew my distress), to raise me a little Money, and to ease your Debt in the most favorable way to you, 'tho so much to my Prejudice. I'm again disappointed however, but can't help once more urging you to think it high time to make me some Remise by which I shall be no Sufferer; I have been one already very considerably, do in your turn take a little to yourself, by making a point of paying me my present Ballance in a *direct* way, even 'tho this Mode should interfere with some favorite Plan you may have adopted. it is but fair that as I have so long bore the burthen, you should come in for a small share of Inconvenience.

Many articles in the inclosed Price Current will pay a good Freight from your place, as you'll perceive on Inspection. I send it for your Guidance.

A great many Ships of the Line are put in Commission, and a hot press for Seamen continues, which makes People imagine War will soon be declared; 'tho these appearances are all we have to judge by. most foreign commodities will rise upon that event considerably. I still remain with great Truth and Sincerity, Sir, Your attach'd Friend and most humble Servant,

HEN: CRUGER, JR.

[Endorsed,] Via New York per *America*.

JOHN PYNER TO AARON LOPEZ

Downs, 10th November, 1770.

Sir,

I HAVE the pleasure of acquainting you of my safe arrival here in 33 Days. Have wrote Messrs. Hayley & Hopkins of my arrival in order to give them all the time I can of disposing of the Cargoe; the Snow has proved verry leakey all the passage, but sails verry well. I shall make all the Dispatch I possible can to get her up to London and hope my Conduct in this, as well as every other matter will prove to your Satisfaction, as you may depend on my studying your Interest the same as my own.

Times are verry likely for a Warr in the Spring; as there is a verry hott press.[1] I have had two hands press'd from me; by an Order from the Admiralty, to impress out of every Vessell, which is done now every day, and every one expects a Warr in a short time. I have not an opportunity of writing to my Wife, but beg you will acquaint her of my safe arrival by a Letter, and you will oblige, Sir, Your Obedient Servant,

JOHN PYNER

P. S. I am informed that Capt. Godfry in the Brig[antin]e arrived here last week.

JEREMIAH BROWN TO AARON LOPEZ

Providence, the 15 Nov., 1770.

Sir,

I TUCK passage on board your Sloop *Mary*, Capt. Daniel Cornell, the 26 October at Quebec, and caim as far as Canso, where I left him and tuck Passage for Boston. I have sum frate on board him with Directions whome to deliver it to. the 5 this Instant I left said Sloop at Canso, all well on board. he had the Misfortune to luse one of your Male Horses in the River St. Lawrance in a Gaile of wind. from Your Humble Servant,

JERE'M BROWN

---

[1] A history of the pressing of seaman has recently been written by J. R. Hutchinson, *The Press-Gang afloat and ashore* (1914).

John Pyner to Aaron Lopez

London, November 26th, 1770.

Dear Sir,

I HAVE now the pleasure of informing you of my safe arrival in 33 days: the Snow was verry leakey but sails fast. I have began unload and hope to have all out in 6 or 7 days and am this day putt up at the Exchange to sail by the 1st of January next. I really find charges verry high here, but shall use your Caution with respect to that, and hope to give you Satisfaction.

We daily expect a Warr to be declared and I think that every matter wears the face of Warr but this I suppose will be determin'd in a few days.

I have apply'd to several Gent. according to your Instructions and have the promise of their freight. You may depend on my doing as I promis'd you when present, and hope you will not have reason to find fault with my Conduct; I shall write you again per first Oppertunity and remain, Dear Sir, Your Obedient Servant,

JOHN PYNER

William Heffernan to Aaron Lopez

Eustatia, December 2th, 1770.

Sir,

I INFORMD you of my being here and the Reson of my coming here by Capt. Snell by va Newyork, sens which I have disposed of som of my Cargo dryd fish @ four ps. Eight, Rice @ twenty Shilings, pipe staves at ten pound per thosend, Shingles @ twenty one Shilings per thosend, some pork @ sixteen ps. Eight per Bbr., and had soald my flowr @ six ps. Eight per Barrel, but yesterday had twenty nine bbrs. turned on my hands it being damaged. Shads hors Mackril Enouns and oyl of turpintine will fetch nothing as yet, nor have I sold half my Cheese. the Sheep soald @ twenty Shiling, loast four of them. last week two of my people left me, and expect the other two will go the first opertunity, as theay are all of a sort, and never desined to return in the Vesel when theay shipt and hands are scarse here and afraid of a winters Coast and ask ten Dolars per month and not to be had at that. markets are so bad to windward that Vasels daly com in here. Capt. Sears arived here yesterday with a Cargo of dryd fish, and two other Vasels all from to windward. Rum is at two and threepenc per Gall, Sugar six ps. Eight. Cocoa not to be had, nor Coffee except in the shell.

I expect to right again in two or three days, ontell then Remain your Obedient Humle Sar't., remain

your Obt. Huml. Sart.

William Heffernan

JOHN WRIGHT TO AARON LOPEZ

Charles Town, December 7th, 1770.

Sir,

I AM now to advize you of the proceeding of Capt. Newdegate of the Brigantine *Charlotte*. you must know that the first of his bad proceedings, to my oppinion, is his sending the Vessell away short of provision under a pretence of their being none to be had (in the Bay of Hundoras), when I had a plenty which he might have had for asking for, with an order on you, which is much like his proceeding in every thing else as I am shure the comeing in here was interely his doings, for am almost convinced that her coming in here was his doings. Am almost convinced that the Cargo of Mahoganey which she had on board when she came in here was yours, altho' threw a Collour of Villaney was consigned to one Mr. Jones, as great a Villain as himself, by which meens the said Joans with bribing the people he gott the Vessell in here notwithstanding. the Capt. I mean Jno. Wright came ashore and gott provision for them, and since which has tried all he could to give Capt. Wright all the Towbl [trouble] that in him lays. you may think much of receiving a letter from a man who has so little acquance with you, butt you must think it concerns every Honest Man when he sees another imposed on by the good oppinion he has of a bad man, which you may think the proceedings of the same may be threw the present Master; butt as have seen the proceeding in the Bay and here which confirms what I now wright to you this, you may depend on from, Sir, your humble Servant,

JOHN WRIGHT

HAYLEY AND HOPKINS TO CHRISTOPHER CHAMPLIN

London, 8th December, 1770.

Sir,

WE are now favour'd with yours of 7th September, 3d and 4th of October, enclosing 3 Bills drawn by Stevenson & Went [1] on Lascelles & Co.[2] £100. at 4 months, £125.17.6. at 8 months and £125.17.7 at 12 months, all which are accepted, and in due course shall be placed to your Credit, but it is impossible to discount them at Four per Ct. Bills not exceeding 2 months may be always discounted here at 5 per Ct. but not under; but when they are so long as 4, 8, and 12 months they cannot possibly be gott done even at 5 per Ct. They must therefore remain till they are due before they can go to your credit, which we wish could be otherwise, as you seem so desirous of their passing to your credit in this year's account. We are getting ready the Goods you desire for your Spring Trade, and we hope to have them all ready for Mr. Lopez's Snow, who we expect will sail about the time he mention'd to you; but the demand for Goods is at present so unusually large, that we doubt

---

[1] Of Barbadoes.

[2] Lascelles and Daling, of London. The rate for the twelve months bill was thirty per cent.

you will find many articles dearer than you expect, however you may depend upon our taking all possible care that the whole shall be executed on the best terms and with the utmost attention to your particular patterns and instructions.

The Bill which you remitted us for £110 on Rob't Brown, which was noted for nonacceptance, was nevertheless paid when due, and is placed to your credit, as is also that for £222. on Rob't Udney, James & Co. This last was protested, but taken up by Mr. Smith of Bristol, in consequence of our application to him agreeable to your directions. We are in a perplexing state of uncertainty here with respect to a Spanish War, on which it is impossible to form any judgment, but we should think a very little time must determine it. We are etc.

HAYLEY & HOPKINS

Orig. per Robson.

CHARLES HINCKLEY[1] TO AARON LOPEZ

Esteemed Friend,

THIS wates by the Hand my Nefew, Mr. Jabez West, to informe, he has enterd into Partnerships with me, to keep, a Retailing Shop, European and West India-Goods, and he informes me when at your Store in Automn, you informed him you expected a large supply, soon, and would serve us as reasonable as we can be in Boston. Sir, upon that Incouragement, and hearing your goods are arived, Mr. West now wates on you. if you'd give Credit, for sutch good as he shall judge proper to take, either for said Company and also on my Private Account, I shall endevour to honor his Ingagements, and it is my present purpose to turne my Trade to your Town in lue of Boston, if I am as well us'd. Pray excuse Hast, from Your Friend and Very Humble Servant,

CHA. HINCKLEY

Lebanon, 24 December, 1770.

---

[1] Son of Gershom and Mary (Buel) Hinckley, of Lebanon, Conn.

Ebenezer Shearman to Aaron Lopez

Cape Necholas Mole, December 25, 1770.

Sir,

I take this opertunity to inform you that I have sold the Sloop *Salley* for 400 Dollers and the Amount of my Sailes is 4878 Liver. my Sope and Sperits or Corgils [cordials] and White oak Staves I cant sell and shall send them and the affects in Capt. Sayer for Rhodeisland, the affects in Indego. the flour that was put on board for super fine 10 of them is common, and one of them is so dammadge that am affraid I shant be able to sell it, and the Onion I lost 100 bunchs roted. the Reson I sold the Sloop *Salley* under what I was orderd is that I carrey'd away my Main beam on the Pasage 2 Shrouds and Fore Stay, and should ben obleag'd to git all new stand rigen for on the Pasage was obleag'd to git up the Cables for Shrouds and the Vesell prov'd very leakey. the fais of the Markit is much allterd from what it was. fish is fell from 30 Livers to 24 Do., and Poark from 10 Peas of 8 to 8 Peasis of Eight. Indego is 7 Levers 10 Sous p[er pou]nd. What my Poart Charges is I cant tell yet. this is the secon Letter Concluding with Your Most Obedeant humble Servant,

Ebenezer Shearman

Hayley & Hopkins to Christopher Champlin

London, 21 January, 1771.

Sir,

Since our last of which the above is Copy, we have received your favours of 17th October 4th and 6th November. We have therewith a Bill on Lascelles & Daling for £292:13:3 at 8 Months sight which is accepted and in due course shall be placed to your Credit but it is impossible to discount it on the terms you propose so it must lay by us till it becomes due. We now enclose your Account Current as usual to the end of the Last Year, ballance then in our favour being £978:1:7 is carried to your debit in new Account which if upon examination found free from Error please note in conformity, of which shall be obliged by your acquainting us in your next. We have shipp'd the greatest part of the Goods you desired on board this Vessel the *Jos'h* Capt. Pyner as per Invoice and Bill of Lading enclos'd amounting to £1780.11.11 on which we have made £1825 Insurance premio etc. being £45.18. We hope they will arrive with you in good Season. What remains to compleat your orders shall be dispatch'd as fast as possible, but we shall not be able to execute your order for Tea which you desire may be shipp'd, if it should be orderd, to Boston New York or Philadelphia. We believe the Merchants at all those three ports have in general forebore sending their orders for that Article, if there is any going it is not done openly, but we suppose there may be some who will endeavour to get it underhand. We think thus circumstanced it is not your meaning to have any. we dont know that there is a single Chest going to your Colony. We are, etc.

HAYLEY & HOPKINS

(Copy) Original per Pyner.
[Endorsed,] Per Capt. Gilbert.

JOSHUA HART TO AARON LOPEZ

Charles Town, 15th February, 1771.

Dear Sir,

YOUR kind and obliging favour of the 20th Ulto. which was handed me by Capt. Earl, I have now before me, and am happy to find your goodself and family continue enjoying a perfect State of health. May the same be long attended with every other desireable felicity.

Youl please accept of a small Cask Sour Oranges as a token of our sincer Friendship. Mrs. Hart joins me in our sincer thanks for your kind favour of the salmon which came in due season. Mrs. Hart and family joins me in wishing you and family, your Brother Abram and family, the Widow Lopez and Children, and Mr. David Lopez and the rest of your worthy family, a Merry Purim, and may the good of Israel set a Blessing on you all and am With Sincerity, Your Assured Friend, and Most Obedient Servant

JOSHUA HART

P. S. youl please excuse my curtailing being friday afternoon, therefore not able to enlarge.

HENRY CRUGER, JR. TO AARON LOPEZ

Bristol, February 20th, 1771.

Dear Sir,

I CATCH this oppertunity to inform you the parcel of Oil received per the *Ellen*, Captain Clark, on the joint Account of you and my Father, is sold at £27 per ton. the sales shall be soon made out and sent you.

The underhand and I may say stupid management of the Broker who had the disposal of the 60 Tons that arrived with yours hurried me into a sale 30/ or 40/ under the value of the Oil. There is no guarding against, nor punishment for such people. however considering the late Season of the Year £27 is no bad price.

I wish, Dear Sir, you would listen to my advice and contrive to dispatch a small Vessel here early next fall with 50 or 60 Tons of white and brown Oil. I think you might be certain of obtaining £30 per ton for the White and £26 or £27 for the Brown. I received some white early this fall and sold it all at £32 per Ton. I remain with Respectful Regard, Sir, Your most Obedient Servant

HEN: CRUGER, JR.

BENJAMIN ALLEN TO AARON LOPEZ

Green Island in Jamaica, March 8th, 1771.

Dear Sir,

THESE may searve to let you no that I am still in green Island with my fish and flower on hand, which I look upon to be the grates part of my Cargo att preasent which I cannot dispose of att aney rate, omiting Cash as it is not to be had hear. Should have sailed by the time apointted had not David Cuningham Esqr. disapointted me of forty Caskes of Molasses which he had prommest me, and after leting me have tenn of them cam and told me I could have no more as he intended to disstill all he made. have now on board about forty Casks. Expect to git fifteen or twenty more in about tenn dayes, and if my goods will not sell shall leave them with Capt. Benjamin Wright and git hom as fast as I can, as I no you expect to see the Sloop *Abigail* in the month of May. Begging you will forgive my long tarrey by reason that I would not trust out my good and tak my pay in rum nowing that you have no call for it, as Rum is the onley payment they will make hear for aney goods that thay by, and you may depend on it, Sir, that I shall make all the Dispach that I can. Wee have an od sett of peapel to deal with hear. Am, Sir, your ever humbel Sarvent to searve,

BENJ'N ALLEN

N. B. the Sales that I have made amounts to four hundred and fifty pounds. the Lumber have deliverd to Capt. Wright as per Order which came to a good market. I think it sold for 12 and 14 pounds per thousand.

BENJ'N ALLEN

[Endorsed,] Per favor Capt. Wanton, Ship *Polley*.

HENRY CRUGER, JR. TO AARON LOPEZ

March 16th, 1771.

Dear Sir,

BEING without any of your late favors have nothing particular to say by this Bearer only that she is my ship, *The Aaron* that Holmes did command, but now Capt. Gough. She is making me a full freight out to Boston: what they will freight her back with I yet know not. I have desired my friend John Hancock Esq. to whom she goes consign'd, to correspond with you on that subject: as perhaps you may think fit to load her for me with Logwood, Mahogany, etc. if you can serve me I shall always be mindful of the favour. The strong talk again of War inclines me to think a Cargo of Logwood would not be a bad Speculation, especially if you ship it at a peacable Freight. thirty five Guineas are now given to insure against War a Twelvemonth; the people say it is unavoidable. the Turks and Russians will bring us in. this is all that at present occurs, save to assure you that I am with unalterable respect and esteem, Sir, Your most humble Servant,

HEN: CRUGER, JR.

DANIEL TILLINGHAST TO AARON LOPEZ

Sir, Providence, March 20th, 1771.

I HAVE sent you by Mr. Marsh 1 Hhd. Rum q[uantit]y, 117 gallons, and have hear inclosed your Distilling Account, which leaves a Ballance due to you of 67 gallons of Rum. when I wrote you last I omitted the order you drew in favor of Mr. Eddy for 100 gallons, which makes it short of what I wrote you than. you'l please to examine the Account and if you find it right creditt me accordingly. should have sent the whole Ballance but had no Cask that would hold it. if you want any more Rum and have any Molasses by you should be glad to exchange. I am just out, must gett some in a few days. should be glad to know the lowest Cash Price for Molasses at Newport. Please to send my Account by the Return of Boat and you'l oblige your Most Humble Servant,   DAN'L TILLINGHAST

WILLIAM CHASE TO AARON LOPEZ

Sur, Sunbury in Georgia,[1] 2 April, 1771.

I AM to sail for Barbados to day. have had but bad marketes hear. alltho I have staid so long have sold a

---

[1] No such port is listed in the modern gazetteers.

bout half your Cheas att about 6d li. the oyel att three pounds 10/ per Bl. Shall do the best I can with the rest. Shall right you a gain from Barbados. Remain Sur your Friend and Humbel Sarvant,

WILLIAM CHASE

BENJAMIN WRIGHT TO AARON LOPEZ

Savlamar, the 10th April, 1771.

Dr. Couzen,

MY last was per Sloop *George,* Capt. Green, who parted this Island the 17 ulto. hope he is safe arrived with you long before this and came to a good market. You have annexed duplicate of the Invoice Bill of Lading and Account Sales of the Sundries per Brigg *Cæcelia,* Peter Mackay, Master. You have also inclosed a Copy of my Letter to Hayley & Hopkins your friends in London, ordering you a further Insurance of One Thousand Pounds Sterling, which hope will meet your Approbation. You have likewise Mr. William Hull of St. Anns Letter to me in answer to my Letter to him, wherein I desired him to give me a particular Account of your matters in that Parish. His answer was not so satisfactory to me as I could wish, and am of opinion it will be less to you my good Master, as I am fearfull your Interest is suffering in that part of the Island.

I am really sorry I cannot give you my assistance there at this time, as I am in a fair way to dispatch the *Diana* in a good Season. Have now on board between Eighty and Ninety Hhds. Sugar and some Rum on freight. Have Sixty Puncheons Rum ready to ship on board on your own Account, am dayly collecting, but find the people very backward in payments. my Cargoe sticks on hand, therefore I must be obliged to purchase some Rum on the strength of my little Credit, as I am determin'd the Brigg shall sail in all May, if no unforeseen accident happens, sooner if possible. I find it will not answer any good end to keep the *Diana* here till I piddle off her Cargoe and wait to collect her debts, as it will take a long time to do it, and you are very sensible it will be attended with a greater expence to keep so large a Vessell here, two or three months. I am therefore determin'd to purchase some Rum to prevent my falling much short of the quantity I advised Messrs. Hayley & Hopkins I should ship, as you will see by the Copy of my Letter to them. I find a much greater quantity of Rum shippd this year for London market, than has been for many years past. I wish you may not become a sufferer by ordering so large a quantity to that market; I think it will not be amiss to ship ten Hhds. good Sugars on your Account provided I get them seasonable and good, which shall be the case or I shall nor purchase any. Markets much the same as when I wrote you by Green. Capt. Buckley has been very sick but is now much recovered. His people have been complaining, and two run away from the Brigg. He is very poorly mann'd, and works very hard himself. I should have been much put to my shifts to have got the *Diana* unloaded had not the *Cæcilia* been here. Her hands have given all the assistance in their power. Mr. Watts the Carpenter has justly merrited my displeasure, and I shall not forgive him for his treason. you sent him here to build us a long boat to load the Brigg. I am well perswaded he told you that he had taken every article sufficient to compleat her, but when he began to sett her up he had not plank enough by one half. I was obliged to buy Nails, Oakum and plank. He brought no Knees to secure the Boat. I have likewise been under the necessity to hire ten days carpenters labour, and after all I believe I shall get the Brig to Sea before he will have her done. He well understands the Custom of your wharfe, that is to say, work as little as possible, and if it answers a good end employ those Blood Suckers. my advice is to feed them well and give them Grogg enough, then you be a mighty good Man. Further sayeth not on this subject.

Poor Ben Allen begins to squeek. he wants me to take his Vessell and Cargoe into my hands and dispatch him. he could not conceive there was so much trouble and expense attending the Disposal of a small Cargoe and collecting it in. tis true the poor fellow arrived here at a dull Market, but I arrived here at a much worse, by reason I came after him and found him selling many articles at this place. the Old Fellow is not hard mouth enough for this place. Modesty is not looked on here a Virtue. I am daily in expectation for the arrival of the *Charlott*. I want her Cargoe much. time will not admit of more at present. My best Compliments to your good Lady, and am with Esteem, Your Most Humble Servant

B. WRIGHT

HENRY CRUGER, JR. TO AARON LOPEZ

Bristol, 12th April, 1771.

Dear Sir,

I HAVE only time by this Vessel, that I am dispatching in a great hurry, to own the Receipt of your esteem'd and agreable Favor of 25 January.

I am obliged to you for recovering that little matter from Mr. Goldthwait, and for your pains with Mrs. Freelove Saunders, who treats me unjustly in every word and action, also for the 6 Guineas from Heffernan with which your Account is debited. I lament the bad success of your little Brigantine; there is no guarding against imprudent Men, nor expences incident to old Vessels, nor stress of Weather, nor bad concerted plans: pity, but I had had your orders to sell her right out.

I now inclose you account sales of the first parcell of Oil sent to me by my father on your and his joint Accounts, Neat Proceeds £404.3.10 Sterling, one Moiety of which is to your Credit with my thanks. It had sold better by 2 or 3 £ per Ton if it had arrived 2 or 3 Weeks sooner.

The last parcell is sold, the White from £26 to £26.10.0, and the brown from £24 to £24.10 per Ton. amongst the latter are 6 Casks blubber or Whale Oil, they are not yet all gauged off. per my next the Sales and particulars shall be rendered.

Accept, Sir, my warmest acknowledgements for your

Friendly Attention and chearful Assistance in my concerns with John Channing. I am persuaded you have been instrumental in rescuing me from a dangerous Debt; and may be from a total loss of it. I am imprest, Dear Sir, with a grateful sense of your Conduct, which is all that I have time to say now, except that I remain with undissembled Esteem Your most Obliged Humble Servant,

HEN: CRUGER, JR.

BENJAMIN WRIGHT TO AARON LOPEZ

Salamarr, 28 April, 1771.

Dr. Couzen,

THE preceeding is what I wrote you per the *Polly*, Capt. Brenton Wanton, who left this Island the 18 Inst. Hope he may meet with a short Passage and arrive safe. Since which I have mett with trouble on account the Officers of the *Diana* differing and the Mate leaving the Brigg, and has carried away his Servant, and two more of his Sailors has taken their departure. likewise Dan'l Watts Esqr., by Profession a louzy Carpenter, has enloped before your long Boat was near finish'd. You cannot immagine how much I am distress'd for want of a Carpenter and Sailors to dispatch the *Diana*. the London Ships offer Sixteen Guineas for Seamen for the Run. Should I be drove to that Extremity it will reduce the freight Bill much. I can but express my Surprize that you and Capt. Buckly should ship a Second Mate which doth not understand Navigation, which is the case as I am inform'd, and how I shall provide a Mate is more than I can at present advise you as yet. The *Diana* will be entirely loaded by the twentieth of May, should no farther misfortunes befall me, but when she will sail cannot say as that depends on getting a Mate and Sailors. I used every method in my power to get Morgan the Mate to tarry by the Brigg and proceed on the voyage, but all to no purpose. I believe him to be a person that cannot be depended on. bad Tidings still hangs on the end of my Penn. I now acquaint you I shall not ship on board the *Diana* for your Account so much as I expected, for this reason the Brigg cannot carry so much as I expected by a considerable Quantity. therefore have taken so much freight on board, am obliged to shut your own Goods out. you are very sensible that my Payments here comes in so slowly prevented my getting your own Goods in first, and you well know Sugars must be stowed under the Rum, which obliged your goods to be the last on board, but you may rest assured that I shall ship per first opportunity the deficiency of what I shall fall short in the Brigg, to compleat the Sum I order'd insured, for your Account, and shall advise Messrs. Hayley & Hopkins timely as they may transfere the Insurance, and as your Brigg goes full freighted it cannot make any great difference to you. I shall have near forty Puncheons Rum by me after the Brigg is loaded. therefore do not think I have not been able to collect the Quantity I advised your friends in London I should have ship'd them per the *Diana*. tis not the case notwithstanding your two Cargoes to me are not more than one-half sold. I shall surely ship to Bristol ten Puncheons Rum for your Account and address them to Henry Crewger Esqr. agreeable to your request, and advise him timely to cover your property. in regard to your matters at St. Anns cannot meddle with as yet. Martin Luther's with Daniel Moore Esqr. that affair must stand till Luther sends me the Account Current. please advise him the same. Have been looking for the *Charlotte* this some days past. Hope no accident has happen'd to her. I am much in debt here to dispatch the *Diana* as my Cargoe sticks on hand. flatter myself you will not see or even suffer me to be carried to Prison, as I am pushing to serve my Couzen.

I am very sorry the *Abigail* has been so long detain'd, but we cannot make people buy our Goods if they dont chose to purchase. I am affraid your Vessell to Kingston will be later than she was last year which will be to your disadvantage. Should I be able to go to St. Anns and should receive any thing for you, what am I to do with them? please to be very particular in your Instructions, and I will be equally as particular in executing your Instructions. Markets are very low and Cash very scarce. No articles in demand. Should you build a Ship for this trade let no Carpenter alter the Dimentions I gave you, and order her to be built burdensom to carry a large Quantity of Goods, to let you share some Proffitts with your Industry, but at same time please to observe I do not mention this to intice you to build a large and expensive Ship, but these small Vessells will not answer for this trade. We have advanced the freight from 3/6 to 4/3. time will not admit of more at present. Capt. Peter Wanton will sale by the last of May. by him shall be able to repeat some more Grievances. I have sent six bottles Olives to be equally divided between Mrs. L[opez] and W[right], share and share alike. Could not get any more in this place. I am, Dr. Sir, Your Most Obedient Humble Servant,

BENJAMIN WRIGHT

[Endorsed,] Per the *Abigail*, Capt. Allen, Q. D. C.

ABRAHAM REED TO AARON LOPEZ

Sir,

I HAVE put on board Cory a dozen hats for you the which I have had ready a long time, but several thing has from time to time fell out so thay have not ben sent be fore. I have also a dozen Boys hats that are fur'd on the uper side of the Brim that will be ready by the next time Cory goes to Newport. shoud be glad if you will send me Silk nuf to line them, and I will send them by him. as to the flannel it is not come to hand the men war to have sent it according to agrement but did not, wherefore I had concluded not to take it but insist on the money but I find it is like to make a Breach between us if I dont take the Cloth [from] a Letter which I had from him a day or 2 since I shall [try] next week to see him again at which time shall get the Cloath or the money. If I am oblig'd to take the Cloath I must alow you for being kept out. I will come and see you for a settl[ement very so]on. I have sent a hat for your little

Son in among the hats by Cory. I am, Sir, your Very Humble Servant,

ABRAH. REED.

Dartm., April 30, 1771.

N. B. their is 6 hats in a Paper with yours in the Box for William Giles. Should be glad if you will let him have them.

HENRY CRUGER, JR. TO AARON LOPEZ

Bristol, 21st May, 1771.

Sir,

SINCE my last respects have none of your esteemed favors. My Father has remitted me a Bill on your Account £184.3.5 Sterling at 40 Days sight. it was accepted 17 Instant when due will be to your Credit.

I now hand you herewith Sales of Oil received per New York, which you are a Moiety concerned, Net Proceeds £150. Stg. to your Credit in the Account Current inclosed on which is still a ballance in my favor £4047.9.1 Sterling that is pass'd to your Debit in a new Account. if you find it right, pray note the same in Conformity.

You have also inclosed a price current for your Guidance. I wish you would, Dear Sir, make me a handsome remittance in Bills direct. it is high time some such thing was done. I have already suffered enough by the *round a bout payments* you have made my Father for me. I remain, with great regard, Sir, Your most humble Servant,

HEN: CRUGER, JR.

JOHN STEVENS TO AARON LOPEZ

Bristol, May 25, 1771.

Sir,

WE arived in your Ship *Benjemin* after a tagous passeg of 54 Days haveing nothing but Rpated gales of wind the whole Time. I was ex[t]reamly glad to find the Ship meet so quick a Sale. Capt. Potters I supose got home befor this time, whose behavour I think none of the best, though I forbear to mention perticlours as his falings are not unknown to you, men Charecters being a thing so tender. I should not mention this but for good Reasons given me on the passeg. I thought of coming out to you myself if an Afair of mine in Law did not hinder, and when it will be ended is not known to me. I am now going out this place mate of the ship *live Oak*, Captain Lunberry, to South Carolina to pass a few months. at my Return if I can settle my Afair, I intend to come to Roadisland, when I hope you will give me some small place in your Servic. as to public Afairs hear there is Nothing but putting Lord Maires in the Tower with Aldermen, and hissing the King in the Streets. what the end will be time that brings all things to pass will show. I have nothing more metaril to write you. I am wishing you Health and prosperity and Remains your Obliged Humble Servant,

JOHN STEVENS

JOHN MALLARD TO AARON LOPEZ

Bristol, 1st June, 1771.

Sir,

I HAVE already had the pleasure of addressing you per this Bearer, who being detain'd by contrary Winds, affords me an opportunity of owning receipt of your esteem'd favor dated 8th March and 17th April. the first cover'd Augustus Johnston on Joseph Sherwood for £52.14.8 Sterling which is noted for non Acceptance.

The Bill of £184.3.5 Sterling, handed me in your last, I had before received from my Father, as formerly wrote you.

I note what you have been so kind to do in my Affair with John Channing, for which am very thankful as I doubt not you did your best, rather than submit to such hard Terms for me, as your last mentions. its Cruel Usage! pray correspond frequently and fully with my Father on this Matter. to him I lately sent the Account Current properly proved on which was, and is, a Ballance in my favor of £5281.6.10 Sterling for your Guidance. I remain with Regard, Sir, Your most humble Servant, By Procuration of H. Cruger, Junior,

JOHN MALLARD

HAYLEY & HOPKINS TO CHRISTOPHER CHAMPLIN

London, 8th June, 1771.

Sir,

SINCE our last of which the above is Copy we have received your favour of the 18th and 22d April with the following Bills vizt.

Stevenson & Went on Lacelles & Darling	£89. 1.11
Jno. Inglis on the Commissioners of the Navy	7.13. 6
do. . . do	2.10. –
Fra's Levett on Rich'd Oswald	20. –. –

All which are accepted and in due course shall be placed to your Credit. We are very sorry the Spring Ships for your port had so long passages. we hope they arrived soon after the date of your Letters now before us. The Order you sent us for Fall Goods shall be attended to. The Goods are getting ready and shall be shipped, as many of them as can possibly be gott ready on board Scott via Boston, and the rest by the first Vessels for Newport; but Goods in general and low pric'd Woolen Goods in particular will be very scarce and dear. You may depend upon our endeavours to gett the whole on the best terms and as early as possible. We shall particularly attend to what you write about the Gunpowder. We have not the least trace of remembrance of Mr. Isaac's having seen your Invoice. We believe he did desire us to send some Manchester Goods for him at the same prices at which you ordered yours and this is all we remember of the matter. however, Sir, be assured no person shall in future have recourse to any of your Invoices. Inclosed you have Invoice for some Goods shipped for your Account at Bristol on board the *William*, Captain Rotch, amounting to £24.18.6, on which we have made £25 Insurance premio, etc. being 15/3. We are, etc.

HAYLEY AND HOPKINS

Original per Jarvis.

JOHN FREEBODY, JR., TO CHRISTOPHER CHAMPLIN

New York, June, 1771.

Sir,

I FIND that I am like to make a longer Tarry than I expected, and for fear that you should want Money before my return, I have sent it you by Capt'n Warner, consisting of Forty-Six half Johannes's three Doubloons and three Pistoles, for which you have his Recpt; I find that several People here is a collecting all the Doubloons and Pistoles that they can get: which makes them very scarce. Several Gentelmen have promis'd me if they should receive any dureing my Stay here to reserve them for me. I shall endeavour to collect all I can and if I should return timely for you; you shall have the Refuseal of them. I conclude in hast and am, Sir, Your Humble Servant,

JNO. FREEBODY, JR.

1 Doublon	£5.12.8	3 John's a 64/6	£9.13.6
1 do.	5.13.4	1 do.	3. 4.0
1 do.	3.19.0	1 do.	3. 5.0
1 Pistole	1. 9.0	1 do.	3. 5.3
1 do.	1. 8.8		19. 7.9
1 do.	1. 8.4		3.3
	£19.11.0		19.11.0

Flour	20/ to 21/.	Molasses	1/10
Beef	55/	West India Rum from 3/6 to 3/7.	
Pork	88/	Jamaica Rum	4/4 to 4/6.
Bread	20/		

[Endorsed,] Per Capt. Warner.

[Memo.] Johnston & Freebody, New York.

George Sears to Aaron Lopez [1]

Newfound Land, St. Johns, July 11, 1771.

Sir,

THIS may inform you that after a passage of 17 days we arived safely at St. Johns whare I find Markets much as usual, except Bread and flour which is in very great demand. when we arived here Bread and flour was 16/ it is now rise to 21/ Bread 23/ flour and like to continue scarce. If it should sute you to send me some, it will help to get of some other dull goods. I have sold three or four hundred pounds Sterling, but they being not all deliver'd cannot send you the Bills by this oppertunity, but shall send them by next which will be soon. the Snow is so shole in the Hole that she will not sell. I allways understood at Home she wass better then nine foot Hole. But I have agree'd to take a Freight of Fish for the Streights which will be about £300 Sterling, and have the greatest assurance of having a nother from thence to London. If you insure it must be from the Bay of Bulls in N Found Land to Leghorn, Naples, or Civita Vichia, one of those ports they being not far distant and the Merchant not yet concluded which. the Snow is to sail about the middle of next month. I shall be gladd of a line from you per first Oppertunity to know your Intentions. you may relie on my takeing all possible care and panes for your Intrest in the Sale of the Cargo, and am your Humble Servant,

GEO. SEARS

P. S. I sold 40 Sheep at 16/ the remain[der] at 10/6, they being small and poor.

Anchors and Cables there is a great Quantity at Market which makes them so very low. If you should send me any Bread and flour in a Schooner of those Dementions she would likely sell, a high Deck long quarter deck eight foot 8 inches Hole or 9 foot.

G. SEARS

---

[1] Original in the Newport Historical Society.

Price Currant.

N. E. Rum	1/6	Tobbacco	4d, 4½d, 5d.
Cordials	3/	Pitch Tarr and Turpentine	15/
W. E. Rum	2/1 to 2/3	Anchors	4½ and 5
Jamaca	3/ to 3/6	Cable and Hawsers	40/
Molasses	1/2	Hhd. Staves 110/ bbl. do. 55/60	
Brown Sugar	35/ 40/	Sper Candles	1/4
Coffea	1/.	Chocolat	1/.
Pork	55/ to 60/	Sheep 10/6 16/	
Indian Corn	2/9	Strong Beer 30/	
Bohea Tea	4/	Soap 5d if hard.	
L Sugar	8d		

[Endorsed,] Per favour of Capt. Turner.

HENRY CRUGER, JR. TO AARON LOPEZ

15th July, 1771.

Sir,

Preceding is duplicate of my last Respects, and since am favor'd with yours of 24th May. I observe with pleasure your intentions of sending an early Cargo of Oil to my Address the approaching Fall. be assured you will find your Account in it. I note what you say respecting my Ship *Aaron*. I had some hopes you might have help'd her to a Freight, but they all vanish'd upon reading your last. I fancy her destination will be to Carolina.

Herewith you have Copys of my Letters to my Correspondent in Jamaica when I returned him the £100 Bill under protest that he had received on account of £150 Bill sent him formerly in same Situation. I will again write him shortly in the most pressing manner, to urge a Settlement: and I hope he will not be backward in using all proper means for your Security, as I don't know a better person there to entrust it to; but 'tis a hard Matter *to recover Money* in that Island, even from the best of them.

Your said favor cover'd a Bill of Exchange, of which had before received the first of same set, and advised you accordingly.

I am afraid John Channing's Affairs will turn out very bad, but there's no help for such things. I persuade myself your Activity and Zeal for me, in that Matter will do a great deal, and if my whole debt can any way be secur'd, that you will not fail doing it.

I have received a Letter from Captain Benjamin Wright, dated Savannah la Mar, 29 April, 1771, wherein he requests me to make £110 Insurance for you, on 10 Puncheons Rum he had ship'd for your Account on board the *King George*, Captain Smyth, bound here; which have accordingly done, and I debit you £5:7:0 Stg. for Cost of the same as per Account inclosed. in the *Copy* of his said Letter, he mentions £150 to be insur'd, which apprehend must be an Error in copying, because in general, £10 a Puncheon is the Value Rum is insur'd at from Jamaica. I have therefore gone according to his original Letter. the *King George* is soon expected.[1] Jamaica Rum is now 7/8 to 7/9 per Gallon.

Inclosed is a Price Current, which brings me to conclude with Regard, Dear Sir! Your humble Servant,

HEN: CRUGER, JR.

ABRAHAM SARZEDAS TO RIVERA & LOPEZ[2]

Savannah in Georgia, 25th July, 1771.

Gentlemen,

MY last to you per Capt. Peck coverd a Recipt for Two Tierces of Rice on your Account to pay for the Error of the Accounts remitted from the Mole, which I hope is safe to hand.

Notwithstanding my firm resolution of ever more plowing the Ocean and absent my self from my dear Family; I find (allthough very desagreable) that Nessesity obliged me ones more to go and reside at the Mole St. Nicholas to enable me to provide them confortably, as my Children advances in age, so I find the wants the greater. While Life doath last its my duty to do my best for their aducation, etc., etc.

---

[1] She arrived about August 5.
[2] Original in the Newport Historical Society.

Influenced by those motives which must in the Eye of every good man appear laudable I am to quit my family within a fortnight for the Mole for one year at least, if God grants me life and health its probably much more, which must cheafly depend on the Business I shall have; its boath my Duty and Interest to offer you and your friends, my Sarvice dureing my Residence there. Should you think me worthy of being intrusted with your Consignement, depend that my study shall be ponctuality and dispatch so as to merit your aplause; This being the nedfull, permit me to take my Leave, and to wish you and good Family health and felicity and to subscribe, Gentleman, Your most obliged humble Sarvent to command,

AB'M SARZEDAS

[Endorsed,] Via Ch's Town.

THOMAS ROGERS TO CHRISTOPHER AND GEORGE CHAMPLIN

Nichola Mole, 28th July, 1771.

Gentlemen,

THIS will acquaint you of my arivel yesterday after a very Pleasant Passage but to very bad Markets, their being hear know in the Road upwards of Forty Vessels to load with Molasses, and not one hhd in the Harbour at present to be sold, the last Vessel load that was sold hear was for 23 Sous per gallon. have not sold any part of my Cargo yet. Things are know selling hear at the follow[ing] Prices: Boards at 110 Livers per M, Shingles at 20, Fish at 18 per Barrel, Rice at 18 per Ct. I am afraid it will be some time before shall be able to procure a Load of Molasses, as the Traders hear [are] takeing the advantage of the times, finding Molasses in great demand, bring 5 or 6 Hhds. of bad Sugar in every Craft, and unless you take the Sugar with the Molasses they will not let you have it. from Gentlemen your most Humble Servant,

THOS. ROGERS

[Endorsed,] per favour of Captain Weeden.

THOMAS ROGERS TO CHRISTOPHER AND GEORGE CHAMPLIN

St. Nichola Mole, 21st August, 1771.

Gentlemen,

I'M sorry to inform you that Molasses has rize to 24 Sous within this day or two and I have only the Three Thousand Gallons on board bought at 23 Sous. their is none at Market now, but I do exspext the next that arives will be sold at 25 Sous if not more, at which price shall be oblidge to take my Molasses as could not agree for it on no other terms then thee price current when it arives which I'm in hopes will be in about 15 days, at which time shall sail if not disappointed. I have 14 Cask Rice on hand that cannot sell at any price. Shall ship you 4 hhds. Sugar by Capt. Norris who will sail about the time I do. I am, Gentlemen, Your Most Humble Servant,

THOS. ROGERS

the next Vessel that sails will be Capt. Barron in whom Capt. Dupey comes Passenger.

[Endorsed,] Per favour of Capt. Lawton.

HENRY CRUGER, JR. TO AARON LOPEZ

Bristol, 23d August, 1771.

Dear Sir,

SINCE the above few Lines, have received your esteemed and obliging favour of 28th June. thanks for your Zeal and Activity with the Sloop *Draper*. when my father's Bills on that transaction appear in your favour, your Account Currant shall have Credit for the same, with my sincere Acknowledgements, which I now offer to your good self for your Alacrity and ready Compliance in the providing of a Cargo for my Ship *New York*, Captain Jones.

No further news yet from Jamaica respecting the protested £100 Bill. it is a shocking Country for a Man to have Money in, Experience makes us wise! I remain with respect, Dear Sir, your most obedient Humble Servant,

HEN: CRUGER, JR.

P. S. My Broker just brings an Account of his having sold your ten Puncheons of Rum at 7/8 per Gall:

Inclosed is Price Currant for your Government which is all that in my present hurry offers. Dear Sir, Adieu!

H. CRUGER

JOSHUA HART TO AARON LOPEZ

Charles Town, So. Carolina, August 28th, 1771.

Esteemed Friend,

I FLATTER myself these will find you your worthy Spouze and family in a perfect state of health as this at present leaves me Mrs. Hart and family. My chief Motive of writing to you via New York is to desire you that you will per first Vessell for this port ship me ten hhds of Chioce, free from Stillburn and good proof, Jamaica Rum on my own account and risque, not to exceed in price 2/6 Sterling prime cost, of which beg and intreat you you'l look for such good Rum as above mentioned, if it suits you. It intirely depends on chance Rum being at present 21/ this Currency per Gallon. If Vessells should not arrive in Season probably it will rise much higher for which reason should you think proper: you mout address some to your friend Mr. Russell which I make no doubt but it may turn to advantage this Country Rum sold this day at 13/3 per Gallon. think it will rise: You may depend shall remit you the amount of what the rum comes to per said Vessell, or pay any person here you may think proper to order to receive: I must inform you that Dollars has rose to 32/6, half Joe's weighing 9 dwt. to £13, of which you'l [take] notice: Had they been any Vessells for your port I should have shipd you Rice, tho' very high at present, it being £3.10 Cash, and expect the new Crop will break its thought at the same price. have not to add but that the Great God may grant you and your worthy family health, and that he may write you and them in the Book of Life, and believe me to be with pure and disinterested Love and regard, Dear freind, Your freind and humble Servant,

Joshua Hart

be pleased to make my best Respects acceptable to your Sister Lopez and her worthy family, to your Brother Abraham and his worthy Spouze and family, to your Brother David, and all inquiring freinds, particularly to Hasan Truro.

Peleg Green to Aaron Lopez

Saint Anns Bay, September 6th, 1771.

Sir,

THIS my second serves to inform you of our Sircumstancies at St. Anns, which is but indeferent in the Molasses way: I am very sorry to inform you that shall not be able to git Load of Molasses here, for it is not posoble to git 40 Hogshead Molasses in the Island for the Cash, which it gives me a great deal of unesiness to think of being disapointed in our expectation, as I know you want a Load of Molasses very much this fall. I have got now on board sixteen Hogshead Molasses, and expect to git about 10 or 15 more, which will be all: that we shall be able to git here, then shall proseed to the Cape St. Nicolas Mole by Captain Benjamin Wright orders, which you desired me to follow in every Degree, which I shall with a Deal of Pleasure. I have dispatch the Ship *Jacob* Long Boat to Savanna Lamar, for some Hogs Lard that Captain Wright has upon hand, which I amigine will answer very well at the Mole. So with what Good Money we can git, I may well say Good money for there is but very little Good pasing, and the Hogs Lard, am in hops to purches forty Hogshead of Molasses at the Mole besides what we have on board. I need not acquaint you of the Prices of Good here as Captain Wright will be able to inform you more perticeulaly than I can. I expect to sail for the mole 20 Instant if nothing happen more then we no of at present, and shall use all posible means that lys in my Power to dispatch your Vessell. have nothing more to ad shall conclude. am Sir your Humble Servant and yours [to] serve,

PELEG GREEN

SAILING ORDERS FOR CAPTAIN PELEG GREEN

You are, as Master of the Sloop *Mary* on her intended voyage from St. Anns, Jamaica, (where she now rides at Anchor) to St. Nicholas Mole on the Island of Hispaniola, and from thence to Newport Rhode Island, to follow the Instructions herein contain'd.

Vizt. You are, your vessell being ready for sea, to embrace the first Oppertunity of a fair Wind to proceed, *immediately*, for St. Nicholas Mole as above mentioned, on your arrival there, you are to vend the sundry articles which are fully mention'd in your Invoice, on the best terms you posibly can, taking care not to trust any body, and when sold you are, to invest the nett proceeds, (as likewise the Cash mention'd in the aforesaid Invoice) in good Mollasses, on the proper account and risque of Mr. Aaron Lopez of Rhode Island. (but in case you find the Mollasses extravagantly dear so as you think no Profitt may be obtained thereon, then, you are hereby impowered to deliver unto the aforesaid Gentleman all the Dollars you have in your hands,) which when done you are to sign, and forward, to me in Jamaica a bill of Loading for whatever you may take on board, at the aforesaid Port of St. Nicholas Mole, and on compleating your Cargoe, you are, immediately to proceed to the Port of Newport in Rhode Island, and where on your safe arrivall, you are to deliver your Cargoe, to the hands of Mr. Aaron Lopez there, or to his Assigns and so wish you and your Sloop to your desired Ports in Safety. St. Anns, the 4 October, 1771.

[BENJAMIN WRIGHT]

Abraham Lopez to Aaron Lopez

Jamaica, Savanna La Marr, October 21st, 1771.

Sir,

I AM now to acknowledge the Receipt of two of your favours of the 31st of May last and of the first of July, with Duplicate to the former covering a Receipt in my favour from Mr. William Cozzen's for his Dividend received that year from the Executors of Bernard Senior Esq. dec'd amounting to £68.3.6¼ Sterling. I am realy sorry I did not at that time explain myself to you in regard of the Delivery of said bill so clear as I ought to have done, which woud have set aside all manner of Doubt. the Expression I made was not done with an Intent to offend my good friend Mr. Lopez, so far from any meaning of that kind, I am extremely obliged to you for the Trouble you have taken on the occasion. should I not acknowledge this, as well as many other favours, I shou'd look on myself to be ungratefull, and at all times you express yourself so obliging with the greatest Warmth towards me and all my family, that never cou'd given me any room ever too imagine than to shew you the same Complaisance, as I have received from you.

I am obliged to you for acquainting me of my letter of 29th April last safely got to your hands. on sight thereon you sent instructions to an ingenious Blacksmith in the Country to have the same made; at last you have obtained an Answer to two letters you have wrote him; that he will soon come to town, and will call on you, as they are altogether so triffling; I make no doubt to oblige you, he will soon make them, which I should be glad off, as the Season draws so nigh to put the Mill about. I shoud be glad to have them here this side Christmas, for I can hardly do without them. when I know the Expence shall pay Captain Wright with thanks.

I must once more importune on your goodness to settle this matter for me with the Executors of Andrew Cozzens. herein inclosed you'l receive his Account Current as it now stands; ballance due in his favour £46.5.2½ Currency, for the Payment of which you'l receive herein inclosed George Robert Goodin and William Bosleys Esqrs. their first bill of Exchange drawn in my favour on Messrs. Mure Son and Atkinson, at 90 Days after sight for £33. — 10½ Sterling, which Sum is equal to said Ballance. (The second bill will be sent inclosed in the Duplicate of this) taken the Receipt in full of all Accounts as it now becomes a total Settlement of the whole Demand against the Estate of Bernard Senior Esqr. I beg you'l excuse all this Trouble I have given you, and I remain with my best Compliments to self, and all your good family, wish you all health and Happyness, at all times ready at your Commands, from Sir, Your most Obedient and very humble Servant

[UNSIGNED]

[Memo.] from Abraham Lopez.

[Endorsed,] Per favour of Capt. Gamble, Q. D. C.

PELEG GREENE TO AARON LOPEZ

St. Nicholas Mole, October 27th, 1771.

Sir,

THIS convaence serves to inform you that I arrived here the 18th of October where I find Markets very loe indeed and Molasses very high Molasses is now from 25 to 26 Soues and chief of it enguaged before I came in but as my vessell is chart[er]ed and our expences verry high I thought proper not to wate for Molasses to fall as it [is] uncertin when it will, and have laid out all my Double Loone and Pistoles for Molasses, which amounted to 23 Hhd., but was oblige to give 26 or ells wate week or 10 day, which is much wors then giveing 26 Soues according to my calcalation as our Vessell is chart[er]ed. the two Negros that Capt. Wright shipped by me on your account, I have sold them but very loe, as one of them was sick the whole Pasage from Jamaica. I sold the well one with the sick one to git him of, and got for both 320 Peases of Eight. But the flouer which I brought is very bad indeed, and I beleave it was when I brought it from Rhode Island; for we had many Barrill returnd in Jamaica after they was sold. I have reason to think they was bad before shippd becau[s]e they never got wett on our Pasage. I have offerd them for 3½ Peases Eight per Barril but could not git it. I am now a starting of them out of one Barril into another in order to git the bad from the good, and shall put them of at sum Rate if possible: the Current Price for Candles is 45 but very sloe at that. I have sold six Boxes at that and have 7 more upon hand: I shall not lay out any of my mild mony, as Molasses is so very dear: I shall have on board in all 57 Hogshead Molasses. I have nothing more to acquant you of at present, but have 3 people sick and buried Thomas Ash in Jamaica.

So wishing these may find you and your family all well I conclude. am sir your most Humble Servant,

PELEG GREENE

PETER R. LIVINGSTON TO CHRISTOPHER CHAMPLIN

New York, 11 Nov. 1771.

Dear Sir,

I FIND one of your Name under the New Port head has meet with a large double decked Sloop the 22 of last Sept. off Hispaniola lat. 22, long. 71, with her Mast lashed along side and some Mens Shirts and a Womans purple and white Gown hanging on the Rails. by the description I am fearful it is one I am concerned in. She left this the 14 of June last bound for New Orleans and was to go thro' the windward passage. She had a Woman passenger on board, was loaded with flour and dry goods, was a verry large Sloop, believe she would carry about 1100 barrels of flour. She had on board now 841 barrels flour and about 50 barrels Beef and Pork and 2500 lb. of Powder. What I want of you is to be so kind as to enquire of Capt. Champlin and to gitt as particular a discription of her as possible he can give, particularly if she had a head or no, and if she had, whether he could distinguish what it was. As I am to leave Town

[in] a day or two I would take it as a particular favor if you would send by the post an answer to this directed to Mr. Thomas Randall, Merchant. Am, Dr. Sir, Yours, etc.

P. R. LIVINGSTON

JNO. FREEBODY, JR. TO CHRISTOPHER CHAMPLIN

New York, December 12, 1771.

Sir,

I HAVE sent you by Capt. Webstar one Tierce of Tea, for which you have his Recpt. inclos'd: the Tea you may depand upon being good, and I hope it will turn out to you satisfaction. I have not yet dispos'd of your Coffe, but I am afraid that I shall not be able to get above 1/4d, but I shall do the best with it that lays in my power, for you. Tea is expected to rise daily as their is a very strick look out kept, by the Men of War, and Custom House Officers, who have this day seis'd 19 Chest: at Flushing, and yesterday a Parcel in a store in this City. I hope this may come safe to your hands. I am, Sir, Your Humble Servant,

JNO. FREEBODY JR.

Molasses from 1/10 to 1/11d	Flour 22/
West India . Rum 4/10 to 5/	Bread 20/
Spirit . . . . . . 5/9 to 5/10	Beef 50/
New England Rum 2/6 to 2/7	Pork 100/

[Endorsed,] Per Capt. Webstar.

ENGAGEMENT OF COOPER

MEMORANDUM That I the Subscriber have this 24th December, 1771, agreed with Mr. John Valentine, that he shall go Cheef Cooper of my Ship the *Jacob*, Henry Davenant, Master, from hence to Jamaica, on the following Terms viz. That he is to be allowed at the rate of Eight dollars per Month till he returns home, provided he embraces the first Opportunity to return home after the Ship *Jacob* compleats her Loading, Unless I may have occasion to load a Vessell of mine this present year with Molasses at Jamaica, as in that case he is to make the necessary Molasses hhds for such a Vessell and tarry in Jamaica till she returns here, taking his Passage in her with the Priviledge of two hogsheads. In that case I agree to allow him at the rate of Ten Dollars per Month from this Day instead of Eight aforesaid till he returns.

JOHN VALENTINE

December 24, 1771.

CULLEN POLLOK TO AARON LOPEZ

Edenton, January 16, 1772.

Dear Sir,

YOUR much esteemed favours by Mrs. Ellis and Captain Weeden came to hand the 6th of this Inst. Captain Weedens Vessel run on the shoals and he narrowly escaped loosing her, which delayed the Letters a fortnight, yours by Captain Winslow came to hand the 10th. Captain English arrived here the 12th, she is gone up Cushy to load with corn and staves as soon as the corn is fit to take on board for so long a Voyage, which will not be untill the last of February.

I am sorry you have been so wrong informed, as to our plentyfull crops, as there never were shorter crops made. Captain English I am afraid will not be able to get his load of corn under 15/ per Barrel, as to wheat I am afraid he will not be able to get any, so that I cannot advise you to send any more Vessels for grain, unless you think it will answear to ship corn at 17*s* per Barrel and that in Money, as there never were so many Vessels here before for corn, and most of them have brought cash, more or less. Staves may be had for goods, but both the Pipe and Barrell staves you mention, are two inches longer than we get for any Market, so that I should be glad you would examine the lengths below, and write me if they would sute, as it would make some difference in stowage.

I am extremely concerned that thus circumstance, your Voyage may not prove as prosperous, as I most sincerely could wish it, however my endeavours, as far as I can, shall not be wanting. please to accept my warmest good wishes for your wellfare and believe me, Dear Sir, Your Real Friend and Most Humble Servant,

CULLEN POLLOK

Permit me, Worthy Sir, to intrude a Line of thanks to my Dearest Friend Mrs. Lopez for three Letters I have received from her since my arrival in Carolina, the last by Captain English accompanied by too many proofs of her Affection; I can only say that I fear such an Accumilation of kindness will take from the merits of my disinterested Esteem. I shall shortly write a long Letter to my best Friend on this subject. mean time present, good sir, my best regards to the most amiable of her Sex your Lady. I am with great Deference,

ANN POLLOK

HENRY CRUGER, JR. TO AARON LOPEZ

Bristol, 1st February, 1772.

Dear Sir!

FOR want of direct conveyances it is a long time since I last had the pleasure to pay you my respects. Could I have foreseen how tedious it would prove, you should have been put to the expence of sundry Packet Letters, or by some round about way have heard from me. The Summer always affords frequent opportunities, so you shall hear from me more regularly for the time to come. After this long interval, I wish I could begin a letter by telling you I had been paid for the £100 Jamaica Bill, but to the shame of all concerned, they have not wrote me a syllable relative to it since my last.

With infinite pleasure I see before me four of your much esteemed favors dated 18th July, 22nd August, 31st October, and 2nd November. their contents are more acceptable and grateful to my Mind, than any of your letters have been for a long time before. I regard it as the forerunner of further Consignments. there is more joy in one *solid Testimony* of a Mans good intentions, than in ninety and nine vacant professions that serve only to raise a poor Devils hopes, and make his disappointments the greater. I never, dear sir, doubted the sincerity of your heart, when you promised me soon to do me Justice; but, my God! *what* have I sufferd for want of that Justice. You have frequently assured me of your ardent endeavors to fulfill your Engagements with me. altho' I gave entire Credit to every thing you wrote me, yet, my distresses made me involuntarily complain: if ever I went too far, I take this opportunity to entreat you to ascribe it to the right, but almost fatal cause, and pardon me.

Permit me, sir, in the first place to return you my best thanks for your general Conduct with, and particularly for your so well dispatching of my Ship *New York*. I am exceeding glad to advise you the great article of Oil turned out to our most sanguine wishes. Thirty five Pounds per Ton I flatter myself will encourage you to send more to this Market. I wish it had been in your power to have made your quantity just double. the particulars of the sale (being at public auction) I will not here trouble you with, as I desired my Father to do it by sending you an extract of my letter to him respecting it. inclosed is the sales of the whole, Nt. Proceeds being £1499.15.7 Sterling. One Moiety will be to the Credit of your good self when received, the other to the Credit of H[enry] C[ruger] of New York.

I wish it was in my power to give you so favorable an account of the Mahogany but it really is quite the reverse. In the first place, Vessel after Vessel has been arriving here for 6 months past, in which space above 500 M feet have been imported. Our Keys and Yards are so crowded, that we are absolutely at a loss for room to put it. from 5*d* and 6*d* a foot, it is reduced to 3*d* and 4*d*, and two Cargoes more are daily expected. this the Owners have taken care to make publickly known. the next remark is that yours (from *a Comparison* I speak) is the worst parcell at present in Bristol. It consists of a great deal of small, rather porus, much shaken, and in general *too short* — especially the very large Loggs — which are four feet shorter than they are coveted to be. I write this upon the assurances and judgment of Dealers in the article. no wonder then, when the best Wood is now selling for only 4*d* by the Cargo, I was satisfied to get 3½*d* for yours. it was getting rid of the whole cargo at a stroke. I despaired of making more. the price is very low to be sure, but still I hope for your acquiescence, if not your approbation. these are the bitters that sometimes are mingled with the sweets of Trade. However, upon the whole, I hope a mixture of Oil and Mahogany may not prove a very unpallatable composition. The Measurer will soon enable me to furnish you with the Sales.

Agreeable to what my father wrote you, he did transmit me a sett of Bills value £597.15.6 Stg., which were at maturity placed to your Credit in account with my thanks. fresh and sincere acknowledgments are due to you from me for your assiduous care, and chearfull attention to my unfortunate concerns with the late John Channing. Good luck seems the lot of some People. I never was of the Party, every year and almost every other connection I make produces something unpropitious. The repitition of Bad Debts quite disheartens me. I refer the settlement of my Debt with H's Executors entirely to your Goodness, and am heartily disposed to make you any pecuniary Compensation for your trouble (by Commission or otherwise) that you shall please to fix.

Pray send a few words to me in your next concerning the nonentity of an Estate that your Capt. Osborne left behind, and also of his Brother who hath administerd. The Captain died in my Debt £350. Sterling, the Brother after flattering me several years with the whole of my Ballance, at length writes me — *You* have recover'd the whole of his Estate, and I shall get — *nothing.*

I believe there was no mistake in the Premium of Insurance made on the *Ellin* about this time twelve month. It was advanced a Guinea per Cent by the apprehensions of a Spanish War. the Account of Particulars was render'd in mine of 4 February last. at foot hereof is a Copy of it for your further satisfaction.

The Cask of old Copper is sold. the Sales shall soon be sent you and by same conveyance (in two or three weeks) the Copper bottom suitable for a still of 54 in: diameter as you are pleased to direct. The few tons of Logwood are not yet disposed of, the price is too low. the Staves are partly sold at a good price. my next I hope will furnish you Sales of whole Cargo.

For three or four things more I must pester you with my warmest thanks, for your trouble in recovering from Mr. Goldthwait 13/9, which is to your Debit for your Account of Disbursements and Money supply'd Captain Jones, which are to your Credit; and for your polite and acceptable present of Apples and Cramberries. The first were all decayed, the latter were the best I ever had.

A few words more, dear Sir, and I have done. You have more than once told me that when ever opportunity offer'd you would be glad to make some gratefull return for the long Inconveniences you have put me to. a fair one offers now for *Ships* are in great demand in Bristol, and a lumbar cargo consisting of 2 in: white Oak b[o]ards for Ship and Boat building, etc., would answer mighty well. I would not encourage you if I did not think so, and I flatter myself you will endeavor by all opportunitys to reduce a Ballance that has cost me so much perplexity and infilicity. I am sure I need not reiterate to you, Sir, that I have for several years past (communibus annis) sunk by you from £300 to £500 Sterling per annum exclusive of the losses sustained by the Rum, etc., and my good Father has from time to time taken in order *to reduce my debt*. This you could not help I well know, but when a Man suffers, he looks to the sole cause of it. by the Ship *Aaron* too, I have sunk much Money. I had never kept her till now, but could never sell her for any thing compared to her first cost, so that I have been sinking hundreds ever since my debt with you became so monstrous. to explain the former part of this last paragraph — I must solemnly protest to you, whatever the amount is of the *annual Interest* you pay me, I lose almost double that by receiving it, for at the time you are paying me only 5 per Cent for the use of my Money, if it were in my own possession, I could make 10, 12½ and 15 per cent of it. This proposition must to you, Sir, be natural and clear, and cannot help persuading myself but that the common honesty and justice which directs every mans actions will incline Mr. Lopez in particular, to make me some, if not ample Amends.

But in these things you of course, Sir, will do as you list; therefore I will only add, that there is at present great Encouragement to send a Vessel here just now with a good assorted cargo. I don't know what to say to you about Oil, you used generally to send it *so late*, but if you can contrive to send 50 or 100 Tons of White to be here about the latter part of November, or sooner, (giving me due notice of its coming in order to *hinder* our Buyers from *sending to London for it*) I should not despair of obtaining you a high and profitable price for it.

I had like to have forgot to render you an Account of £600 Insurance done by my Father's repeated orders on your account, on your Interest a board of the *New York*, Capt. Jones. I am glad to see it neats you much more than was insured. Cost is £16.0.0 Sterling to your Debit.

And now, Sir, I take my leave for the present, with every good wish for your health, happiness and prosperity, being with perfect respect and sincere Esteem

Your most Ob. H'ble Servant,

Hen: Cruger Junr.

P. S. I have credited your Account £1.2.8 by order of Mr. Jacob Rod. Rivera.

January 3d, 1771.

Mr. Aaron Lopes
    To Henry Cruger Junior Dr.

To Cost of £275 Insured on your one half share of 20 Tons Oil per the *Ellis* John Clark Master from New York vizt.

£100 James Laroche
£100 Thomas Longden
£75 Thomas Easton
£275 at 3 Guineas per Cent £8.13.3
         Part Policy . . . .   4. -
        Commission ½ per Cent . . .   1. 7.6
       To Mr. Aaron Lopez's Debit . . £10. 4.9

Henry Davenant to Aaron Lopez

Kingston, February the 16th, 1772.

Sir,

I HAVE the pleasher to inform you of my safe arival hear, in your Ship *Jacob* on the 13th Inst. after a verry tedious Passage of 32 days. we have had verry hard Gales of wind, in one of which we had the misfortune to loose one Hors, No. 2, and fifty Turkeys. the Gale was so sevear we could hardly keep the Decks with safety. I have deliverd five horses; fifty Boxes of Candles; and forty four Barrels of Herrings to Mr. Dolbear, as Capt. Right [Wright] is not in town none of our Horses is disposed of as yet; and verry litle of the Stock sold, but hope they will soon; I should have sailed this day for Savannalamar, but am detained on account of my new Bowspriet, the other being sprung and verry rotten, and had hard work to make him serve us into Port. I have got a new Sparr for £12. this Currency, which is cheap for this Part of the world. I have got him in and partly rig'd and intend to saile on Wednesday. James Smith is still on Board, the Sailor we shipt last, but a verry poor Hand indeed. There is great Prospect of verry fine Crops in the Island at present, and but few Ships hear.

I wish you had shipt four Horses with us, instead of four Passengers, for they have been nothing but a Plage to us except Mr. Gordon. I am, Sir, Your Verry Humble Servant,

HENRY DAVENANT

Post. I have taken on twenty Rum Puncheons, which I am to deliver at Savannalamar, by Mr. Dolbears Order.

HENRY CRUGER, JR. TO AARON LOPEZ

Bristol, 11th March, 1772.

Dr. Sir,

THE preceeding is Copy of my last Respects to you and since I have not been favor'd with any of your acceptable Epistles. this will cover Sales of the Cask Shruff received per Ship *New York*, nt. proceeds £13.9 Stg. it will also include Invoice of the Still Bottom ship'd to the care of my Brother, who will be desired to forward it to you. it amounts, with Charges to £24.16.0 Stg., which after deducting the proceeds of Shruff, leaves a Ballance of £11.7.0 Stg. to your debit in Account Currant. that I will soon furnish you with, for your Government.

It is not in my power by this Ship to furnish Sales of the Mahogany, nor the Dab of Logwood, 'tho it is sold. The Oil is all paid for. a few thousands of the Staves remain unsold. I hope my next will put a finishing stroke to the whole.

The unaccountable Conduct of the People in Jamaica still leaves us room to complain of them. the Bill of £150 is yet unpaid, at least to me.

I have very little to trouble you with at present. *Ships are still in great demand,*—I cannot help hoping you will do something the ensuing summer for me: it will be reviving my broken spirits.

My Father lately remitted me a Bill of £84.2.7 Stg., which he says I must at maturity place to the Credit of your A/C,—that shall be done accordingly. this is all that at present occurs, save to assure you of my steady Regard and Attention in all your Commands, being with much Esteem, Dr. Sir, Your most obedient Humble Servant,

HEN: CRUGER, JR.

BENJAMIN WRIGHT TO WILLIAM BOURK

Savanna La Marr, Jamaica, March 14th, 1772.

Sir,

I AM favourd with yours under the 28th December, 18th and 26th January, to which I now reply that I have exerted myself as much as I am able concerning your mistake in clearing out, and have prevailed so far as to prevent any of your securities being hurt here, but could not obtain a new clearance without the delivery of the old one up, so you must manage matters wherever you go in the best manner you can. You have likewise inclosed the Governours passport, Captain Robinson Bill of Lading, and your present account with me, for the amount of the latter please to transmitt me per the earliest opportunity, two orders on Mr. Lopez, the one to stand void on the others being accomplished, and both to be of the same tener and date. The article of postage in your account is by reason of your letters coming by the way of Kingston; I have now with me the *Ocean*, Captain Peters, and the Ship *Jacob*, Captain Davenant, both which Vessells are now ready to take in and hope to dispatch them soon for London. Your observation concerning Ramson is nothing more than I expected. I hope the Beef will please you, it is the best and cheapest I could get. Be oblidgeing enough to inform me per the first opportunity what Cargo you have got in for Mr. Lopez that I may advise him thereof. I remain Yours, etc.

BENJAMIN WRIGHT

To Captain William Bourk of the [Brigantine] *Minerva* at Honduras Bay, per the *Ann*, Captain Robinson.

Peleg Greene to Aaron Lopez

Newbern, [North Carolina,] March 21th, 1772.

Sir,

THIS my second serves to acquaint you that I have got but 1100 white oak Staves and 1000 white o. Heading and 1800 red oak do. on board yet and that is all Mr. Ellis has got by him but he tell me that he expect them down every day which is very uncertin and what to due in this case I cannot tell but he tell me he will borrow about 2000 the day after tomorrow which will be one days work for me and then shall be idle again exsept overhalling the Vessell. I have tryd the whole Town through and cannot purches any Heading or Staves, for here is three Vessell now loading for Jamaica who has enguaged all in the place. But I am in hopes I shall sail the second of them. I am determined to wate till the 21th of April and if Mr. Ellis cannot dispatch me by then I shall think it proper as the Season will be so far spent to make up the Rimainder of my Cargo with fright which I belive I can git for Jamaica and make the best of way to Jamaica. Staves is still £4.15 and £5 and Heading at £7: Tarr 8/. Corn 15/ per Barril. Turpentine 12/6. Hogs Lard at /6d, and Pork at £4.5 to 4.10.

Captain Thomson arrived here the 12th of this mounth from Charleston who saild from Kingston the 7th febuary last and inform me that white Staves was then at £14 per M which imagine by that time Captain Peters must have been nigh his Port if nothing happend, but he was not arrived when Captain Thomson sailed. I am in hopes he will arrive at good market for Lumber. it must have been very high or els Captain Thomson would have not proseeded here for a load of Lumber for that market. if this should be true the Ship will make a great Voyage which beleve it is.

have nothing more to acquaint you of at present but shall conclude am, Sir, your Humble Servant, and yours to Serve,

PELEG GREENE

Joshua Hart to Aaron Lopez

Charles Town, 27th March, 1772.

Dear Sir,

ITS with satisfaction and pleasure I acknowledge the receipt of your esteemed favor of the 5th Ulto. which now lays before me and note the Contents: am extream glad to find that you and every branch of your family injoyd a perfect state of health: the continuance of which shall be my daily prayers to God to continue.

Inclosed you have Bills of Loading and Parcells for 3 barrells of Choice Rice markd and numberd as per Margin which I wish safe to your hands: and as youl find theres a Ballance due as per Account at foot of £5.6.6 our Currency to me I beg and intreat youl give it to my Wifes two daughters Rebecca and Sarah who lives at Father Allens: I should have sent you some ground Nutts or Potatoes for your Acceptance, but none being come to Market that was any way good: I would not purchase any. having not of moment to add, but that I wish you and every one of your family a Merry Pascua de Pesah, and that you may see many of them with felicity and happiness: Mrs. Hart and daughters joins me with my freindly Salutations to you Mrs. Lopez and dear Children and believe me to be with pure and disinterested regard, Dear Sir, Your Esteemed Freind and humble Servant,

JOSHUA HART

P. S. please give my best respects to your Sister Lopez and her good family, to Mr. Ab: Lopez and his family, to your Brother David Lopez to Domini Truro, to Father Allen and his family, and all inquireing freinds.

Cullen Pollok to Aaron Lopez

Edenton, April 7, 1772.

Dear Sir,

MY first to you was immediately after Capt. Riply's arrival, by post, a coppy of which sent by a Vessel to Falmoth, with orders to the Captain if he could not get a better opportunity to put it into the Post office, and am a good deal surprised you had not received either before the date of your last, which was handed me by Captain English the 22nd past, and informed me that he should with Captain Ripley be ready to sail in a few days.

I presume before this you have received mine forbiding the comeing of Captain Toby, expecting I should be able to get a Vessel here, but being disappointed, I must desire you to procure me a Vessel, on as easy terms as you can, to come here and take a load of corn for New York she must not be above four hundred and fifty barrels, nor draw more than nine feet loaded, and must have thirty working lay days, as soon as you have procured such a Vessel please to inform me by a line to the care of Mr. Lowther at New York that I may not freight another there, where I expect to be by the first of May unless some unforeseen accident happens.

Captain English arrived so soon after my receiving your favour that I left the purchasing of the staves to him. I believe they have both staves on bord, but do not know if they have contracted for any others, but I shall know before this goes from here, but as I am going up the Country for eight or ten days, I leave this for fear the Vessel should sail before my return.

I am extremely sorry it has not been in my power to send the papers necessary in those causes before now; it has been entirely owing to want of opportunity, the papers were too bulkey to be sent by Post and the Post also too uncertain as we often find it here. I am much afraid it will not be in my power to be in Rhode Island before the middle of your Court, as Mrs. Pollok has been so very ill that she is not yet able to leave her Room, but I still hope to set out in fortnight. I have wrote to Mr. Honeyman what to do in those sutes, and believe unless I can get a better opportunity than this I shall not send my proofs by this, who is Captain Weeden whose Vessel is very bad, unless he stays untill towards the 20th, when the weather will be more settled but bring them my self.

Your sloop arrived some time ago at Newbern. I sincerely wish she had come here, it would have saved you £80. which Captain English and Ripley must pay in money for lighterage, and she might have been loaded here immediately, and every thing done to her you desired. Captain Riply and English are just come into the Bay and will sail in two or three days. they have both a quantity of goods left, and do not know what to do with them. Captain Riply has received the money from Coll'r Dry, but was obliged to go to Brunswick. I am very sorry your Vessels have been delayed so long, but they came too late, and draw two much water in proportion to their burden; but am in hopes their corn will go in the better order to Market. having nothing more to add that I can recollect, I must conclud with my Most sincere best wishes to you Mrs. Lopez, and all your Friends at the point. I am, Dear Sir, Your Most Sincere Friend and Most Obedient Servant,

CULLEN POLLOK

HENRY DAVENANT TO AARON LOPEZ

Savanna La Marr, 6 oclock, Munday Morning, the 13 of Aprill, 1772.

Sir,

In my last per Captain Brayton, I advised you I should saile for London this day being the 12 of Aprill, but as my remainder part of Cargo did not come on board till late in the Weak, and not haveing my complement of Peple shipt to my desire, and my Fyerwood not comeing out of the Cuntry so soon as it was prommised, has retarded my Saileing. however, tomorrow Morning, if possible I shall saile; My Cargo consists of, Vizt.

Hodgsets of Sugar and tearses on Freight	104
A. 1. to. 6. Your own Account Tearses	6.
Sugars in Hodg[sets] and Tearses	110
Rums in Puchions on Freight	70.
A. 1. to. 62. on Your own Account, Punchions	62.
Rums in Punchions	132

A. 1. 15 Peices of Mahauganey
Do. Logwood, eight Tons and one 13th.
DW. therteen Plancks of Mahauganey, on Freight.

I am Your Verry Humble Servant,

HENRY DAVENANT

Post Script. I desier it as a favour that youl right me verry pertickeler, if the ship *Orion* should be sold in London, who is to come home with me Passengers. Now Sir, in my opinion, none has a Right to their Passage home in me from London but them, who shipt, to go the Voyage round in her, at Rhode Island, and none of them that has or may ship in her since her Departure from Rhode Island, but shall follow your Directions on that Head, when I have the Pleasher to receive your further Orders in London. Yours,

HENRY DAVENANT

HAYLEY AND HOPKINS TO CHRISTOPHER CHAMPLIN

London, 16th May, 1772.

Sir,

SINCE our last of which the above is Copy, we have received your favour of the 15th February desiring £1400 Insurance on the Sloop *Adventure* to Africa and America which we have effected as per account herewith premium etc. being £125.2.6 is to your Debit. We hope it is done in such a manner as to provide for all the circumstances you mention and will meet your approbation.[1] Inclosed you have Invoice and Bill of Lading for a few Goods shiped for your Account on board the *Charlotte*, Capt. Rogers,

---

[1] The policy was on the *Adventure*, "at and from Newport to the coast of Africa, during her stay and trade there, and from thence to her port of discharge in British America or the Island of St. Croix. If the vessel is sold on the coast the risk on cargo to be continued on such other vessel or vessels as may carry the slaves to market, and 4 per cent in that case to be returned on the £400 insured on vessels and freight." The insurance on vessel "and freight valued" was £400, and on "cargo," £1000; the rate was eight guineas per cent. *Hayley and Hopkins to Christopher Champlin*, May 16, 1772.

amounting to £55.3.7, on which we have made £56 Insurance, premium, etc., being £1.10.9. We are, etc.

HAYLEY AND HOPKINS

Per Rogers.

C[HRISTOPHER] AND G[EORGE] C[HAMPLIN] TO CAPTAIN SAMUEL SNELL

Newport, May 12th, 1772.

Sir,

WE flatter our selves this will meet you in safety upon the Coast in a fair way of making us a Voyage, as from the accounts up to January, and the price Capt. Gardner in Mr. Wickhams Ship obtained for his rum Slaves was much lowered, At the Castles with whom he traded, Colo. Wanton's Brig, Mowit Master, is arived here, cleared his owners £500 Stg. Capt. Brigs carried to Barbados 230 Slaves sold 210 of them at £33. Stg. round, left 40 on the Coast will make a good voyage. We don't doubt of your giting the same price if the Slaves are good in kind which without doubt you will endeavour to procure. Capt. Clark will deliver you this. Capt. Hicks in the Ship will not sale till June. Mr. Hazards brig not till August. these are the only vessells we kno of that can follow you from Newport and before they git down flatter our selves you will be near finishing. Lin Martin is gone to Philadelphia to fit cannot sale from thence 'till July. We have wrote to London for a Guarantee on a House at the Granados and St. Kitts, from both which places we shall be informed the price of Slaves before we lodge our orders at Barbados for you which will enable us to limit the price at Barbados. you'll write us by all occassions. keep your Business to your self. there is two vessells will leave Boston in [a] month for the Coast, that in June and July 3 or 4 vessells will sale near together.[1] Capt. Gardner informs his owners

---

[1] "By the inquiries which I have made of our oldest merchants now living, I cannot find that more than three ships in a year, belonging to this port [Boston], were ever employed in the African trade. The rum distilled here was the main spring of this traffic. The slaves purchased in Africa were chiefly sold in the West

after laying two months on the Coast alone he coud not make any trade with the blacks, and finally sold to the Castles at 130 to 150[1] for women and 140 to 160 for prime men. is likely to make a fine voyage. therefore we earnestly recomend to you as soon as you receive this to sell all the rum you may have on hand to the Castles on the best terms you can for prime Slaves, and make all the dispatch of, for when those vessells I mention to you git down the Castles will be filled which will be within a month after this letter or 6 weeks at most, and shoud you tarry 'till they git down the chaunce will be lost. in this you'll act as things appear as we cannot judge how the trade is at this distance, but to lay a long time on the Coast to piddle with blacks must be against the voyage. keep it an entire secret what vessells are coming down on the Coast, as it may make the Castles indifferent about buying if they kno it. We wish you health and success and are, Your Friends and Owners
C. & G. C.

DAVID PEREIRA MENDES TO AARON LOPEZ

Kingston, Jamaica, 22d May, 1772.

Dear Sir,

I HAVE the pleasure to acquaint you of my safe Arrival in Montego Bay, the 24th ultimo (and in this town the 16th Instant) after a very dismal, and melancholy Passage of 29 days. I am thank God in very good Health. I have since my arrival to Jamaica felt the good effe[c]ts of my voyage to North America, more than ever I did there. I

Indies, or in the southern colonies; but when those markets were glutted, and the price low, some of them were brought hither. Very few whole cargoes ever came to this port. One gentleman says he remembers two or three: I remember one, between thirty and forty years ago, which consisted almost wholly of children. At Rhode Island the rum distillery and the African trade were prosecuted to a greater extent than in Boston; and I believe no other sea-port in Massachusetts had any concern in the slave business. Sometimes the Rhode Island vessels, after having sold their prime slaves in the West Indies, brought the remnants of their cargoes hither for sale. Since this commerce has declined, the town of Newport has gone to decay." Jeremy Belknap in 1 *Mass. Hist. Collections*, IV. 196.

[1] That is, gallons of rum.

pray God for the continuance that I may have no occasion to cross the Seas again. I beg leave to return you my unfeigned thanks for the kind treatment I receiv'd from you during my residence in New Port, your politeness, good nature, and benevolence, cannot help to gain you the Esteem of every person, they have captivated my Heart, together with that of every Gentleman of your acquaintance. thrice happy should I be if I could be favoured with an opportunity of making some returns to the many obligations to which your Civilities have laid me under, in the mean while, please to accept this tribute of Gratitude.

I found my Brother Abraham in a very poor state of health. he is just come out of a dangerous fit of sickness. he seems to be very anxious of seeing his Wife, and throwing himself at your feet. I shall dispatch him by the latter end of next month, in the manner I promised you, and shall write you by him more copiously upon that subject. I beg that you'l lett Mrs. Lopez partake with you in the assurance of my best respects. Please to make my best Compliments acceptable to Don Francisco, and Don Manuel. I hope they are well, and that they have met with all the Success, due to their Just Cause, and Remain, Dear Sir,

*Your most humble Servant,
David B'ma Mundus*

Peleg Greene to Aaron Lopez

Green Island, Jamaica, June 10th, 1772.

Sir,

I EMBRACE this present opportunety of enforming you of my safe arrival at Savanna La marr to the address of our mutual friend Captain Benjamin Wright, to which Gentleman I delevered my credentials agreable to your Instruction I am now in this Port so far in my way to St. Anns in order to collect your outstanding Interest there, which wish to succeed in. from whence shall proseed again to Savanna Lamarr, where if no oppertunity presents itself of Captain Benjamin Wright disposeing of the *George*, shall emedeately proseed for Carolina agreeable to your entimation I received from you there. the Sloop is very unfit for the Voyage owing to the Badness of hir Sails and upperworks being very defective. so should I arrive at Carolina I hope to receive a Letter from you relative to her destenation which permits me to hint as follows: the Sloop to take in a Load of Lumber at Newbern, from there to the Back Side of Rhode Island, there unladen the Cargo and Proseed up the River in order to be rebuilt, as I think such a Step absolutely nesessary before she will be fit for a west Indian Voyage. I hope you'll pardon the fredom of this intamation and favour me with a Line at Newbern for my goverment. Should you chuse hir to be repaired at Carolina, a new main sail and jibb will be unavoidably necessary, the Expence of which will be very [great] there. therefore I presume the best method be of hir proseeding as above and comeing down the River as a new vessell to recive hir outfits at Newport. If you are determined she shall not come near Rhod Island permits advising your sending a new main sail and jibb so as to met me at Newbern, as it will save the extraordinary expence of buying them there which Demention shall put down in Post Script in feet. Sir, Your most obedient Servant   PELEG GREENE

N. B. the dementions of the Main Sail is as follows the Hights of the Mast 44 feet and Length of the Boom 49 Do. the hights of the Jibb 62 feet and the Bowl Split 25 feet.

SAMUEL SNELL TO CHRISTOPHER CHAMPLIN[1]

Annamaboe, June 16, 1772.

Sir,

THIS is the first opportunity that I had had to right to you sence I left home. Capt. Dun sailed when I was at the

---
[1] Copy supplied by Mr. John H. Storer.

mines, and I have had no opportunity to right till now. I maid no stop to windard as I thought it best to perseed down the coast as soon as possable. We had six weeks passage from land to land Cape Verd. I sold 10 hhd of Rum at the mines for gold; I maid no traid at Cape Coast. We arrived heare 24th day of May. Capt. Morse sold his cargo at the mines and Capt. Roggers sold his at Cape Coast, Capt. Bardine has sold all his cargo so that there is no Rum heare at preasant to sell but what I have. I have sold 45 hhd. I give but 160 for slaves as yet. I should due very well if there wase any black traid, but there is none and they are about going to war which makes it worse. I saw Mr. Brew But we had no talk about the sloop. I have Bought a Long Boat. The Boat That this Sloop Brought Out I shall goe to Leward with my vessail. In 2 or 3 days Time which I hoop to Disspose of the Best Part of my Rum if not all Before I return up again we are all well and harty at preasant Thanks be To god for it. Sir: with esteam your most obedt and humble servt

SAMUEL SNELL

HAYLEY AND HOPKINS TO CHRISTOPHER CHAMPLIN

London, 20 June, 1772.

Sir,

WE have rec'd your favours of the 8, 30 April and 8 May advising receipt of your Account Current. We hope your next will acquaint us was found free from Error. We are sorry the Caudle Cup was not agreable to your intentions. If you should return it we will endeavour to get the Maker to take it back.[1] The Bill you enclose us for £450 is accepted and when paid shall be placed to your Credit. We shall endeavour to procure a Guarantee on some good house at the Grenadaes and St. Kitts for your Sloop *Adventure*, Capt. Fell, but we are not able to get it in time for this Vessell but hope to send it you by the next. We now not

---

[1] It cost £18.17.6.

how to give you any Guide that can safely be depended upon for Speculating in Oyl or Ashes. The price of the former has been very high this year. White Oyl at this time would sell for £36 per Ton, but there is no dependence to be placed on its continuance. When the new Oyl comes it will most probably be under £30 per Ton; if the Fishery should be large it will certainly not exceed £28 at the utmost. Ashes are at present very heavy a large Quantity now here and very little demand. We expect the price will not be more than 28/ for pott and 36/ for pearl, but all this merely conjecture and will depend upon the Quantity that comes.

The Goods you write for are getting ready and shall be dispatched in the first Vessell for your port. We know not who that will be, for the one Mr. Lopez talks of is not yet arrived here. We have now credited you 12/6 for the damask Table Cloth wanting. We are etc.

10 July, 1772.

Sir,

INCLOSED is a Letter of Guarantee for your Guinea Cargo, upon which you may place all confidence. We doubt we shall not be able to procure one for St. Kitts, the Merchants in that Trade all seem averse to such Engagements. Mr. Lopez's Ship *Jacob* is now here and will return to Newport. We propose shipping your Goods on board her and are, Sir Your very humble Servants,

HAYLEY & HOPKINS

[Endorsed,] Per Capt. Gardner via Boston. Snell & Co. Guarantee.

HENRY DAVENANT TO AARON LOPEZ

London, the 12th July, 1772.

Sir,

TIS with great pleasher I acquaint you of my safe arival in your Ship *Jacob* in London, from Jamaica, after a Passage of Elleven Weaks. we have met with no accident thanck God, but I must confes, I expected she would come to peices with us in several violent Gales I met with in the cours of my Passage. our Sugars are half unladen; but the Rums are greatly in our way, as they will not be taken out, till thirty days after the Ship is reported. Messrs. Hayle & Hopkins are worthy Gentlemen, and treat me with great Politenes. you may depend shall make all the dispatch home that I possible can, as I hope to saile some time in August. I did expect to have the Pleasher of finding your further orders hear. Capt. Birk nor Capt. Peters are arived as yet. I am with the greatest Respect Your Verry Humble Servant,

HENRY DAVENANT

[Endorsed,] Per Capt. Gardner via Boston.

HENRY DAVENANT TO AARON LOPEZ

London, the 13th of July, 1772.

Sir,

THE News of my Arival hear on the 1st Inst. after a Passage of elleven Weaks, will be I fancy verry agreable to you. we have met with no Accident thanck God, tho we have had violent Gales for the time of ear, I ever saw. we have got half our Sugars out, but most of our Rums will be in till the thirty days are out. after reporting the Ship, I got in, in good time, haveing scarce either Water or any Provisions on board. I must be forst to get some light Canvas and light Cordage we have had so much bad Weather, especially in the Gulf of Florida. You may depend of my makeing all the dispatch to get home with the Ship, posible I can, and hope to saile from hear in all August. As I have got four of Captain Piners Peple on board, and no Dout shall have most of Captain Peters allso, besides some of ny own, I shall be forst to lay in a great Deal of Provisions which is a verry dear artickel hear at preasant. I have discharged all my Peple but three. I am, Sir, Your Verry Humble Servant,

HENRY DAVENANT

[Endorsed], Per Ship *London*, Capt. Chambers, Via Newyork.

HENRY CRUGER, JR. TO AARON LOPEZ

Bristol, 14th July, 1772.

Dear Sir!

THE last of your agreeable favours that I have received is dated 13th March; they coverd the 2ds of two Setts of Bills drawn by my father on me in your favour, the one for £70.14 Stg. the other for £84.2.7 Stg. both of them are passed to the Credit of your Account Current with my thanks.

I now enclose you the miserable Sales of Mahogany, etc., part of the old *New York's* Cargo. the Neat Proceeds is £425.15.3 Sterling, one Moiety of which is passed to your Credit, the other to that of H. C. of New York. These Articles, low as they sold, woud not sell for as much now. this for your government.

I now take the liberty to hand your Account Current, ballance whereof up to 31st December last, is, in my favour, exclusive of Interest, £2452.15.11. Sterling, which on examination, if you find right, please to note in Conformity with me. on the back of the Account is the particulars of what has been put to your Credit since that period. this for your government. Do, good Sir! contrive to pay me off this fatal ballance! if I were not distressed for the want of Money, more than ever Man was, I would not, *could not*, say half so much.

In spite of all I have written, am unable yet to get any further satisfaction from Jamaica concerning the returned Bill of £150.

In longing, anxious expectation of soon hearing from you to the purpose, I subscribe with sincerity, and respectfull regard, in all your commands, Dear Sir! Your attached Humble Servant,

HEN: CRUGER JR.

George Sears to Aaron Lopez

St. Johns, Newf[ound]land, July 17, 1772.

Sir,

I ROTE you from Ferreland informing you of our passage of 14 days there from thence we stopt at Bay of Bulls but sold nothing at either place of any Value. I have been here a Week today. I have sold 16 Hhds. N. E. Rum at 1/6, all the Lime @ 21/, all the Lumber at the prices below, all the Bricks. Mollass. I have sold but one Hhd., it not being in such Demand as I rote you from Fereland. I cannot yet inform you wheather I shall charter the Brigg or sell. Mr. Bulley will give her a Freight imediately if his own Brigg does not arive in three or four days. the goods that I left with him last Winter are not all sold, Tobacco and Brown Sugar some on hand. Shall remitt home the Bills agreeable to Directions as soon as Oppertunity offers. the last Vessell here from Lisbon saild 6th June. Captain Ripley was not there. the Price of Salt at present is from 9/6 to 10/6 per Hhd., which is 6 Bushels Likely to be dearer. by next oppertunity shall give you an Account of Mr. Bulleys Sales which I could not get yet. I am, Sir, your Humble Servant,

GEO. SEARS

Price Currant

Bread and flour 18/ Likely to be dearer for that reason have sold none.
Corn 3/6
Soap 4d. dull.
Loaf Sugar 7d. Brown Do. dull.
Rum 1/6 Quick.
Molasses 1/2 dull
Lime 21/ Tarr 11/ and 12/
Briks 18/ bbl. staves 55/

Oak boards 60/ Pine Do. 42/6
Tea 3/ Coff 9d to 10d.
Any Quantity of Hay quick at 4/6 or 5/
Jamaca Rum 3/8
Common West India 2/ to 2/3. Very dull
Large merchantable Fish 13/6
Small ditto 11/6
Likely to be cheeper.

Philip Minis to Aaron Lopez

Off Cape Bonaviste on Cuba, 17th July, 1772.

Sir,

THIS serves to acquaint you that I left Kingston about 20 days since, when I left your Son in Law Mr. Abraham

Pereira Mendes in a very bad state of Health and it was thought was inclineable to go into a Consumpsion if so suppose it will soon terminate in Death, which I hope not as he is a young man and may reform. Messrs. Harts & Pollock knows me to whom pray tender my best Respects. I am Sir Your Most Humble Servant,

PHIL MINIS

PELEG GREENE TO AARON LOPEZ

Green Island, Jamaica, July 25th, 1772.

Sir,

I EMBRACE this oppertunity of informing you of my safe arrival from St Anns and other out Ports, but what success I had in collecting your out standing Interest shall not mention, as Capt. Wright will be the bearer who will inform you of my whole Proseedings. I am now in this Port where I shall take my water in and some more Balast as soon as the Brigg is dispatch, which my boat and all hands is imployd, which shall accomplish on the 26th and then shall make all posible speed to dispatch the Sloop which will be about the 29th, and shall proseed to Newbern, North Carolina, according to our mutual friend Capt. Wright instructions which you desired me to follow in every perticuly. Sir, I am sorry to tell you that the calcalation of this voyage turns out so much to your disadvantage, the Sloop being so small and very much out of repair, so that hir outfit and mens wages will be most as much as a Carolina Cargo, and especially when I com to put on a new deck which must unavoidably have before she can proseed any voyage so I beg you would consider the condition I am in in regard to the disbursements which she unavoidably must have, mens wages being very high in these parts and provision likewise, you must need think that my drogeing round the Island must be very expencif where every thing is so very dear. so I beg you wood consider all these disadvantages when I render my account of disbursments. hav nothing more to rite but shall conclude hoping to find a Letter lodgd at Newbern for my goverment.

wishing these may find you and your lady well and all your children, am, sir, your Humble Servant,

PELEG GREENE

FROM C[   ] D[   ] TO DAWSON

Dear Sir,

THE Accounts you sent me so long ago, have not had a Perusal 'til within a few days. When I first received them I was in a state of health that wou'd not admit of attention to any kind of Business. Since that I have been either in the Back Country, or my time has been wholly taken up with affairs of another sort of which indeed I have had more on my hands than my present weak Constitution can well bear for the late frolicks we have had here of burning the King's Vessell,[1] etc., have occasiond trouble to me beyond expression.

I cannot possibly entertain a Doubt of the Justness of the Accounts. I am persuaded they are fairly and equitably stated; but at the same time I see with pain that the small Capital I advanced in that Concern is totally sunk, or to define it more clearly, I have drawn my support from that Capital, instead of drawing it from my Labours. Tis true many circumstances occur'd very unfavorable to our original views of which the Disappointment of Messrs. Wombwells was by far the greatest, that alone was sufficient to produce all these unhappy Consequences to my small fortune — it did not affect you so much because the Stipulation gave you a clear and certain annual Profit. it wou'd be absurd at this Time for me to regret that Stipulation, but yourself I am perswaded will allow it has turn'd out a very heavy charge. Had our trade gone on in an uninterrupted course, I trust our Management wou'd have been such as our Profits wou'd have easily borne the Stipulation — the Interruption therefore has been most fatal to me.

---

[1] The *Gaspee*. Arnold, *History of Rhode Island*, II. 312.

The great Loss I have sustained by the Landau, a transaction I did for our mutual Advantage, and the charge of paying the hire of a Clerk during my stay in England (where I did much more benefit to the Concern than I wou'd have done at Moncks Corner, at that time very poorly supply'd on account of Mr. Wombwells Disappointment) are things too you will take into your consideration; and I am persuaded you will then make your charges on the settlement as easy as the nature of them will admit. What those charges ought to be, or how I shall determine on the Value of your Time, I am really at a loss. I cannot make a proposal with any degree of propriety — but I will hope from the light in which I now see our affairs, that I shall draw a Sum not less than two hundred pounds Sterling, with which I shall be satisfied. If you think well of this Proposal I will sign any Discharge you shall draw up and if my Proposal is [in]admissible yet do me the justice to believe that I have no intention it shou'd [be] an ungenerous [one.]

I propose to embark for England in the latter End of September or beginning of October. By Durfee's Vessell which brings this Letter I wish I may hear from you, and I wish further that our concerns cou'd be finally clos'd before I go. I am very infirm, and it must be highly satisfactory to you, as well as to me to have them finish'd.

I have not been in Newport for this Month past, so that I had not an Oppertunity of showing Mr. McNeile and your other Friends during their short stay those Civilities I wish'd for. Mrs. D. joins my Regards to Mrs. D. and I am Very truely Yours, etc.

C. D.

Middletown, Rhode Island, 7 August, 1772.
[Endorsed,] To M. Dawson per Capt. Munro.

George Sears to Aaron Lopez
July 30, 1772.

The Freight of Mr. Bulleys which I had some expectation of, am not likely to get. no one has yet made an offer for the Brigg. make no doubt but I shall get a Freight for her.

a Vessell sails in three weeks for England, shall then send Home the £340 to Hayley & Hopkins for account of Mr. R. Rivera. I expect Capt. Allen every moment should be gladd to see him as I have party ingaged the Brigg he is coming in. I have not sold the Negro am in expectation of selling soon.

Bread and Flour I have sold but little as it's not quick at 18/. I think best to keep it a little longer. Merchantable Fish is like to be very plenty and cheap. the price at present is 11/6 small 12/ large which is very high. from Sir your Humble Servant,

GEO. SEARS

WILLIAM SAMUEL JOHNSON TO AARON LOPEZ[1]

Stratford, August 5th, 1772.

Dr. Sir

I AM favour'd with yours of the 28th of July, the moment of my return from N. York, where I have been some time; and am very ready to commence such action as you mention for Don Manuel de Valladares's Monies, on the Terms I mention'd to you, which I doubt not you will recollect, that I would run the hazard of my own Fees and trouble if the Gent'n themselves, or anybody for them, would advance or engage to repay, the necessary expences of such suit, viz. the actual Disbursements to the Sheriff, the Court, Witness's, etc. These expences will indeed amount to but a trifle, but actually to advance Monies on the hazard of the Event of the Suit I have ever consider'd as a species of Champerty forbidden by our Law, and dishonourable to its Professors, and have therefore never done it; but my own Fees I have a right to suspend on any Condition I think proper, and have no objection to hazard them on the Event of this suit, if upon the whole you think it expedient to bring one. Capt. Sistare, you observe, will be entitled to call for the original Bill of Lading, and a circumstance so important, I should imagine, would not be forgotten, nor neglected, by his

---

[1] The original is in the Newport Historical Society.

Counsel; and if it should be called for and we not be able to produce it we must infallibly fail. You also know that Mr. Shaw expects to absorb the Monies in Charges and Expences occasion'd, as he says, in a great measure, by the Detention consequent upon the former Arrests made at the suit of Don Manuel, etc., and by the suits for Salvage. Capt. Sistare will also have the benefit of the objection that he was not holden to return to Spain nor to account for the Monies and Merchandize by him received, until the Suits for Salvage were determined. These are the Objections which at this moment occur against bringing such suit, at present; nevertheless if you think it expedient and adviseable I will proceed upon the Terms I have mention'd. I am sorry that Mr. Ingersoll's and my Depositions did not come to hand in season. According to my Promise I saw them perfected before I left New Haven, viz. the day after I parted with you, and left them to go, as was proposed, by the then next Post to Col: Babcock. When you write Don Manuel I beg you will present my respectful Compliments to him, and assure yourself that I am with great regard and esteem, Dear Sir, Your most obedient and most humble Servant,

SAMUEL SNELL TO CHRISTOPHER CHAMPLIN [1]

Tantom Road, August 7, 1772.

Gentilmen:

I RECEIVED yours by Capt. Clark and I make no dout that if nothing happens to us but what we shall due as well as our nabours. My rum wase all gone before Capt. Clark arrived. I have maid my trade mostly with the whits as there is no black trade going I have disposed of my rum to the whits at 140 for women and 160 for men. I have ben

---

[1] Copy supplied by Mr. John H. Storer.

from Annamaboe this two months with my vessail and I am going up as soon as possable to wood and water I cant tell you when we shall sail up the coast as the trade is stopt by reason the blacks is agoing to war but as soon as I can get my slaves from the whits I shall sail. I have ben something unlucky, I lost my long boat soon after I got hure she went a shoer in a hard squal and the third of this month Capt. Roggers boat came on bord of me, and two of his people and my cooper and John Heman took his boat in the night and his gon of so that I never expect to see them any more my maits is both sek at preasant but I am in hoops that they will recouer soon. Mr. Champlin has ben sek this two months but he has got about againe. The vessail is now under sail that I am agoing to send this letter by. I am well and harty myself at preasant thanks be to God for it. hooping Gentlemen you are the same. Gentilmen, I am your most obdt and most humble sarvant

SAMUEL SNELL

HENRY DAVENANT TO AARON LOPEZ

London, the 20th August, 1772.

Sir,

THIS with my kind Respects to you and Mrs. Lopez, will inform you of the misfortune I have met with in being forst to stay behind my Ship; and purely on Account of another person, who I was partly concerned with in a Bond of £200, York Currency which I was forst to give in New York before I could get out of Prison, there. the Bond is now became due, and the Person who realy in justis ought to pay it, is obsconded, and poor me is forst to stand liable; but Sir as its impossible for me to pay it: I have been forst to serrender myself up a Prisoner, in the King's Bench; and have deliverd up every thing I have, except the Vallue of £20, which is alowed me, and what is that to begin the World with, that has a wife and Children and out of Buisnes. however I shall intierly rely on your Goodnes; and hope youl give me my old Ship againe, or some other; I realy want it: and hope youl extend your favours to me once more. Inclosed is my Accounts from the time I took charge to the 17th of July, and hope they will meet with your Aprobation. Sir, my Affares will be all setled the 26th of this Month, after which shall be a free man. You may depend Sir that I will proceed for New York, or Rhode Island in the first Ship that sailes, after Capt. Peters, in the *Jacob*, which will be in about 12 days. Can ashure you Mr. Hayly is my good Friend and does all in his power to serve me; and my Famely; I am Sir Your much obliged Humble Servant,

HENRY DAVENANT

PELEG GREENE TO AARON LOPEZ

Newbern, No. Carolina, Sept. 13, 1772.

Sir,

I ARRIVED here the 27th August where I found no Instruction lodged for my Government so for that Reason I due not know how to conduck Matters but from the intemation I had from you about puting a new deck have tryd to git Plank but cannot exsept I git it sawd by Hand and then it will be greene which will by no means due so for that Reason have concluded to cork hir decks which have begun upon and find it turn out much better then I expected and am in hopes shall git hir overhald by the last of this month and if I have no orders by that time, I shall begin to think you have given me the Sloop and shall emedately pick up a Cargo of Staves, Heading and Shingles, and some Tarr, and the remainder in Stock if any to be got by that time. as for Pork it will not be in season till the first of december and that will not due to wait so long and amigine it will be very high then — and proseed directly to Jamaica where I hope shall mete our mutual Benjamin Wright to whom shall deliver my Cargo if you think I am not caperble of disposeing of it and am in hopes giting some offer for the Sloop this time for this Trade will only pick your Pockit for she carris so little it is impossible to clear any thing by it. a vessell that wood carry about 40:000 of Lumber and draw about 9 ft. 2 in. of water might make a very good hand of it but a little Vessell will not except a man should come here in the winter and take a Load of Pork and Corn and Naval Stores and Stocks and then a man might due something better for this is the dulles time of the hole year.

the Negros I received at Jamaica all got in in good Health only Homer had two bad Places on one of his Thighs which wood not heal up but in Good Health other ways but however no[ne] of them fetch as mush I expected by reason of many cuntry born Negros was sold at Vandue and at Six months Credit which makes a great ods but however I have sold four of them named as follows —

Jack	at 70	Prices of Goods here	
		white Staves	at 90/
Cudjo	at 70	Heading	at £7
		Shingles	at 12/
Homer	at 50	Pitch	at 15/
		Boards	at 60/
Newbuary Boy	at 57:10	Red oak Staves	70/

the Molasses have sold at 2/ but the barril of Sugar unsold. I have nothing more in pertickerly to rite but shall be rady to sail by the first of November by which time I hop you will send the main Sail and Jibb if you dont I must wate till I recive a Letter from you before I can venture to buy duck here which will come very high indeed. Mr. Ellis has got some but it cost him 14 1/2 dollars a bolt in the west indais. Shall conclude. am Sir, Your Humble Servant,

PELEG GREENE

[Endorsed,] Per favour Capt. Cannon.

SAMUEL WARD TO AARON LOPEZ

Westerly, 29th September, 1772.

Sir,

SOME Persons have taken up on my Beach a Cask of Wine which I should have demanded as my Property as by Law wrecked Goods for which no Owner appears belong to the Lord of the Manor, but hearing that a Block Island Boat had thrown out some Casks of Wine of yours I imagine that the Sea more merciful than the custom house Officers hath spared one of them, and as I should be glad of an opportunity of alleviating your Loss tho in a small degree I spoke to one of the Men who took it up. He seems willing upon my representation that if upon your acquainting me with the marks and size of the Cask you lost this appears to be one of them you should have it, allowing what is handsome for taking up and securing it: He desires you would write to me as soon as possible. I am, Sir, Your most humble Servant,

SAM WARD

HENRY CRUGER, JR. TO BENJAMIN WRIGHT

Bristol, 1st Oct., 1772.

IN consequence of something Aaron Lopez Esqr. has lately wrote to me on this Subject, I must inform you that in the beginning of the year 1769, Mr. Mendez remitted me from Jamaica a Bill of £150 Stg. drawn by Daniel Moore on Robt. Alexander and Robt. Maitland of London and endorsed by Ph: Ph: Livingston of Kingston; this Bill was protested; and not having a good opinion of Mendez, I would not return the Bill to him; but to my Correspondent and Countryman Nath'l Grant, begging of him to do the needful. he recover'd a Bill from Moore for £100 Stg. in part of the protested one, and sent it to me; this Bill *also* proved bad; and I returned it to Mr. Grant with Protest, so long ago as 20th February, 1771, it was a draft of Lewis Cutbert on Sam'l Bean, since that, I have never heard a syllable more from Mr. Grant on the subject.

Now I must request of you, Sir, as this Bill is the property of our worthy friend Mr. Lopez, that you will find out where the blame lies; whether Mr. Grant had ever received it, why he does not remit it; or please to speak to Mr. Moore about it, and know whether he means to pay the Bill; and pray is not Mr. Livingston as an endorser liable? I suspect every thing is not cleverly managed; therefore, for the Interest of our friend, do make some Enquiries, and see if you can get Mr. Grant to remit the money.

I shall be glad to hear from you on this subject, and am Sir, Yrs etc.

H. CRUGER, JR.

HENRY CRUGER, JR. TO NATHANIEL GRANT

Bristol, 1st Oct., 1772.

I HAVE already wrote you a few lines by this Bearer. the present is only to make an enquiry about the Bill of £150, drawn by Robt. Alexander & Robert Maitland with a protest for non payment I returned to your hands *so long ago as March 1769.* I am the uneasier about this Bill, as the person on whose Account it was remitted to me, is often calling on me for a settlement, being informed the Drawer of it (Mr. Moore) is very capable of paying it, and so is Mr. P. P. Livingston the *Endorser*, if this is the case; for God's sake! why are they not instantly compel'd to do Justice? I beg of you Mr. Grant to give me some satisfaction on this head, that I may no longer suffer the bad opinion of my correspondent in No. America, who frequently hints that he imagines I neglect his Interest in this matter; wherefore I must entreat you to insist upon Mr. Moore or Mr. Livingston's paying you the Bill with Cost and Damages, and remit me the same without further loss of time. I lament their want of honor to do it before; from such connections God forever deliver me. . . .

HENRY CRUGER, JR.

GEORGE SEARS TO AARON LOPEZ

St. Johns, Newfoundland, October 4th, 1772.

Sir,

I HAVE not had an Oppertunity of writeing to you before this sence Captain Allen saild who I hope has got safe home. Captain Ripley arived here the Evening after Captain Allen saild, which was sooner then I expected according to the accounts I had. he lay here about three weeks before I could sell the Brigg, she being two shoal in the Hold for this Trade, otherwise could have sold her exceeding well. the most I could get was £501, as I had given my word I would not take £500, but from your writeing I thought better to take that price then send her home again and she would not carry Fish enough on Freight to make any great hand of it. the Salt I sold at 8/9 per Hhd. which is very low oweing to several large Vessells ariveing in a short time of each other, but none sold on better terms then my self. Capt. Ripley went from hence for Trepassey about 18 days since to deliver the Brigg and some goods I sold at same time amounting to £536.7.5, the first Bill of this Sett I ordered him to give you, the second I have received here, the third is left in good hands and I expect it here soon. I expected Capt. Ripley would have com to this Harbour againe for a passage, therefore did not wright by him. nor I did not think it prudent to send Bills or the Cash he brought with him, as I expected he would com round in an open Boat, to this Harbour again as tis not common to get a Passage there. you have here inclos'd a Receipt for the Money Captain Ripley brought, which I have delivered Captain Gideon Manchister. Likewise the second Bill of James Jackson's and the first Bill of the Sett James Goss on John Goss for £169.15.6 which I hope will com safe to hand. I have sent to London all the first Bills of the Setts as you ordered, £340 for Account of Mr. Rivera to Hayley and Hopkins in the Ship *Vestal,* John Temple Master, bound for London sailed August 30th., £161.16.3 to William Steade, £400.9.8 to Hayley and Hopkins on your Account in the Ship *New Race Horse,* James Drew Master, sailed this day bound for Teingmouth. As there will be an other Oppertunity soon for England, I think better to send the second Bills from hence to London and bring the third home with me. As I wass beginning the first day of this month to part load the *Dianna* with W. India Fish for Rhode Island I frieghted her to Mr. Robert Bulley for Barcelonia, with Liberty to touch at Malaga or Alic[ante] at 2/3 per

Quintal. If no farther than Malaga 2/, which is the same as last years Frieghts. Mr. Bulley prommisses to do all in his power to get her a Frieght for London and by all accounts there is no Danger but she will get one. we have one thousand Quintals now on board and hope to saile in 10 or 14 days. If it should so happen there is no Frieght to be got, I shall give Captain Buckley Orders to load with Salt and proceed Home to Rhode Island and to send a Line to Hayley and Hopkins as soon as he knows wheather he shall get a Frieght or Load with Salt for Rhode Island. With them you may leave Orders for Insureance accordingly. With regard to loading the Brigg for Lisbon the Accounts of Markets at that place are so bad, that it would be Madness to think of it without I was a mind to sink a good Deale of Money for you. the Merchants here will not ship ther own Fish they have on hand. there wass great hopes last year on Fish. 'tis likely it will be so againe this year there being so much old Fish left on hand. I suppose you have heard of a great number of Marchants and two Banks failing in England. I have a List of there Names. Beleave it will not effect me or any House here. Mr. Bulleys Friend is faild at home, but Bulley wass a small Ballance in his Debt, therefore it will not hurt him. I hope to be ready to com home in two or three weeks at farthest. I have not much goods unsoald. Caezer is not sold yet. Vessells of proper Dementions are much wanted and have been this 5 or 6 Weeks I could have sold or chartered half a Dozen, of such Dimentions as I gave you last year—50 or 51 foot Keele, 21 foot Beem, 8 foot 6, 8 foot 9 or 9 foot Hold, or a little larger in this proportion, Briggs or Schooners tho Briggs seem rather to have the preference. they will hardly ever fail of selling any year while the Fishery is carried on, there Sides not too tumble too much to hender them from hawling in fish as they make Bankers of them after they have been to Market. they should be all trunells [1] where Spikes are us'd, as they dont like to see a Spike in Bottom or Waste. From, Sir, your humble Servant,

GEO. SEARS

---
[1] "Treenail commonly pronounced trun'-nel."

P. S. Since I finished Mr. Bulley tells me he thinks he wants to send the Brigg as high as Naples or Leghorn. If so the price will be 2/6. he tells me he allways insures to any Port in the Streights as it makes no Odds with the Insurers.

G. SEARS

I agreed to give Captain Manchester 3 Dollars to bring this money which I have not paid.

SAMUEL SNELL TO CHRISTOPHER CHAMPLIN[1]

Annamaboe, Oct. 6, 1772.

Sir:

I WROTE you by Capt. Johnson the 26th Sept. and this comes by Capt. Roggers, the next that sails from heare will be Capt. Bardine. I cant tell you Sir when I shall saile but as soon as I can git my slaves from the castles, I shall sail, as I only weight for them, if the trade groes better I shall sail soon, if not I must stay longger. Trade never was none to be so dul as it is now, not heare. I have but 15 slaves on board yet, I got one hande out of Capt. Johnson before he sailed.

Gentlemen with esteame, your most obdt and humble servant,

SAMUEL SNELL

HAYLEY AND HOPKINS TO CHRISTOPHER CHAMPLIN

London, 31st October, 1772.

Sir,

ON the other side is copy of our last. We have now only to advise you that the Bills mentioned in our last on Wraxall & Hall for £100 on Deane, Munckley & Co. for £200, and on Greenwood & Higginson for £100, are all accepted and when paid shall be placed to your Credit; and to return your Bill and protest for £32 on David Paris Esqr. for the Charges

---

[1] Copy supplied by Mr. John H. Storer.

thereon we debit you 8/6 we hope you will be no sufferer, but be able to recover the Amount with Damages.

The Bill we advised you, to have noted for non acceptance, on William Innis for £23 is paid and placed to your Credit. (Copy Original per Welshman.)

HAYLEY AND HOPKINS

TILLINGHAST & HOLROYD TO AARON LOPEZ

Providence, November 23, 1772.

Sir,

WE herewith send you all the Shakes we can yet get in we expect a quantity in from several hands which we look for daily, as fast as they come, will send them down. here is also a parcel of Cedar pails. shall send 2 or 3 dozen more as soon as they come which will be in a little while. we could not procure the Hoop poles you requested, and as for Hoops they bring them in so poor we are afraid to send such as generally come to market here. if we could get them that we approved of ourselves within the limited time, we would be glad to send them to you; but we don't love to have any difficulty about them as they are a precarious article.

we would be glad of a bag of pemento if you have any. the Endico is not such as we could wish but possibly we may get it off.

Mr. Jenckes has been with you we suppose but have not seen him since. if you have given him an order on us for the money will pay it him for the Endico. We are, Sir, your humble Servants,

TILLINGHAST & HOLROYD

P. S. your affair with Allen is not yet determined.

Mr. Aaron Lopez,   Dr.

To 43 Cedar pails at 12/ per dozen	£2. 3.–
To 20 Shakes hhds. at 7½ per s.	2.12.6
	£4.15.6

TILLINGHAST AND HOLROYD TO AARON LOPEZ

Providence, November 25, 1772.

Sir,

WE wrote you monday last and sent a parcel of Shakes and pails, but find thro' the neglect of the boatman they are not yet delivered. we now add to them 30 more Shakes which came in yesterday: and are sent by the same Boat by Mr. Justice. We can have a parcel made by a Cooper in Town which are reckoned better than the Country ones and are valued at 3/ per s here, at which price we must take them in lieu of Casks. if they will suit you at the price to be discounted as Cash will send them down next trip. these now last sent are some of them longer than the common size which shall charge all together at 2/9 per s. Your humble Servants,

TILLINGHAST & HOLROYD

30 Shakes at 2/9 per s. . . . .£4:2:6.

HENRY CRUGER, JR. TO AARON LOPEZ

Bristol, 1st December, 1772.

Dear Sir,

I HAVE the pleasure of seeing before me your two much esteemed favors of 21st July and 25th September.

In your first favor you advise of your intentions to consign me your new Ship of 160 Tons; in your next, you order £1800 Stg. insurance on her and her cargo and freight, which was accordingly effected by good underwriters, and the Account Cost is herewith, amounting to £54.16.0 to your Debit in Account. she (the *Henry*) does not yet show herself; but as the wind is got fair, I hope soon to see her. Oil is in great demand, and notwithstanding you gave so high a price for it, I flatter myself I shall render you a *gaining* Sales. I wish to God she may make her appearance, so that we may sell it before any more arrives, a deal will depend upon that. the Ship we cannot think of selling 'till towards Spring. in winter time trade is dead, and Vessels of course out of demand.

I return you my sincere thanks, Sir, for the continuance of your care and attention to my unfortunate concerns with the Estate of the late John Channing; and as to the two Osbornes—what shall I say of them? Peace to their Manes! they deceived me, abused you, and berogued many. their flagitious principles proved them Brothers. let you and I make a Merit of Necessity, and not only forgive the Injuries and Injustice we receiv'd from them, but pray God also to forgive them, and be merciful unto them.

These Impositions and Abuses are enough to banish all confidence from amongst Mankind; but, blessed be Nature's God, who hath provided a something, a grave oblivion, in which we may bury all remembrance of past sufferings, and be again happy by looking forward.

Your Account has Credit for £2.1.7 additional Disbursements on the Ship *New York*, Captain Jones.

Immediately upon receipt of your favor, I wrote a letter to Mr. Nath'l Grant, and another to Capt. Wright (Copies of them you have herewith) desiring (in the strongest terms) they would send me some satisfactory account of the protested Bills returned to Mr. Grant; I join with you in easily believeing [the] Conduct of the parties, and the neglect of this Bill, are occasioned more by the want [of honesty] than the want of abilities to pay it. for my part, I can [only] with truth declare, I seldom have fallen into the hands of any one [   ] Person *in that Island*, but I have suffer'd by them.

Agreeable to your proposal, Dr. Sir, I do now send you my Order on Nath'l Grant for the Amount and Damages on said Bill of £150, drawn by Daniel Moore, and for the *Damages* of the £100 which was remitted *in part*. I wish with all my heart Captain Wright may be able to recover it and punish the Delinquents. they are a disgrace to the name of Merchants.

Let me conclude this letter (as nothing else occurs) with thanking you kindly, Sir, for the Attention you paid to my recommendation of young Wyatt, the Collectors favorable answer to you has made all his friends extremely happy; if you would do me the honor to make my acknowledgments and respectful compliments to him, you will further oblige, Dear Sir, Your affectionate Humble Servant

HEN: CRUGER JR.

DORCAS EARL TO CHRISTOPHER CHAMPLIN

Newport, the 1 m. 1, 1773.

Friend Champlin,

As its my principle not to contract debts beyond my ability to comply with in a short time, am very uneasey that I owe thee. thought I would [ask] if thee was uneasey as its some time sence did not know but thee would think me thoughtless of the debt when its not the case but its out of my power to pay the money at present tho have Effects of our own in the shop, and as I dont sel on creidit am in hopes of making pay in time if thou art willing to alow me that privilege, for altho thee told me when I took them I might make payment as I sold them, yet I could not be easey without ecknowleging the debt and tel thee the goods are cheif of them yet on hand. as I have not an assortment they sel but slowly, and as I have not money to purchase more must be content and do as well as I can with what goods I have, if thou art not uneasey, which I beg thee would let me know.

I dont like to be in debt or I might have more goods; but the fear of not selling so as to make payment soon, and the thoughts of having peoples money in my hands to their Disadvantage, makes me afraid of venturing more untill I know thy mind, which will be a Satisfaction to me, and ecknowleged as an additional favour done thy Friend

DORCAS EARL

Stevenson and Went to Christopher and George Champlin

Barbados, January 7th, 1773.

Gentlemen,

WE wrote you of the 6th of November per Captain Steele via Philadelphia in answer to your favour of the 11th September. since which we are favoured with yours of the 6th October advising us that you had heard of Captain Tuells arrival and that it was possible he might be with us in November, but he does not yet appear. soon as he does we will deliver him your letters, and you may depend on our rendering him our best Services. Negroes keep up with us and good Slaves will command a high price. we sold Captain Wantons Cargo which Captain Rogers brought in a few weeks past at £36 and £35 Stg. round, but they were prime, and such Slaves will always meet a good and ready Market. Slaves have been high at Carolina, but by the last Accounts they were fallen, and from the low price of their Rice it was the opinion of the Factors that slaves wou'd still fall. we shall be happy if Captain Tuells slaves arrive in order, so as to enable us to take him up, as it will give us real pleasure to render you our best Services, being with respect, Gentlemen, Your most hmble Servants,

STEVENSON AND WENT

Joshua Hart to Aaron Lopez[1]

Charles Town, 8 Feb'y, 1773.

Dear Sir,

I HAVE your much esteem'd favor of the 8th ultimo covering an Account and Bill of Lading for 8 Quarter Casks of white and Two of Red Lisbon. the Red might answer very well here, but the People in this Province are quite unacquainted with it, and the white comes to dear for this Markett, as I might have bought better here for less Money,

---

[1] The original is in the Newport Historical Society.

and about three months since I purchased a Quantity of much the same Quality as yours from Uriah Woolman, a Merchant of Philadelphia, at 20 Dollars. since then I have been offerd to be imported from the same City, any Quantity I liked at 18 Dollars.

The 4 Kegs of Cordials your Brother sent me I have sold to some of [my] Country Friends for the great Price of £26.17, this Currency, to pay which I have sent by Capt. Earl, Sixteen Dollars, which with 17/ I paid for Freight and Wharfage is the Amount. I should not have been able to obtain so large a Price but bye Connections in the Country and selling them for a long Credit; I am very sorry to be oblig'd to inform you that I cannot undertake a Commission Trade. You well know my incapacity, and haveing no Clerk to keep my Accounts, I must therefore decline it; but I shall in the propper Season for Cordials, send for a sufficient Quantity of Anniseed as will answer mine and my Friends purpose. in the mean time please to inform me how he will sell the same per Gallon.

I should have sent you Rice for the Cost of the Wine being $238\frac{1}{2}$ dollars, but its now at 60/, and by the Account I have it can be bought for less with you. I have therefore deferd it, hoping that in a short time it may fall in the Price, when I shall execute your order but if that does not happen, I will send you dollars or Johannes's which will be most agreable.

I thank God that my Family is well and particularly that my Daughter Hester is restored to a good State of Health. You will please to make all our kindest Salutations acceptable to your Lady and every Branch of your worthy Family, and believe me to be very Sincerely, My Dear Sir, Your Oblige Friend and Very Humble Servant,

Joshua Hart

[Endorsed,] Per favor of Capt. Earl.

HAYLEY AND HOPKINS TO CHRISTOPHER CHAMPLIN

[London,] 10 February, 1773.

Sir,

WE confirm the above Copy of our last respects and have now to acknowledge receipt of your favours of the 4th and 10th September; 22d October, 5th, 21st and 26th November and 3d December with the following bills —

Robert Scarlett on Wm. Reynolds	£386.12.2	N
S. Barrett on Peter Holmes, Liverpool,	55.— —	N
Do. . . . . do. . . . do.	35. 8.10	N
Alexander Simson on John Noble Bristol	183.— —	
Peter Ewing on Wm. Innis	100.— —	
Arch George on Dean & Co. Bristol	50.— —	
John Bowman on Mayne & Needham	100.— —	N
Do. . . . . do.	150.— —	N
Wm. Barnett on Serocold & Jackson	30.— —	N
Benj. Mowat on Wm. Miles, Bristol	50.— —	
Jas. Grant on Robert & William Grant	20.— —	
John Bowman on Mayne & Needham	150.— —	N
do. . . . . do.	100.— —	N
do. . . . . do.	100.— —	N
do. . . . . do.	52.— —	N

of which the 10 Setts marked N are noted for Non acceptance and we fear will be returned with protests which will be a great disappointment to you as well as to us, but cannot be helped. You may depend upon our taking care to forward the needful protests without delay on such as are not paid when due. The other 5 Setts are accepted and when paid shall be placed to your credit.

We are obliged to you for recifying our omission of not charging the Morocca Shoes, they were 1 doz. 12/, 1 doz. 15/, [and] 1/2 doz. 22/ 11. in all £1.18. for which we now debit you. We are glad to see you had so good a prospect of recovering the money for the protested bill of £100 on Allen and Marlar. We now enclose you the other bill on the same House for £192.05.—with protest which hope you will be no Looser by, the cost of this protest being 5/9 is to your debit. We have applied to Captain Shand for the ps. of Silk, but he informs us he undertook to gett it done himself and that he shall do so and bring it back to you. The premium for insuring a Vessell from Rhode Island to Jamaica and London warranted to sail from Jamaica on or before the 26th July is £6 per Ct.

The Goods you desire are getting ready and we propose sending them in Shand, who we expect will leave London in about 10 days or a fortnight. The Boston Ships will none of them sail a Week before him, so that your Goods will arrive this Spring in pretty good season.

We now enclose your Account Current to the 31st December last, ballance then in our favour being £3805.16.9 is carried to Your debit in new Account which if upon examination found free from Error please note accordingly of which shall be obliged by your informing us in your next. We are very respectfully, Sir, Your most Humble Servants

HAYLEY & HOPKINS

Endorsed, Per Capt. Cartwright, via Boston.

STEVENSON AND WENT TO CHRISTOPHER AND GEORGE CHAMPLIN

Barbados, Feb. 16th, 1773.

Gentlemen,

WE have the pleasure to inform you that Captain Tuell in your Sloop *Adventure* arrived here the 14th Instant from the Coast with 94 Slaves, and as our demand keeps up we took of two purchasers to view them, and finding them healthy and in good order we obtained £35 Sterling a head, round, which we think a very good price and hope it will give you satisfaction. We shall dispatch Captain Tuell in the course of six weeks with our own bills agreeable to your desire. We are with respect, Gentlemen, Your most hum. Servants,

STEVENSON AND WENT

SAMUEL TUELL TO CHRISTOPHER AND GEORGE CHAMPLIN

Bridgetown in Barbados, February 22th, 1773.

Gentillmen,

THIS comes to inform you, of my arivel heare the 13th of this month with 94 Slaves on board, all well and in good order, which I have sold, the hole of them, all round to Messrs. Stevenson and Went, the 16th of this inst. for 35 pound Starling, and am to be despatcht in six weeks, from the time sot. I ask'd 36 pound round for them, but I found after standing out two or three days, that I cood not obtain no more then 35£, and then I struck, according to your orders, which I hope will be agreable to you. I had seaven weeks passage wanting one day. I purchest in all 95 Slaves. I lost one before I left the Coast, so that I have sold 81 Cargo. I rote you two or three lines the 16th of this instant by the way of Boston which this comes the same way. Gentill Men, with Esteem your Most Obedient Humble Sarvent,

SAMUEL TUELL

[Endorsement,] Boston April 5th 1773. Rec'd and forwarded by Sirs Your humble Servants,

THOMAS STODDARD & Co.

CULLEN POLLOK TO AARON LOPEZ

Edenton, March 9, 1773.

Dearest Friend,

It is now some time since I rec'd your most welcome favours. the two Vessels are both in the bay waitin a wind. Captain has good success in collecting and am in hopes will continue to have. I wish it had suited to send for the plank as it was already. I'm much obliged to you for your kind concern for my disappointment at York indeed it was vexatious but I have long learnt to laugh at such things. if the Captain had done as he might he would have taken the wheat on board, but Providence has wisely ordained that

[no] Situation in this world shall be without its Alloy, much less a poor Carolina Planter.

I have lately been informed by a line from Mr. Chaloner that one of my causes at S. Kingston was tryed, and that judgment had gone against me, but that Mr Marchant said my cause was good and had renewed the Sute, but does not say what they had done in the other, nor what sum they had recovered. I have wrote to him to write to me more particularly and to Mr. Marchant desiring him to write me also and shall esteem it a favour if you will put them in mind of it. . . .

my absence from home two Sumers, with the death of my Steward, and the loss of a most particular Friend, by a fall from his Horse, which fractured his skull, and dyed two days before I came home, he was a Gentleman of the Law possesed of every Virtue, and of a Liberal Education. he was the only one of that Profession, that ever I knew, whose accquaintance with the most vilinous part of Mankind had not deprived of the feelings of humanity, for the better part, and whose sentiments were as delicate as possible. within these few days, the loss of my oldest acquaintance in the Province, and most intimate Friend and Relation, a Man for every Virtue inferiour to none, that if it was not for my only comfort, and some few Friends (tho none in this Province) I should hold this World very cheap; all these things I am afraid will confine me at home this year, tho you may depend on seeing me next very early, by the permission the Almighty God. All these thing are sent by Providence to wean us of our two great fondness, for this World by the time we are to leave it, and ought to be looked on as favours from Heaven. but why should I trouble my dearest Friend, because I know his unbounded goodness will excuse it. Everything you was so kind to send by Captain Riply came safe to hand for which I return you many thanks. I shall take it as a favour if you will inform me what I can get a good House Carpenter to come here for by the Month one who understands weather boarding in the manner of Mr. Brindlys or Mr. Dudys House.

I should be much obliged to you also to procure me 100 li. of Fowl meadow grass Seed. I am afraid you will not get it unless you give notic in the papers but I would begrudge no expence for it; also 50 li. of orchard grass seed such as grows on Mr. Marchant's Lot.

Having nothing more to add I must co[n]clude with a tender of my most sincere good wish to your most amiable Spouse, Mr. and Mrs. Rivera, and all your sweet little Family, whom I doe most sincerely love and be assured, Dearest Sir, that I am Your Most Sincere Friend and Most Obedient Servant,

CULLEN POLLOK

BENJAMIN WRIGHT TO AARON LOPEZ [1]

Savanna LaMarr, Jamaica, the 14 March, 1773.

Dear Cousin,

I IMBRACE this Opportunity, being the first that offer'd, to advice you of my safe arrival here, with a passage of thirty days; during which I really suffer'd in body and mind on account of ———. kind Providence favoured us with an easy time off our Coast that brought your horses in good order, without any considerable mortality with the Poultry; my being so very late brought me to a glutted market, that laid me under many inconveniences, but I cannot complain of what Sales I have made; as I think the prices are tollerable, of which you shall have a Sketch in course of this Epistle. I now congratulate you on the safe arrival of the Brigantine *Charlotte*, Capt'n Ebenezer Shearman, who arrived here safe.

I am now favour'd with your much esteemed favour of the 17th and 21st January per the *Charlotte*, Capt'n Ebenezer Shearman, who arrived here the 3rd Instant, after tutching at St. Nichola Mole, and landing all your Spermacaeti Candles and the greatest part of your hoops and left them with Capt'n John Dupuy; I received from Capt'n

---
[1] Original in the Newport Historical Society.

Ebenezer Shearman two hundred and eight pounds Fifteen shillings Cash; which have pass'd to your Credit. I wish your common flour per *Charlotte* had been disposed of at the Mole, as its quality will not answer here. In answer to a Paragraph in your letter, where you hope Capt'n Stephen Bardin has sweetned my mouth with a purse of Pistoles, poor young man I am much afraid he is no more; I cannot hear any thing of him; I have had advise from all parts of this Island but no account of the poor young fellow. my disappointment in the Tenders miscarrying will be attended with bad consequences: I shall not be able to procure more than sixty or seventy hogsheads Mollasses, and that not till the last of April; it will not be in my power to prevent your looseing your Gaspee voyage with the *Charlotte* as the Crops here are very late, and such a whet season that our London ships will not sail so soon as they did last year by near three weeks; time has been when disappointments of this kind wou'd have made me very unhappy, but I am determind not to frett: I notice your memorandum for the quantity of Sugar, Rum, Piemento, etc., etc., which shall pay regard too, altho I shall be sorry to see the *Charlotte* go home in ballast; but as the intention of Orders is to have them fulfill'd, I must mortify my self and act against your Interest. I am sorry there is no vent for the keggs of honey you put on board and must return them per Shearman.

I am in hopes to remitt your correspondents Messrs. Hayley and Hopkins near one thousand pounds Sterling in unexceptionable bills of Exchange. I shall be under the disagreeable necessity of shipping some produce to London on your account as I must take it in payment. in regard to your proposal in sending a cargo of Mules to this place can assure you should you be fortunate enough to land a Cargo of Mules here in good order they wou'd meet with an agreeable market: but to say what they woud average cannot, as that depends on the quality and the order they arrive in; such a Cargo as you mention will sell here at any season of the year and as you are not a stranger in trade to this Island you will naturally suppose that between December and the month of June wou'd be the most likely to receive prompt payment for them.

At my arrival here I met with a letter from Henry Cruger of Bristol, desireing me to apply to Nathaniel Grant of Kingston to know what was become of Daniel Moores bill of Exchange for one hundred and fifty pounds Sterling endorsed by Ph: Ph: Levingston, which bill was forwarded by Mr. Cruger to Nathaniel Grant under protest, desireing him to do the needfull. I immediately made application agreeable to request, and herein inclose you a Coppy of Grants letters to me on the subject. You have likewise inclosed Coppy of Capt'n Peleg Clarks letter informing me what his Slaves averaged, and his opinion what time your Brigantine *Ann*, Capt'n Inglis, might be in this Island. Slaves still are in demand and sell very quick and at a high price; but how long it may continue is more than I can pretend to say. was I to give you a particular account of the marketts here and the quantitys of Lumber now on hand it must appear to you a romance. my friend Dolbeare writes me that good Codfish at Kingston is from 7/6 to 12/6 per Ct., and Capt'n Shearman tells me it is still lower at Nichola Mole.

I now inform you there is introduced into this port from Philadelphia two large ships which are to be established ships for London, and one ship from Boston likewise to be a yearly ship; they are all under the direction of a new established house here, (namely) Inglis & Blair. I find I have potent power to encounter; therefore must beg you will order matters so as your large ship may be in this Port by the 10th January, provided she comes with *only* half a Cargo; she being so very large I must begin in time her load or she will be very late. I must recommend it to you to have the clear boards for her Cabbin put out of the weather to have them properly season'd. I'm confident Staves next year will not be very high here; shou'd it be convenient for you to procure about Twenty six thousand of good hoops on our joint account of the following dimentions, thirteen thousands, fourteen feet long, and thirteen thousands, twelve foot long, I think I can insure you thirty-three dollars per M, shoud they be very good in quality I dare say they may command thirty-six dollars per M, with a proviso they can be here by the 1st of January next, as my brains are much confused at present I must conclude with wishing you all may Escape the Gallows this time, notwithstanding you are all a parcell of Rebells. my respects to Mrs. Lopez and am with Esteem, Your Cousin,

BENJAMIN WRIGHT

Horses 1 . . . . . . at £55
        2 . . . . . . at £40 each
        1 . . . . . . at £36.15/

Sperm. Candles . . . . at 3/1½ per lb.
Keggs Tallow Cagg and all together at 1/ per lb.
Shadds . . . . at 23/9 per barrell.
Boards from £6 to £7 per m.
White oake Staves and heading at £12 . . per Do.
Red Oake Ditto . . . . 10 . . Do.
Fine flour . . . . at 30/ per Ct.
Common flour . . . . at 25/ per Ct.
Codfish no sale what little have sold 25/ per Do.
Shingles that very good . . . . . . 45/ per m.
Lamp Oil . . . . at £7 per barrell.
Pork . . . . £5.5/ to 5.10/ ditto.
Bass . . . . from 32/6 to 35/ per bbl.
Geese . . . . 6/3 each
Turkeys . . . . 7/6 do.
2 Quarter Casks Wine at £ 11 each.
Some Oysters . . . . at 3/1½ each kegg.
Ditto of the Keggs Biscuit at 7/6 do.
Mackrell . . . . from 42/6 to 45/ each.

WILLIAMS & CO. TO CHRISTOPHER CHAMPLIN

Sir,

YOUR favor of the 2nd Inst. is to hand. We note the Contents. Are much obliged to Mr. Gibbs for his recommendation. Should be glad to render any friend of his every service in our power; but its impossible to say, with any kind of certainty, what demand Vessels may be in next fall, or if freights may be easily got. Thus much would observe; At that season of the year, viz. September and October, a good Vessel has not wanted for a freight, to the Eastward; especially when the Owner would load 1/2 or 3/4. The common freights per Bushel to Cadiz and Lisbon are 12d Sterling and 5/ per Bbbl. If they go up the Streights, rise in proportion to the distance and different ports they toutch at: The last years Wheat have been heigh 6 at 7/ per Bushel, Flour 16 at 18/ per Ct. Can at that season of the year dispatch a Vessel of her burdon in 3 or 4 weeks at most, especially if we have warning of her coming. The customary Commissions are 5 per Ct. for sales and 5/ per Ct. for purchasing there cargoes: Can at any time sell in a few weeks 20 to 40 Hds. of Country made or West India Rum. The retale price for the Country made is from 2/3 to 2/6. Spermacetie Candles is a very good article; as are some of your very best bright Muscovado Sugars: 10 to 20 Hds. of Melasses might be readily turnd into Cash. As to her being registerd in our Names, we are not inform'd suficiently of that matter to answer it fully. Expect to be in Newport this Summer when will make it my business to confer with you more fully on that and other matters. We are Very Respectfully, Sir, Your Very Humble Obedient Servants

THOS: CH: WILLIAMS & Co.

Annapolis, 15th March, 1773.

N. B. Bills Cash or such Articles as will command Cash must be had for purchasing the cargo. If Effects in hand, wou'd at any time advance four or five hundred pounds on them, if not meet a ready sale.

HAYLEY AND HOPKINS TO CHRISTOPHER CHAMPLIN

London, 23 Mar., 1773.

Sir,

ABOVE you have Copy of our last, since which have none of your favours. Our Motive for troubling you at present is to return you with protest, the Bill on William Reynolds for £386.12.2, and those on Peter Holme of Liverpool for £55. and £35.8.10. for Cost of the former we have debited you 5/9, and for the 2 latter 11/2. By Captain Burke who we expect to sail in about 10 days, we ship a few Goods remaining to complete your Orders and are etc.

Copy, Original per Hood.

Since writing the above, the Bills you remited us on Mayne & Needham are become due and they have paid 3 of them for £100 each, which are placed to your Credit, the others being 2 of £150 each and one for £52 are protested, but as Mr. Mayne assures us they will also be paid in a few days, we dont return them by this Vessell but shall keep them till Burke sails, which will be in about a week, and if they are not paid before he sails, they shall be returned you. We are, etc.,[1]

HAYLEY AND HOPKINS

30 Mar. 1773

TILLINGHAST AND HOLROYD TO AARON LOPEZ

Providence, March 25, 1773.

Sir,

WE have sent you 15 Shakes of 42 Inches and 18 of 46 In. if any more come in to us seasonably, we shall send them to you. these of 46 Inches are 3/ per s. the others 2/7½ per s.

the remainder of the Lime lays now ready on the wharff. wish the boatman would have taken it in now, as it may take damage if any rain would come on it, tho we covered it with boards, but choose to have it away as soon as possible, as we are crowded for room. this we charge you at 15/

---

[1] On March 30 they wrote: "We now enclose Invoice and bill of lading for a few Goods shippd for your Account in the *Minerva*, Captain Burke, amounting to £147.10.9 on which we have made £150 Insurance, premio etc. being £3.17.9. Mayne & Needham have not yet paid the remainder of Mr. Bowmans bills on them, but they make a point of our not returning them by this Vessel and promise certainly to pay them very shortly. We therefore think it eligible to keep them yet a little while which we hope you will approve."

per hhd. but we cannot get any more under 18/ they have raised the price lately, and have been backward in bringing it, till t[hey] had fixed the new price; if we send you any more [it] will be 18/. We are with great regard, Sir, Your most humble Servants

TILLINGHAST AND HOLROYD

PELEG GREENE TO AARON LOPEZ

Ocrecock Barr, April the 27th, 1773.

Sir,

I IMBRACE this present oppertunity to inform you of my safe arrival here after a teages Pasage of 16 days which will backward our Voyage very much; but by the blessing of God hope we shall make up loss time in coming home. I had very heavy Gales of wind the most part of my Pasage. I got once within a days sail of my Port when I took a Gale of wind and drove me of 7 days but thanks be to God I got in at last without any damage, and shall proseed up to Edenton as soon as wind and weather will permit and deliver my Credentials to our friend Joseph Reply who I shall assist all that in my Power lies to dispatch the Sloop in order for another Trip. I have not hered any thing from Capt. Reply senc I arrived it being very inconvenient to hear from the Country this time a year nither am I able to acquant you anithing of the Market but shall rite you by the first oppertunity after I git up the Country. have nothing more to acquant you of at present but shall conclude with my steady atention for your interest. Am, Sir, your Humble Servant,

PELEG GREENE

SMITH AND ATKINSON TO CHRISTOPHER CHAMPLIN

Boston, May 3d, 1773.

Sir,

YOUR favour under the 29th Uito. came in course. we are sorry the Patney Chints etc. were not arrived they must come to hand soon after the date of yours as they were forwarded by the first Waggon. the other Goods were sent by the Providence Waggon monday last and the Invoice by the Coach to Providence. we sent you a ps. of white figured drawboy with the Goods last week. we have not any white Effegine nor any assortment of Blond Laces. they were very scarse in London last winter which prevented our R. Smith from getting a quantity at prises which would answer here. when you are in want of any future articles your Commands will oblige, Sir, your obedient Servants,

SMITH AND ATKINSON[1]

THOMAS DOLBEARE TO AARON LOPEZ

Kingston, Jamaica, 15th May, 1773.

Dear Sir,

THE Bearer of this Captain Parkinson of the Sloop *Hero*, comes to your port with a Load of Mohogany, who I beg leave to recommend to your best advice and assistance, as he belongs to a Friend of mine here, Mr. Philip Cox, from whom you'll receive a Letter per this conveyance. Per the Instrument of agreement accompanying this you'll perceive that the Mohogany is consigned to Mr. Eleazer Trevett, upon his giving you full and sufficient security for the Amount of the Money due Mr. Cox, for the goodness of which he entirely depends on your judgment. I must therefore beg, Sir, that you would be particular in this matter, as Mr. Cox has nothing here to secure himself with respect to the performance of the agreement in dispatching the Sloop with the Goods as there inserted in five weeks. tho' Mr. Trevett may not be nicely exact in the compliance of shiping every article, Mr. Cox will not mind it, (so that he dispatches the Vessell by the five weeks) but no doubt

---

[1] "You (we doubt not) are convinced that we cannot afford to sell the prime of our goods at 50 pr. ct. on interest for any long time. The use of the money is the only intention. We find but few goods imported here this fall." *Smith and Atkinson to Christopher Champlin*, October 4, 1773.

you'll get him to come as near it as possible, per the Agreement you'll see the whole matter set forth. should Mr. Trevett not be able to give good and sufficient Security for the Mohogany, you'll please to dispose of it to the best advantage for Accompt of Mr. Cox, and if you should not be able to dispose of it so as to send per the Bearer, the Articles as per Agreement with Mr. Trevett, be pleased to send a Cargo of White pine Boards, and other Articles as you may be able to advance upon the esteemed Value of the Mohogany. you'll also see per the agreement that Mr. Trevett on giving you good and full security, but not without, has liberty to go to Boston if it is found it will be more advantageous than by selling the Mohogany at Newport.

the inclosed is an Order on Captain Thos. Tillinghast for £2.13.4 1/2 which be pleased to receive for my Account. Mr. Harry Cruger's Bill on Nathaniel Grant Esq. in your favour, I am to receive the Money for the 28 Current.

Your particular attention to the Mohogany will very sensibly oblige me, and for which be pleasd to satisfy yourself, and any favours shewn Captain Parkinson or my Friend will be esteemed as conferred on Your most Obedient Servant,

THOS. DOLBEARE

Fish 20/
Alewives 25/
Boards 100/

Staves — a glut.
Spe. Candles 3/1½.

FELIX O'HARA TO AARON LOPEZ

Gaspey, 29th May, 1773.

Sir,

YOUR much esteem'd favour per Capt. Earnshey, with the sundry articles wrote for, is come safe to hand, for which I return you thanks and shall take care to remitt you in due season. Your Memoir is familiarly written. I am sory it could not have been presented dureing the Parlements sitting. I hope I have in some measure remedy'd that disapointment, as I impartially represented the matter to Generall Carleton, in a Letter, bareing date 15 September last, which letter though voyd of both art and diction, I flatter myself will be found a true representation of the matter, which I make no doubt His Excellency will lay before the Lords of Trade, (we expect him out this Sumer). Give me leave to return you my gratefull thanks, for the favourable oppinion you are pleas'd to entertain of me. I must confess it is but little I have in my power, but even that little shall be vigorously asserted in favour of Equity, (for I shall not mention the word Liberty) for under that spacious name are commited the most horible Licentiousness, the makeing publick Fisheries, private property is so impolitick a Step, that nothing but partiality could oblige Government to adapt, which I am far from thinking is the case, if matters are properly represented. I have allready loss'd ground in the esteem of these engrossers. I would not wish to have a friend of their narrow dispositions. I am not sufficiently independent to oppose the current of opposition against me on this occasion. Neither so necessitous as to oblige me to act beneath the dignity of an honest man. I am, Sir, Your much oblig'd Humble Servant,

FELIX O'HARA

P. S. please send per Capt. Fry, or Mr. Greens vessel who comes to load fish, 2000 20 p'y Nails, 1000 6 p'y do.
Please to excuse haste, this being our Harvest day.

[Endorsed,] Per Capt. Fry.

STOCKER AND WHARTON TO CHRISTOPHER CHAMPLIN

Philadelphia, June 18th, 1773.

Sir,

WE have before us your favor of the 1st Instant by which we find the Bread per Captain Anthony was receiv'd in good order.

Herewith please to find Invoice and Bill of Lading for 150 Barrels Bread shipt per the Sloop *Peace & Plenty*,

Joseph Anthony, Master, on account of Robert Grant Esq. & Co. Contract, amounting to £188.15.1, which we have no doubt will give you satisfaction. there is not a Barrel of Mess Beef to be bought in the City, nor is it often brought here for sale.

At Lisbon, Vessels meet with much better dispatch than at Cadiz, as they are often times clear for sailing in twelve to sixteen days, and at Cadiz they are kept from four to six weeks, some times longer.

Your Vessel will stow two hights of Flour between Decks on their bildge, and it is that we usually put there, tho' we have put Wheat now and then between Decks in bulk; that is built up Rooms, the same way as we do when put in the Hold, and if the Decks are very tight the Vessel will carry it safe. Masters Wages out of this Port is from £7.10. to £8. this Currency per Month (we always allow the latter price to our Masters and a present of five or six Gallons Spirit a Voyage), besides the privilege of carrying 18 Barrels Flour Freight free; or the same bulk in any other Goods.

The usual Commission here for shiping Goods and drawing Bills for the reimbursment is 5 per ct. so that a Commission on a third or more of the Cargo of the Owners Property will clear him, in our Opinion, if any charge of procuring Freight. the expense of loading will lay on the Owner, tho that is not heavy in this Port, as we can get a Vessel that will carry 2000 Barrels of Flour loaded, that is the Goods taken of the Wharf (if Flour) for about £12, and stowed away by people accustomed to that business. We remain with Offers of our best Service, Sir, Your Very Humble Servants,

STOCKER AND WHARTON

Flour 17/9 to 18/
Bread 16/6 to 17/. it has fell 6d within a Day or two.
Molasses 20 1/2 to 21d.

Rum Continent 2/2
West India 3/2 to 3/3.
Exchange 65/ to 66½ per ct.

Benjamin Wright to Aaron Lopez.[1]

Montego Bay, the 19 June, 1773.

Dear Cousin,

I COULD not let this oppertunity slip without informing you I am yet above the surfice of the Earth *but* how long I may remain uppermost, I cannot say. I am now here after your money from Samuel Johnson. I have met with indiferent sucksess have received only forty pistoles and them verry bad money. Capt. Tennant tells me if he can posibly receive any more of that worthy Gentlemans cash he will gladly pay the remainder. I cannot with propriety make any greate dependence on receiving any more, as my tarrey here in this Island will not be long, [if] an Oppertunity should offer soon for the continant. I hope by this Capt. Shearman in the Brigantine *Charlotte* may be arrived. he left this Island the 23 ultimo with a fair wind and pleasant weather. the *Jacob*, Capt. Peters, saled the 11 inst. for London by him and Capt. Hervey I transmitted to Messrs. Hayley and Hopkins for your account upwards of twelve hundred pounds Stg. in bills of Exchange which hope will meet with due honour. I have transmitted the above mentioned per the *Jacob* abought six hundred pounds Stg. in produce which I sincearly wish to a good market. I cannot refer to any of my former letters, nither can I give you the exact Amount of the above mentioned bills and produce transmitted for your Account, as I am a great distance from my books, and pappers. you may depend I am not far from the Amount. I have some prospect of settling the bills of Exchange returned under protest by Henry Cruger to N. Grant of Kingston. I have paide greate attention to that matter as it has lane dormant for such a length of time. you cannot have the least conception of the trouble that attends my haveing these matters to settle in so many different ports which are so distant from each other. I really undertake them with satisfac-

---
[1] Original in the Newport Historical Society.

tion notwithstanding they are so ferteging. I wish you may not fret at the expences attending these Journies at this wet Season of the Year.

I now acquaint you I have inguaged a Commander for the Ship *Ann* and have come under writings to deliver her at Savana la Marr the dangers of the Seeas excepted. please to pardon my presumption in takeing so much consequence on me and dwo not intierly condem me before you hear my reasons for takeing such a step. My dear Cousin, the face of things have greately altered sence last year. I have had labour to compleet the *Jacobs* Load, after keeping her here two months longer then I did last year, and greately to my Mortification there is so many Vessels introduced into this Island lately that many of them have taken in Sugar into this Island lately that many of them have taken in Sugar at 3/9 per Ct. and many of them will not be able to get more then one half there load. this surpriseing alteration has raised my Apprehentions and I have thought it really necessary by some means or other to strengthen my Interest and fix matters in such a manner as to be ceartain of a load for our ship *Ann* and not leave that grand point to an uncertainty. to affect which I have given Capt. William Tomlinson the command of our new Ship knowing his Intrest to be good for four hundred hogsheads yearly. I am positive I can supply the remainder in good season to make her an early ship. as I am now speaking of Capt. Tomlinson I shall indeavour to give you his Charactor impartially as I am well acquainted with him and his famely from my first knowing this Island. Imprimus and first of all, he is a thurrough Seaman and one of a tollarable Address. he understands business verry well and a man of greate Oeconomy. he is a maried man, his wife is of Boston. he intends setling in Rhode Island. I flatter myself his Connections may be of service in puting of my American cargoe. I find the *planters* are well pleased at my giveing him a Ship. they asure me they will do every thing in their power to serve us. your pretended friend Abraham Lopez is pleased to say *it* was the most prudent step I could have taken to procure our ship a Load next year when there is every way so bad a prospect. I think I have sofficiently trespaced on your patience. I did not intend saying half so much when I set down to write. had nature been as kind to me as it has been to my Cousin I might have put all I have said into one half the lines I have made use of. we must not all expect to shine in life, therefore I am thankfull I can convey my meaning at any rate so as to be understood. my best respects to your vertious partner and famely in genneral. . . . I am, Dear Cousin, with Esteem your humble Servant,

BENJAMIN WRIGHT

[Endorsed,] Per the *Hampden*, Capt. Brown.

GEORGE SEARS TO AARON LOPEZ[1]

St. Johns, N'f'Land, July 8, 1773.

Sir,

WE arived at Trepassey in thirteen days there I sold about £480, wass detaind there 4 weeks by bad weather and head winds. from thence went to Fereland sold nothing, have been at this Harbour three days. I never saw such a Stagnation in Trade as here at present oweing to the Failours in England, the Merchants are much in want of goods but not willing to draw Bills yet, by reason they have a great Quantity of Fish on hand and great quantitys caught this year. the Markets low in every part of the Streights, which must make Fish very low here. I have purchased 800 Qtls fine large White Fish at 7/6. this Fish should Capt. Story arive would serve for part of his Cargo, or if the Brigg should not sell it will ballast her, for Rhode Island, except I shall be obligd to take more Fish, as there are but few I dare risque. there Bills and Fish will be very cheap. I have had this day an offer for the Brigg, but not likeing the man shall wait for another. by the Quantity of Fish here I think Freight must be high this season. no Oile to be bought at present, last sold £18 per Ton, Salt has been

[1] Original in the Newport Historical Society.

18/ per hhd. all this Spring, still worth 17/. Hope Capt. Story may arive soon. tis expected it will be high all the season. this is the first oppertunity I have had to write sence I came here. Should you receive this before Capt. buckley sails you may send 50 or 100 Boxes Tallow Candles they will be 10d or 12d in the Fall. 10 Boxes Spermacity Candles will sell for 2/. Mr. Bulley had about £2000 p[r]otested last year but still carrys on Trade as usual not quite so extensive. I am sorry to inform you Pork is fell to 60/ per bbl. Last year 95/. Bread and Flour I sold all at 18/ 'tis now a Drug not worth 14/.

Geo Sears

Molasses 1/3 — 10 hhd. sold
Rum 18d — 25 sold
Corn 3/   250 bush'l sold

Coffea 9d — dull
Other goods much as la[s]t year.

Coppy of the above by Capt. Crawford.

Bewickes, Timerman and Romero to Stocker and Wharton

Cadiz, 15 July, 1773.

Sir,

THIS will be delivered you (God willing) by Captain Thomas Foster, who intends for your Place. We are acquainted with said Commander these many Years, and always known him to support the Charecter of an honest industrious Man. he had the Misfortune some time ago to loose his Vessel at Moyodore, whereof he was Chiefly Owner, and has now fixt on going to America to seek for employment. We therefore take the Liberty to introduce him to your Favors, and if you can assist him yourselves, or recommend him to the Notice of any of your Neighbours we shall ever acknowledge the same, as a signal token of your Friendship, and on the like and all Occasions, shall endeavour to demonstrate our Gratitude, and make you all the return in our Power. Being very truely, Sirs, Your most Obedient humble Servants,

BEWICKES, TIMERMAN AND ROMERO

JOSHUA HART TO AARON LOPEZ

Charles Town, 26th July, 1773.

Dear Sir,

BY Captain Munro I with pleasur answar'd your much esteem'd favour, which I hope has come to hand and that it found you in company of Mrs. Lopez injoying perfect health. I have also remitted per said Munro the amount of the Cask of Anneseed water, that was shipped by your Brother Abraham.

I omitted in my last to acquaint my friend about the Rice. I am much indeted to him for his kind offer of executing any orders that I shuld have, as for shipping the Rice on my own account will no ways answar, for their is no article that I want at present that will answar in any way, which I am sorry for as I am convinced my worthy friend would spare no pains to serve me.

I would with pleasure have shipped the Rice on your own account by this Conveyance but did not know wether it would answar your Markets for its a very exhorbitent price at presant — 10/ per 100 lb. I dont know when it will be less, for we shall have a very bad Crop this Year, by Reason of the great drougth we have had. it has intirely burnt up the corn, and the Rice is not much better. its that maks our last years Rice so high. my friend will pleas to let me know if it will sute him to have it shiped on his own account as I will with pleasur comply with his orders, in any thing.

Sence my last to you I have had the pleasur of receiving the coppy of your kind favour, by the way of new york forward[ed] by Mr. Hendricks, which I soposed was by accident mislaid. I am thoroughly convinced that the Neglect was not my friends.

I shall be glad to render you or yours any Servis in my power. In the interim I am with my best wishes to your self and Spoues and every Branch of your family. Mrs. Hart and Hetty and family joines with me in wishing you and Mrs. Lopez and all your good family well over the Fast. I remain, Dear Sir, Your assured friend and most Humble Servant,
JOSHUA HART

my Respects in perticuler to your Brother Abraham and David family.

[Endorsed,] Per Captain Earl.

NATHANIEL RUSSELL TO CHRISTOPHER CHAMPLIN

Charlestown, So. Carolina, July 28th, 1773.

Sir,

I RECEIVED your favor by Captain Earl with a Negro fellow for Sale who I have sold for £325. Currency, three months Credit. I have been fully determin'd for some time past not to sell another Negro except they were enter'd here and Duty paid. I had rather loose the whole commissions I have made on selling Negroes than be detected in smugling one the Shipper would be no Looser by paying the Duty as the Negro could then be expos'd publickly and no person will give so much for them under those Circumstances, they being always liable to be seized for the Duty. I must beg you never to send me another except you intend to pay the Duty. I am with Respect, Sir, Your most Humble Servant,
NATHANIEL RUSSELL

[Endorsed,] Per Captain Earl.

STOCKER AND WHARTON TO CHRISTOPHER CHAMPLIN

Philadelphia, August 6th, 1773.

Sir,

WE have before us your favor of the 20th July per Capt. Anthony.

With regard to the price of Wheat when the new crop come to market in any plenty, which will not be until the middle or latter end of October, that is very uncertain; we are of opinion it will not be so low as 6/6; for tho' the last Crop is said to be a tollerable good one yet the Farmers having been used a long time to great prices the most of them are become wealthy, and therefore will keep back their supply unless they can obtain what they call a good price. add to this we dont think the crop either in Spain or Portugal has been so good as that of the last year: indeed the price will depend in a good measure on the Orders receiv'd early from those places. as to the purchase of Wheat before the arrival of the Ship that will depend on the quantity at market and the price some little time before she may be expected. but it is our opinion that Flour will answer from this Port full as well as Wheat, at lest we have generally found it so. We have corresponded with Mr. Horne's House tho we have not done any business together, and there are those we would prefer. It is very probable we shall have orders from some Houses that we have already done business with perhaps for a quarter or a third concern, and we should have no objection to ship a quarter and if not too inconvenient a third on our own accounts. those Houses that we have had any thing to do with have paid the Freight either in heavy half Joes or a Bill as we have orderd, the Master to receive it; and if the Cargo arrived to a tollerable brisk Market would return Bills for about half the amount perhaps two-thirds, the remainder as fast, they say, as they are in Cash. if it is orderd in heavy half Joes the advance comes the heavyer on them and therefore will make it the less, but if the amount is to be sent to London, unless they sell for Cash or very short Credit, they will not immediately advance much on the Cargo, for they generally give their own Bill either on their own Houses or their Banker, which soon becomes due, whereas if they are sent to America the time is so long before they get to hand they have a good chance of placing funds in London out of the Cargo to take up the Bills, and therefore in that case the advance comes very light. Exchange at present is high tho the sale is not very brisk — the last Bills 40 days obtain'd 67½ pr[emium] but in the fall of the year we do expect it will be down perhaps to 60 may be under.

We have reason to believe Flaxseed [1] will bear as good a price this year as it did last, for they have none of the old seed left on hand in Ireland; but there is no article comes to this Market so fluctuating as that and therefore there is no forming a Judgment of the price, for we have known a difference of 1/6 to 2/ per bushel in the course of two or three days. We beleive this article will answer here full as well as any other and the quantity cannot be too large and we think it will pay the Ship a good freight. it is thought our Crop of seed will fall short of the last year, so that it may probably be worth your attending to.

Flour lately took a start from 18/3 to 19/6 occasiond partly by some imprudent people purchasing, and the Mills wanting water, and now as the Country is busy are afraid it will be very little lower until the new comes to Market. We remain with respect, Sir, Your Very Humble Servants

STOCKER AND WHARTON

---

[1] "At an early period of his [Hugh Orr, 1717-1798] residence in Bridgewater, observing that our farmers had not been in the habit of preserving their flax seed for market, he endeavored to inculcate among them the expediency of preserving and preparing that article for exportation. The suggestion, however, instead of being favorably received, excited in many instances considerable animosity. Having imbibed the chimerical idea that seed exported to Europe would enable them to cultivate flax to an extent that might eventually prove subversive of our own cultivation; some, even of those who were allied to him by the ties of friendship, actually destroyed their flax seed, lest it should fall into his hands. But impressed with its importance, and resolving to accomplish the interesting object, he became himself the purchaser; and having constructed a curious and useful machine, of which he was the original inventor, for the purpose of cleaning the flax seed, and having accumulated a large quantity, conveyed it to Boston, whence he exported it to Scotland, and received a profitable return. Thus he became the first exporter of flax seed from the county of Plymouth, if not from New England, and to the exertions of this gentleman are we indebted for the introduction of that valuable article of commerce, which had not before been considered worth preservation." 1 *Mass. Hist. Collections*, IX. 266. In 1758 the trade in this commodity to Ireland had grown to such proportion that an intention of laying an embargo on it produced a protest from Ireland. Sparks MSS., v. I. 34.

Peleg Greene to Aaron Lopez

Barbados, August the 11th, 1773.

Gentlemen,

I IMBRACE this present oppert to acquaint you of my safe arrival after a teages Pasage of thurty eight days and to add to our trouble find Markets very bad indeed by Reason of so many Vessell arriving before us and still keep comeing in. we have not discharged any of our Cargo yet but shall begin this day to land the boards which I beleave is sold. but the Shad Mr. Hart is going to put in a Store he has hired to retail out, which I am afraid will not due as the weather is so hot here they may be apt to hurt. but if the Pickle does not leake out and the fish keep good he may git rather more for them I beleave: as for our Herrings I fear has leekd all the Pickle out. we have got at two barril and them with no Pickle in. but how the rest will turn out I cannot tell. it is no wonder that the Pickle is out for puting so many board on the deck it has racked hir all to peases. for when we come to open the Hatches the fish and Lumber looked if it had been rafted all the way which caused the hoops to fly and let the Pickle out. but am in hopes there is not many of them so. if you remember that was one perticuler thing I desired, not to put board on deck. for I was very sensible the bad consequence wood attend it. for I am very sensible it prolong[ed] our Pasage five or six days for when it blow anything of a Breese to carry hir deck under water which a small breese wood due we could hardly keep hir free and many times oblidge to brig due, which if the boards had been of deck could have made very fine weather of it. I am afraid the friaght of them boards will not pay the damage of the Cargo but I can not tell how bad it will be before we brake up the hole which I should have done long ago had I had the conduckting of it for if the Pickle is out of them as it is more likely to be out of them to the bottom of the hole then them two we got out first they will be growing worse and worse every day. but am in hopes they will turn out better then I expect. have nothing at present to acquant you of shall conclude with steady attention for your interest and useing all means that lays in my Power to assist the Gentlemen to whom I am addressed to to dispatch the Sloop, tho my young Master Samuel dont care to take any of my advise. if he had our Cargo would been sold long ago and for as much as he will git for it now. for eight or ten Sail of Vessell arrived sence we did with Lumber. Am, Gentlemen, your Humble and yours to serve,

PELEG GREENE

HAYLEY AND HOPKINS TO CHRISTOPHER CHAMPLIN

London, 14th August, 1773.

Sir,

SINCE our last of which the foregoing is Copy we have received your favour of the 18 June with the following Bills —

Alexander Brymer on Robert Grant & Co. . . £150.–
John Lawson . . on Commissioners of Victualling 16. 5.–
Jno. Stevens . . . do 8. 8–
James Bates . . . do 12.10.–

All which in due course shall be placed to your Credit.

Inclosed you will find Invoices and Bill of Lading for the Goods shiped for your Account in the *Tristram*, Captain Shand, amounting to Mark £1688.3.6
LR 650.–.6
On which together we have made £2400 Insurance, premio, etc., being £60.10.6. We hope they will arrive with you in good Season and prove to your Satisfaction. The India Company are just shiping a large Quantity of Tea for America upon their own Account, for which reason the Merchants here have unanimously agreed not to execute any orders for that article this Fall, as when the Companys Quantity arrives, Tea must be cheaper in America than in England, and you'll be able to supply yourself

cheaper than we can ship it. what you order of that article is therefore ommited, which we hope you'll approve. The small additional Order for Goods received by Sheldon did not come to hand in time to permit there being procured for this Vessell; but you may depend upon having them by the next Opportunity and are, etc.,

HAYLEY AND HOPKINS

(Copy) Original per Shand.

NATHAN MILLER TO CHRISTOPHER CHAMPLIN

[Warren,] Munday morning, the 16 August, 1773.

Sir,

THE tide was small on Satterday I dare not lanch the Ship. But they are rissen so much that they will now answer. I shall lanch tomorrow morning if I here nothing more from you. it will be high Warter at seven oclock and ten minnits and if you send me any thing about it pray if you limmit me at a time only say that you will be at the Expence of geting her a floate if she stops at the end of her ways. I dont want you should take any Resque or Trouble on you if it is a suteable time, but it will be unreasonable for you to ask me to lanch in a bad Tide, and if the Vessel stops to git her off at my own Expence. You must send 140 lb. of Ocom. Do let it be good. from Your Very Humble Servant,

NATHAN MILLER

STOCKER AND WHARTON TO CHRISTOPHER CHAMPLIN

Philadelphia, September 13th, 1773.

Sir,

BY Captain Anthony, who arrived yesterday we are favord with yours of the 3d Inst. by which we find your new Ship is launched, but detain'd up the River by contrary Winds.

We have this Minute receiv'd a letter from our good Friends Messrs. Bewickes, Timerman & Romero of Cadiz, a Copy of which we inclose for your perusal; if you think

Capt. Foster who those Gentlemen recommend will answer your purpose for a Commander for your Ship, we beleive he will thankfully accept of her. he seems a middle aged Man has no family, and we believe our Friends would not recommend him if they did not know him to be worthy of it. if you think of accepting of him he can go in Capt. Anthony, if he should be here on receipt of your Letter; or he can go to New-York, etc., by the Stage. your answer by return of the Post to this will be satisfactory.

We apprehend the Ship will carry the quantity of sixteen or seventeen hundred barrels of Flour; if we can't readily procure Freight for her it is very probable we may interest one of our Lisbon Friends one third in the Cargoe, ourselves a third and you a third. We dont expect Flour will come very plenty to Market until November. it will then, perhaps, be as cheap as any time this year, but before that a Cargoe may be procured if you think it will be of any Advantage to your Scheme to have the Vessel to return early, so that this of dispatching her early from Rhode Island lays with yourself. probably it may be worth attention, as you want a full Load of Salt, to send her to St. Ubes,[1] from Lisbon, for it. this should be left to the discretion of the House she is addressed to.

The Freight the Ship makes will no doubt be immediately remitted to London. the Salt will be shipt on Account the Cargoe, and the remainder forwarded as fast as they are in Cash, and some Houses will some times advance a part. We remain With much respect, Sir, Your Very Humble Servants,

STOCKER AND WHARTON

P. S. the Ship should be provided with a Mediterranean pass. we believe they can be had here, if you have not got them.

Flour 18/6 to 19/ Scarce at present; Continent Rum 2/2; Molasses 20*d*.

---

[1] Better known as Setubal, on a bay of the same name, in Portugal.

Cullen Pollok to Aaron Lopez

Edenton, Sep. 20th, 1773.

Dear Sir,

YOUR most obliging favour of July 30th I received some time past, and acknowledge my self much obliged to you for the letters from Mr. Marchant. he also mentions two Chaises charged in one year. if there are two chaises charged in the whole account it is a double charge, for George Pollok never had but one. I remember it very well, it is in this Town now; but Mr. Scollay must prove his Account somehow; it is very difficult you know to prove a negative   it is impossible for me to prove Mr. G. P. never had two chaises, and it would be for Mr. G. P. if he was alive. it lyes with them to prove he had. I am much obliged to you for the trouble you have been at to procure me a Carpenter, but I have given over all thoughts of building and I shall not want them. as soon as the grass seed can be procured I shall be very glad of them.

I intend next spring to save 1000 barrells of herrings, if you think it would sute you I will engage you that quantity at fifteen shillings our money per Barrell to be delivered by the middle of May,   if not I must trouble you to send me two Vessels that will carry 500 Barrells each, to be here by the first of May to sail from here to Jameca. I should be glad one of the Captains was a Person I could consign the whole to. . . .

Be assured, Sir, that I am Yours Most Sincerely,

CULLEN POLLOK

Thomas Dolbeare to Aaron Lopez

Kingston, Jamaica, 2d October, 1773.

Dear Sir,

YOUR kind Letters of the 24th June and 10th August, are now in my Hand, the Contents of which add so greatly to the obligations I am already under, that quite at a loss how to attempt an acknowledgment in which I am sensible my best endeavours must fall far short of what the occasion requires: I can only say, that I am fully sensible how greatly I am obliged, and how little able to return so many favours, which will always remain firmly fixed in my remembrance.

The Sloop *Hero*, Captain Forrester, arrived here the 21 Ult. in 38 days. when I read the conduct of the Trevetts I lamented that I ever thought of troubling my good Friend with so bad Men. I did something suspect them, but could not think they were so egregiously wicked. I hope ever to retain a lively sense of what a deal of trouble you have had in this matter. I *think* I may say, you will never have any more from my quarter. I could have wished you had taken the Mohogany on their non-compliance, and sent a Load of Common Boards, for I really did not think upon your puting yourself to the advance of £527 or I never would have sent her that way. I shall get the money of Mr. Cox and transmit Hayley and Hopkins as soon as possible. Mr. Cox says he wishes you had sold the Mohogany for the most it would fetch, and let him know his loss at once. I don't think it adviseable ever to ship Hard-pine Boards to this Island, for they won't fetch more than White pine, and cost nearly 100 per Ct. more. my respects to Mrs. Lopez and the Family, tho' unknown, and believe that I am, with the most perfect sincerity Your greatly Obliged and most Obedient Servant,

THOS. DOLBEARE

THOMAS DOLBEARE TO RIVERA AND LOPEZ

Kingston, Jamaica, October 8, 1773.

Gentlemen,

I HAVE before me your Friendly and obliging Letters per Forrester and Campbell under 24th June and 10th August, the contents of which lays me under the most sensible obligations, and I hope in some future day to evince the sincerity of them. Yesterday the Brig *Ann*, Capt. Einglish, arrived from the African Coast with 104 Gold Coast Slaves in pretty good Order, after being a long while expected. The conditions Capt. Wright will acquaint you I fully objected to when proposed, but Mr. Winn concluded after a considerable time, that it was better to take her up at 4.8.12 than to leave it in the discretion of the Captain as he might think himself at too great a Liberty and I wrote Captain Wright accordingly on the 3d Ult. Mr. Winn departed this transitory Life at 29 Years of age, after a short illness. I have therefore, Gentlemen, to secure your interest Messrs. Peatts & Westmorland Merchants here to indorse my Bills, who are good and approved, of which Gentlemen you may enquire of Messrs. Malbones. the day of sale is 13th inst. and rest assured Gentlemen there will be nothing [wanting] on my part to make the Voyage successfull. We have authentic enteligence of a Contract being made between the Kings of Great Britain and Spain whereby it is settled that the Spaniards are to be supplied with Negroes, at Kingston in the Island of Jamaica for Cuba and the Main at £60 per head, to be continued for 5 years, that they are allowed 3 bbl. flour to every Negro, that the duty of 30/ Currency to be taken off and 2/6 only to be paid on importation, when it is to commence and other particulars is not yet transpired. the planters here are much disgusted. Capt. Einglish would have benefited materialy if he had arrived in August as I expected. be pleased to excuse haste. I shall write per the next opportunity more full. our Markets for America produce low. I have only to add that I am, Gentlemen, Your most Obedient Servant,

T. DOLBEARE

[Endorsed,] Per Capt. Forrester.

JOHN O. KELLY TO CHRISTOPHER CHAMPLIN

Warren, October the 20th, 1773.

Sir,

SINCE I have seen you, I bought 20 Casks of flaxseed, which I am to pay for this week, or else it will be sold to

Providence people, whom plauges me about getting away what they can from me, as I am confident they will give 7 shillings per bushel for it, before Newport men will have it, as they are collecting for Newyork. You told me you would give me but 1 Dollar a Bushel for Seed deliver'd in Newport, and freight, which is a thing I cant get it for.[1] all to about 10 Casks I have in my own Store, which belongs to you. in regard of the Ballence due on Book Accountt and my order of forty Dollars in feavor of Kinnicutt, but however, if you doant think Ile run away to Ireland, or else I ant worth 100 Dollars, send them to me, by Capt. Shearman, with a Box of Glass six by eight which I shall discount the whole with you as soon as I can get my flaxseed together, etc., etc. I doant think I shall draw one Copper more on you, until you have Vallue received of the above Sums mentioned. Sir, I am [with] due Respect Your most humble Servant,

JOHN O. KELLY

N. B. Doant stress your self as I know perhaps, you will be very loath to trust an Irish man with the above; if you think you cant conveniently do it, without hard thoughts.

THOMAS DOLBEARE TO LOPEZ AND RIVERA

Kingston, Jamaica, 22d October, 1773.

Gentlemen,

MY last was under the 8th Current per Captain Forrester, acquainting you with the arrival of the Brigantine *Ann*, Captain Einglish from Annamaboe; this will acquaint you with the sale of her Cargo. 57 were sold the first day averaging £63 and 4d 1/2, clear of duty, 14 the third day

---

[1] "The seed Cant be purchasd Deliverd at the Harbour under 5/ or 6 shillings per Bushel, as there never was so much Salt giveing for Seed as they give this Year, two Bushels and half and 3 giveing for one of Seed. Nither could the Seed be Collected in 14 Days as they wont Thrash the Seed in general until they want the Salt to salt their winter's provision." *Asa Champlin to Christopher Champlin*, September 17, 1773.

at £51, 22 the fifth day at £32, the remainder at £8 only. had there been five times as many, and the Negroes good, they would have sold at the price they did the first day. there were a number of old men, but the Boys went off very high. I find there are 14 Privelege Slaves which I think is large, and will take from the Cargo considerably. I shall conform to the terms accepted, tho' the decease of Mr. Winn and the uncertainty of the goodness of the Negroes laid me under some disadvantage. I have acted from principle, Gentlemen, in the sale of this Cargo, and I hope it will be satisfactory, my intent has been that it should. I am now at Port Royal dispatching a Vessell, that I am much in haste, but hope in a few days to be at leisure, when I shall write you.

We have this day accounts confirming the Negro Contract with the King of Spain, but we find the 27/6 is not to be taken off.

I have only to add, Gentlemen, that I have a full sense of the obligations under which you have laid me and that no future day shall erase the remembrance of them, being with the most perfect sincerity, Your very Obedient Servant,

THOS. DOLBEARE

[Endorsed], Per Capt. Leech, via Hispan'a.

WILLIAMS AND COMPANY TO CHRISTOPHER CHAMPLIN

Philadelphia, November 1st, 1773.

Sir,

THIS for your Information, that our Market at Baltimore unexpectedly keeps up, tho' still under this from 5 at 10 per Ct. Seede time is now over and a great deal of flour, etc., may be expected down. The Crops are good in general which believe will lower them. Our last letters from Europe particularly from England and Barcelona, give accounts of the heigh Markets, some Cargoes of American Wheat has sold in London from 60 to 65/ per Quarter, that is 8 Bushels winchester measure; as heigh in Barcelona. It has not exceeded 50/ in Lisbon and per the last accounts from there that Market was much in the Wane. I woud always prefer Shipping to an Eastern Market in the Spring of the Year, for if there is any Scarcity it is from May till July before there own Crops comes in. Shou'd you think of furnishing us with Rum, Molasses, etc., for a spring cargo, the sooner it is in hand the better chance it will have for being sold well. 20 to 40 or 50 hhds. of Molasses may easily be rund of at the heighest price, as may 20 or 40 hhds. of your Rum and a few hhds of good Sugars. Lofe Sugar is now in demand. Bad Muscovado Sugars will never sell. Shou'd you not choose to load her wholly, there is not the least doubt but we can get 1/3 or 1/2 ship'd on freight. We are, Sir, Your Very Humble Obedient Servants,

THOS. CH. WILLIAMS AND CO.

At Baltimore

Flour	17/6	Corn	2/9 to 2/10
Wheat	6/9 to 6/10	Exchange	67½ at 70 per Ct.

My Compliments to Messrs. Fowler & Gibb: Wou'd have wrote them per this oppertunity but the Vessel sails. Communicate what part of this to them you may think will be of service.

[Endorsed,] Per Capt. Antony.

STOCKER & WHARTON TO CHRISTOPHER CHAMPLIN

Philadelphia, November 4, 1773.

Sir,

THE within we wrote in expectation of its being in time for Capt. Anthony. We find that Flaxseed is pretty plenty in this part of the Country and those that have taken it in within twenty or thirty Miles of the City having given a Dollar to Eight Shillings. there is no article that comes to this market so fluctuating as is Flaxseed and therefore it is impossible to know the proper time to sell. We have had two of the principal Seed buyers with us for the preference when it comes but we dont purpose making a very precipitate Sale. We are of the Opinion it will be best to dispose of it, say for the highest Price given this Season with this reservation not to be under something certain, if we can get any good hands to make such Agreement with us but we doubt if they will. We are with Respect, Sir, Your very humble Servants,

STOCKER AND WHARTON

HENRY DAVENANT TO AARON LOPEZ

St. Johns, November the 6th, 1773.

Sir,

THIS will inform you of my safe arrival at St. Johns, after a Passage of Twenty one days, and without any accident except the los of Six Sheep; they being over crouded in the Arnings; the Snow is unladen, and most of our cargo of Fish, etc., on board, and do expect to saile for Rhode Island the 20th of this Inst. the Snow is a fine stif Vessel, and sails verry fast; and has been much admierd hear. I expect to have fifty, or sixty Passengers, between Decks at 40/. Sterling per Man; have got thirty at this present time, which has pay'd their Passage to me. I should have been hear ten days before I was had it not been for some heavy gales of wind. I am, Sir, Your most Obliged Humble Servant,

HENRY DAVENANT

P. S. if you had sent Molasses, instead of Sheep, twould have answerd much better for your Intrest. it is now 2/6 per Gal. and Rum 2/3.

[Endorsed,] Per favour Capt. Tileston, the Scooner *Polly*, via Boston.

STOCKER AND WHARTON TO CHRISTOPHER CHAMPLIN

Philadelphia, November 20, 1773.

THE present serves to advise that since that of the 16th the Pilot Boat (out of which a Pilot went into your Ship) is come to up to Town, the person that is in her says they met with the Ship the 11th Inst. considerably to the Southward of our Capes, and that he was four days after he left the Ship before he got in, and as she does not yet make here appearance he apprehands the spurt of Southerly Wind that bro't him from the Capes to Town did not bring her so far as the Capes. The wind for many days has been at N. W. and now it is at N. E., and both unfavorable for her. The next Market Day after we heard she had a Pilot on board we engaged with our Millers for 1000 barrels of Flour at 18/6 in order to have what we could depend on and in clean casks, as well as to give the Ship dispatch and get her out of the way of others we daily look for. Flaxseed sells in small parcels at 9 to 9/6, tho no great quantity has yet come to town nor has the Spirit of buying yet caught fast hold of the Purchasers. We think the price will advance but not as high as 12/. We remain with much respect, Sir, Your Very Humble Servants,

STOCKER AND WHARTON

P. S. Since the above we hear the Ship was seen within fifteen or twenty Miles of this and is expected up the next Tide.

THOMAS DOLBEARE TO RIVERA AND LOPEZ

Kingston, Jamaica, November 20, 1773.

Gentlemen,

SINCE my last, I have yours covering a Letter to Captain Einglish, who I purpose dispatching for Mole Cape Nicola with the £800. about the 13th of next Month, as I told him when the Cargo was deliver'd me. I find the £800. on Cargo, with the nearly £800 privelidge, the Captains Coast Commissions, and the Duty of 30/ per head there will be £1900. at least, to pay Captain Einglish in Money. I think there are generous Priveliges allowed out of your port. the gross Sale of the 102 Negroes per the *Ann*, is £5187. this Currency; out of which the 14 Privelige are to be taken. Negroes continue in demand, the Spaniards are now here on purchase, one of them bro't 100.000 Dollars, but they appear to expect them at low rates, for they as yett, have offered but £38. Sterling, to have the first choice, which will never do, for if I recollect right, the *Ann's* Cargo averaged the first day with the Duty £45.15/ Sterling. it appears by what I have been able to collect, that England and Spain's Monarchs have adjusted and concluded the Contract for a certain number of years; what number we have not yet understood. they are to send their ships to what of the English West Indies they may chuse, and not to be limited to this Island as was reported, that they can give from 270 to 290 Dollars per head, but about £25 Currency per head. they will be obliged to pay their Priests for Baptising. they purchase them to sell per feet and inches, so many feet and inches making a piece, as they term it; how many, I have not yet learnt. they have 3 Barrells flour to every Negroe which will be a great cover to large quantitys of Contraband Goods. the Factury at Port Rico is to be thrown up. the Spanish King has lent the Company £60 m Dollars on certain conditions. this is all I have yet been able to gather. as new matter arises I shall be informing you. prime Negroe Men £64 and Duty Women £62 and duty. I remain, with the most perfect respect, Gentlemen, Your most Oblig'd Obedient Servant,

T. DOLBEARE

£3687.--		74	Negroes of Brig. *Ann*
72.	for 8 refuge at £9.	28	do. of Ship *Cleopatra*
£3759.	Brig. *Ann's* gross Sale	102	
1428.	Ship *Cleopatra's* do. one refuge of £9 included	14	Privelige deducting
		88	Negros of the two Cargoes.
£5187.	the Gross Amount.		

WILLIAM BARRON TO CHRISTOPHER CHAMPLIN

Philadelphia, November the 22, 1773.

Sir,

I THOUGHT proper to acquant you of my safe arvial after a long Pasag of fifteen days the Tusday after I left Newport I had a verry hard gail of Wind from North to N. N. E. with much rain but the ship maid extreem good weather and on the Thursday fowling got the Poilet on board then the wind shifted to the Northward and blowing verry hard brought the ship under hur courses and she being light was put to the Southward as far as the Lattude of 37.44 North. Notwithstanding we barred the courses as long as we could and sence I have got into the River the Wind still continud to the North which has been the case of our not geting up the River sooner. I have delivrd the Letters to Mr. Wharton he has not had time to mention aney thing to me about the Voige but he will right to you by the Post to morrow. I have just know seen a Capt. of a snow from Lisbone one of my acquantes out Nine Weaks which informs me salt is cheaper at Lisbone than at S. Urbes, and likewise informs me the Markits is verry dul and he tells me that their is nothing to be don in the freight way except to Iarland and that with salt. but I have not had much time to talk with him as yet. But shall be better able to acquant myself soon and shall acquant you by the next and evry oppertunity. the ship[1] dont sail so will close to the wind as I expected but she sails verry well from the wind and stars extreem well she maid sumthing more water at sea then when I left Newport, and I think it will be proper to try the seams when the Cargo is out which will be tomorrow their is James and the frenchman is good for nothing except to hall and pull they cant stear I am in hops I shall leave this verry soon and Sir you may depend on my making all the Dispatch that is in my Power. and Remain Sir your most humble Servent,

WILLIAM BARRON

STOCKER AND WHARTON TO CHRISTOPHER CHAMPLIN

Philadelphia, November 23d, 1773.

Sir,

WE are favord with yours of the 2d and 6th Inst. by your Ship *Peggy*, Captain Barron, who got to this Town Saturday

---
[1] The *Peggy*.

Night, and this morning was entered in the Custom House and is now discharging. We as yet have not had an offer for the Seed, but we told one of the Buyers that he might have it giving us the highest price it sold for this Season; he is to give us his Answer by tomorrow Noon. We find another purchaser has refused to take a hundred Hhds. from a Neighbour of ours on them terms. rather than sell at the price going now which is about 9/3 we will put it in Store a few days, tho it seems to be the Opinion of many people that it will not be higher this year.

The Ship, we mentiond in a preceding Letter we purposed to address to Messrs. Parr, Bulkeley & Co. of Lisbon, a well established and good House, and who we have great reason to think will render you Satisfaction in the execution of your business.

The Cargoe will be shipt on a joynt account of those Gentlemen you and our selves, each one third, so if any primage to be abated for your part (which is only reasonable) it can be charged in the Captains Account at Lisbon, because the whole no doubt will be included in the Sale. We remain With respect, Sir, Your Very Humble Servants,

STOCKER AND WHARTON

STOCKER AND WHARTON TO CHRISTOPHER CHAMPLIN

Philadelphia, November 26, 1773.

Sir,

SINCE ours of the 23d Inst. we have received yours of the 16th Inst. and observe what you say respecting Seed. We have great reason to believe that there is not two thirds the Orders this year for that article as there was the last, and many of them are limited at a lower price than is now going.

There is generally from ten to twelve thousand hhds shipt from hence yearly, so that what comes from your Port cannot affect the price much. We have tryd several of the principal buyers and the highest offer we have had is three pounds ten shillings per hhd including the Cask, not one of them can we get to take it upon the terms of allowing us the highest price this Season. it is not customary to do it, tho we believe it has been done by a House to one or two particular people, and from all we can gather we have reason to think that person is tired of that method. from several we have had an offer of the medium price, but we would rather take what is going at present than accept of that. the purchasers seem to understand each other this year better than we ever knew, for they seem all to speak the same Language, and to know the conversation that passed between us and either of them. it has sometimes happend that the price is higher at the last of the season than any other time, but it is by no means a certainty, and is often then the lowest, for in bad weather the seller is as willing to get clear of it as the purchaser is to receive it, lest it should remain on hand until the next Season.

The price we have been offerd say £3.10 per hhd leaves £136.10.—. for Freight besides paying the Insurance, upon a supposition that the Cost of 48/6 your Currency (Dollars at 6/.) included the Cask, and this to have in her way is a pritty clever setting of. Our Calls for Money at this Season are considerable and not a barrel of Flour or any other produce can be purchased without; yet as you seem to be of opinion the price will be high we will keep it a few days longer, tho' we must confess it is our opinion it will not exceed if it gets so high as 10/ per bushel. £3.10 including the Cask which here sells for 4/. is not quite 9/6. Captain Whitman we find has been offerd 9/3 but he stands out for a better price.

The Ship made a begining yesterday and if the weather continues favorable we hope to dispatch her the last of next week. the firm of the House at Lisbon is Parr, Bulkley & Co. We purpose to ship the ten barrels of Flour by order of Mr. Brymer, per the first that will carry them. We remain with respect, Sir, Your Very Humble Servants

STOCKER AND WHARTON

Post Office Account

New York, November 29th 1773.

At Ten Days sight pay to Messrs. Beekman Son and Goold Three Hundred and Thirty one Dollars and one Quarter or Current Money equal to that in your Province for Value rec'd and place it to Acct. of Money remitted in part of the Sum due from you to the Gen'l Post Office without farther advice from your humble Servant 331¼ Dollars.

John Foxcroft

To Thomas Vernon Esqr. Post master at New Port.

331¼ Doll. is	£99.7.6
½ Mo. Interest	— 5.
due	£99.12.6

[On the reverse of sheet:]

Newport, December 6th, 1773.

Accept to pay the Contents

Thos. Vernon

Newport, January 25, 1774.

Rec'd the Amount of this Draft with the Interest to this Date in Behalf of Nicholas Brown & Co.

Per Geo: Benson

Nathaniel Russell to Christopher Champlin

Charlestown, 1st December, 1773.

Sir,

You have herewith Account Sales of your Negro sent me by Earl, Nett Proceeds £296.15. which I would have sent you by this opportunity but cannot possibly get it chang'd into hard money. Bills of Exchange has been so very scarce that all the Dollars and Heavy Gold has been sent to Great Britain for Remittance. if you can draw on me or order it in produce, if that will not suit you, I will desire Capt. Durfee to pay it you when he is in Cash on my Account. I am with Respect Your most Humble Servant,

NATH'L RUSSELL

Sales of a Negro man received per the *Nancy*, Capt. Earl, on Account of Mr. Christopher Champlin of Newport.

1773.	August 1. By Wm. Johnson for 1 Negro man	£325.0.--

Charges.

1773.	To Cash paid his passage	£12.—	
	To my Commission 5 per Ct.	16. 5	
	Nett proceeds to your Acct. Currt.	296.15	
			325.--

Errors Excepted.

NATH'L RUSSELL.

[Endorsed,] Per Capt. Munro.

THOMAS DOLBEARE TO RIVERA AND LOPEZ

Kingston, Jamaica, 7 December, 1773.

Gentlemen,

HERE with you have the Account Sales of Brigantine *Ann's* Cargoe with the 29 of the Ship *Cleopatra's* Disbursments, etc. as I could not determine the proportion of Disbursements due from the Ship *Cleopatra* I have carried the whole to the Debit of the Brig *Ann;* leaving the proportion to be settled by you. when I wrote you via Hispañola, my meaning of the Negroes averaging £63 the first Sale, clear of Duty, was, clear of the Sale Duty of 20/ the Import Duty of 10/ per head youll find debitted in the Account of Sales. the inclosed is Captain Einglish's Receipt for the £800, and the Bills of Exchange for £1983.5.11 Sterling or £2776.12.4 Currency. your directions to me were to send Spanish Doubleloons of 13½ dwts and Johannes to the Mole, but, a few days since, receiving a letter from Mr. John Dupuy of Mole Cape Nichola that no Money but Johannes and Dollars would answer, there being Difficulty in passing Doubleloons, I concluded on sending Dollars, as 2½ Currency was to be gained, Dollars passing here at 6/8 and there at 11 Bitts or 6/10, which noncomplyence I hope youll not construe to an inatention to your Interest, but a disposition towards it.

The restriction under which you laid me with respect to the Security and which I cant but think any more than a prudent Act, obliged me to gett Messrs. Peatts & Westmoreland of the place to draw the Bills giving them half the advantage, which they did on the Condition of this Cargo of Negroes being carried on under the Firme of T. D. & Co. which is the reason of the Accounts being under that Signature. Negroes continue at £64 and Duty for Men, Women at £62 and Duty of 20/. two Ships have arrived this week with 700 Negroes from Annamaboe. endeavours on my part have been that this Voyage should be successfull. how far I have been an Instrument towards it doubtless youll form a Judgement. I can only say that if my hearty good Wishes wou'd have avail'd I think they were not wanting. I shall allways esteem myself with the truest Sincerity, Gentlemen, Your most Obliged Obedient Servant,

T. DOLBEARE

P. S. this day two Months the Brig arrived in the Harbour.

[Endorsed], Per the Brig *Ann* Capt. Wm. Einglish. Q. D. C.

THOMAS DOLBEARE TO AARON LOPEZ

Kingston, Jamaica, 9th December, 1773.

My good Sir,

PER this conveyance I have wrote you in Copartnership with Mr. Rivera. your letter to Mr. Cox I delivered, and he appears amazed at the Trevetts atrocious conduct, indeed I have often lamented my troubling you with so trifling affair, and as it has turned out, with such scandalous Fellows. The prodigious trouble you have had really pains me. however to make amends in some degree, I must desire, that in whatever commands you may lay me under in future, you'll never think you are troubling me. about six weeks since I remited between two and three hundred pound Currency to Messrs. Hayley and Hopkins. Mr. Cox having been very ill prevented his giving me the Bills for the remainder. he is now recovered and promises them per the sailing of the first Vessell that sails for England. the Man you bo't the Alewives of must have deceived you, for there were not 10 bbs. of good in the whole, and as I bo't them I have sufferd by them, tho' I took em at 20/. they were not above half full and they were mostly decayed. Markets here very low, best Fish 12/6, Alewives 17/6, Sper. Candles 3/1½, Carolina Staves £7 and £8, and all the outports gluted. at Savanna la Mer, common Boards are at £7, and scarce. I remain, Dear Sir,

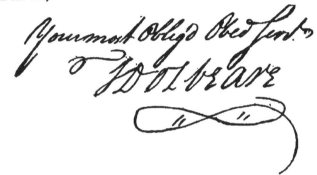

[Endorsed,] Per Kent, via Boston.

WILLIAM BARRON TO CHRISTOPHER CHAMPLIN[1]

Philadelphia, December the 10th, 1773.

Sir,

I RECEIVED your letter by Capt. Anthoney and am verry sorry to hear the ship has cosst so much money more than you expected. I am allmost loaded and shall sail in 2 days and you may rely on my making all the despatch that is in my power and shall do all that is in my power to

[1] Copy supplied by Mr. John H. Storer.

employ the ship in the parting way for as long a time as
you shall think proper. If I think it for your interest and
by what I have learnt from Capt. Bulkley, a brother of Mr.
Bulkley in Lisbone that there is freight to be got from
Ireland. My frenchman is run away and has taken several
jackets and shoes from the people, likewise a pr. of silver
buckles from the boy, and five dollars from the black boy,
notwithstanding all the men on board in their cabins. I
did all my endeavour to catch him again but could not.
If he should come that way and you can take him I hope you
can punish him according to the law, he was not worth
his vittles on board the ship. I have been detained sumwat
longer than I expected on account of the flower was on the
[1] I have been informed by Mr. Morton which I make no
doubt but he has alreddy informed you by the post. I
should have wrote by the post but Capt. Whitman is going
so soon and I thought it would save the postage. I shall
observe your instructions in every degree and shall do nothing
without first counselling with Mess [1] It will make
little ods with me how long the ship is out if I can get good
employment for him, only on my family's account, and if
I should stay longer from home than I expected when I
left it and they should want anything I hop that you'l
please to let them have it. My mate is well, and the people
and likewise myself, and hoping that this will find you in
the same good health as when I left you and remain, sir,
your most humble sevt.

WILLIAM BARRON

STOCKER AND WHARTON TO CHRISTOPHER CHAMPLIN

Philadelphia, December 10, 1773.

Sir,

WE wrote you under date the 4th Inst. at which time
we had little doubt of procuring Flour for the *Peggy* so as
to dispatch her by this time, but we find ourselves greatly

---

[1] Illegible.

mistaken.   for we never knew more difficulty in geting that article then there has been for a fortnight past.

What we bought lately we were obliged to give 19/ for and still want about 200 barrels to fill the Ship. we offerd 19/ for some this day but we understand some other buyer has given three pence more for it. We bought about 60 barrels of Burr Midlings, which is esteemd by our Bakers quite equal to common Flour, at 16/ per bl., and we do expect will sell at Lisbon for a better profit than the Flour. we got it a bargain as it generally sells within a triffle as much. If we can come across 50 or 60 barrels more as cheap we will purchase them.

We have the Flaxseed still by us as 9/6 or 9/7 is the highest we have been offerd, and it is now rather slack as considerable quantitys are in Town for sale, and the purchasers seem determined not to raise the price. we had thought of selling it this week but will keep it a few days longer to give you a chance of doing better. it will however be a mortification to be obliged to take less than we could have had some time since. Captain Anthony has deliverd his seed to Mr. Carson as usual but the price is not fixt. he will no doubt settle it with him before he leaves this. We remain with respect, Sir, Your Very Humble Servants
STOCKER AND WHARTON

[Endorsed,] Per Cap. Whitman.

STOCKER AND WHARTON TO CHRISTOPHER CHAMPLIN

Philadelphia, December 17th, 1773.
Sir,

WE wrote you the 10th December Inst. by Capt. Whitman and are since without any of your favors. We have it now in our power to inform you that your Ship *Peggy* left the Wharf the 15th Inst. and Capt. Barron went away in the Pilot Boat the night following being obliged to wait for two Hands. He has been very unfortunate with his people, one, a French Man run away several days since and stole from the people several of their Cloths and some Cash, and two others, the best Hands he had, eloped the day before the Ship left the Wharf (their Names John Perry and John Douglass) and are in debt to the Ship £5.18.1 this Currency. We must confess these people leaving the Ship is not more than we expected and what we told Capt. Barron we were afraid would happen, for we have had many instances of their runing away because our Wages is generally much higher than out of any other Port, and the Captain took all the pains man could do to keep them, but to no purpose. he was obliged to ship three Hands in the room of those that are gone and his Vessel is now but pooly manned with Seamen, tho People enough. Herewith please to receive Invoice of the Cargo shipt on board the *Peggy*, William Barron, Master, for Lisbon, one third on your account, one third on account Messrs. Parr, Bulkley & Co. and the other one third on our account, amounting to £3280.5.3, one third of which we have charged to you. The Cooperage is higher than on any Cargo we ever ship'd, as it was mostly what we call back Millers Flour, and turning in and out of Store and roling a considerable distance, and the Casks not being very strong (tho the Flour fresh and good), that the expence of Cooperage was much encreased. Also please herewith to receive the Ships Disbursments amounting to £62.3.2 which we likewise charged to your account. We wish we could inform you of our having disposed of the Flaxseed and are sorry to say that you[r] sanguine expectations of the price we are afraid will opperate against you. Seed has been sold with a few days as low as 8/6 some parcels of very good at 9/ and there is a great deal in the Town unsold. We offerd yours at 70/ per hhd including the Cask, which is the price we were once offer'd but cannot get it at present, nor do we think we ever shall. We are realy sorry we did not take the Price, which we think was high, when we had it in our power. It will be wrong now to force the sale and therefore shall wait a few days rather than sell it under 70/ notwithstanding we realy want the Money as we are providing Cargoes of Flour for two Vessels we hourly look for.

We remain with much Regard, Sir, Your very humble Servants,

       STOCKER AND WHARTON

P. S. Through mistake we delay'd sending the 10 bbls Flour by Capt. Anthony. he will however lend you as many and we will send them by Capt. Greenold.

HAYLEY AND HOPKINS TO CHRISTOPHER CHAMPLIN

[London,] 20 December, 1773.

Sir,

THE above is copy of our last, since which we have received your favour of the 9th September, enclosing a bill for £445.5.6 drawn by Robert Scarlett on Wm. Raynolds which is noted for Non Acceptance, and we dare say will be protested when due; of which you may depend due care shall be taken. We are, Sir, Your very humble Servants,

       HAYLEY AND HOPKINS

Since we wrote the foregoing we have received your favour of the 25th October enclosing a bill of Stevenson and Wents for £146.13.5, which is accepted and when paid shall be placed to your credit. Your large bill of those Gentlemen's which is noted for Non Acceptance they tell us will also be paid when due which is on the 3d of March next. We have agreable to your directions made the following Insurances, the Accounts of which you will find herewith.

> £1000 on the Sloop *Adventure* and Cargo from Rhode Island to the Coast of Africa and America, premio, etc., being £78.15.6.
> £1600 on the Ship *Peggy*, Rhode Island to Philadelphia, and her discharging ports in Spain Portugal or Italy, premio, etc., being £72.10.6.

We hope they will both make you successful Voyages.

The order you enclose us for Goods shall be putt in hand immediately and all possible dispatch given to it so as to have the whole ready for the first Spring Ship. We are sorry to see Shand was not arrived, it is very unlucky for such of our friends as have Goods on board him. We hope shortly to hear of him and are as before

H. & H.

Dr. Mr. Christopher Champlin for the following Insurance. On 11/16th of Sloop *Adventure*, Robert Champlin, Master, and Cargo, at and from Rhode Island to the Coast of Africa, during her Stay and Trade there, and from thence to her port or ports of discharge in British America.

£300 Vessell
700 Cargo.

£1000 Insured	at 7 Guineas per Ct.	£73.10.—
	Policy	5. 6
	Commission	5.—.—
		£78.15. 6

On the *Peggy*, Barron, at and from Rhode Island to Philadelphia, and at and from thence to her port or ports of discharge in Spain, Portugal or Italy, to return 9/6 per Ct. if she discharges without the Streights.

£1000 Vessell valued
600 Cargo

£1600 Insured	at 4 per Ct.	£ 64.—.—
	Policy	—.10. 6
	Commission	8.—.—
		£72.10. 6

[Endorsed,] Per Capt. Gorham via Boston.

STOCKER AND WHARTON TO CHRISTOPHER CHAMPLIN

Philadelphia, December 30th, 1773.

Sir,

WE are sorry to inform you that we have your seed still by us and are realy at a loss to know what to do with it; that article is now selling at 8/4 to 8/6 and the buyers seem very confident it will not be higher. it gives us real pain we did not sell it when we were offerd a price that would have left you a handsome profit; it distresses us to think of taking the price going and shall therefore hold out a little longer, unless we can obtain 9/ or upwards for it, altho' the Money at present would be of great Service to us. Our Navigation is now interrupted by the Ice so that there is little expectation of any more seed coming to Market this Season, but the quantity already shipt and to be shipt from hence will exceed the quantity exported last year, near 2000 hhds. it is expected; so that you were wrong in counting upon a Short Crop as that is not the Case, by which we are afraid you will suffer considerably. we will do all we can however to make the loss as light as possible, for if we can get a higher price by trusting it a little time we will dispose of it on these terms, tho it is not, as we said before, very convenient to us.

The Ship *Peggy* left our Capes the 19th Inst. with fair Wind and she is stiffer the Pilot says by much than Capt. Barron expected. We advised his keeping at lest half his Ballast in, which no doubt has been of use. the Captain did not write to us but the Pilot says she sails pretty well. We have no late Accounts from Lisbon but we are of Opinion her Cargoe will pay a Freight and leave some profit to the concernd.[1]

We have shipt per Captain Grinnell ten barrels Flour by order of Mr. Brymer. the Vessel we believe is gone down and the Captain purposes to follow her by Land this Day.

We hope soon to hear from you in the mean time, and always, we remain with much respect, Sir, Your Very Humble Servants,

STOCKER AND WHARTON

P. S. Captain Grinnell went without signing the Bills and by that means the Inv. was left. it is here inclosed.

STOCKER AND WHARTON TO CHRISTOPHER CHAMPLIN

Philadelphia, January 18th, 1774.

Sir,

WE wrote to you the 15th Inst. since then we have had some conversation with the Owners of a Vessel in the Flaxseed way respecting yours, which if we would agree to Ship,

---

[1] The *Peggy's* cargo consisted of 70 bbls. middlings, 1358 bbls. flour, 605/4 bbls. and 52 half bbls. She reached Lisbon January 24, 1774.

they would send the Vessel to any port we inclined. this however we told them we could not undertake to do without your Orders. they at last offerd us 8/9 per bushel for it with the liberty if you chose it of our shiping it on your account, if not they would oblige themselves to take it and pay us that price, and as no vessel has gone from hence to Dublin they agree to go to that port tho' a bad place for a Vessel to lay.

We offerd it at 9/ and on those terms, but whether they will agree to it or not we dont know. a friend of ours that had a consignment of 350 hhds. from N. York has orders from the Owner to ship it, but they can only get room in the Vessels now loading for 200, and it is in hopes the Owners of this Vessel we are speaking of procuring the remainder of that quantity on freight, with a small parcel or two beside, that induces them to make the proposal to us. We have thoughts of leting it go even at 8/9, lest when you give orders to ship it we may not get a Vessel to carry it, especially to Dublin; at which port we could put it into a safe and good hand, Mr. Rowland Norris, and we think there is a chance of that being a better Market than any other. According to the present appearance we think it advisable to let it go on the above terms at 8/9; provided the Gentlemen continue in the mind, and we hope it may meet with your approbation; it will be absolutely necessary that you let us know what you determine upon, whether you risk it or not, by the first post, and if you do we advise your having it insured as the Dublin Harbour is rather dangerous. The Post is not in but momently lookt for. if we determine with these Gentlemen respecting the Seed before the Post goes out, we will mention it. We remain with respect, Sir, Your Very Humble Servants,

STOCKER AND WHARTON

Since the above we have seen the Owners of the Vessel and had a further conversation respecting the Seed and are afraid they mean to decline purchasing, as they have been spoken to by a person that is desirous to ship 300 hhds. to know if they will take them in; and his plan is for the Vessel first to go to the Harbour of Loughsweily[1] and to proceed to Dublin or to any other port in the Kingdom where there is the chance of the highest market. at Loughsweily the Vessel is intended to be addressed to Mr. Redman Conyngham of the House of Conyngham and Nisbitt of this city, and of equal credit to any on the Continent. We dont know for certain whether this is fixt upon but have some reason to believe it is. We are realy afraid there will be no other Vessel puting up for freight, at least there appears some danger of it, and therefore we think it advisable to ship it on your Account, unless we can make the conditional agreement as mentiond in the preceeding.

STOCKER AND WHARTON TO CHRISTOPHER CHAMPLIN

Philadelphia, January 22d, 1774.

Sir,

WE wrote to you 18th Inst. and advised we were in treaty with a House here for your Flaxseed since when we have agreed with them for it at the price of 8/9 per bushel unless you choose to ship it your self, and we have it at our option to do either any time before the Vessel sails, which if the Weather is favorable she may depart in about a fortnight; we therefore hope to have your answer before that time otherwise we shall be much distressed to know how to determine agreeable to your mind, but our own judgment will lead us to ship it rather than take the above price. . . .

STOCKER AND WHARTON

PARR, BULKELEY AND CO. TO CHRISTOPHER CHAMPLIN

Lisbon, the 25th January, 1774.

Sir,

WE have the pleasure of owning receipt of your most esteemd favor of the 2d and 25th November, handed us last Night by Capt. Wm. Barron of your Ship *Peggy*, who

---

[1] Lough Swilly in Donegal.

has on board 1424 blls. and 52 half Blls. flour, with 70 Blls. of Burr Midlings in thirds, with your good self, and our mutual friends Messrs. Stocker and Wharton the Shippers at Philadelphia, the whole amounting to £3280.5.3. in the disposal of said Cargo be assur'd on our activity, and utmost deligence and altho' sales of Flour is at present dull at 3$800 per Qu[intal], yet we are inclined to think it will be brisker soon.

The Philadelphia Gentlemen write that our supplys will be short this year by some thousand of Barrels. Respecting the Net Proceeds of your third of this Speculation, we observe you would have it remitted together with the freight Mony to your friends Hayley and Hopkins of London, deducting there from Amount of Ships Port Charges and the Cost of about Six thousand Bushels of Salt. The Five hundred Pounds you ask for, to be first remitted, will be forwarded before your Ship sails from hence, and of which per first Packet we intend advising your said London friends. As soon as the Sales is closed, and a final remittance made to Messrs. Hayley and Hopkins, we will hand you your Account Current. Respecting our being again concern'd in the *Peggy's* Cargo, we have wrote Messrs. S[tocker] and W[harton] that we shall have no objection; but that a quarter part, would be more agreable, as we are pretty largely engag'd throughout the Continent, and with none more than this proportion. Lisbon and a market for the Chance of Speculating, is the Plan that we have laid down to all our friends, and they have found their Accounts by it, having at times made noble hits. It is very true that here are abuses in the Measure of Salt, our Shippers from long experience, does as much justice as any of them. this Article is very cheap say 1$700 per Moy[1] and is under the St. Ubes price. It does not answer so small a Ship as yours to go round there to load on account of the high Charges in taking out the ballast, etc., which let serve for your government.

---

[1] A measure only used for salt, and of uncertain quantity; but in this case meant from 16½ to 18 bushels. See p. 487, *infra*.

Captain Barron we observe is allowed the customary Primage, which you did well to mention. Whilst the *Peggy* is unloading, we will be at work in looking out for a freight for her, and should we find employment for her, that will be for your Interest will acquaint Captain Barron thereof, and consult with him, in every respect towards the promoting your Interest. We coud get the *Peggy* full for London, but that is an expensive Port and an uncertainty of Employ afterwards. Be assurd on our best endeavours for your Interest flattering ourselves to give entire satisfaction and refering to our next remain truely, Sir, Your Obedient humble Servants,

PARR BULKELEY AND Co.

Flour,	3800	Corn,	220
Wheat,	460	Exchange,	66¾

[Endorsed,] Per Capt. Harper, Via Philadelphia.

Rec'd under cover and forwarded by S. Y. V. H.

STOCKER & WHARTON.

PARR, BULKELEY AND Co. TO CHRISTOPHER CHAMPLIN

Lisbon, 5th February, 1774.

Sir,

WE last paid you our respects of 25th Ulto. per Casson and Harper advising the safe arrival of your Ship *Peggy*, Captain Barron, which and the further contents we here by confirm. This per Captain Gensell serves to advise you that we have wrote to your friends Messrs. Hayley and Hopkins, acquainting them that before the *Peggy* sails from hence we should wait on them with a remittance of £500 Stg. on Account of your third concern in the Cargo and the freight money, and that for the remainder of the proceeds of your effects we should forward to them good bills as expeditiously as we became in Cash. We have the pleasure to advise you that have given the *Peggy* a freight to Falmouth and Baltimore in Maryland, and back to Lisbon, (and if required to proceed to Cadiz,) and which we expect will make out to her One hundred pounds Stg. per Month, or thereabouts. we engage for the quickest dispatch at every place; the Ship carries about as much Wine and fruit to Falmouth and Baltimore as will ballast her, for which has £100 Stg., and is to bring a full loading of Flour at 5/ Stg. per barrell. Captain Barron thinks she will exceed 1600 Blls. if carefully stowed, and the freighters are to pay half Port Charges. It is a freight that we wou'd accept of for our own Ships, and no doubt you will approve thereof. when the Ship returns we will exert ourselves in the sale, with a proviso, you do not in the sequel contradict it. By the 20th of this Month we are expecting the Ship *Pitt*, Captain Cheesman, from Marseilles, which is chartered to go round to Falmouth and Philadelphia for the sake of the Flour Freight. she carry's 1700 Blls. flour, and went a Trip for us last Spring and which performed in 4½ Months with ease. Your Ship has more and purely to make it come up to your limits that you might be satisfied. here was no freights stirring except to Hambro or the Western Islands, which there is no touching in the Winter Season. When the Ship returns we may be able to get her a freight. please favor us with your Commands in this respect and remain assuredly, Sir, Your most humble Servants,

PARR, BULKELEY AND Co.

Flour	3$800 per Qu. slow table	Corn	220 per Alquier
Wheat	460 per Alquier	Exchange	66½d per $

P. S. One days work will discharge the *Peggy*, and we expect to get her away in 8 or 10 days. they are briskly at work in boxing the Lemons nothing else delays her.

STOCKER AND WHARTON TO CHRISTOPHER CHAMPLIN

Philadelphia, February 9th, 1774.

Sir,

WE have before us your favor of the 26th February and hope in a few days after you wrote that letter ours of the

18th January got to hand. had the Seed been our own we would most undoubtedly have sold it when we were offerd 70/ a Cask for it including hhds.; but if you will please to look over your letters to us on the subject you will find they convey to us the most sanguine expectations of the price being 12/ per bushel, and advised our keeping it some time. the offer we had was soon after it came here, and when we refused that which your letters will justify, we had it not in our power to obtain near the same price after, and when we mention'd that we should keep it but a few days longer, we undoubtedly meant to sell it and made an offer of it; but we found a glut of it had then come to market and the buyers were blowing upon it and talked of 8/ to 8/3—and indeed some at 7/6—and after refusing about 9/5 the thoughts of accepting of 8/3 or thereabouts was grating enough, especially was we were in hopes of geting at least that at any time, and laying out of the Money was an inconveniency to none but ourselves, induced us to try a little longer in hopes something better would turn up. respecting our confering with Capt. Anthony we believe he could have mentioned to you that we did; but he put his Seed into the hands of Mr. Carson as usual, who we believe did not allow him the highest price that should be given the Season, but the price then going, which we believe was a good deal under 10/.

We endeavord very hard to agree with some of the purchasers to allow us the highest price that it should be sold at, and not under the price then going, but they rejected the proposal with some warmth.

Save that we refused accepting Conyngham and Nesbits first offer of 70/ per hhd., we have acted as we would have done most certainly as if it had been our own, and we beg you to think our conduct has been very disinterested in this affair, for we had nothing in view but to serve you otherwise we should have acted a very different part. And it gives us great pain to find you so uneasy and embarrassed in this matter, as we see no great occasion for it, because we have not hinted, or at least did not intend to hint, an uneasiness at our being in advance for the Ships cargoe more than the Money would be useful, having made some engagements in the way of our trade, which Sum would have assisted us in fulfilling with more ease. Our letters of the 18 and 22, January will inform you that we had agreed with Bayard, Jackson and Co., Owners of the Snow *Dickinson* to ship the Seed in that Vessel, or they to give the price of 8/9 per bushel if you had rather sell than ship it. Our Navigation is still interrupted by the Ice, as it has been upwards of four weeks, and likely to continue eight or ten days longer. The Snow *Dickinson* wants to be hove down, the Owners are now about it tho at considerable expence, so as that she may be headed as soon as the navigation is clear, and will proceed to Letterkenny in the Harbour of Loughswely, to address of Mr. Redmond Conyngham, who will have the liberty to send her to any port, if the market is more inviting.

We continue of the same opinion still that it is better to ship it than sell it at 8/9, and in order to give you a double chance it shall go on our joynt accounts, as shall your third of the Cargoe by your Ship to Lisbon; and the proceeds of the Seed we shall order into the hands of our friends Messrs. Mildred and Roberts of London, and when the Sales of both Flour and Seed is finished we can settle the profit, should any happen to either, or the loss, if the adventures should prove unfortunate; by this step your Account with us will be so near a ballance that the difference can't make you *very uneasy*, nor shall we, as this affair has turned out, think much of our advance; tho' the Money will be much longer going from Ireland than that upon the footing it was put, will be from Lisbon. at any rate we dont purpose to sell the Seed at 8/9, and therefore if the plan we have laid down is not agreeable to you, and you would rather take all the Seed, or all the Flour, or the whole of both, we are content; only fix the matter by return of the Post. We shall get the whole Amount of the Flaxseed insured, and please to let us know if there is any done on the Flour. if you should conclude to take a half of each we will settle our

Books in that way as soon as we have what quantity of seed there is at 8/9 per bushel. We would observe that many of the hhds. dont hold seven bushels, several being short of what they are markt.

There is no obtaining Money upon the Seed here from the friends of any House we may consign it to, nor should we like to accept of it, if there was no other reason than being confind to discharge it with their Friend, which we must do on them terms, and suppose the Gentlemen here gives us liberty to draw on their friends in London in a month or six weeks after the vessel sails, that might be a means of making a precipitate sale to place funds out of the Seed in London to take up the Bill, so that upon the whole it is better to suffer some inconvenience here on account of the advance than not give it every chance of a market.

The last Accounts from Lisbon was the 11th November then Flour was selling at 3$500 per Quintal which would scarcely pay a freight, but as there has not so much gone from hence as usual we are in hopes some little profit will be left to the adventurers. We remain With respect, Sir, Your Very Humble Servants,

STOCKER AND WHARTON

PARR, BULKELEY AND CO. TO CHRISTOPHER CHAMPLIN

Lisbon, the 14th February, 1774.

Sir,

HAVING this moment learnt of Captain Cornell at St. Ubes bound to your Port we embrace this oppertunity to acquaint you that the last of the Lemons are going on board the *Peggy*, and that we expect to get her away on Thursday next. We are certain she will have the quickest dispatch at Falmouth, the same at Baltimore, having wrote our friends as pressingly as if the Ship was our own, so that there is a great chance of the Voyage being compleated within the 5 Months. Every thing bids fair for it. Captain Cornell we understand has made a very poor hand for some time with his Snow. What do you think when the Ship returns from Baltimore (and no sale here for her, nor a good freight) of her proceeding from hence to Falmouth and Boston on Joint Account with Wine, Oil, and Lemons, and again here with Flour from Philadelphia in thirds with Messrs. Stocker and Wharton. Your sentiments hereon will oblige us. Flour we are selling at 3$800 per Qu. it is a good price, and altho it goes off slowly are in hopes not to have a Barrell of yours left when the *Peggy* returns. by the first Packet we intend remitting your London friends the £500 Stg., and nothing else occuring at present for your Interruption, remain most respectfully, Sir, Your obedient humble Servants

PARR, BULKELEY AND CO.

STOCKER AND WHARTON TO CHRISTOPHER CHAMPLIN

Philadelphia, February 17th, 1774.

Sir,

OUR last was under date the 9th Inst. in which we wrote you pretty fully respecting the Seed, determining to ship it rather than sell at 8/9, and yesterday your favor came to hand dated the 8th Inst. We observe you had rather ship it than sell at 8/9 and therefore we are well pleased we reserved the choice. The Vessel will be full in two or three days and be ready to depart as soon as our navigation is open. What we mentiond in our last letter we here confirm, that your third of the *Peggy's* Flour and this Seed we will take a half concern in, or we will take the whole of either which you please; and as we shall order the proceeds of the Seed into the hands of our friends Messrs. Mildred and Roberts of London, we can, when this is done, settle the affair between ourselves without its interfering with the plan you are upon with the *Peggy*. with respect to our drawing Bills, upon the presumption of a remittance being made to London out of the proceeds, is a step we would not choose to take, lest an accident might happen and our

Bills be returned with 20 per Ct. damages, for there is no knowing where the Vessel will discharge; and if the Market should be dull the seed will probably sell upon a Credit of three to six months; this is the information we have receivd for we never shipt any on our own accounts. we are likewise informed that for two or three years last past it averaged about 60/ per hhd., save the latter part of last season, when some sold for £4.10 to £5. owing to two or three people having a good deal by them and bought up all they could lay their hands upon, and by that means raised the price. The Commission in Ireland we are told is 2½ per Ct. and the Charges about 12d per hhd., freight to Ireland 12/ per hhd., Insurance 2½ per Ct., and a half per Ct. for effecting it; the same Commission as on Flour or any other Goods, and porterage 6d. tho' on this we shall charge no Commission upon the plan we have proposed, to make the matter as easy to you as possible. We would rather pay Interest ourselves than receive it, our situation in business requiring all the Moneys we can collect, as our connections are pretty extensive; therefore the Interest of Money to people in trade is but a small consideration; yet as this affair of the Seed has turned out contrary to your expectations, and tho' we paid the Cash instantly for the *Peggy's* Cargoe, we dont intend to make a Charge of the Interest, and by the Scheme we have proposed of your taking a half of the Flour and Seed, or if you please, the whole of either, will give you a chance more — and our candid opinion is you had better take a half of each, for then you have two chances.

We have not the least intelligence from Lisbon since we wrote you, so that we are much at a loss to know what is doing there. We sent a Brig of our own with a Load of Wheat that left the Capes of Virginia about the 1st of October, she was not arrived the 11th November, but as that market was not so good as some up the Straits, the Gentlemen she was address[ed] to had partly concluded to send her to Barcelona: as we have heard nothing of her it is more than probable that is the case. We mentiond that the Casks did not contain as much as they were markt, at lest a great many of them, especially those markt WD; for they loose on an avarage one peck a Cask or rather more, and of this there can be no doubt, as the Flaxseed Works where it was sent to be cleand, at that time or since, had no other to mix with it that could cause any mistake; and the greatest part was measured before it was put into the Mill, for as they found them run short they were induced to try many more Casks than is customary to do, and one of our Clerks saw several Casks tryd; and we understand by those in that way, that from experience they have found the Seed from New England and Rhoad Island to run short.

We now enclose Sale of the Seed and instead of 8/9 we have carried it out at 9/ which we have no doubt will be satisfactory to you, and our inducement to do this is because we take a part ourselves or if you choose it, as we have before observed, we will take the whole, or the whole of the Flour; for tho the first Cost of both is too high to expect any great profit, yet we hope either will be attended with some little, and we are at a loss to know which to give the preference to. Net Proceeds thereof being £1065.19.6. is to your Credit.

Since writing the above we find the Seed is all shipt, say per the Snow *Dickinson*, [blank] Johnson, Master, and inclosed is Invoice for the same on our joynt account (supposing you acquiesce to the proposal) amount being £1145.6.7, — and as you determine we can make the Entries hereafter. You will find there was 23 Casks condemnd, we will endeavor to sell them for something and what they sell for your account shall be credited the same. All Seed before shipping is sent to some of the Mills to be cleand, for which 2/6 per hhd is paid, and a deduction of 2½ per Ct. for wastage in cleaning. When the Bills of Lading are signed we purpose to send you one, and we intend to write to London for Insurance. We remain with respect, Sir, Your Very Humble Servants,

STOCKER AND WHARTON

STOCKER AND WHARTON TO CHRISTOPHER CHAMPLIN

Philadelphia, March 12th, 1774.

Sir,

We have before us your favors of the 1st and 5th Inst. confirming the proposal we made of your taking a half concern in the Seed and our holding the same part in your one third of the *Peggy's* Cargoe of Flour, and with you wish the former adventure may prove more fortunate at the market it is going to than it did at this, and it is our opinion it will; for now the Vessels are all saild the quantity shipt from New York, this place, and Maryland is ascertaind, and falls short of what went the last year between one and two thousand hhds: so that we find those that are adventurers in that article have good hopes of its leaving a profit. We are not well enough acquainted with the Trade to Ireland to give you the information you request, but we will make enquiry and let you know hereafter. from what we have understood the price of Seed there is as fluctuating and the profits as precarious as on any article shipt from the Continent, and the greatest part of what goes from hence is on account the people the other side the Water. It has given us a good deal of pain that the Seed fell so short and we have no doubt of your being imposed upon. there was not a Cask of Seed in the Works but yours and the Proprietor of them is a very careful honest Man.

Inclosed please receive a Letter from Messrs. Parr, Bulkley and Co. of Lisbon which came inclosed to us a few minutes after the last Post went out. You will be informed by it of the arrival of your Ship *Peggy*. Mess. Parr, Bulkley and Co. mention the nominal price of Flour to be 3$800 and hopes, with having a little patience, to obtain it. if they do that adventure will leave some profit. they mention they would soon make your Friends in London the remittance you requested and give Capt. Barron their best advice and assistance. Salt was very low selling at 1$700r per Moy which contains from 16½ to 18 bushels.

We observe you had orderd £600 Stg. Insurance on your third the Cargoe per the *Peggy;* the same sum we requested to be made on the Seed, so that no notice need be taken of that in our Accounts, at least the difference can't be much as we do suppose the premium will be the same on both. We remain with respect, Sir, Your Very Humble Servants,
STOCKER AND WHARTON

HAYLEY AND HOPKINS TO AARON LOPEZ

[London,] 6 April, 1774.

Sir,

THE preceding Copy of our last we confirm; since which Captain Allen is arrived from Dunkirk and proposes returning to Newport in Captain Hall. We have paid him £126. 18.11 on the Brig's account, for which you will find his receipt enclosed, and he has delivered us a bill for £95.17.10 for proceeds of his freight to Dunkirk, which is accepted and when paid will be placed to your credit. We hope it will not be long before we have the pleasure of acquainting you with the Sale of his Vessel; He will inform you of the bad state of her Sails and Cables. we hope nevertheless she will not lay long on hand. We have not a Line yet from Captain Buckley.

We have now to acknowledge Receipt of your favours of the 1st and 10th February, and agreeable to your instructions therein we have made the following Insurances, —

£1000 additional on *the Ship Nancy*, Capt. Wright, to Jamaica and London, for 3/4 cost of which we debit you as per Account . . . . £48.15.—
£1400 on the *Deborah*, Davenant, for which we debit you . £35. 5. 6
£ 700 on the *Jacob*, Peters, to Barbadoes and back, for half of which we debit you £15.17. 9

the Accounts of all which you will find enclosed, and sincerely wish them all successful Voyages, particularly we hope you will not be disapointed in your view of the *Jacob's* Voyage. The bill you remitt us for £35 drawn by Captain Wright on ourselves shall when due be placed to your credit. We wish our application to the friends of Mr. Veratt had been more effectual; if your bills had been the only ones in the same situation we think they would have paid them, but they assure us there are several more in the same state and positively they are determined not to pay any of them. The Insurance on the *Neptune* was, as you observe, made in the name of James Burke; but no prejudice can in such cases ever arise, provision is made in all our policies for a change of Master and nothing is necessary in case of accident but a proof of its being the same Vessell on which the Insurance was made. We are much obliged to you for the trouble you have taken in explaining the conduct of your Factors last year which we own had hurt us, but what you now say has removed all difficulty from our minds on that head. May better success attend your future endeavours and guard you from so many unlucky accidents as you experienced last year. The letter you enclosed us for Messrs. Mayne and Co. was forwarded immediately upon our receiving it. We are very respectfully, Sir, Your most Humble Servants,

HAYLEY AND HOPKINS

[Endorsed,] Per Capt. Hall, via Boston.

PELEG GREENE TO AARON LOPEZ

Ocracock, April the 6th, 1774.

Dear Sir,

THIS my second is to acquant you that I have been laying at Ocracock from the twenty first of March with varable winds and weather with continual Gales of wind and so large a sea that no Pilot would carry me over the barr, and on the second of April I issued forth. a Gale of wind from the ENE with squals of wind and rain at 4 am it backned to the NbE and still continued to blow harder and hard then parted my small Cable and found the Gale still increase at day light saw several vessells drove on the barr where there Vessells and Cargo must be intirely lost, if not there life, and finding myself driving directly on the bar for my last bower Cable would not bring hir up, and for the benefit of your Interest and our Life I thought proper to cut the other Cable, run hir on the Point of Ocracock, which was the last place we could save our selfs and accordingly did and thanks be to God save our vessell and Cargo and our Lives which had we drove on the bar must unavoidable been lost. we have met with no other damage but lost our boat we got the vessell off with only takeing the Lumber of Deck. at Meridian the Gale moderated. this day I expect to have all the Lumber on board again, and then shall make the best of my way to Savanna La[Mar] there was fourteen sail of vessells drove on shore, and five of which will be entirely lost, and one drove over the South breakers and gone to see and every soul perished. am, Sir, your Humble Servant and yours to serve,

PELEG GREENE

[Endorsed,] Per favorer Captain Rodman.

CHRISTOPHER CHAMPLIN TO PARR, BUCKELEY AND CO.

Newport, Rhode Island, April 16th, 1774.

Gentlemen,

I AM now to acknowledge your esteemed favours of 25th Jany. 5th and 14th Feby. noticeing the arival of my Ship *Peggy*, your Intention of remitting my Friends at London £500 Stg: by first Packet, and the remainder of my 1/3 of said ships Cargo as fast as your in Cash, all which is agreeable and I doubt not of your punctuallity in this matter. I fell into this Business in some measure to facillitate my remittance to London, as my annual call that way is upwards £5000, which I yearly import. If the Freighting to Lisbon, etc., proves inviting, I shall increase my Concern by building a ship to stow 2000 Barrels. Your contracting for a small Freight to Baltimore and another from thence to Lisbon is much more agreeable than to have returned with Salt, as the quantity lately imported from your quarter has lowered the price with us; and if her passages are short and no delays in the ports some profit will arise. I suppose you mean by the Freighters paying half the Port charges, to include as well as the Custom House Clearing and Entering, half the Piloteage, anchorage, unladeing and relading, the different freight goods, Powder money, etc., that may accrue at any or all the ports she may truck at 'till her final discharge at Lisbon or Cadiz, the duties and customs if any — on the Freight Goods is a material charge on them, of course — as is likewise the primage customary paid the Master at Lisbon, which Messrs. Stocker and Wharton inform'd me was about 1 or 1¼ per ct. on the vallue of the Freights, to be charged to the Freight goods, except my 1/3 of the *Peggy's* cargo, which the Master by agreement was not to take on my part of her Cargo, nor upon any other Goods shiped on my account during his voyage, that suppose the ships Freight to be £300, and the primage 1 per ct. his due would be £3, the two thirds of which would be his due provided I was interested 1/3 of said Freight Goods; but if not concerned the whole woud be his due, chargeable to the Proprietors of the Goods on Freight. this is what I meant by the Captains being intituled to customary Primage. with regard to your proposal of being jointly concerned in cargo to Boston of Wine, Fruit, etc., for the reasons before noted of my falling into this business to raise a remittance for London, it woud not suit me. my present request is this when the ship arives at Lisbon to sell her, if the price I have limitted my Captain to take can be obtained in a few days, the amount to be remitted to Hayley and Hopkins of London with dispatch. If this cannot be done, then load her with salt for my account, with the utmost dispatch, and let her sail for Newfoundland, where I have ordered Capt. Barron to lodge his Cargo in the hands of Mr. George Sears of St. Johns, and from thence come direct to Newport. the least I expect will be 1/6 Stg. per bush. English Measure, which will make a Freight of near £200 for the Ship, for which good bills may be had on London at 40 Days sight, and the ship will be with me to refit at a much less Expence than at any other place, when I will send her to Philadelphia if you will hold 1/3 of Flour, and she shall perform the same voyage over again during the next year. If you chose to be jointly concerned in the Salt to Newfoundland, I have no objection, as your moiety of the neat Proceeds can be remitted in Bills direct to London from thence. This plan I woud have pursued if nothing better can be done. If you or your Friends coud give her a Freight to Boston, equal to £150, I shoud chuse it before the salt voyage, as she woud be the sooner here to refit for the Philadelphia voyage, in which if you exert yourself may accomplish. If the ship shoud go to Cadiz the Freight of course increases. 7/ Stg. is now given for those Markets out of Maryland and Virginia as per advice this Post, and at New York 6/ Stg. for their small Barrels to the France Market — such is the demand for ships this Spring. Youll take care the Freight moneys be remitted to my Friends in London with all dispatch, and that she has the utmost Dispatch at Cadiz, as delays at that port often happen. should this be the case it will make her return here late, and destroy the Philadelphia voyage. you'll give me the earliest notice if you will hold 1/3 from Philadelphia on a new voyage as also Stocker and Wharton that I may conduct accordingly. Freights to and from the Western Ilands I am afraid of on account of the great Risk of the ship laying at those Islands. therefore as I have laid open to you what I think most conducive to my Interest, I shall still leave the Captain at liberty to undertake any other plan that may appear more for my interest with your advice, which may present at his arival with you, doubting not of your acting for the best, in full Confidence of which I am, with much esteem, Gentlemen, Your most obedient humble Servant

C[HRISTOPHER] C[HAMPLIN]

CULLEN POLLOK TO AARON LOPEZ

Dear Sir,   Edenton, April 25, 1774.

Captain Riply informed me some time past, that a Captain of yours had brought [a] Jack Ass[1] from the St[ra]its

---

[1] Spanish Jacks were much esteemed. Washington received some from Spain as a royal gift.

to Rhode Island. I shall take it as a particular favour if you will purchase him for me by all means. I am in hopes he was brought chiefly for me. If you remember when I was at Rhode Island the first time I was one day saying that wanted to purchase one, you said you either had a Vessel going up the Straits soon or had one there then, and that you would give the Captain particular instructions to try to get one.

I am afraid it will be very late in June before I shall have the happyness of seeing you in Rhode Island. I have not as yet sold any part of my Crop nor had any offer. I never knew Markets so low; I have not seen the Captain of your Brig and I am afraid as he is gone up Cushy to Riply and shall go out of Town tomorrow for Hallyfax about Seventy miles and cannot be at home again in ten days.

HAYLEY AND HOPKINS TO AARON LOPEZ

Sir, [London,] 29 April, 1774.

WE are now favoured with yours of the 9th March by Captain Davenant. Allen was sailed from hence before the receipt of this Letter, but we believe the money advanced him was not more than would be conformable with your orders now before us. We shall follow your directions respecting the sale both of the *Neptune* and the *Deborah*, and hope neither of them will lay long on hand. Davenant chusing to return to Rhode Island, we have kept your instructions in view and paid him £54.8.6 on the Snow's Account, for which you will find his receipt enclosed. The Oyl he brought us on account of yourself and Mr. Rivera is landed and shall be disposed of as expeditiously as possible; but the large quantity now in the Buyers hands will not permit us to expect an immediate sale; you may depend upon our not missing any good opportunity. The nominal price is £42.10 for White and we think we shall get about that price for this parcel of yours. The Staves are also landed and shall be taken care off.

The Insurance desired on the *Ann* for Africa, etc., [is] effected and herewith you have the Account thereof, your 2/3 of premio, etc., thereon being £89.6.4 is to your debit. The premio on these Voyages has for some time past been only 7 Guineas several have been done at that rate both by Mr. Lane's house and ours, the first of which was as you observed Mr. Mawdsleys Brig the *Mary*, in doing which our two Houses went hand in hand, and by so doing effected that which neither of us could have accomplished any other way. the great success which the African Vessels have had was the inducement. Since our last Mr. Thomas Dolbeare of Jamaica has remitted us for your Account a bill for £150 on T. and R. Hunt, which is accepted and when paid shall be placed to your credit. In our next we shall transmit Account Sales of the 3 Casks of Indico consigned us by that Gentleman, the money for which will about that time be growing due. We have no Letter yet from Captain Buckley; We suppose he must before this time be returned for America. We are very respectfully, Sir, Your most humble Servants,

          HAYLEY AND HOPKINS

[Endorsed,] Per Captain Frost.

PELEG GREENE TO AARON LOPEZ

Dear Sir,   Savanna Lamarr, April the 30th, 1774.

I IMBRACE this present oppertunity to acquant you that I arrived the 27 Instant, after a Pasage of seventeen days, and at my arrival I delivered my Credentials to Captain Benjamin Wright, Merchant here, agreable to my Instructions, but am afraid that I have not arrived at so good Markitts as I could wish in respect to our Pork, there being so much made this year and I being detained so long at Carolina that there was many barril arrived before me, which makes it rather against us, but however after all our Misfortune of driving asshore and long Detention there, I am glad to inform you that our Cargo comes out in very good order, and likewise the Hogs they were as fatt as Seals. I can't percive that the schooner has recived any

Damage by driveing asshore, for she is as tite as a vessell can be, and dont complain any attall. the greatest Damage was lousing our boat which I was oblidge to buy another, which cost twenty five Dollars, for which sum I drew on Captain Joseph Reply, Merchant at Caushy. as for the perticular prices of Good here I am not able to inform you of, as I have but jest arrived. but as Captain Wright rites by the same convannce I amagine he will rite the perticular. haveing nothing more to rite essencial, only shall make the best of my way home as soon as the Schooner is disposed of agreable to my Instructions, conclude with my steady attention to promote your Interest and am Sir

your Humb'l: Serv.t and yours to Serve

Peleg Greene

PELEG GREENE TO AARON LOPEZ

Savanna lamarr, Jamaica, June the 2th, 1774.

Dear Sir,

AFTER my arrival here and delivering my Cargo to Captain Wright agreeable to my instructions, he perposd a Voyage to me by your desire, which I am very sorry I could not proceed. my Reasons why, is my not knowing it before I saild from Carolina, so that I might have settled my business accordingly, but not knowing but what I should continy the Carolina Trade as I have been there some voyages past and expecting to go there this winter, I left my afairs very much unsettled therefore I could not pretend to undertake. and another reasons is I dont think it would have been prudent for me to undertook that Voyage had I been prepared for it, as I have never been acquanted with that part of the world. it ought to be a man that has been there, as the Navagation is very precareous, and diffecult, and for a man to undertake such a voyage without being well assured of his knowledge of that Country I think woud be a man of bad Princibles. and as Captain Wright dont chuse to send any stranger in hir has concluded to send hir to Rhode Island in hir Ballas about the 10th Inst. Conclude with my ready attention to promote your Interests, Am, Sir, your Humble Servant and yours to serve,

PELEG GREENE

THOMAS DOLBEARE TO AARON LOPEZ

Dear Sir,   Savanna [la] Mar, 13th June, 1774.

THE inclosed Memo. of Pig and Bar Iron I inclose as introductory to the shiping 3 or 400 Tons per annum for a Furnace we have in this Island. you'll be pleased, Sir, to ship this per the first Opportunity as it must be here soon, at the same time acquainting me the lowest Terms on which you could ship 400 Tons Pig Iron yearly to be delivered at Kingston free of any expence. for the inclosed you may draw on me at a Month's sight favouring Captain Wright, or I'll transmit the Amount when to you it may be most agreeable. I shall be much obliged you'd write me full respecting this Pig Iron, as a large Contract is likely to be adjusted. the same kind of Iron that is here mentioned came in the Ship *Nancy*, shiped per Lee and Jones, who can inform you where it is to be had. [I'm] now writing in the Compting Room of our good Old Fr[ie]nd Captain Wright. I remain (in great haste), Dear Sir, Your most Obedient Servant,

T. DOLBEARE

WILLIAM BROWN TO AARON LOPEZ

Sir,   [Dighton, R. I.,] June the 13, 1774.

I [REC]EIVED your favour of the 2 of June wharein you informd me of the fish sent you by Samuel Briggs on examing you found them in much the same ordor as the former passel. Sir, I never under stud that the furst fish was in bad ordor, but only the Bairrills being small not marchantabl which was oing to the fish being unexpecttedly taken on a suding and the wather being warme would not keep, which obligd the oners thair of to make youse of old Bairrils which was a bought 15 Bairril or 20, which I told the man when I agreed for the fish that the Bairrils I thought would not pass and agreed if they would not pass for him to make them marchantable which I expect to due and if not full to fill them up which is to the furst fish and as to the laste fish thair never was beatter fish not beatter Bairrils than thay ware all but 4 or 5 Bairrils which on your finding falt with gives me reson to think that you have got a large surply of fish sum other way and are not in the leest wants of fish and thair fore give me the plee of crowding your Worfe with unmarchantabl goods which is far from my Desine or Desire and I would not have trobld you with one fish this year ondly you rote to me for fish and I new that I was under gratter obbligation to you than aney other Man in Nuporte being in your deat largely and you sent back Speck and Shakes you would not take of me, and what to pay you in I now not which puts me in still gratter desire to be out of your Deat nowing that you recevd of Isaac Tubs seaverel Bairrils of fish this year as small as mine and fownd no falt and mad him as good pay and beatter than ever I had which make me think that you are desposd to be hard with me or that your Cupper or Clarkes are to blame but God grant me to make sum once more and I hope I shall never give you reson to falt me agane but I will cum down as sune as Tanton Corte is over which I shall have sum ocashon to tend on. I should have bin down this weeke. I have sent down the plank and what Knees I have ready, and can a sure that had it not have bin for my missfortaine in the Loss of the Sloope which was sesd and allso 500 Dollr sence by Ebner Alding desest you would have had your Dues longe before this time, as my Nattor is not to ceep aney man out of his money when it can be cum at. I have draw out your accoumpt and find by my accoumpt I am £100 or more in your Deat that is in the way of trade, and what to pay you in I donte know if you wonte take fish nor shingels nor shaken Caskes nor Specks. the Iron pots should have sent you but the fornis which I had concerns in did not begin her blasts till a bought six days a go, which If now mishap befals her can surply you with before longe and aney thing that I can surply you with am ready to sarve you. the 50 Half Bairrils can have mad in three or 4 weekes which if that will answer you will leat me know and I will cum down next week and se all the fish in marchantabl order and take them out of your way if it donte sute you to take them of me. from your Humbl Seruant

WILLIAM BROWN

HAYLEY AND HOPKINS TO AARON LOPEZ

[London,] 20 July, 1774.

Sir,

THE foregoing is Copy of our last respects; We now enclose Account Sales of the 3 Casks of Indico received by Captain Ratsey from Jamaica, for nett proceeds of which we have credited your Account £159.11.10, which we flatter ourselves will be agreable. We have since our last received your favours of the 19th April and 27th May; the former solely to order £1200 Insurance on the *Minerva,* her Cargo and freight from Newport to Newfoundland, which was immediately effected, and herewith you have the Account thereof, premio, etc., being £21.10.6 is to your debit. The Insurance of £1500 on the Snow *Flora* for the same Voyage, ordered in yours of the 27th May, is also done and you are debited for the premio, etc., thereof £26.15.6 as per Account also herewith. we are obliged to you for advising receipt of your Account Current and that you had found it free from error. The £50 bill on Connell and Co. of Glascow was not due till 26th January, under which date it is to your credit in new account. We have credited you also 8/ for the Ream of paper you mention to be wanting in Case

No. 8 per Rogers, and £1.19.8 overcharged on the Commission for settling the loss on the *Cupid*. We beg your pardon for these inaccuracies. We have rectified the charge of the Insurance on the *Nancy* by charging Captain Wright with his ¼ of the whole premium on the Cargo, which was clearly directed in the postscript you refer to, but some how or other overlooked by us. It is with pleasure we can advise you of the arrival of the *Nancy* in a six weeks passage from Jamaica, from whence she sailed the 1st of June; This short passage is very fortunate as it will enable us to gett her away from hence in a more tolerable time than we expected, to which nothing on our part shall be wanting; She will be unloaden about the 15th August, and by Shand or Rogers we shall be able to say what time we expect to dispatch her and what prospect there is of freight for her. The Goods you desire to have shippd in her for your own Account and for the Account of her Owners you may depend upon, and we shall be particularly attentive to what you mention about the quality of the Coal. We have had no Letter from Captain Buckley, but we understand he has been at Gibraltar and is sailed from thence with a Cargo of Mules, towards payment of which we suppose his freight from Newfoundland has been applied. You'll please observe that we have had no Orders for Insurance from any quarter either on his Vessell or Cargo. We are sorry to find the money paid Allen was more than he ought to have taken, but hope you will not have any difficulty in securing yourself; We could not gett rid of him for less, and you'll please observe that when any Master leaves his Vessel in our hands, we have it not in our power to refuse paying any demands he may make against his Owners, as he has possession of the Vessel and our Laws will not force him to quit her till he is fully satisfied. We wish we could give you the agreable Account of the Sale of the *Neptune*, but the bad condition of her Cordage and Sails has hitherto prevented any tolerable offer being made us for her; Captain Allen promised to inform you of her condition which we hope he did for your satisfaction in those particulars, you may depend upon no good opportunity being slip'd of disposing of her. We wish we may do it at a tolerable price. The *Deborah* proved a very unsaleable Vessel for this place, as her dimensions were very unsuitable for any European Trade, the smallness of her Hold in particular was a heavy objection; We wrote down to Liverpool agreable to your directions and two of the Merchants there who are concerned in the African Trade have since her arrival been to view her with thoughts of purchasing her, but they both declined taking her, assuring us that though she was constructed in the manner usual for the Trade from Rhode Island to Africa, sho would by no means suit for the Trade from Liverpool. We own under these circumstances we were afraid we should have been a long while before we should have disposed of her and therefore thought it fortunate that a purchaser offered last week who offered £450 for her. We stood hard for £500 but found it impossible to gett him up higher than £480 which sum we thought it right to accept; and though it is perhaps less than you expected to gett for her, we are nevertheless persuaded that it was better to lett her go than keep her under her circumstances which gave so little room to expect any ready and better price for her. The Oyl received by her is still on hand, the very large quantities which have been continually arriving, and that at the time of the year when the consumption is small, has so entirely damped the market that the Buyers will not purchase more than they want from time to time for present use. We think however we are at the Eve of selling this parcel of yours at £42, in which expectation we hope we shall not be disapointed. We are glad to see Mr. Sears is so clear about the recovery of the money for Bulley's protested bill, in which we hope he will succeed, but we would still renew our caution in respect of him. He is not in high credit here, a great number of his bills have been protested lately. We have not received any remittance from Mr. Dolbeare for your Account save the 3 Casks of Indico and the bill for £150 mentioned in our last, so that there is still between £60 and £70 still to come of the Sum he was to remitt us. We are glad to see Captain Wright had made you a satisfactory Sale of the *Cleopatra's* Cargo of Slaves; We hope he did the like with that of the *Africa*, who we find was arrived there and her Cargo sold; There can be no doubt he must have done well with that Cargo as you had given him a limitation of price. We observe the departure of the *Minerva* for Newfoundland; we wish her a profitable voyage; The £70 Insurance ordered on her for account of Mr. Sears is made, premio, etc., being £1.4.6 as per Account herewith. We were last week surprized with the arrival of Captain Story in the Brig *Venus* in our River with his Cargo of Corn. It seems the markets at Lisbon were greatly overloaded with that article and he thought it best to proceed from thence to London; He tells us the Cargo is sold immediately on arrival at an advantageous price. The particulars he will doubtless acquaint you with himself, as he has not mentioned them to us; He has putt himself under the direction of Mr. Mayne who we hope will be able to procure him a freight from hence some way or other, but at present nothing has offered. We shall be very glad if we can assist him in this matter, but we know of no way at present. The number of Vessels now on the Birth for America leaves no room for any hope of a freight that way. In the Insurance made by your orders on the *Venus* she had liberty to go to New York to load, and a larger premium was given on her for that reason; but as the regular premium from Newport to Lisbon, which was the Voyage she went, is only 2 per Ct. of which we informed the Insurers in consequence of your advice to us, they have returned us the additional premio of £1 per Ct. which we paid for her being to go to New York, and we have credited you £9.-.- for the same being on £900 insured. We are very sorry to see you have so strong grounds for conjecturing that some accident has happen'd to your Brig *Leviathan* on her Whaling Voyage; We hope there is still some chance that she may be safe, though the probability is against her; You may however depend upon it that if you have occasion to call upon your

Underwriters upon her Account they are all of the best sort and there will be no delay or difficulty attending the settlement of the loss according to right. The information you are so obliging to give of the safety of the *Seaflower*, Lewis, was very agreable to the two Underwriters on her, who from what you had formerly mentioned had long ago concluded that they were certainly to pay for her. Having now gone through the material articles in your favour now before us, we shall proceed to give you such particulars as have arisen in your service from other places.

We have a Letter from Messrs. Robert Anderson and Co., of Gibraltar, enclosing us papers extracted from their Court of Vice Admiralty respecting some damage which the Brig *Charlotte* received in a Gale of Wind in their Bay. The principal article is the Cost of a Cable which appears to have been cutt by the Rocks but not lost. We have laid the papers before the Insurers who object that in the state the Cable appears by the papers to have been in, it should have been spliced and they must have paid for any damage it had sustained, but that they cannot think there is any ground for calling upon them to pay for a new Cable, and *that* for a Cable which is certainly considerably larger than the one which was damaged; We only mention these particulars now; The objections have some weight, but the settlement must necessarily be delayed till we have an Account of her Arrival at Jamaica which hope may be soon, as she sailed from Gibralter 11th April; when that Account arrives we will endeavour to settle the Gibralter Average the best we can. We have since our last received several Letters from Captain Wright, with which we have received the following remittances vizt.

Herring & Foot on Wm. Beckford	£1457.2.10
Do. . . . . . Beckford & James	291.8. 7
Jos. Bellamy on E. Minifie	200.-. -

all at 90 Days sight, which bills are accepted and agreable to Captain Wright's directions shall when due be placed, one half of each bill to your credit and the other half to the credit of Mr. Rivera, being in part proceeds of the *Cleopatra's* Cargo; He advises receipt of the protested bill on Serocold and Co. for £230.11.4, and has in return sent us an order on those Gentlemen for nett proceeds of 40 Tierces Sugar on board the *Nancy*, which when received shall be placed to your credit agreable to his instructions. We suppose there is no doubt of their complying with the order, of which you may depend upon being regularly advised. He promises further remittances by the 26th of July Ships and directs us to follow your instructions respecting the Goods you may order to be shippd on the *Nancy* for account of the Owners, which shall be attended to. This being all that at present occurs we respectfully remain, Sir, Your most humble Servants,

HAYLEY AND HOPKINS

Since we wrote the foregoing we have sold the *Neptune* for £450, which considering the condition of her Stores we think a very good price for her, and hope you will have the same opinion of it.

PARR, BULKELEY AND CO. TO CHRISTOPHER CHAMPLIN

Lisbon, 9 August, 1774.

Sir,

THIS serves to confirm what we had the pleasure of writeing you on the 10th March last and at same time to acknowledge receipt of your esteemed favor of 29th April, and it gives us pleasure to find you approve of the freight we gave your Ship *Peggy* to Baltimore via Falmouth and back to Lisbon, from which Voyage we congratulate you on her safe arrival with 1624 bls. flour. she came upon the 7th and we have already taken out 400 bls. and the remainder will be landed without loss of time, and shoud we not in the interim succeed in our endeavours to sell the ship, and seeing there is no freights stiring worth accepting for the streights, we shall immediately in compliance with your order load the ship with Salt on your account for St. John's, Newfoundland,

and which we find to be conformable to your orders to Captain Barron under a later date than your letter to us. Respecting the freight money of this voyage after deducting the Port Charges and Cost of the salt on your Account the Balance in compliance with your directions shall be punctually remitted to your friends Messrs. Hayley and Hopkins of London, to whom on the first Current we had the pleasure to remitt £300 Stg., Ex. 66d per $, is 1090$909 rs. to your debit and is to the extent of what we are in Cash on your account from the Proceeds of your 1/3 concern in the *Peggys* Cargoe from Phila.

Concerning the Primage on your part of the *Peggys* Cargoe we have settled it with Captain Barron, receiving from him 5.200 and crediting you therewith. as soon as we can collect the debts outstanding on the *Peggy's* Cargoe in which you are 1/3 interested we will make a remittance of the Balance to your London friends, and hand you your Account Current.

As to our Markets they have been glutted for some time past with grain and flour and are so yet, but within these few days discovery has been made that our Harvest will not yield so plentifully as was at first expected, from which we may reasonably conjecture that by the time the *Peggy* comes round from Phila. with flour she may find no unprofitable market here. This being all that occurs at present we conclude very truely, Sir, Your

Obd:^t hble servants
Saml Bulkeley & Co

GEORGE HAYLEY TO AARON LOPEZ

London, 10th August, 1774.

Sir,

MY present motive for troubling you with a seperate address is to inform you, that my partnership with Mr.

Hopkins expires on the 31 December next, from which time the Business of the House will as formerly be carried on by myself alone, till such time as I can form a new connection with a prospect of advantage to my Friends and satisfaction to myself. My wish is [to] continue Business with such Gentlemen on whose integrity, and ability to fullfill their engagements I can depend, among which number I cannot be mistaken in placing Mr. Lopez. If agreable to you I would propose the following method for closing your account with Hayley and Hopkins. That you draw four Bills on me payable to them, the one for £4000 payable on the 31 March next, another for the same sum payable on the 30th June following, another for the same sum payable the 30th September following, and the fourth for such sum as may be then remaining unpaid of the ballance of the Account Current which will be furnished you at the close of the present year; The sum in this last bill cannot be mentioned, but it may nevertheless be drawn in the words above mentioned and made payable on the 31 December, 1775, or in any other words to the same purpose as you may approve. Upon these bills being so drawn and remitted your Account with Hayley and Hopkins will be closed, and your remittances from that time and all other transactions in business may center with me alone. This mode will be very agreable to Mr. Hopkins, and I do not see any objection to it on your part. I have given this Subject a good deal of consideration, and the mode I have proposed seems more eligible to all concerned than any other that has presented it[self] to my mind, but if you think otherwise and approve any other method better, please to signify it, and I shall acquiesce. One of my reasons for the proposal is shortning Business, by enabling both you and myself to keep only one account open instead of two, but the most material reason is the removal of a difficulty which lays upon Mr. Hopkins mind, which will by this means be wholly taken away; The largeness of your ballance has for some years past caused him a good deal of uneasiness, and as the partnership between us will now be closed he will be very anxious to have the account closed sooner than may probably be convenient to you: I do not mean to say so large a Ballance is agreable, but convinced as I am of your strict honour, and of your determination to lessen it by degrees as fast as you are able, I have not the least apprehension of the whole being safe, and am therefore willing to take it upon myself in the manner before proposed. If these Bills are so drawn no Commission will be charged on them either by Hayley and Hopkins or my self. I shall only add that I beg the favour of you to keep this proposal to yourself, as there are very few of my friends to whom I should chuse to offer the same terms. I am with real Esteem, Sir, Your most humble Servant,

GEO. HAYLEY

[Endorsed,] Per Captain Shand.

HAYLEY AND HOPKINS TO AARON LOPEZ

London, 11 August, 1774.

Sir,

THE foregoing is Copy of our last respects, since which we are without any of your favours. The *Nancy* is not quite unladen, but as the 30 days are near expired we expect her Rum will now be taken out in 3 or 4 days and we shall then dispatch here with all the expedition we are able, and we hope to gett her away in about 3 weeks and we will do all we can for her, but the prospect of freight for her is but indifferent. She will have 120 Chaldron of Coals on board, for account of her Owners which is a large quantity, but Captain Tomlinson says she cannot do with less. The time of payment of the *Neptune* and the *Deborah* is not yet quite out, but will soon, and you may be expecting the Accounts of both Vessels in our next. We mentioned in our last that Captain Story was looking out for a freight and that we wished it might be in our power to assist him. We are glad we can tell you we have recommended him to a freight from hence to Philadelphia, were we suppose he may be arrived before you receive this. We are happy in an Opportunity of giving you this disinterested proof of our regard for your Interest. In our last we gave you expectation of selling your Oyl in company with Mr. Rivera at £42 per ton; in this however we were not successfull. many Arrivals about that time made the Markett worse and worse, so that we were glad to enbrace an Offer which was made us of £41 for it, and we believe we have done right, the great Quantity now on hand we think must reduce the price. We are, etc.,

HAYLEY AND HOPKINS

By desire of Captain Storey we have made £350 Insurance on your part of the *Venus* and Freight from hence to Philadelphia, as per Account herewith, premio, etc., being £9.0.6. He has left the proceeds in the hands of Mr. Mayne who has wrote to Lisbon to enquire what is to be done with it, and as soon as he receives an Answer we suppose he will pay the Money to us.

We have just received your favor of the 24th June the whole of which shall be minutely attended to. You'll have observed by our preceeding, that we have never received a Line from Capt: Buckley who has been so long sailed from Gibralter, that tis now impossible to make any Insurance on his Vessell. We are etc.

PARR, BULKELEY AND CO. TO CHRISTOPHER CHAMPLIN

Lisbon, 15 August, 1774.

Sir,

THE preceeding we confirm Copy of our last Salutes. Captain Barron who is at present indisposed, considering the season of the year too farr advanced for the sale of salt in Newfoundland by the time he could reach there (and in which we agree with him), have concluded as soon as it pleases God to give him strength to proceed home with the ship in a good ballast of salt, here being only Western Island freight stiring, and which you object to, and as to sale here is no one that will come up to your limits. reffer-ing to our next per Barron we cordially salute you and remain most Respectfully,

       PARR, BULKELEY AND CO.

STOCKER AND WHARTON TO CHRISTOPHER CHAMPLIN

         Philadelphia, August 20th, 1774.

Sir,

WE are indebted for your sundry favors; the last inclosed a letter which we forwarded to Lisbon per Cap. Hart.

The other day we rec'd letters from Ireland giving us account of the arrival of the Flaxseed and with pleasure we inform you to a good market; we have no letter from Mr. Redmond Cuningham to whom it was addressed, but have understood it was selling at 77/6 per hhd. which is a much better price and common, and its arriving late at market too was as it happend a great help to the sale of it, so that we are well pleased that you are like to do better with its being shipt than even if it had sold here at your highest limits. when the sale of that and the Flour is receiv'd we will settle the account. We are afraid our friends Mess. Parr, Bulkley & Co. have kept some of that Flour too long; tho' no doubt they did for the best. the last accounts from Lisbon is realy discouraging, Flour would not sell 3$000r, so that all the Freight will be sunk.

The crop of Flaxseed this year in this Province and we believe in Maryland and the Jerseys is very scanty, so that it is our opinion it will be higher than it was the last year, and therefore if you mean to make a purchase we think you may venture to give as much or more than you did then and the sooner you secure it the better. If you have no objection we will hold a half concern with you in four or five hundred hhds. and we will send you Bills to pay or the Money as you choose, but pray take care that you get measure, and see to the quality of the Casks.

Our last crop of Wheat proved much more abundant than any heretofore, and if the purchasers act prudently the price may be lowerd. We remain with much respect, Sir, Your Very Humble Servants,

STOCKER AND WHARTON

Flour 18/.

PARR BULKELEY AND CO. TO CHRISTOPHER CHAMPLIN

Lisbon, 25th August, 1774.

Sir,

HEREWITH you will receive copys of our last Salutes of the 9 and 15 Current and which we hereby confirm. the £300 Stg. we remitted the 9th to your London friends is something more than we find our selves in Cash from your goods per the *Peggy*, nor have we dispos'd as yet of the remaining 50 barr's flour, unwilling to part with it at the miserable low rates others have sold at. nevertheless the adventure will be ended with the loss of as little time [as] possible. it is the glutted markets that has hinderd the Accounts being liquidated. You prefer'd a freight for your ship to the Streights. we conceive some one that knew very little of the Mediterranean have been your adviser. the *Peggy* from hence to Genova, after lyeing a month or six weeks in loading, wou'd not make more than £120 Stg. freight up, and after lyeing there on the Birth for Lisbon 2 or 3 months woud come down with about £300 Stg. this is look'd upon as a very good thing, and after all cannot be reckond equal to £60 Stg. per month. large Dutch Ships make it do. they sail at a very easy expence of Wages and Victuals, and which we mention for your future guidance. We hand you inclosd bill of Lading and Invoice of 200 Moys of Salt, cost 391$078rs., account of Disbursments on the *Peggy* amounting to 119$116rs. both which sums are at your debit, and to your credit stands the ship freight as per Manifest, amounting 1471$817rs. and further you will receive your a/c respecting only to the *Peggy's* freight from Baltimore ballanced to a point by our remittance on y/a[1] to Messrs. Hayley and Hopkins of 929$315rs., all which please note

---
[1] Your account.

in our conformity. Respecting the Ship returning to Lisbon in 3/3 as before, we are willing, but conditionally the Price of Flour does not exceed 16/ Currency per Cwt. and Ex-[change] not lower than 70 per Ct., and which we shall mention to Messrs. Stocker and Wharton by a Brigg we dispatch in 5 or 6 days. we think it imprudent to extend the limits notwithstanding the favorable appearance of prices being up in the Winter and Spring. in all your Commands we truely are, Sir, Your Obedient Humble Servants,

PARR, BULKELEY AND CO.

Flour 3200	Corn 200
Wheat 400	Exchange 66d per milrea.

HAYLEY AND HOPKINS TO AARON LOPEZ

30th August, 1774.

Sir,

ON the other side is Copy of our last respects. This we hope will be delivered you by Capt. Thomlinson in your Ship *Nancy*, who we now return to you with a better freight than we expected. Inclosed you have Invoice and bill of Lading for the Goods shipped on board him for his Owners' Account amounting to £929.17.7, on which we have made £955 Insurance. We have also made £3000 Insurance for account of the Owners on the Ship and freight, premio, etc., of both together being £99.8. The amount of the Goods and the two sums insured as above amount to £1029.5.7 for your 3/4, of which we debit you £771.19.2; Inclosed you will likewise find Invoice and bill of Lading for Goods shippd for your own Account in the *Nancy* amounting to £2745.3.5, on which we have made £2800 Insurance, premio, etc., being £70.10.6. We hope they will arrive with you in safety and in pretty tolerable season. The expences on the *Nancy* this Voyage will be very heavy. we have paid Captain Thomlinson £210. on the Ships Account as per his receipt enclosed, besides which he has left us a large amount of Tradesmens bills, both together he tells us will amount to between 6 and 7 hundred pounds. All Accounts relating to her shall be forwarded as soon as we are able, but it will be some time first as we dont expect to begin recieving the freight till the latter end of next month. Having settled with the Buyers of the *Neptune* and the *Deborah* we enclose you their accounts, nett proceeds of the former being £288.14.5 and of the latter £662.13.1 which we flatter ourselves you will approve, and if upon examination they are found without Error please note them in conformity, as you will also the enclosed Account Sales of the Staves received by the *Deborah*, for nett proceeds of which have credited you £37.4.9. By direction of Captain Storey we have applied to Mr. Mayne for the proceeds of your part of the *Venus's* Cargo, which he has not yet paid us, but promises to do it in a few days, so that our next we suppose will acquaint you with the Sum he pays us. We are very much obliged to you for the generous offer you make us of a part in the *Nancy* upon so equitable terms, and likewise for the shares you propose our taking in the other two Vessels designed for the Jamaica Trade. There are not two Gentlemen in America with whom we would so soon enter into such an Engagement as yourself and Mr. Rotch, but it is utterly incompatible with our general plan of business to become Owners of Shipping. We confine ourselves as far as we are able to our Commission business, which is as much as we find ourselves able to manage properly, and no temptation of profit would induce us to enter into a West India connection further than it falls in with our No. American Trade. We sincerely wish your plan may turn out as advantageous as you expect. Such part of it as you may think proper to place under our Management here you may depend upon it we will execute with the same Zeal as if it was wholly our own concern, for we desire upon every occasion to prove ourselves, Sir, Your most Humble Servants,

         HAYLEY AND HOPKINS

31st. Mr. Mayne has this morning paid us £600 for your Account which is to your credit.

Stocker and Wharton to Christopher Champlin

Philadelphia, September 8th, 1774.

Sir,

We have before us your favor of the 30th August and find you were on the look out for Flaxseed, and wish you may succeed to procure it on reasonable terms. we are of opinion it will bear as good a price here as it did the last year. it is certain in this Province the Crop falls short of the last year.

We can expect no kind of information from the Delegates in Congress as they are sworn to Secresy, so that we must wait with patience until they have entirely finished the business they have met on. We however can hardly think that a Non Exportation can take place to Ireland, unless it becomes general, that is an intire Suspension of Trade. it is the Opinion of a very great Number that a Non Importation from Great Britain would answer a good purpose.[1] the times are very precarious, and if it should be found necessary to shut up our Ports, either partially or all together, it must be submitted to; therefore this consideration should be attended to in making purchases. The other day we receiv'd account sales of the Flaxseed, Nett Proceeds, £1066.2.7 Irish; when it is remitted we shall know the Amount in Sterling, and after being furnished with Sales of the Flour and the Remittance for your third sent forward we can settle the difference of profits on both adventures.

The last account from Lisbon was very discouraging for our produce, with but very little hope of an amendment.

---

[1] The first intimation of what was being done in the Continental Congress was the publication of a resolution adopted on September 22: "*Resolved unanimously*, That the Congress request the Merchants and others in the several colonies, not to send to Great Britain any orders for goods, and to direct the execution of all orders already sent, to be delayed or suspended, until the sense of the Congress, on the means to be taken for the preservation of the liberties of America, is made public." This resolution was circulated as a handbill. *Journals of the Continental Congress* (Library of Congress edition), I. 41. The handbill is reproduced in the same volume, p. 43.

should any alteration take place this Fall for the better we will hold a third in the *Peggy's* Cargoe from hence, and very probably we shall have orders to interest some of our Lisbon Friends another third.

Our Exchange has been favorable for a long time, say 72 to 76 per Ct. they are rather on the decline, and as soon as Produce comes plenty to Market which will be in a few weeks, they will fall.

Our Farmers are now very busy preparing the ground for the next crop. the last was the finest we ever had for Wheat and Rye. We remain With respect, Sir, Your Very Humble Servants,

STOCKER AND WHARTON

CHRISTOPHER CHAMPLIN TO STOCKER AND WHARTON

Newport, September 17th, 1774.

Gentlemen,

YOUR favor of 8th Inst. I have before me, noteing the Nt. proceeds of our seed. do you mean exclusive of Insur[ance]? or is it still to be charged? what is the common exchange between Ireland and London? we have many bidders after seed; our country engrossers will not deliver it here under £3 N. York money per cask including cask. I have agreed with several at that price. I lost the buying 40 cask this day, by endeavouring to get it 58/ per cask. another steped in and bid 60/; that I find unless I finally comply shall not obtain a quantity, and I fear 64/ will be finally given. I shall buy all I can at 60/ per cask. do you mean to ship it to Ireland, or sell it? write me by first post, as I shall be obliged to ship it in different Coasters and at different periods — at least a month distant from the 1st to last time of shiping — to prevent the storeing here, as it is sent in at different times, from many quarters having a Vessel last year of my own [I] tarryed till collected the whole, but by our Coasters it can be shipped only as it comes in. I have endeavoured to keep the seed from being sent in till about the time Anthony returns. If it is required sooner say when, and whither I may continue to buy at 60/ N. York per Cask. If the *Peggy* shou'd arive in time will send it in her. Seed ought to fetch 10/ with you to make it worth attending too. If a prospect of giting a good price at Ireland, it may be well to ship, unless 10/ coud be had with you. all the information you can send me will be necessary, as the time draws near. I am, Gentlemen, Your most humble Servant,

CHRIS: CHAMPLIN

[Endorsed,] Per Capt. Anthony.

PARR, BULKELEY AND CO. TO CHRISTOPHER CHAMPLIN

Lisbon, 24 September, 1774.

Sir,

WE had the pleasure of writing you the 26th Ulto. per Captain Barron of your Ship *Peggy* who we hope is arrived in a good State of health. we handed you bill of lading and Invoice of 200 Moys Salt, Account Port Charges and Disbursements, also Manifest of the Ships freight and advised of a remittance of 929$315 to your friends Hayley and Hopkins all which we confirm and crave your reference to the further contents.

Before us is your truely esteemd favor of the 6th July and finding Salt was a glutt at Newfoundland we are glad that did not order the *Peggy* to try St. Johns with her Cargoe; by late advices from Phila. we find a liklyhood from a plentifull harvest throughout the Continent of flour being at or under our limits of 16*s* per cwt. here this article is looking upwards, and very likely to leave a proffit in the Winter and Spring. Yellow Conecticut Corn, and good red Wheat, also bid fair for a favorable exit. as yet we have not put off the 50 Bls flour per the *Peggy* last Voyage, nor collected sufficient from the debts to make a further remittance to your London friends. we hope it will not be long ere we have the pleasure. Whenever you have an opportunity of recommending Consignments to us we'll be gratefully thankfull to you for them, and you may rest assured of our acting in such an honorable manner as to give intire satisfaction. at your service we truely are, Sir, Your assur'd friends and obedient Servants,

PARR, BULKELEY AND CO.

Flour 3$100 to 3$600 as in quality. Corn   200 to   240
Wheat   420 to   480   Ex[change] 65¼

STOCKER AND WHARTON TO CHRISTOPHER CHAMPLIN

Philadelphia, September 27th, 1774.

Sir,

WE have before us your favor of the 17th Inst. and find you had the promise of 200 Casks of Seed which would stand in 66/ our Currency per Cask d'd here. we suppose this includes the Cask otherwise we are afraid it will leave us but little profit. however we have no objection to your continuing to purchase as you propose until you secure four or five hundred hhds, and doubt not you will exert your self to procure them on the very best terms. We have still reason to believe that this province, and we believe the Jerseys too, will produce a much less quantity of that article than they did the last year; but we are informed that Maryland and Virginia will do pritty well. You know better than us what the Northern Provinces can furnish. We are in hopes the price here will be 10/ or near it, and we think we had better sell at that than ship it. however of this we shall perhaps be better able to form a good Judgment by and by. it matters not when you ship it, but we think you should not loose an opportunity lest you should be perplexed to get a Vessel to bring it.

No Vessel lately from Lisbon or Cadiz; the first that arrives shall make enquiry of the Captain about the *Peggy*.

The Congress is still sitting; they keep their Intentions secret, save that the other day they published a Resolve which is here inclosed, and will shew that they intend in part that a Non Importation from Great Britain is necessary for the preservation of the Libertys of America. it is impossible to judge what they will determine upon, but we think a Non exportation will not take place until after they have heard the fate of their other measures. When any thing new transpires shall take the liberty of informing you. in the meantime and always we are with much respect, Sir, Your Very Humble Servants,

STOCKER AND WHARTON[1]

STOCKER AND WHARTON TO CHRISTOPHER CHAMPLIN

Philadelphia, Oct. 18., 1774.

Sir,

WE have this minute received your favor of the 11th Inst. and find the information we gave you had perplexed you a good deal. what we mentiond was the report of the Town and said to be the opinion of the Members of the Congress. Our next letter we hope would get to hand to prevent your parting with what Seed you had purchased, at an under price, and at the same time might perhaps been a sufficient hint for your buying from others at a low price before they recovered from their surprise. We remain with respect, Sir, Your Very Humble Servants,

STOCKER AND WHARTON

P. S. In a letter rec'd the other day from Mess. Parr, Bulkeley & Co. "on the 17th Inst. arrived the *Peggy*, Cap. Barron, from Baltimore, with 1624 barrels Flour. we generously offer'd the Cap. the additional Freight of 1/6 Stg. per barrel to proceed to London, having rec'd advice that the prices there for Wheat and Flour were favorable, but the Captain did not choose to go, having rec'd orders

---

[1] "We wrote to you under date the 1st Inst. and have since understood that the Congress does not mean to prevent the export of Flaxseed to Ireland and therefore we think you had better keep on purchasing until you secure three or four hundred hhds, unless we should find it advisable to request you to stop your hand.

"There is nothing more fluctuating than the price of this article, and therefore we can form no Judgment what it will be, or whether we had better sell here or ship it. Some people imagine it will be as high as 10/ or upward. But very little has yet come to Market and has sold from 8/ to 9/." *Stocker and Wharton to Christopher Champlin*, October 8, 1774.

from Mr. Champlin to take a loading of Salt for St. John, etc., etc."

We think he did right. S. AND W.

STOCKER AND WHARTON TO CHRISTOPHER CHAMPLIN

Philadelphia, October 25th, 1774.

Sir,

Our last respects was under date the 18th Inst. to which we refer you. being without any of yours the present serves to advise that it is expected the Congress will break up to day or tomorrow.[1] their proceedings will we believe be out tomorrow. Flaxseed is not prohibited to be sent to Ireland, so that we hope you have made tollerable progress in the purchase of that article.

Unless the Acts of Parliament be repealed by the 10th of September next a Non Exportation is then to take place to Great Britain, Ireland and the West Indies, except Rice to Europe; the Slave Trade to be discontinued after the first of December next; which is a most excellent resolve.[2]

Flaxseed is worth here about 10/. it is as you know a most precarious article to deal in, but we think, it will not be low this year at this Market. We remain with respect, Sir, Your Very Humble Servants,

STOCKER AND WHARTON

P. S. if the Ship *Peggy* comes here, we will ship for ourselves and our friends, 2/3 of her Cargo, you to hold a third.

STOCKER AND WHARTON TO CHRISTOPHER CHAMPLIN

Philadelphia, October 28th, 1774.

Sir,

We wrote to you by last Post, but had not time fully to answer your letter. we find you had agreed to ship the

---

[1] It dissolved on the twenty-sixth.

[2] This refers to the Association or non-importation agreement entered into by the members of the Continental Congress, October 20, 1774. See *Journals of the Continental Congress* (Library of Congress edition), I. 75.

Seed you are purchasing on our joynt account in the Brig *Britannia*, Edward Fare, Master, at such Freight as is usually given from hence. there is no ascertaining this exactly as 11/ to 12/ Irish, according to the plenty or scarcity of Vessels is given here. we have no doubt we could at this time charter a Vessel at 11/ or under, and we are confirmed in our Opinion by a Gentleman of veracity who is well versed in that Trade. We have to observe that the Shippers of small parcels generally pay 12/, but to secure the Freight the Owners of the Ship often gives them their passages or perhaps a part as they can agree. therefore we think the Freight in the *Britannia* should not be more than 11/.

You dont mention when you think the Vessel will sail, tho we suppose you did intend to dispatch her before the first of December, at which time you understood the Non export was to take place. it is impossible to form a true Judgment what port the Seed will do the best at this year. We have however been consulting a friend of ours whose opinion we rely much on, and he thinks as it will go early that we had better order her to Dublin, as it can be carryed from thence to other places if the Markets should be encouraging, in small Craft on pritty reasonable terms. a better Judgment can be formed by those that ship late, than those that ship early, as they know the different Ports each Vessel is bound to, and can order the Vessel to proceed accordingly. We therefore advise her going to Dublin, and now inclose a Letter for our friend Mr. Rowland Norris of that place whose probity, and attention to the Interest of the concerned we have not the least doubt of. we have requested him to order the Vessel to any other Port if he finds such Step will advance the Interest of the Owners of said Cargo; an adequate Freight being allowed to the Vessel according to the time and risk, and our half of what you may ship we have desired him to remit to London. Should she be sent forward we have requested him to give the same directions to the House she may be ordered to, as he receives from you and us, and also attend to the directions he may receive from the Owner of the Brig respecting her and his part of the Cargo. As the Congress has broke up and published as much of their proceedings as they thought right, we would send you one of the Pamphlets, did an oppertunity offer; but no doubt your delegates will furnish you with them.

We have left Mr. Norris's Letter open for your perusal which please to seal and forward with yours. We remain with respect, Sir, Your Very Humble Servants,

STOCKER AND WHARTON

P. S. had not you better agree with Mr. Fowler to ship the whole Cargo on a joynt Adventure you and us one half and he the other, or in thirds. Let us know how we are to make you a remittance. Exchange is here 69 to 70 per Ct.

Please to put a Cover over Mr. Norris' Letter.

SCOTT AND FRASER TO AARON LOPEZ

Gothenburg, 29 October, 1774.

Sir,

SINCE ours of the 4th June, we have not had the pleasure of hearing from you. We have given up all hopes of seeing your Vessell from Jamaica which we have been in daily expectation of these three months past. If you have not alter'd her Voyage she must inevitably be lost, which we would be sorry to hear. Give us leave at present to state the situation of our market: at our India Sale in September Boheas sold at about 14d sterling per lb.; Congo 2/2 to 2/6, as in quality; common green or Singlo 2/; Hysan 4/6 to 5/. New Herrings, tho' as yet very scarce, could be shippd fit for the West Indies at 10/6 or 11/ per Barrel.

Should your Schooner appear, which we have very little hopes of, we have still on hand a sufficient Quantity of Bohea to supply her with, altho that article is now much in demand and the Price started 6 per Ct. owing to very considerable orders coming in since the Sale. Notwithstanding this speculation has not taken place, we shall be glad to hear you have resolv'd on another; nothing shall be wanting on our part to render it advantageous. We are Sincerely, Sir, Your most Humble Servants,

SCOTT AND FRASER

STOCKER AND WHARTON TO CHRISTOPHER CHAMPLIN

Philadelphia, November 4th, 1774.

Sir,

WE have yours per Capt. Anthony and shall endeavor to get a Freight for the Ship *Peggy*. we wish you had orderd her here as soon as her salt was out. we would have given her two-thirds of a Freight to Lisbon, the other could have been shipt on your own account. We have an order for half a Cargoe of Wheat and Flour for Bristol. we dont know if we can get it here for the price limited, and have wrote to Virginia to endeavor to get it bought there. if we succeed, and nothing better offers for the Ship, we could give her that Freight; but the detention with you will make her very late. you should not part with the Matts she brought under the Salt as they are rather scarce, but have them washed and dryed.

You dont mention what quantity of Seed you have secured or expect to get, in your last letter. We hope it will be upwards of 300 hhds. it is selling here in small parcels at 11/6, and have no doubt of its obtaining 12/ and upwards for any tollerable quantitys. we hope Mr. Fowler and you have agreed to let the Cargoe in thirds. we think it will answer in Ireland, but was it here now we could be certain of a profit. We have wrote to our friend at New York to endeavor to make a purchase there for us, if he succeeds, would you have an objection to the Ship loading there for Bristol? Vessels are very plenty. We remain With much respect, Sir, Your Very Humble Servants,

STOCKER AND WHARTON

Flour 16/9 to 17/.
Wheat 6/6 to 6/8.

P. V. THRELFAL TO CHRISTOPHER AND GEORGE CHAMPLIN[1]

Grenada, November 18, 1774.

Gentlemen,

WE are duly favor'd with yours dated the 28th Septr. advising Sale of your Slaves at St. Kitts. We as well as you think it a little extraordinary the Factors did not write you per your Vessell.

We are in great hopes our late Act will be soon repealed, when she shall be enabled to sell Slaves as usual, you may depend on being regularly advised when we have an alteration which must be for the better. . . .

P. V. THRELFAL

STOCKER AND WHARTON TO CHRISTOPHER CHAMPLIN

Philadelphia, November 22d, 1774.

Sir,

THIS day comes to hand your favor of the 12 Inst. per Whitman and find you purposed to dispatch the *Peggy* the 25 Inst., therefore shall be providing her Cargoe in order to give her dispatch. The last accounts from Spain, Portugal, and England, were very encouraging for our produce; Flour at Lisbon 3$500 and on the rise, in England their Crops were very indifferent and Wheat at Bristol was worth 6/6 to 6/9 per bushel. We have an order for half a Cargoe. if you can purchase a load of good sound and full grain Wheat, say eight to ten thousand bushels put on board, Commission and all charges included at three shillings and eight pence Sterling per bushel, and can procure a Vessel to carry it to Bristol, Lisbon, or Cadiz, as we may hereafter direct, you may secure us a Cargoe, provided it be agreeable that we make the payment in Bills at 60 days on London or Bristol, one half when we receive the Bills of Lading, or when you inform us the Cargoe is shiping, the remainder in one two or three months after as you can

---

[1] The original is in the Rhode Island Historical Society.

manage it; or rather than fail we would send Bills for one quarter part to begin to make the purchase, tho' this we would rather not do. in case you can make the purchase do charter a good Vessel and see that she is well denaged[1] proper Corn Rooms and well lined or matted. the Wheat must be clear of Fly and Garlick. Your answer soon will oblige us. the price we have limited is above what you say it can be bought at and have no doubt you will get it as low as you can.

We have wrote to Dublin this day, as we find a Vessel will sail for some part of Ireland in a day or two, informing Mr. Norris that the Brig will soon sail. Seed is worth here 12/6 to 13/. We remain With much respect, Sir, Your Very Humble Servants,

STOCKER AND WHARTON

STOCKER AND WHARTON TO CHRISTOPHER CHAMPLIN

Philadelphia, December 5, 1774.

Sir,

OUR last respects was under date the 29th November and have now to advise that the *Peggy* is just arrived, but too late to enter this afternoon. You may depend we will give her all the dispatch in our power, but Flour geting up to 18/. and more purchasers than we ever knew, is a disagreeable circumstance. We wish she had brought the Flaxseed in preference to its being shipt to Ireland, for we are of opinion this is the best market. we are not so sanguine in our expectations from the Irish market as you are. they can be supplyd from Holland at about 70/ to 80/, and will no doubt when they find there is a scarcity in America send to Holland for what they may want. if they have not time to do this we do think it will be high — tho not so much as you expect. Your next we hope will inform us that you have bought the Cargoe of Wheat we

---

[1] Dunnaged.

wrote for. We remain With respect, Sir, Your Very Humble Servants,

STOCKER AND WHARTON

Seed 13/6 to 14/.
Exchange 67½ per doll.
We shall call for the £100 on Mr. Hughes.

ORDER

Rhode Island, December 16th, 1774.

Sir,

PLEASE supply His Majesty's Ship *Rose*, under my Command, with Four Hundred pounds of fresh Beef.

JAS. WALLACE

HENRY GARDNER TO CHRISTOPHER CHAMPLIN[1]

Philadelphia, the 23d December, 1774.

Dear Sir,

I HAVING an oppertunity make boald to acquaint you that we are now lying at Ready Island and have ben heare this three days wating for a wind to go to sea. We left the Sitty the 20d December. We have got in sixteen hundred and two Barrels of flower in all. We loaded the ship in fore days and a half. The Ship is vary tite and has ben ever sence we left Rhodeisland. Sir, thear was a Negro belonging to Mr. Miller the Mastmaker that hid him self on bord the ship and run away we never found it out until after our arival at Philadelphia. after we had ben out 4 days he maide him self nown to Sirlone, and he give him vittels and water. Sirlone kep it privit until he got on shore. Capt. Barron saw in one of the Newspapers a Negro prince Miller advartiseed, mistrusted that he came with us, so I keep a Lookout for him, catcht him, put him in jaile. that advartisement was two Dollars Reward, but I understud by Capt. Carronton that he had put out advartisements ten Dollars Reward. the Negro will come hince with Capt. Momford. Capt. Momford paide me

---

[1] The original is in the Rhode Island Historical Society.

two Dolers that was the first advartisement But the last was ten Dollers Reward so I should have eight Dollears more. Sir, I should be glad if it lay in your way that you wold git it for me. Sir, I am well and harty so no more at preasan. I remain, Dear Sir, your most umble Sarvant

HENRY GARDNER

PELEG GREENE TO AARON LOPEZ

Annamaboe, December the 25th, 1774.

Dear Sir,

I GLADLY imbrace this present oppertunity to acquant you of our safe arrival here after a tedious Pasage of 140 days after stoping to windard as we run down along we tuched to almost every Port runing down but purchased only 12 Slaves with all our trouble, but at our arrival here found times to be very good thanks be to God for it. there was only one Rum man that is Captain Johnson of Boston and he had almost done before we arrived. Shall mention some of the Perticuler which may be of servis to you as you carry on this trade, in regard to the Prices of Slaves. our Captain gives for Prime men slaves 190 Gallons and 200 do. and for Prime women 170 and 180 Do. to the whites; and the Black trade is very good at present which give us a great Prospect of a good Voyage and Dispatch. Ive had a good oppertunity of gitting acquanted in this trade, as we tuched all the way down the Coast, and have improved every hour of time, and have been in the Long boat ever sence we arrived here which is not common for a second mate, and am glad to tell you without vannity that I think myself capable of taking charge of a Vessell in this trade with what experience I have already acquired for I find the trade very easy, and hope you will think of your faithfull six years servant against his Return, if it should please God to speare his life, as I am confident that I am capable of taking Charge of Vessell about 100 or 120 Hhd which is full bigg for Dispatch, and it will be a good time of the year when we return, as we expect to be at home in July if nothing happens, and the Vessell thats now fitting and on their Pasages will all be off the Coast that time of course. have nothing more to mention only please to give my Complements to your Lady and famly likewise to Mr. Lavary and family and to Miss Wright. Shall conclude with my sincere wishes for your wellfare. am, Sir, Your Humble Servant and yours to serve,

PELEG GREENE

[Endorsed,] Via Barbadoes Captain Clarke.

CPSIA information can be obtained
at www.ICGtesting.com
Printed in the USA
LVHW081319100420
652961LV00012B/77